PARABLES
OF OUR LORD

WILLIAM ARNOT STUDY SERIES

Parables of Our Lord
Lesser Parables of Our Lord
Studies in Acts
Studies in Proverbs

PARABLES
OF OUR LORD

by

William Arnot

KREGEL PUBLICATIONS
Grand Rapids, MI 49501

The Parables of Our Lord by William Arnot,
published by Kregel Publications, a division of
Kregel, Inc. All rights reserved.

Library of Congress Cataloging in Publication Data

Arnot, William, 1808-1875.
  The Parables of Our Lord.

  Reprint of the 1865 ed. published by T. Nelson,
London.
  1. Jesus Christ—Parables.   I. Title.
BR375.A73   1981   226'.806   80-8065
ISBN 0-8254-2119-5   AACR1

Printed in the United States of America

CONTENTS

Contents

Introduction: Parables in Luke 15

INTRODUCTION

WE have been accustomed to regard with affectionate veneration the life-work of the Reformers, and the theology of the Reformation. Of a later date, and in our own vernacular, we have inherited from the Puritans an indigenous theology, great in quantity and precious in kind,—a legacy that has enriched our age more, perhaps, than the age is altogether willing to acknowledge. At various periods from the time of the Puritans to the present, our stock of sacred literature has received additions of incalculable value. So vast and varied have our stores become at length, that an investigator of the present day can scarcely expect to find a neglected spot where he may enjoy the luxury of cultivating virgin soil : so ably, moreover, have our predecessors fulfilled their tasks, that a modern inquirer, obliged to deal with familiar themes, cannot console himself with the expectation of dealing with them to better purpose. It does not follow, however, that a contribution to the literature of theology is useless, because it neither touches a new theme, nor treats an old more ably

The literature of one century, whether sacred or common, will not, when served up in the lump, satisfy the craving and sustain the life of another. The nineteenth century must produce its own literature, as it raises its own corn, and fabricates its own garments. The intellectual and spiritual treasures of the past should indeed be reverently preserved and used ; but they should be used as seed. Instead of indolently living on the stores which our fathers left, we should cast them into the ground, and get the product fresh every season—old, and yet ever new. The intellectual and spiritual life of an age will wither, if it has nothing wherewith to sustain itself, but the food which grew in an earlier era ; it must live on the fruits that grow in its own time, and under its own eye.

Nor will a servile imitation of the ancient masters suffice. A mere reproduction, for example, of the Puritan theology would not be suitable in our day ; while the truth, which constitutes its essence, remains the same, it must be cast in the moulds of modern thought, and tinged with the hues of modern experience.

Engineers surveying for a railway lay down the line level, or as nearly level as the configuration of the surface will permit ; but an engineer's level is not a straight line ; it is the segment of a circle,—that circle being the circumference of the globe. The line which practically constitutes a level bends downwards continually as it goes forward, following the form of the earth, and at every point being at right angles to the radius. If it were produced in an absolutely straight line, it would, in the course of a few miles, be high and dry above the surface of the earth, and entirely useless for the practical purposes of life. Such would sacred literature become if in blind admiration of the fathers, the children should simply use the old, and not produce the new. As we advance along the course of time, we are, as it were, tracing a circle ; and he who

would be of use in his generation, must bend his speculations to the time, and let them touch society on the
level at every point in the progress of the race. To throw
a new contribution into the goodly store does not, therefore, imply a judgment on the part of the writer that the
modern theology is better than the ancient. We must
make our own: it concerns us and our children that
what we make be in substance drawn from the word
of God; and in form, suited to the circumstances of
the age.

Still further, the accumulations of the past should be
used by those who inherit them, as a basis on which to
build. It is the business of each generation to lay another
course on the wall, and so leave the structure loftier
than they found it. The Bible, like the world, is in-
exhaustible; in either department hosts of successive
investigators have plied their tasks from the beginning,
and yet there is room.

Some observations are here submitted, more or less
strictly introductory to a treatise on a specific branch of
Scriptural exegesis—the Parables of Our Lord.

1. Analogy

As the husbandman's first care is neither the fruit nor
the tree which bears it, but the soil in which the tree must
grow: so an expositor, whose ultimate aim is to explain
and enforce the parables of Jesus, should mark well at the
outset the fundamental analogies which pervade the works
of God, and constitute the basis of all figurative language,
whether in human teaching or divine.

The Maker and Ruler of the universe pursues an object, and works on a plan. His purpose is one, and he

sees the end from the beginning: the variations, infinite in number, and vast in individual extent, which emerge in the details of his administration, are specific accommodations of means to ends.

The material and moral departments of the divine government are, like body and soul of a human being, widely diverse from each other; but one Master administers both with a view to a common end. The two departments are different in kind, and therefore the laws which regulate the one cannot be the same as the laws which regulate the other; but in both one designer operates towards one design, and therefore the laws which regulate the one must be like the laws which regulate the other. From the duality of creation, there cannot be identity between the physical and moral laws; but from the unity of the Creator there must be similarity.

Nor is it only between the two great departments of the divine government generically distinguished, that analogies may spring: within either department, analogies innumerable may be found between one species and another, and even between individuals of the same species. Between two parts of the material world, or two portions of human history, or two processes of mental effort, analogies may be traced, as well as between the evolutions of matter and the laws of mind.

It is not strictly correct to speak of the similitudes which we have been accustomed to admire in literature, as "creations of genius;" the utmost that is competent to genius is to observe and exhibit the similitudes as they lie in nature. An observing eye, a suggestive mind, and a loving heart constitute all the necessary apparatus; with these faculties in exercise, let any one stalk abroad upon the earth among his fellows, and analogies will spring spontaneously around him, as manifold and as beautiful as the flowers that by daylight look up from the earth, or the stars that in the evening reciprocate from heaven the gentle salutation.

Analogy occupies the whole interval between absolute identity on the one hand, and complete dissimilarity on the other. You would not say there is an analogy between two coins of the same metal, struck successively from the same die; for all practical purposes they are identical. Although the two objects are thoroughly distinct, as all their sensible qualities are the same, we are accustomed to speak of them not as similar but the same. In order that a comparison may be effective either for ornament or for use, there must be, between the two acts or objects, a similarity in some points, and a dissimilarity in others. The comparison for moral or æsthetic purposes is like an algebraic equation in mathematical science ; if the two sides are in all their features the same, or in all their features different, you may manipulate the signs till the sun go down, but you will obtain no useful result : it is only when they are in some of their terms the same and in some different, that you can bring fruit from their union.

We stand here on the brink of a great deep. For wise ends the system of nature has been constructed upon a line intermediate between the extremes of sameness and diversity. If the measure of difference between classes and individuals had been much greater or much smaller than it is, the accumulation of knowledge would have been extremely difficult, or altogether impossible. It is by the combination of similarity and dissimilarity among sensible objects that science from its lowest to its highest measures becomes possible. If all animals, or all plants had been in their sensible qualities precisely the same there would have been of animals or vegetables only one class: we could have had no knowledge regarding them, except as individuals: our knowledge would at this day have been less than that of savages. Again, if all animals or all plants had been in their sensible qualities wholly dissimilar—all from each, and each from all, it would have been impossible to frame classes; our knowledge, as on the opposite supposition, would have been limited to our observation of individuals. In either case Zoology or Botany would have been impossible. Man, endowed with intelligence, could not, in such a world, have found exercise for his faculties. It would have been like a seeing eye without a shining light. The power would have lain dormant for want of a suitable object. Ask the Botanist, the Naturalist, the Chemist—ask the votary of any science, what makes accumulated knowledge possible; he will tell you, it is the similarity which enables him to classify, accompanied by the diversity which enables him to distinguish. Wanting these two qualities in balanced union there could be no analogy; and wanting analogy, man could not be capable of occupying the place which has been assigned to him in creation.*

---

* But in order to employ analogy with effect more is needful than to make sure that the two objects or acts compared are similar without being identical: the design for which a comparison is made enters as an essential element, and decisively determines its value. Between two given objects an analogy may exist, good for one purpose but worthless for another. Given two balls, spherical in form and equal in size, the one of wood and the other of iron; and let the question be, Do these two objects bear any analogy to each other, real in itself and capable of being usefully employed? The question cannot yet be answered: we must first ascertain for what purpose the comparison is instituted. The two balls are like each other in form, but unlike in material; whether is it in respect of their form or their material that you propose to compare them? If one of them rolls along a gently inclined plane, you may safely infer that the other, when placed in

In suggesting probabilities and throwing out lines of inquiry, analogy is of unspeakable value in every branch of science; in sacred apologetics its specific use is to destroy the force of objections which may be plausibly urged against facts or doctrines otherwise established; but it is as an instrument for explaining, illustrating, fixing, and impressing moral and spiritual truth that we are mainly concerned with it here.

God's word is as full of analogies as his works. The histories, offerings, and prophecies of the Old Testament are figures of better things which have been brought to light by the gospel. The lessons of the Lord and his apostles teem with types. Almost every doctrine is given in duplicate : the spirit is provided with a body; a body clothes the spirit. Every fruitful vine has a strong elm to which it clings; every strong elm supports a fruitful vine.

One important use of analogy in moral teaching is to fix the lesson on the imagination and the memory, as you

---

the same position, will follow the same course ; for although different in other features they are similar in form. But you cannot infer that because one floats when thrown into the water the other will float too, for in respect to specific gravity there is no similarity between them. Again, let two pieces of wood, cut from the same tree, be brought together, the one a cube, the other a sphere; you may safely conclude, if one swim in water that the other will swim too, because though of diverse forms they are of the same specific gravity ; but you cannot conclude, if the one roll on an inclined plane, that the other will roll also, because though of the same specific gravity they are of diverse forms. Two objects may be compared for the purpose of inferential analogy, although in nine of their qualities they are wholly dissimilar, if they resemble each other in one, and that the quality with respect to which the comparison is instituted. Again, although two objects be similar in nine of their properties, and dissimilar only in one, no useful analogy can be instituted between them if the object for which the comparison is made have respect to the one point in which they are dissimilar. An acquaintance with such simple rudiments would go far to correct blunders both in the construction and the exposition of analogies.

might moor a boat to a tree on the river's brink to prevent it from gliding down during the night with the stream. A just analogy suggested at the moment serves to prevent the more ethereal spiritual conception from sliding out of its place.

In practical morals analogy is employed to surprise and so overcome an adverse will, rather than merely to help a feeble understanding. In this department most of the Lord's parables lie. When a man is hardened by indulgence in his own sin, so that he cannot perceive the truth which condemns it, the lesson which would have been kept out, if it had approached in a straight line before his face, may be brought home effectually by a circuitous route in the form of a parable. When the conscience stands on its guard against conviction you may sometimes turn the flank of its defences unperceived, and make the culprit a captive ere he is aware. The Pharisees were frequently outwitted in this manner. With complacent self-righteousness they would stand on the outside of the crowd, and, from motives of curiosity, listen to the prophet of Nazareth as he told his stories to the people, until at a sudden turn they perceived that the graphic parable which pleased them so well, was the drawing of the bow that plunged the arrow deep in their own hearts.

A man may be so situated that though his life is in imminent danger, he cannot perceive the danger, and consequently makes no effort to escape. Further, his mind may be so prejudiced that he still counts the beam on which he stands secure, although a neighbour has faithfully given warning that it is about to fall; it may be that because he stands on it he cannot see its frailty. Let some friend who knows his danger, but wishes him well.

approach the spot and hold a mirror in such a position that the infatuated man shall see reflected in it the under and ailing side of the beam that lies between him and the abyss. The work is done: the object is gained: the confident fool, made wise at length, leaps for life upon the solid ground.

Although the faculty of perceiving and understanding analogies is inherent in humanity, and consequently co-extensive with the race, it is developed in a higher degree in some persons and in some communities than in others. The common opinion, that the inhabitants of mountainous countries possess this faculty in a higher measure than the inhabitants of the plains, seems to be sustained by facts. Within the borders of our own island it is quite certain that the Scotch and the Welsh employ figures more readily and relish them more intensely than the English. How far the difference may be directly due to the physical configuration of the country cannot perhaps be accurately ascertained; but doubtless the mountains contribute indirectly to the result, by rendering access more difficult, and so producing a greater measure of isolation and simplicity.

It is an acknowledged and well-known fact, moreover, that the inhabitants of eastern countries are more prone to employ figurative language than the peoples of western Europe; but it is difficult to determine how far this characteristic is due to the meteorological and geographical features of the continent, and how far to hereditary peculiarities of race.

Looking merely to the physical features of their country, you might expect that the inhabitants of Palestine would possess in a high degree the faculty of suggesting and appreciating analogical conceptions; the peculiar history

and jurisprudence of the people must have tended power
fully in the same direction.   Accordingly, as might have
been expected from the circumstances of the nation, it
appears in point of fact on the whole face of the Scriptures, that as the institutes of the commonwealth were
symbolical, the language of the people was figurative.
They were at home in metaphor.   It was their vernacular.
The sudden and bold adoption of physical forms in order
to convey spiritual conceptions, did not surprise—did not
puzzle them.   "Ye are the salt of the earth," "Whereso-
ever the carcase is, there will the eagles be gathered together," fell upon their ears, not as a foreign dialect, but
as the accents of their native tongue.

It might easily be shown that no other characteristic
connected with the form of the Scriptures could have done
so much to facilitate their diffusion in all climes, and in all
ages, as the analogical mould in which a large proportion
of their conceptions is cast; but this is scarcely denied by
any, and is easily comprehended by all.   In another point
of view, less obvious, and not so frequently noticed, the
prevalence in the Scriptures of analogical forms, attaching
spiritual doctrines to natural objects and historic facts,
has served a good purpose in the evidences and exposition of revealed religion.   The more abstract terms of a
language are not so distinctly apprehended as the more con-
crete, and in the course of ages are more liable to change
The habit, universal among the writers of the Scriptures
from the most ancient to the latest, of making abstract
moral conceptions fast to pillars of natural objects and
current facts, has contributed much to fix the doctrines
like fossils for all time, and so to diminish the area of controversy.   All the more steadily and safely has revealed
truth come down from the earliest time to the present day,

that it has in every part of its course run on two distinct but parallel tracks.

2. Parables

The parable is one of the many forms in which the innate analogy between the material and the moral may be, and has been practically applied.* The difficulty of constructing a definition which should include every similitude that belongs to this class, and exclude all others, has been well appreciated by expositors and frankly confessed. The parables of the New Testament, after critics have done their utmost to generalize and classify, must in the end be accounted *sui generis*, and treated apart from all others. The etymology of the name affords us no help, for it is applied without discrimination to widely diverse forms of comparison ; it indicates the juxtaposition of two thoughts or things, with the view of exhibiting and employing the analogy which may be found to subsist between them ; but several other terms convey precisely the same meaning, and therefore it cannot supply us with the distinguishing characteristic of a class. As far as I have been able to observe, hardly anything has been gained at this point by the application of logical processes. The distinctions

---

* Christ made it his business to speak in parables ; and, indeed, one may say, the whole visible world is only a parable of the invisible world. The parable is not only something intermediate between history and doctrine ; it is both history and doctrine—at once historical doctrine and doctrina history. Hence its enchaining, ever fresher, and younger charm. Yes, the parable is nature's own language in the human heart ; hence its universal intelligibility, its, so to speak, permanent sweet scent, its healing balsam, its mighty power to win one to come again and again to hear. In short, the parable is the voice of the people, and hence also the voice of God.— *Die Gleichniss-reden Jesu Christi, von Fred. Arndt,* vol. i. 2.

which have been successfully made are precisely those which are sufficiently obvious without a critical apparatus ; and in regard to those comparisons which bear the closest affinity to the parable, and in which, on account of the rainbow-like blending of the boundaries, logical definitions are most needed, logical definitions have most signally failed. Scholars have, for example, successfully distinguished parables from myths and fables ; but this is laboriously to erect a fence between two flocks that in their nature manifest no tendency to intermingle; whereas, from some other forms of analogy, such as the allegory, the parable cannot be separated by a definition expressed in general terms, which shall be at once universally applicable and universally understood.

Into all parables human motives and actions go as constituents, and in most of them the processes of nature are also interwoven. The element of human action is generally introduced in a historic form, as " a certain man had two sons ;" but some of the similitudes of Scripture, which by general consent are reckoned parables, lack this feature, as for example, the Lost Sheep.* "What man of you, having an hundred sheep ?" For my own part,' while there are some that, on the one hand, I can with confidence include, and some that, on the other, I must with equal confidence keep out, I see not a few lying

---

* It is not, however, by the universal consent of critics that even this is admitted as a genuine parable. Schultze boldly excludes it ; but he excludes also all the group in Matt. xiii. except the Tares. By one arbitrary rule after another, he cuts down the whole number of our Lord's parables to eleven.—*A. H. A. Schultze, de parabolarum J. C. indole poetica com.* Men have good cause to suspect the accuracy of their artificial rules, when the application of them works such havoc. Better that we should have no critical rules, than adopt such as separate on superficial literal grounds, things that the judgment of the Church and the common sense of men have in all ages joined together as substantially of the same class.

ambiguous on the border. My judgment inclines to what seems a medium between two extremes,—between the decision of some German philosophical expositors who are too critical, and the decision of some English practical preachers who are not critical enough. I would fain eschew, on the one hand, the laborious trifling by which it is proved that the parable of the Sower is not a parable; and, on the other hand, the unfortunate facility which admits into the number almost all similitudes indiscriminately. I shall adopt the list of Dr Trench,* thirty in number, as being on the whole a fair and convenient medium ; although I could not undertake to demonstrate that these only, and these all possess the qualities which in his judgment go to constitute a parable. Some that are included can scarcely be distinguished by logical definitions from some that are excluded ; but so far am I from considering this a defect, that I deem it a necessary result of the impalpable infinitesimal graduation by which the fully-formed parable glides down into the brief detached metaphorical aphorism, in the words of the Lord Jesus during the period of his ministry.

Certain figurative lessons, differing from the parable on the one hand, and the allegory on the other, may be found scattered up and down both in the Scriptures and in secular literature, whose distinguishing characteristic is, that they are not spoken but enacted, and which I am disposed to regard as more nearly allied than any other to the parables of our Lord.

They seem to constitute a species of simple primitive germinal drama. Some examples occur in the history of the Hebrew monarchy before the period of the captivity. At Elisha's request, Joash, King of Israel, shot arrows

---

* Notes on the Parables.

from a bow, in token of the victory which he should obtain over the Syrians. Left without instructions as to the frequency with which the operation should be repeated, the king shot three arrows successively into the ground, and paused. Thereupon the prophet, interpreting the symbol, declared that the subjugation of the Syrians would not be complete (2 Kings xiii.) Another specimen may be observed, shining through the history in the reign of Jehoshaphat, when a prophet named Chenaanah made a pair of iron horns, and flattered the King of Israel by the symbol that he would push the Syrians till he should consume them (2 Chron. xvii. 10). About the time of the captivity, and in the hands of Ezekiel, this species of parable appears with great distinctness of outline, and considerable fulness of detail. When a frivolous people would not take warning of their danger, the prophet, godly and grave, took a broad flat tile, and sketched on it the outline of a besieged city, and lay on his left side, silently contemplating the symbol of his country's fate (chap. iv.) The strange act of the revered man attracted many eyes, and stirred new questionings in many hearts. Equally graphic is the representation of Israel's captivity, in the dramatic parable recorded in chap. xii., where the prophet personally enacts the melancholy process of packing his goods, and escaping as an exile.

From the subsequent history, we learn that this significant act arrested attention ; the people gazed in wonder on the sign, and anxiously inquired into its meaning.

It is eminently worthy of notice that the lavish and bold imagery of Ezekiel effectually served the immediate purpose for which it was employed ; it attracted the people's regard, explained the prophecy to their understandings, and fixed the lessons in their memories. It is true, indeed, that they did not repent ; but this only shows that parables, even when dictated by the Spirit, have not inherent power to convert ; even God's word may, through the hearer's sin, remain a dead letter in his hand. It emerges incidentally in the history that the preaching of Ezekiel was eminently popular ; crowds came out to hear and see.

The ultimate spiritual success lies in other hands ; but in as far as the instrument is concerned, it is proved, from the experience of this ancient prophet, that the mastery of analogies draws the people round the preacher's feet, and brings his lessons into contact with their minds and hearts.

In modern times, much argument is employed to prove that the drama may be pure in itself, and effectual as a moral educator,—argument which, however excellent it may be in theory, has hitherto proved impotent in fact. But from the beginning it was not so ; Ezekiel was a dramatist ; he acted his prophecies and his preachings on a stage. The warnings were in this form clearly articulated, and forcefully driven home ; if they failed to produce the ultimate result of repentance, the obstacle lay not in the feebleness of the instrument, but in the wilful hardness of the subject whereon the instrument was plied. Dramatic representation in the simplicity of its infancy was a golden vessel of the sanctuary, employed in the service of God; long ago it was carried away into Baby-lon, and profanely used as a wine cup in the orgies of idols Whether it shall ever be wrenched from the enemy, puri-fied, and restored to the service of the temple, I know not.

In the general history of the world, the most interesting parable of this class that occurs to my memory is one attributed to a North American Indian in conversation with a Christian missionary. The red man had previously been well instructed in the Scriptures, understood the way of salvation, and enjoyed peace with God. Desiring to explain to his teacher the turning point of his spiritual experience, he had recourse, in accordance, perhaps, with the instincts and habits of his tribe, to the language of dramatic symbols rather than to the language of articulate words. Having gathered a quantity of dry withered tree leaves, he spread them in a thin layer, and in a circular form on the level ground. He then gently laid a living worm in the centre, and set fire to the circumference on every side. The missionary and the Indian then stood still and silent, watching the motions of the imprisoned reptile. It crawled hastily and in alarm towards one side, till it met the advancing girdle of fire, and then crawled back as hastily to the other. After making several ineffectual efforts to escape, the creature retired to the centre, and coiled itself up to await its fate. At this crisis, and just before the flames reached their helpless victim, the Indian stept gravely forward, lifted the worm from its fiery prison, and deposited it in a place of safety. " Thus," this simple preacher of the cross indicated to the missionary,—" Thus helpless and hopeless I lay, while the wrath due to my sin advanced on every side to devour me ; and thus sovereignly, mightily, lovingly did Christ deliver my soul from death."

3. Parables of Our Lord

Metaphorical language, as we have seen, is deeply rooted in the fundamental analogy which subsists between the several departments of our Creator's work ; and the parable is a species of figure which, for all practical purposes, is sufficiently distinguished from others, although it is scarcely possible to isolate it by a complete logical definition. Nor is it enough to say that those specimens which are found in the record of Christ's ministry belong to the species ; they may be said to constitute a species by themselves. The parables which are known to literature beyond the pale of the evangelic histories are either very diverse in kind, or very few in number. The practical result is, that while we treat the parable as a distinct species of analogical instruction, we must treat the parables spoken by the Lord as a unique and separate class. As the Lord's people in ancient times dwelt alone, and were not reckoned among the nations, the Lord's parabolic teaching stands apart by itself, and cannot with propriety be associated with other specimens of metaphorical teaching. Logically as well as spiritually it is true, that " never man spake like this man."

But, when setting aside all other forms of comparison, we confine our regard to the parable, and, setting aside other specimens, we confine our regard to the parables spoken by the Lord, other questions arise concerning the internal and reciprocal relations of these peculiar compositions ; should they be read and considered as so many independent units miscellaneously scattered over the evangelic record, or should they be classified according to the place which belongs to them in a system of dogmatics? or can any method of treatment be suggested different from both of these extremes, and better than either ?

It is doubtless competent to any inquirer to frame the doctrines which the parables illustrate into a logical scheme, and in his exposition to transpose the historical

order, so that the sequence of the subjects shall coincide
with his arrangement.   This method is lawful in regard
to the parables particularly, as it is in regard to the contents of Scripture generally ; but, as a method of prosecuting the inquiry, I think it loses more on the side of
topical and historical interest than it gains on the side of
logical precision.   As the Bible generally is in its own
natural order, both more engaging and more instructive
than a catechism compiled from it, although the compiler
may have been both skilful and true ; the parables of
the Lord, in particular, taken up as they lie in his ministry, are both more interesting and more profitable than a
logical digest of the theology which they contain, however
faithfully the digest may have been made.

Any one may observe, as he reads our Lord's parables,
that some of them are chiefly occupied with the teaching
of doctrine, and others with the reproof of prevailing sins ;
but when on the basis of these and other subordinate
distinctions, you proceed to arrange them into separate
classes, you are met and repelled by insurmountable
difficulties.   When Bauer, for example, has arranged
them in three divisions, dogmatic, moral, and historic,
he is compelled immediately to add another class called
the mixed, as dogmatic-moral and dogmatic-historic,
thereby proving that his logical classification has failed.*

By abandoning, for the purposes of exposition, the
order in which the parables have been recorded, and

* In reference to Bauer's classification, Limbourg Brower (de parabol. Jesu.)
observes that the distinction between parables that are dogmatic and parables that are moral cannot successfully be maintained, because of the intimate
union maintained in the discourses of Jesus between the revelation of truth
and the inculcation of duty.   This remark, in connection with its ground, is
decisive not only against the particular division to which it is applied, but to
all divisions, in as far as they pretend to be logically distinct and complete.

adopting a classification on the basis of contents or form, some incidental advantages are obtained; especially some otherwise necessary repetitions are avoided, and some subordinate relations are by the juxtaposition more easily observed; but the loss is, I apprehend, much greater than the gain. The temptation to bend the freely-growing branches of the parable, that they may take their places in the scheme, is by this method greatly increased; while historical sequences and logical relations, lying more or less concealed in the record, are in a great measure thrown away. Accordingly, I prefer the method of maintaining in the exposition the order which the evangelists have adopted in the narrative. Besides the advantage of preserving in all cases the historical circumstances whence the parable sprung, we discover, as we follow this track, several groups associated together by the Lord in his ministry, for the sake of their reciprocal relations, and reverently preserved in their places by the evangelical historians. The seven in Matt. xiii., and the three in Luke xv., constitute the chief of those dogmatic groupings formed to our hand in the ministry of the Lord. I refer to them here as examples, but defer the exposition of their sequences and relations, until it can be presented with greater advantage in connection with the examination of their contents.

A question, on some of its sides difficult, meets us here, regarding the reason why the Lord employed parables in the prosecution of his ministry. On the one hand, it is certainly true, as may be proved from all history, that comparisons between material and moral facts or laws, spring up naturally in human converse; and further, that the truth expressed in parables, if not in all cases immediately palpable, is better fitted both to arrest attention at first, and to imprint the lesson permanently on the learner's memory. But the use and usefulness of the parable in this respect are obvious and undisputed; it makes spiritual truth more attractive and more memorable. The difficulty does not lie on this side; it adheres to a second function of the parable, in some respects the opposite of the first, —the function of concealing the doctrine in judgment from closed eyes and hardened hearts. In some instances and to some extent, the parables, while they conveyed the doctrine to one portion of the audience, concealed it from another. In those cases "they are like the husk which preserves the kernel *from* the indolent, and *for* the earnest."* It is the method, not unknown in other departments of the divine government, of making the same fact or law at once profitable to the humble, and punitive to the proud. Not only the Lord's word, but also the Lord himself, partakes of this twofold character, and produces these diverse effects; the same rock on which a meek disciple surely builds his hope, is also the stone over which scoffers stumble in their final fall.

The judicial or penal function of the parable was indicated by the Lord in express terms when he explained the meaning of the sower in private to his own disciples (Matt. xiii. 11–17; Mark iv. 10–13). In these cases, however, the wilful blindness of men's hearts appears as the sin which brought down the punishment, and the obstacle which kept out the blessing. Every word of God is good; but some persons maintain such an averted attitude of mind, that it glides off like sunbeams from polar snows, without ever obtaining an entrance to melt or fructify. To one of two persons who stand in the same room gazing on the same picture in the sunlight, the beauty of the land

---

* *Gerlach in Lange.*

scape may be fully revealed, while to the other, on account of a certain indirectness of position and view, it appears only as an unpleasant dazzling glare. So, of two Jews who both eagerly listened to Jesus, as he taught from the fishing-boat on the Lake of Galilee, one found in the story the word of the kingdom, refreshing as cold waters to a thirsty soul, while the other, hearing the same words, perceived nothing in them but incoherent and tantalizing enigmas. For the right comprehension of the parables in particular, as of revealed truth in general, a receptive heart is a qualification even more peremptorily and essentially necessary than a penetrating understanding. "If any man is willing to do his will, he shall know of the doctrine, whether it be of God" (John vii. 17).

Each of the parables contained some characteristic, or presented some aspect of Christ's kingdom. His kingdom was not of this world, and therefore it was intensely distasteful to the carnal Jews of that day. The idea did not readily enter their mind; and when it did in some measure penetrate, it kindled in their corrupt hearts a flame of persecuting rage. It was necessary that the Lord should, during the period of his personal ministry, fully develop and deposit the seed of the kingdom; but it was necessary also that he should remain on earth until the set time when his ministry as prophet should terminate in his offering as priest. Now, if he had at any period displayed all the characteristics of his kingdom in terms which the mob and their rulers were able to comprehend, the persecution that ultimately crucified him, would have burst prematurely forth, and so deranged the plan of the Omniscient. It was necessary, for example, in order to provide consolation for his own disciples in subsequent temptations, that the Lord should predict his own death

and resurrection; but this prediction when uttered in
public, was veiled from hostile eyes under the symbol,
"Destroy this temple, and in three days I will raise it up"
(John ii. 19). More generally, it was necessary that such
features of the kingdom as its spiritual character and its
expansive power should be made known to true disciples
for their instruction and encouragement, but hidden for a
time from persecutors in order to restrain their enmity.
Parables served the twofold purpose. Tender, teachable
spirits caught the meaning at once; or, if they failed, they
asked and obtained an explanation from the Master in
private; while those who had not the single eye, were for
the time left in darkness. It was their own hardness that
kept out the light; their own hardness was employed as
the instrument whereby judgment was inflicted upon
themselves.*

4. Interpretation of the Parables

Of the parables in particular, as of the Scriptures
generally, it is true that faith is necessary to the full
appreciation of their meaning. That you must understand the Scriptures in order to have faith, and have faith
in order to understand the Scriptures, is indeed, a circle ;

---

* In Matthew (xiii. 13) he speaks in parables, "because (ὅτι), they seeing, see not:" and in Mark (iv. 12), and Luke (viii. 10), "that (ἵνα) seeing
they might not see." Two different objects were effected at the same time,
and by the same act, corresponding to those two terms; it is true that the
Lord employed parables, as one employs pictures to teach a child, *because*
his auditors were children in understanding; and it is also true that he veiled
his doctrines under metaphor *in order that* those who were children in
understanding but in malice men, might not perceive his drift, and so might
not violently interfere to suppress his ministry. Thus according to the explanation which he gave at the moment, "Whosoever hath, to him shall
be given, and he shall have more abundance; but whosoever hath not, from
him shall be taken away even that he hath" (Matt. xiii. 12).

but it is not a vicious circle. As you approach from without, you may perceive that the Bible is the word of God, and that the Christ whom it reveals is the Saviour of sinners ; standing now on your new position, and recognising your Instructor as also your Redeemer, you will discover in his word a length, and breadth, and height, and depth, which were formerly concealed. In our day, as well as when the parables were first spoken, it is to his own disciples that their true meaning is made known.

Another cognate requisite to the true spiritual comprehension of these divine sayings, is sympathy with the view which Jesus took and gave of human nature in its fallen state. He spoke and acted not only as the Teacher of the ignorant, but also as the Saviour of the lost: if we do not occupy the same stand-point, and look upon humanity in the same light, we shall stumble at every step in our effort to comprehend what the Speaker meant.

These two qualifications are supreme; and they apply alike to divine revelation as a whole, and to each of its parts ; there are others which are important though subordinate, and which bear more specially on the particular department of Scripture exegesis with which we are here engaged, the Parables of the Lord.*

1. The faculty of perceiving and appreciating analogies
It is certainly not necessary that an interpreter of Scrip-

---

* The Parables of the Kingdom are, as it were, a picture gallery, and we walk up and down it, examining each picture by itself. We must not forget, however, that these are heavenly pictures that hang around us,—that heavenly things are here exposed to view. A heavenly interpreter walks by our side : we must have a heavenly sense if we would grasp the meaning of what we hear and see. If our study quicken this sense within us, so that it shall grow clearer and sharper before every picture, a rich treat awaits us, for the heavenly Gallery is great.—*Dräseke, vom Reich Gottes,* i., 270.

ture should be a poet; but to possess in some measure that eye for parallels which constitutes the basis of the poetic faculty, is a most desirable qualification for one who proposes to help his neighbours in the study of the parables. It is, indeed, true that a man who possesses only a very small measure of this or of other mental gifts, may read these lessons of the Lord with spiritual profit to himself; but the pictorial theology of the New Testament is not safe in the hands of a teacher who is signally defective in the faculty to which it specially appeals. Learning, and zeal, and faith combined may, in this department, expend much labour to little purpose, for lack of power to perceive the point of the analogy. But, on the other hand,

2. A stern logic is as necessary as a lively imagination. Deficient in the analogical faculty, you cannot in this department go quickly forward; but deficient in the logical faculty, you will go forward too fast and too far. We need a well-spread, well-filled sail; but we need also a helm to direct the ship in the path of safety. Restraining, discriminating judgment, is as necessary as impulsive power. Every one who possesses even a moderate acquaintance with the literature of this department will, I am persuaded, acknowledge the justice of this observation. Some expositors of the parables, especially in more ancient times, remind one of the *Great Eastern* in the Atlantic when her rudder was disabled. There is plenty of impelling force, but this force, for want of a director, only makes the ship go round and round in a weltering sea. From the pages of those commentators, whose imaginations have broken loose, you may cull fancies as manifold, as beautiful, and as useless as the gyrations of a helmless ship in a stormy sea.

3. Some competent acquaintance, not only with the Scriptures, but also with the doctrines which the Scriptures contain, arranged in a dogmatic system, is necessary as a safeguard in the interpretation of the parables. A scientific acquaintance with natural history is necessary not only in order to an intelligent appreciation of the contents of a museum, but also in order that you may turn to good account your miscellaneous observation of nature; in like manner, although a correct exegesis of Scripture supplies us with our only true dogmatics, the knowledge of dogmatics, scientifically arranged, contributes in turn to a correct exegesis. This remark has been drawn from me by my own experience in the study of this deparment of theological literature. If we would avoid the mistakes into which his own contemporaries fell, we must read the Lord's parables in connection with the fuller exposition of divine truth which he commissioned and inspired the apostles to give. Except in some cases where an explanation is subjoined, or the circumstances exclude all uncertainty, it is not safe for us to lean on a parable as an independent evidence of a dogma. The pictorial illustrations and the more direct doctrinal statements of Scripture should go together for reciprocal elucidation and support. More especially it is extremely dangerous for a theologian, when he has a purpose to be served and an adversary to be refuted, to grasp a parable in the sense which suits his view, and wield it as a weapon of offence; in such a case he will probably do more execution upon himself than upon his antagonist. The importance of this point will be more fully seen when we consider the parables in detail.

4. Some knowledge of relative history, topography, and customs should be at hand for use; but, at the same time,

these things should be resolutely kept in their own place They may be good servants, but they are bad masters. Through a signal defect in the knowledge of oriental antiquity, an interpreter may permit some beautiful allusions to slip through his hands unperceived ; but, on the other hand, it ought to be frankly conceded, and, if necessary, firmly maintained, that the profitable use of our Lord's parables does not depend on rare and difficult erudition. If a deficiency in this department infers the risk of baldness in the exposition, a redundance supplies a temptation to pedantic display. It is one thing to place some ancient eastern custom in such a position that a ray of light from its surface shall pleasantly illumine a feature of the parable that was lying in the shade, and all another thing to make the parable a convenience for the exhibition of a scholar's lore.

With more immediate reference to the exposition herewith submitted, it is enough to intimate that it is neither a compend of criticism, nor merely a series of sermons. I have endeavoured to combine the substance of a critical investigation with the direct exhortation which becomes a minister of the gospel, when fellow-sinners constitute his audience, and the Bible supplies his theme. On the one hand, no important difficulty has been consciously slurred over without an effort to satisfy the judgment of a studious reader ; and, on the other hand, no opportunity has been omitted of pressing the gospel of Christ on the consciences of men.

Introduction: Parables in Matthew 13
(Matthew 13:1-3)

" The same day went Jesus out of the house, and sat by the sea side. And great multitudes were gathered together unto him, so that he went into a ship, and sat; and
the whole multitude stood on the shore. And he spake many things unto them in
parables."

IN Matthew's narrative, the first specimen of that
peculiar pictorial method which characterized
the teaching of our Lord, is not an isolated
parable occurring in the midst of a miscellaneous discourse, but a group of seven presented in one
continuous and connected report. Nor is the grouping
due to the logical scheme of the Evangelist; we have
here, not the historian's digest of many disjointed utter-
ances, but a simple chronological record of facts. In this
order have these seven parables been recorded by the
servant, because in this order they were spoken by the
Lord. It does not in the least detract from the soundness of this judgment to concede that some of them were
spoken also in other circumstances and other combina-
tions. There is no ground whatever for assuming that
one of our Lord's signal sayings could not have been

spoken in one place, because it can be proved that it was spoken at another. From the nature of the subjects, and the form which Christ's ministry assumed, it might be confidently anticipated that the parables and other sharply relieved similitudes would recur, in whole or in part, in different discourses and before different assemblies: with this supposition accordingly the facts agree, as they may be gathered from a synopsis of the several narratives.

Among the later German critics, it is distinctly conceded by Lange that these seven parables were spoken by the Lord in the order of Matthew's record, although some of them appear to have been spoken also at other times. If it could have been proved that none of the parables had ever been spoken a second time, the circumstance would have constituted a non-natural and inexplicable phenomenon.

A measure of logical order and reciprocal relation has always been observed in this cluster of parables. While some of the relations, and these the most important, are so obvious that they have been observed alike by all inquirers, in regard to others a considerable diversity of opinion has prevailed. Some, in the sequences of the group, look only for various phases of the kingdom, presented in logical divisions and sub-divisions: others find here, in addition, a prophetic history of the Church, like that which the Apocalypse contains. For my own part I am disposed to confine my view to that which I consider sure and obvious,—the representation of the kingdom of God in different aspects, according to a logical arrangement, not pronouncing judgment regarding the soundness of the prophetic view, but simply passing it by, as being from its nature difficult and dim.

The first six readily fall into three successive well-defined pairs, and the seventh stands clearly designated by its subject as an appropriate conclusion. The *first* pair exhibit the RELATIONS of the kingdom to the several classes of intelligent creatures with which, as adversaries or subjects, it comes into contact: the *second* pair exhibit the PROGRESS of the kingdom from small beginnings to a glorious issue: the *third* pair exhibit the PRECIOUS-NESS of the kingdom, in comparison with all other objects of desire: and the remaining *one* teaches that the good and evil which intermingle on earth will be completely and finally separated in the great day. Thus—

I. RELATIONS....
1. *The Sower;* the relation of the kingdom to different *classes of men.*
2. *The Tares;* the relation of the kingdom to *the wicked one.*

II. PROGRESS......
1. *The Mustard-seed;* the progress of the kingdom under the idea of *a living growth.*
2. *The Leaven;* the progress of the kingdom under the idea of *a contagious outspread.*

III. PRECIOUSNESS
1. *The Hid Treasure;* the precious-ness of the kingdom under the idea of *discovering what was hid.*
2. *The Goodly Pearl;* the precious-ness of the kingdom under the idea of *closing with what is offered.*

IV SEPARATION..
The Draw-net; the separation between good and evil in the great day.

It is not a valid objection to this division that in several cases, if not in all, the subjects reciprocally overlap each other; it is, in the circumstances, natural and necessary that they should. Thus, in regard to the first pair, the work of the adversary appears in the sower, and the contact of believers with unbelievers appears in the tares; but I think these are in either case incidental and subordinate, while the leading idea of the first is the reception given to the gospel by different classes of men, and the leading idea of the second is the wile of the devil in his effort to destroy the work of Christ.

We must, however, beware of giving too much and too minute attention to the sequences and mutual relations of the parables. Most of them, in point of fact, are found in the narrative as isolated lessons, each complete in itself and independent of others. Even in this group, although the connections are interesting and obvious, they are not essential. The meaning of each specimen may be substantially discerned without reference to its place in the series. By studying each apart you may learn the lesson well; but by studying all together you may learn the lesson better.

On the face of the narrative it appears that the first four were addressed to a multitude congregated on the margin of the lake, and the last three more privately to a smaller circle of disciples in a neighbouring house; but there seems no ground for supposing that the two portions were separated from each other by any considerable interval of time or space.

I freely concede that there is some ground for the distinction between the more outward and obvious aspects of the kingdom presented in the first four, and the more inward and experimental matters which, in the last three, were subsequently communicated to a more private circle; but the distinction, though real and perceptible, does not appear to me so fundamental and so deeply marked as to justify those who make it the turning-point of their exposition.

There is a parallel which the thoughtful reader of the Scriptures will not fail to observe, although a prudent expositor will beware of attempting to trace it too minutely, between the seven parables of this chapter and the epistles to the Seven Churches of Asia, in the beginning of the Apocalypse. The two groups agree in this, that both represent by a series of examples various features of the kingdom, and various obstacles with which it must contend: they differ in that, while the examples given in the Gospels are pictures drawn by the imagination, the examples given in the Apocalypse are facts taken from history. But as all the characteristics and vicissitudes of his Church were present to the Head from the beginning, it was as easy for him to exhibit an image of its condition through the ministry of Matthew, as to record examples after they emerged in fact, through the ministry of John. In both cases—alike in the pictures presented to the Galilean crowd and the registered events sent to the Asiatic Churches—the Master's design is to exhibit the kingdom on all its sides, that the observer's view, whether of beauties or of blemishes, may be correct and full.

I subjoin for the reader's information the view of those who see in this series of parables the subsequent historical development of the Church, as it is briefly and clearly expressed by Lange: " We .... trace in the parable of the sower a picture of the apostolic age; in the parable of the tares, the ancient Catholic Church springing up in the midst of heresies; in the parable of the mustard-bush resorted to by birds of the air as if it had been a tree, and loaded with their nests, a representation of the outward Church as established under Constantine the Great; in the leaven that is mixed among the three measures of meal, the pervading and transforming influence of Christianity in the mediæval Church among the barbarous races of Europe; in the parable of the treasure in the field, the period of the Reformation; in the parable of the pearl, the contrast between Christianity and the acquisitions of modern culture and secularism; and in the last parable a picture of the closing judgment."

The parallel which the same critic institutes between the seven parables of this group and the seven beatitudes of the Sermon on the Mount, is an attractive study, and some of the coincidences are obvious and beautiful; but this line of observation should be jealously kept subordinate to the primary substantial lesson which each parable contains. On the one hand, I desire that these secondary and incidental views should not by their beauty draw to themselves a disproportionate share of our attention; and on the other hand, I am disposed to respect every earnest, sober, and reverential suggestion which any believing inquirer may throw out, regarding the lateral references and under-current secondary meanings of the Lord's discourses; for they possess a length and breadth, and height and depth, which will exercise the minds of devout disciples as long as the dispensation lasts, and pass all understanding when it is done.

The Sower
(Matthew 13:1-9, 18-23)

"The same day went Jesus out of the house, and sat by the sea side. And great multitudes were gathered together unto him, so that he went into a ship, and sat ; and the whole multitude stood on the shore. And he spake many things unto them in parables, saying, Behold, a sower went forth to sow; and when he sowed, some seeds fell by the way side, and the fowls came and devoured them up : some fell upon stony places, where they had not much earth : and forthwith they sprung up, because they had no deepness of earth : and when the sun was up, they were scorched ; and because they had no root, they withered away. And some fell among thorns ; and the thorns sprung up, and choked them : but other fell into good ground, and brought forth fruit, some an hundredfold, some sixtyfold, some thirtyfold. Who hath ears to hear, let him hear. . . . . Hear ye therefore the parable of the sower. When any one heareth the word of the kingdom, and understandeth it not, then cometh the wicked one, and catcheth away that which was sown in his heart. This is he which received seed by the way side. But he that received the seed into stony places, the same is he that heareth the word, and anon with joy receiveth it ; yet hath he not root in himself, but dureth for a while : for when tribulation or persecution ariseth because of the word, by and by he is offended. He also that received seed among the thorns is he that heareth the word ; and the care of this world, and the deceitfulness of riches, choke the word, and he becometh unfruitful. But he that received seed into the good ground is he that heareth the word, and understandeth it ; which also beareth fruit, and bringeth forth, some an hundredfold, some sixty, some thirty."

THE parable is, in our language at least, so uniformly associated with this name, that it would not readily be recognised under any other designation; but " The four kinds of ground" (viererlei Acker), the title which seems to be in ordinary use among the Germans, is logically more correct, inasmuch as it points directly to the central idea, and expresses the distinctive characteristic.

At this period a great and eager multitude followed

the steps of Jesus and hung upon his lips. A certain divine authority, strangely combined with the tenderest human sympathy, marked his discourses sharply off, as entirely different in kind from all that they had been accustomed to hear in the synagogue. Finding that instincts and capacities hitherto dormant in their being were awakened by his word, "the common people heard him gladly." At an earlier hour of the same day on which this parable was spoken, the circle of listeners that encompassed the Teacher had become so broad and dense, that his mother and brothers, who had come from home to speak with him, were obliged to halt on the outskirts of the crowd, and pass their message in from mouth to mouth. In these circumstances, the Preacher's work must have been heavy, and doubtless the worker was weary. Having paused till the press slackened, he privately retired to the margin of the lake, desiring probably to "rest a while;" but no sooner had he taken his seat beside the cool still water, than he was again surrounded by the anxious crowd. At once to escape the pressure and to command the audience better when he should again begin to speak, he stepped into one of the fishing-boats that floated at ease close by the beach, on the margin of that tideless inland sea. From the water's edge, stretching away upward on the natural gallery formed by the sloping bank, the great congregation, with every face fixed in an attitude of eager expectancy, presented to the Preacher's eye the appearance of a ploughed field ready to receive the seed. As he opened his lips, and cast the word of life freely abroad among them, he saw, he felt, the parallel between the sowing of Nature and the sowing of Grace. Into that mould, accordingly, he threw the lesson of saving truth. Grasping the facts and laws of his own material world, and wielding them with steady aim as instruments in the establishment of his spiritual kingdom, in simple yet majestic terms he said, " Behold, a sower went forth to sow."

Whether a sower was actually in sight at that moment in a neighbouring field or not, every man in that rural assemblage must have been familiar with the act, and would instantly recognise the truth of the picture. The sower, with a bag of seed dependent from his shoulder, stalks slowly forth into the prepared field. With measured, equal steps, he marches in a straight line along the furrow. His hand, accustomed to keep time with his advancing footsteps, and to jerk the seed forward with considerable force, in order to secure uniformity of distribution, cannot suddenly stop when he approaches the hard trodden margin of the field. By habit the right hand continues to execute its wonted movement in unison with the sower's steps as he is turning round; and thus a portion of the seed is thrown on the unploughed border of the field and the public path that skirts it. Birds, scared for a moment by the presence of the man, hover in the air till his back is turned on another tack, and then, each eager to be first, come swooping down, and swallow up all the grain that found no soft place where it fell for hiding in. Even if it should happen in any case that no birds were near, the seed that fell on the way side was as surely destroyed in another way : the alternative suggested in Luke's narrative is, that "it is trodden under foot of men."

But while the portion of the seed that fell on the way side was thus certainly destroyed, it does not follow that all the rest came to perfection : " Some fell upon stony places, where they had not much earth: and forthwith they sprung up, because they had no deepness of earth: and when the sun was up they were scorched; and because they had no root, they withered away." The stony places are not portions of the field where many separate stones may be seen lying on the surface, but portions which consist of continuous rock underneath, with a thin sprinkling of soft soil over it. Here the young plants burst through the ground sooner than in spots where the seed found a deeper bed: but when the rains of spring have ceased, and the sun of summer has waxed hot, the moisture is quickly exhaled from the shallow stratum of soil, and forthwith the fair promise dies.

But yet another slip there may be " between the cup and the lip:" even from the seed that falls on deep, soft ground, you cannot count with certainty on a rich return in harvest. Although the plants should without obstruction strike their roots deeply into the soft, moist earth, and rear their stalks aloft into the balmy air, they may be rendered barren at last by the simultaneous growth of rivals more imperious and more powerful than themselves. Unless the grain not only grow in deeply broken ground, but grow alone there, it cannot be fruitful: " Some fell among thorns; and the thorns sprung up and choked it." Besides those plants that are more correctly denominated thorns, we may include under the term here all rank weeds, varying with countries and climates, which infest the soil and hurt the harvest. The green stalks that grow among thorns are neither withered in spring, nor stunted in their summer's growth; they may be found in harvest taller than their fruitful neighbours; but the ear is never filled, never ripened, and the reaper gets nothing in his arms but long slender straw adorned at the top with graceful clusters of empty chaff. The roots of the thorns drank up the sap of the ground, while their branches veiled off the sunlight, and thus the good seed, starved beneath and overshadowed above, although it started fair in spring, produced nothing in the autumn.

As Truth is one and Error manifold, so in regard to the seed sown, the story of failure is long and varied, the story of success is short and simple: " Other fell into good ground, and brought forth fruit, some an hundredfold, some sixtyfold, some thirtyfold." The design of the picture is to reveal the various causes which at different times and places render the husbandman's labour abortive and leave his garner empty. This done, there is no need of more. The seed, when none of these things impeded it, prospered as a matter of course, under the ordinary care of man and the ordinary gifts of God.

Three distinct obstructions to the growth and ripening of the seed are enumerated in the parable. The statement is exact, and the order transparent. The natural sequences are strictly and beautifully maintained. The three causes of abortion—the way side, the stony ground, and the thorns—follow each other as the spring, the summer, and the autumn. In the first case the seed does not spring at all; in the second it springs, but dies before it grows up; in the third, it grows up, but does not ripen. If it escape the way side, the danger of the stony ground lies before it; if it escape the stony ground, the thorns at a later stage threaten its safety; and it is only when it has successively escaped all three that it becomes fruitful at length.

In this case, the Lord himself gave both the parable and its explanation; he became his own interpreter. The Master takes us, like little children, by the hand, and leads us through all the turnings of his first symbolic lesson, lest in our inexperience we should miss our way. The Son of God not only gave himself as a sacrifice for sin; he also laboured as a patient painstaking teacher of the ignorant: he is the Apostle as well as the High Priest of our profession. His instructions have been recorded by the Spirit in the Scriptures for our use; we may still sit at his feet and listen to his voice. He has taken his seat on the deck of a fishing-boat while the waters of the lake are still, and is discoursing to a congregation of Galileans from the neighbourhood who stand clustering on the shore. Let us join the outskirts of the crowd and hear that heavenly Teacher too.

He speaks in parables: he fixes saving truth in the forms of familiar things, that it may be carried away and kept. We look with lively interest on the scene which these words conjure up before our eyes; but we should look on it reverently: it has not been given to us as a plaything. Gaze gravely, brother, into this parable, for " thou art the man" of whom it speaks: it reveals the way of life and the way of death to thee. If a traveller who possesses an accurate map of his route turn aside from it and perish in a pit, it will not avail him in his extremity to reflect that he carries the correct track in his hand. Alas! a literary admiration of the parable-stories which Jesus told in Galilee will not avail us, if we do not accept himself as our Saviour from sin.

From the Lord's own exposition here and elsewhere recorded, we learn that the seed is the word of God; that the sower is the man who makes it known to his neighbours; and that the ground on which the seed falls is the hearer's heart. The main drift of the parable concerns the ground, and to it accordingly our attention must be chiefly directed. The lesson, however, is drawn, not from the inherent, essential properties of the soil, but from the accidental obstructions to the growth of grain which it may in certain circumstances contain: some notice, therefore, of the seed and the sower in their spiritual signification is not only profitable at this stage, but peremptorily necessary to the full apprehension of the instruction which the parable conveys.

SEED has been created by God and given to man. If it were lost, it would be impossible through human power and skill to procure a new supply: the race would, in that case, perish, unless the Omnipotent should interfere again with his creating power. For spiritual life and food the fallen are equally helpless, and equally dependent on the gift of God. The seed is the word, and the word is contained in the Scriptures. When we drop a verse of the Bible into listening ears, we are sowing the seed of the kingdom.

The seed is the word, but the Word is Christ : " In the beginning was the Word, and the Word was with God, and the Word was God .... and the Word was made flesh and dwelt among us," (John i.) Christ is the living seed, and the Bible is the husk that holds it. The husk that holds the seed is the most precious thing in the world, next after the seed that it holds. The Lord himself precisely defines from this point of view the place and value of the Scriptures,—" They are they which testify of me" (John v. 39). The seed of the kingdom is himself the King. Nor is there any inconsistency in representing Christ as the seed while he was in the first instance also the sower. Most certainly he preached the Saviour, and also was the Saviour whom he preached. The incident in the synagogue at Nazareth (Luke iv. 16-22) is a remarkably distinct example of Christ being at once the

Sower and the Seed. When he had read the lesson of the day, a glorious prophetic gospel from Isaiah, " he closed the book, and gave it again to the minister, and sat down. And the eyes of all them that were in the synagogue were fastened on him. And he began to say unto them, This day is this scripture fulfilled in your ears." As soon as he had taken from the Scriptures the proclamation concerning himself, he laid them aside, and presented himself to the people. The Saviour preached the Saviour, himself the Sower and himself the Seed.

In the beginning of the Gospel, when the chosen band of sowers first went to work upon the ample field of the world, taught of the Spirit, they knew well what seed they ought to carry, and were ever ready to cast it in where they saw an opening. One of them, and he the greatest, formed and expressed a determination to know nothing among the people save Jesus Christ, and him crucified. Twice in one chapter (Acts viii.), we learn incidentally, but with great precision, what kind of seed Philip the Evangelist carried always in his vessel, and cast into every furrow as he passed along. When a large congregation assembled in the city of Samaria to hear him, " he preached Christ unto them;" and when, on a subsequent occasion, he was called to deal with an anxious inquirer alone in the desert, " he opened his mouth and began at the same scripture"—He was led as a lamb to the slaughter—"and preached unto him Jesus." This is the seed sent down from heaven to be the life of the world.

The SOWERS, although they have become a great company in these latter days, are still, like the reapers, " few" in relation to the vastness of the field. The Lord's message to Ananias of Damascus concerning Saul, immediately after his conversion, graphically defines the office of a minister as a sower of the seed: " He is a chosen vessel unto me, to bear my name before the Gentiles, and kings, and the children of Israel" (Acts ix. 15). A vessel for holding Christ and dropping that precious seed into human hearts wherever an opening should appear—this is the true idea of a minister of the Gospel. Nor is the work confined to those who, being trained to it, and freed from other cares, may thereby be capable of conducting it on a larger scale. As every leaf of the forest and every ripple on the lake, which itself receives a sunbeam on its breast, may throw the sunbeam off again, and so spread the light around; in like manner, every one, old or young, who receives Christ into his heart may and will publish with his life and lips that blessed name. In the spirit of the Lord's own precept regarding the harvest, we may all be encouraged to adopt and press the prayer that our Father, the husbandman, would send forth sowers into his field.

We turn now to the GROUND, and the various *obstacles* which there successively meet the seed and mar its fruitfulness.

I. THE WAY SIDE.—" When any one heareth the word of the kingdom, and understandeth it not, then cometh the wicked one, and catcheth away that which was sown in his heart. This is he which received seed by the way side." A path beaten smooth by the feet of travellers skirts the edge, or, perhaps, runs by way of short cut through the middle of the field. The seed that falls there, left exposed on the surface, is picked up and devoured by birds. Behold in one picture God's gracious offer, man's self-destroying neglect, and the tempter's coveted opportunity!

The analogy being true to nature is instantly recognised and easily appreciated. There is a condition of heart which corresponds to the smoothness, hardness, and wholeness of a frequented footpath, that skirts or crosses a ploughed field. The spiritual hardness is like the natural in its cause as well as in its character. The place is a thoroughfare; a mixed multitude of this world's affairs tread over it from day to day, and from year to year. It is not fenced like a garden, but exposed like an uncultivated common. That secret of the Lord, " Enter into thy closet," and "shut the door," is unknown; or if known, neglected. The soil, trodden by all comers, is never broken up and softened by a thorough self-searching. A human heart may thus become marvellously callous both to good and evil. The terrors of the Lord and the tender invitations of the Gospel are alike ineffectual. Falling only upon the external senses, they are swept off by the next current; as the solid grain thrown from the sower's hand rattles on the smooth hard road side, and lies on the surface till the fowls carry it away. The parallel between the material and the moral here is more close and visible in the original than it appears in the English version. But our language is capable in this instance, like the Greek, of expressing by one phrase equally the moral and the material failure: " Every one that hears the word of the kingdom and does not take it in" ($\mu\dot{\eta}$ $\sigma\nu\nu\iota\acute{e}\nu\tau\sigma\varsigma$). The cause of the failure in both departments is, that the soil, owing to its hardness, does not take the seed into its bosom.

The seed is good: " The word of God is quick and powerful;"—that is, it " is living, and puts forth energy."* Like buried moistened seed it swells and bursts, and forces its way through opposing obstacles. A heart of clay, smoothed and hardened on the surface, may hold it out for a lifetime; but a heart of stone could not keep it down, if it were once admitted, for a single day.

"Behold the Lamb of God, which taketh away the sin of the world;" "If any man thirst, let him come unto me and drink;" "Believe on the Lord Jesus Christ, and thou shalt be saved;"—these and many such great solid seed-grains rain from heaven upon us in this land: shall we close all the avenues to our hearts and so leave that seed lying on the surface till the enemy carry it away? or shall the groanings which cannot be uttered, the convictions of sin in the conscience, rend at length the seared crust, that the seed may enter and occupy the life for God?

If privileged and professing hearers of the Gospel come short of the kingdom, the fault lies not in the seed—the fault lies not often or to a great extent even in the sower, although his work may have been feebly and unskilfully done. If the seed is good, and the ground well prepared, a very poor and awkward kind of sowing will suffice. Seed flung in any fashion into the soft ground will grow; whereas, if it fall on the way side, it will bear no fruit, however artfully it may have been spread. My father was a practical and skilful agriculturist. I was wont, when very young, to follow his footsteps into the field, further and oftener than was convenient for him or comfortable for myself. Knowing well how much a child is gratified by being permitted to imitate a man's work, he sometimes hung the seed-bag, with a few handfuls in it, upon my shoulder, and sent me into the field to sow. I

* Ζῶν γὰρ ὁ λόγος τοῦ Θεοῦ, καὶ ἐνεργής.—HEB. iv. 12.

contrived in some way to throw the grain away, and it fell among the clods. But the seed that fell from an infant's hands, when it fell in the right place, grew as well and ripened as fully as that which had been scattered by a strong and skilful man. In like manner, in the spiritual department, the skill of the sower, although important in its own place, is, in view of the final result, a subordinate thing. The cardinal points are the seed and the soil. In point of fact, throughout the history of the Church, while the Lord has abundantly honoured his own ordinance of a standing ministry, he has never ceased to show, by granting signal success to feeble instruments, that results in his work are not necessarily proportionate to the number of talents employed.

Nor does the cause of failure, in the last resort, lie in the soil. The man who receives the Gospel only on the hard surface of a careless life, is of the same flesh and blood, endued with the same understanding mind and immortal spirit, with his neighbour who has already become a new creature in Christ. Believers and unbelievers are possessed of the same nature and faculties. As the ground which has been trodden into a footpath is in all its essential qualities the same as that which has been broken small by the plough and harrow, so the human constitution and faculties of one who lives without God in the world are substantially the same as those which belong to the redeemed of the Lord. It was the breaking of the ground which caused the difference between the fruitful field and the barren way side. So those minds and hearts that now bear the fruits of faith were barren till they were broken; and those on which the good seed has often been thrown, only to be thrown away, may yet yield an increase of a hundredfold to their owner, when conviction and repentance shall have rent them open to admit the word of life.

Felix the Roman governor was a specimen of the trodden way side. His heart, worn by the cares of business and the pleasures of sin passing in great volume alternately over it, presented no opening for the entrance of the Gospel. Paul, accordingly, when called to preach before him, did not, in the first instance, pour out the simple positive message of mercy: he reasoned of righteousness, temperance, and judgment to come; thus plying the seared conscience with the terrors of the Lord, in the hope of breaking thereby the covering crust and preparing a seed bed for the word of life. But the earth, in that case, was as iron, and refused to yield even to an apostle's blow. From the heart of Felix the message of mercy was effectually shut out. The jailer of Philippi was doubtless equally hard in a more vulgar sphere, but his defences were shattered: in that night of visitation his heart was rent as well as his prison, and over the openings, while they were fresh, the skilful sower promptly dropped the vital seed, "Believe on the Lord Jesus Christ, and thou shalt be saved." The word entered, and its entrance gave life.

At this point the parable addresses its lesson specifically to those who have lived without God in the world, and who have lived in the main comparatively at ease They have not a real heart-possessing, life-controlling religion, and they have never been very sorry for the want of it. They have no part in Christ, and no cheering hope for eternity. They are not ready to die; and yet they cannot keep death at bay. They know that they ought to care for their souls, but in point of fact they do not care; they know there is cause to be alarmed, and yet they are not alarmed. They neither grieve for sin nor love the Saviour; yet perhaps a dark cloud-like thought sometimes sweeps across their brightest sky—We have not yet gone in by the open door of mercy, and while we are delaying it may be suddenly shut.

The case might be understood well enough by those whom it concerns, if the same amount of attention were bestowed upon it that is ordinarily devoted to other branches of business. See the hard dry road that runs along the edge of a corn field: you are not surprised to find it barren in a harvest day; you know that grain, although sown there, would not grow, and you know the reason. The reason why the Gospel does you no good may be as clearly, as surely seen. Cares, vanities, passions, tread in constant succession over your heart, and harden it, so that the word of Christ, though it sound on the surface, never goes in, and never gets hold. Think not that the saints are by nature of another kind: they were once what you are, and you may yet become what they are, and more. "Break up your fallow ground." Look into your own heart's sin until you begin to grieve over it; look unto Jesus bearing sin until you begin to love him for his love. Tell God frankly in prayer that your heart is hard, and plead for the Holy Spirit to make it tender. The saints already in rest, and disciples in the body still, were once a trodden way side like yourself, as hard and as barren. Place your heart, as they did, without reserve in the Redeemer's hands; bid him take the hardness out and make it new. Invite the Word himself to take up his abode within you; throw the doors widely open that the King of Glory may come in. When Christ shall dwell in your heart by faith, a godly sorrow underneath will soften every faculty of your nature, and over all the surface fruits of righteous-ness will grow.

II. THE STONY GROUND.—A human heart, the soil on which the sower casts his seed, is in itself and from the first hard both above and below; but by a little easy culture, such as most people in this land may enjoy, some measure of softness is produced on the surface. Among the affections, when they are warm and newly stirred, the seed speedily springs. Many young hearts, subjected to the religious appliances which abound in our time, take hold of Christ and let him go again. This, on the one hand, as we learn by the result, was never a true conversion; but neither was it, on the other hand, a case of conscious, intentional deceit. It was real, but it was not thorough. Something was given to Christ, but because all was not given the issue was the same as if all had been withheld. In the rich young man the seed sprang hopefully, but it withered soon: he did not lightly part with Christ, but he parted: he was very sorrowful, but he went away.

A Christian parent or pastor, diligent in his main business and fervent in prayer for success, observes at length in some young members of his charge a new tenderness of conscience, an earnest attention to the word, a subdued, reverential spirit, with frequency and fervency in prayer. With mingled hope and fear these symptoms are watched and cherished: the symptoms continue and increase: the converts are added to the Church, and perhaps their experience is narrated as an example. This is not a deception on the part of either teacher or scholar: it is a true outgrowth from the contact of human hearts with the word of life. Man, who looks only on the outward appearance, cannot with certainty determine in whom this promise of spring will be blasted by the summer heat, and in whom it will yield a manifold return to the reaper. When you cast your eye over the corn field soon after the seed has

sprung, you may not be able to detect any difference between one portion and another; all may be alike fresh and
green.   But, if some parts of the field be deep soft soil,
and other parts only a thin sprinkling of earth over unbroken rock, there is a decisive difference in secret even
now, and the difference will ere long become visible to all.
Come back and look upon the same field after it has lain
a few days without rain under a scorching sun: you will
find that while in some portions the young plants have
increased in bulk without losing any of their freshness, in
others the green covering has disappeared and left the
ground as brown and bare as it was when the sower went
forth to sow upon it.   Where the earth is soft underneath,
and so permits the roots to penetrate its depths, the towering stalks defy the summer's drought; but where the roots
are shut out from the heart, the leaves wither on the surface.

If the law of God has never rent the " stony heart " and
made it " contrite," that is, bruised it small, you may, by
receiving the Gospel on some temporary, superficial softness of nature, obtain your religion more easily and quickly
than others who have been more deeply exercised; but
you may perhaps not be able to hold it so fast or retain
it so long.   Testing trials are the method of the divine
government, discipline the order of Christ's house.   He
that endureth to the end shall be saved, but he that falls
away in the middle shall not.   The fair profession that
grows over an unhumbled heart " dureth for a while," but
does not endure to the end.   When tribulation or persecution ariseth because of the word, the religion which
reached no further than the surface cannot maintain its
place there; it withers root and branch.   The inward affection, such as it was, and the outward profession together

disappear. From him that hath not shall be taken even that which he seemeth to have.

In the earlier centuries of the Christian era the profession of faith, when lightly assumed, was frequently and suddenly scorched off the so-called Christian's lips by the pitiless persecution of heathen governments: in subsequent ages, and down even to our own day, Papal fires have burned fiercely in many lands, and before them every faith has faded except that which is of God's own planting, and grows in the secret depths of believing souls. Nationally for several generations we have enjoyed freedom; but let us beware. The divine law, " All that will live godly in Christ Jesus must suffer persecution " (2 Tim. iii. 12), has not been repealed. Nor is this merely a caveat thrown in to keep our theology correct; it is a present and pressing truth. In every season and in every climate the sun of persecution is hot enough to kill the religion which grows in accidentally softened, natural affections, over a whole and unhumbled heart. Experience incontestably establishes the fact, although it may be difficult for philosophy to explain the reason of it, that slight persecutions have often been as effectual as the heaviest in blasting the deceptive appearance of religion, which, under favouring circumstances, grew for a time in the life of an unrenewed man. In point of fact, a sneer from some leading spirit in a literary society, or a laugh raised by a gay circle of pleasure-seekers in a fashionable drawing-room, or the rude jest of scoffing artisans in a work-shop, may do as much as the fagot and the stake to make a fair but false disciple deny his Lord.

Young disciples, whose faith and hope are bursting through the ground, should be, not indeed distrustful of the Lord, but jealous of themselves. " Let him that thinketh he standeth take heed lest he fall." Deeper sense of sin, clearer views of the Gospel, warmer love to Christ,—these are the safeguards against backsliding. Strive and pray for these. Do not keep Christ on the surface; let him possess the centre, and thence direct all the circumference of your life. "Whosoever will save his life," by keeping its central mass all and whole for himself, "shall lose it; and whosoever will lose his life for my sake," opening and abandoning it to Christ from its circumference to its core, "shall find it." It is then only his own, when he has without reserve absolutely given it away.

It seems to have been after the manner of the seed on stony ground that king Saul's faith grew and withered. It came away quickly at first, and presented a goodly appearance for a while; but the ground, broken and softened on the surface by Samuel's ministry and the call to the kingdom, was rocky underneath, and the rock was never rent. When he was seated on the throne, with the thousands of Israel coming and going at his word, he began to feel the restraints of piety irksome, and to count the rebukes of the aged prophet rude. The sun of prosperity scorched the green growth of religious profession that had suddenly overspread his outward life. Michal, his daughter, better acquainted, probably, with the kingly airs of his later than with the pious confession of his earlier days, seems to have partaken of his inward hardness while she had no share of his superficial piety. Like him, she was ungodly in the depths of her soul; but unlike him, she disdained to wear the outward garb of godliness. When she exerted all the force of her irony in order to make her husband David ashamed of his own zeal in dancing before the Lord, she truly reflected the inner spirit though not the external profession of her father's court. That taunt from the supercilious, curling lip of the royal princess, who had honoured him by consenting to become his wife, was a burning ray of persecution streaming on David's defence-less head. If his religion had been confined to the surface, while the pomp and circumstance of royalty occupied his heart, it would have died out then and there, as the tender sprouting corn, whose roots rest on a rock, dies out under the scorching sun of Galilee. But David's faith was deep, and it ripened rather than withered under the scornful glance of the worldly-minded princess, as corn, growing in good ground, fills better and ripens sooner where the sky is cloudless and the sun is fierce.

That deep-seated stony hardness of heart which defies all the efforts of human cultivators is often broken small by the hand of God. It appears that Lydia, through natural temperament or association with Christians, or both together, had attained some measure of spiritual susceptibility, for she confessed the truth and attended the prayer-meeting by the river side; but the seed of the word which had sprung on the surface of her life had not yet struck its root so deep as to withstand persecution if it should arise. She is described as a woman who sold purple and worshipped God: she had an honest business and a true religion, and were not these enough? No; the next fact of her history was the cardinal point of her life,— "whose heart the Lord opened that she attended to the things that were spoken of Paul." The seed from that skilful sower's hand went in and took possession, but it entered at an opening made by the power of God. Whether the rock was rent by the dew of the Spirit dropping silently, or by some stroke of Providence falling on her person or her material interests, we know not. If ordinary providential methods were employed, we know not, of the many instruments that lie close to the Ruler's hand, which he was pleased to use in that particular case. Perhaps the child of this honest and religious woman died, and her bosom, bereft of its treasure, rent with aching. Perhaps, on the day that Paul was there, she came to the meeting for the first time in widow's weeds, and the stroke that tore her other self away had left a wide avenue open into her heart. Perhaps,—for small instruments do great execution when they are wielded by an almighty arm,—an adverse turn of trade had left the hitherto affluent matron dependent on a neighbour's bounty for daily bread. Were other dealers, less scrupulously honourable than herself, underselling her in the market? Was her foreman unsteady? for, being a woman, she must needs depend much on hired helpers. Or did a living husband grieve her more than a dead one could? By some such instrument, or by another diverse from them all, or without any visible agent, the Lord opened Lydia's heart, and the word of life entered in power. Henceforth she was not her own; Christ dwelt in her heart by faith, and her life was devoted to the Lord her Redeemer. Deep in that broken heart the seed is rooted, and now no temptation, however intense and long-continued, shall be able to blanch its green blade or blast its filling ear. Lord, increase our faith. When trouble comes, whether under the ordinary procedure of God's government or more directly from his hand, whether in the form of bodily suffering or spiritual convictions, possess your soul in patience and wait for the end of the Lord. "No chastening for the present seemeth to be joyous, but grievous; nevertheless afterward it yieldeth the peaceable fruit of righteousness unto them which are exercised thereby" (Heb. xii. 11).

III. THE THORNS.—In the application of the lesson this term must be understood not specifically, but generically. In the natural object it indicates any species of useless weed that occupies the ground and injures the growing crop: in the spiritual application it points to the worldly cares, whether they spring from poverty or wealth, which usurp in a human heart the place due to Christ and his saving truth.

The earthly affections in the heart which render religion unfruitful in the life are enumerated under two heads,— "The care of this world," and "the deceitfulness of riches;" the term riches includes also, as we may gather from Luke's narrative, the pleasures which riches procure.

Both from our own experience in the world and the specific terms employed by the Lord in the interpretation of the parable, we learn that all classes and all ranks are on this side exposed to danger. This is not a rich man's business, or a poor man's; it is every man's business. The words point to the two extremes of worldly condition, and include all that lies between them. "The care of the world" becomes the snare of those who have little, and "the deceitfulness of riches," the snare of those who have much. Thus the world wars against the soul, alike when it smiles and when it frowns. Rich and poor have in this matter no room and no right to cast stones at each other. Pinching want and luxurious profusion are, indeed, two widely diverse species of thorns; but when favoured by circumstances they are equally rank in their growth and equally effective in destroying the precious seed.

In two distinct aspects thorns, growing in a field of wheat, reflect as a mirror the kind of spiritual injury which the cares and pleasures of the world inflict when they are admitted into the heart: they exhaust the soil by their roots, and overshadow the corn with their branches.

1. Thorns and thistles occupying the field suck in the sap which should go to nourish the good seed, and leave it a living skeleton. The capability of the ground is limited. The agriculturist scatters as much seed in the field as it is capable of sustaining and bringing to maturity. When weeds of rank growth spring up, their roots greedily and masterfully drain the soil of its fatness for their own supply; and as there is not enough both for them and the grain stalks, the weakest goes to the wall. The lawful, useful, but feeble grain is deprived of its sustenance by the more robust intruder. Under the ground as well as on its surface, might crushes right. Robbers fatten on the spoil of loyal citizens, and loyal citizens are left to starve. Moreover, the weeds are indigenous in the soil : this is proved by the simple fact of their presence, for certainly they were not sown there by the husbandman's hand. The grain, on the other hand, is not native; it must be brought to the spot and sown ; it must be cherished and protected as a stranger. The two occupants of the ground, consequently, are not on equal terms ; it is not a fair fight. The thorns are at home; the wheat is an exotic. The thorns are robust and can hold their own ; the wheat is delicate and needs a protector. The weeds accordingly grow with luxuriance, while the wheat stalks in the neighbourhood, cheated of their sustenance under ground, become tall, empty, barren straws.

2. Thorns and thistles, favoured as indigenous plants by the suitableness of soil and climate, outgrow the grain both in breadth and height. The outspread leaves and branches of the weeds constitute a thick screen between the ears of corn and the sunshine. Under that blighting

shadow, although the stalks may grow tall and the husks develop themselves in their own exquisite natural forms, no solid seed is formed or ripened. On the spot which the thorns usurped, the reaper gathers only straw and chaff.

How vivid on both its sides is the picture, and how truthfully it represents the case! The faculties of the human heart and mind are limited, like the productive powers of the ground. Neither the understanding nor the affections are endowed with an indefinite capacity of reception. The soil, even where it is rich and deep, may be soon exhausted, especially where the more gross and greedy weeds have taken up their abode. You are convinced of sin and begin to cry for pardon; you plead the Redeemer's sacrifice and righteousness; you grieve over your own backsliding, and come anew to the blood of sprinkling; the twin emotions, confession and prayer struggle together in your breast, "Lord, I believe; help thou mine unbelief." Thus far, it is well. The field has been broken; the seed has been covered in the ground; the covered seed has sprung; the sprung seed has grown apace and now seems near maturity. The evil spirit that seeks to spoil this fair promise seldom comes in the form of speculative unbelief. When you begin to fall away, you do not begin by abjuring your religion, or denying the Lord. You do not pull the grown but unripe corn up by the roots and cast it over the hedge: the harvest is marred in a more secret and silent way. The kingdom of the wicked one, cunningly in this matter imitating the kingdom of God, "cometh not with observation." Weeds spring up among the wheat. At first they are small and scarcely perceptible; the inexperienced, apprehending no danger, are put off their guard. The first leaves which these bitter roots put forth are generally smooth, tender, and apparently harmless, giving to the inexperienced eye no indication of their rough and ravenous nature. But these thorns, if they are not watched, curbed, and killed, may yet cause the loss of the soul.

If you are poor, anxieties about work and wages, clothes and food, wife and children, become the thorn plants, harmless in appearance at first, which in the end may choke the seed of grace in your heart. If you are rich, the pleasure which wealth may purchase, or love of the wealth itself, may become the bitter root, which in its maturity may overpower all spiritual life within you, and leave only chaff, to be driven away in the great day of the Lord. Watch and pray: these cares and pleasures present themselves at first in humble and submissive guise; it is by their gradual growth that they are enabled to inflict a deadly injury. Their roots, if not checked, silently drain all the sap of your soul, and the kingdom of God within you, although never formally abjured, is permitted to sink into decay. Your time, your memory, your imagination, your affections, your thoughts, late and early,—all that constitutes your life, instead of being devoted first to the kingdom of God and his righteousness, are usurped and absorbed by the things that perish in the using. When you betake yourself to the word, to prayer to communion, your heart, already searched, drained, scourged by the greedy roots of rank earthly lusts, is a sapless, impoverished, shrivelled thing, where faith in God and loving obedience to his law can no longer grow. Thus perish many bright promises; and high above the ruin, living and abiding for ever stands the word of Christ a witness against all who have been undone by neglecting it, "No man can serve two masters."

Worldly cares nursed by indulgence into a dangerous strength are further like thorns growing in a corn field, in that they interpose a veil between the face of Jesus and the opening, trustful look of a longing soul. It is the want of free, habitual exposure to the Sun of righteousness that prevents the ripening of grace in Christians. Unless we turn our eye often upward, and expose the struggling, springing seed of faith to the beams of the Redeemer's love, there will be no steady growth of grace, and no ultimate fruit of righteousness. It is thus that insinuating, overspreading, domineering cares quench both hope and holiness : they hinder the simple, tender, confiding look unto Jesus which is necessary to the increase or maintenance of spiritual life. The love of Christ freely streaming down from heaven through the Scriptures and by the ministry of the Spirit, when freely admitted into an open, willing heart, by degrees turns fear into hope, doubt into faith, and the feeble struggle of a child into the strong man's glorious victory; as unimpeded sunlight converts the minute mustard seed into a towering tree, and the tender sprouts of spring into the golden treasures of harvest. A thickly woven web of cares and pleasures interposed between the soul and the Saviour is a chief cause of failure in " God's husbandry."

Nor is the harvest safe although the thorny shade that overhangs it be not completely impervious and constant. Fitful glances of sunshine now and then will not bring the fruit to maturity. Stand beneath the branches of a forest tree on a day that is at once bright and breezy : you may observe on the ground at your feet a curious network of flickering light trembling and dancing about in perpetual motion. The sunbeams that penetrate at intervals through openings among the agitated branches are barren though beautiful. The grass that gets no other light grows slim and pithless, bearing no seed-knot on its slender top. Sunlight admitted now and then through apertures in the leafy awning is not sufficient for the processes of nature; the grain field must get its bosom opened without impediment permanently to the sun. It is thus that snatches of spiritual exercise do not avail to promote the growth, or even to preserve the life of grace in a heart that in the main is habitually overshadowed by a crowd of overgrown imperious worldly cares. Evening and morning you may open the Bible and bend the knee, but the tender plant of righteousness in your heart is not effectually revived by these brief and fitful glances. Before the drooping leaves have had time to feel the genial warmth, another cloud has closed the orifice and left them again in the chill damp shade. Even the Lord's day, as a gap left open between earth and heaven, is not by any means so wide as it seems; for the memory of the past week's business and pleasure stretches over on the one side, until it meet, or almost meet, the anticipation of the next week's business and pleasure, so that even on the Sabbath the world still overshadows the soul of its votary. Shut out, except at short and uncertain intervals, from the Light of Life, he passes through the summer of his probation with a well-proportioned but empty form of godliness; and the Lord, when he comes at the close to gather the wheat into his garner, finds on that portion of the field only the rustling chaff of a hollow profession, instead of the fruit unto holiness that grows on living souls.

Some lessons suggest themselves in connection with this portion of the parable, and claim a brief notice at our hand.

1. As the thorns are indigenous and spring of their own accord, while the good seed must be sown and cherished; so, vain thoughts, lodged in our hearts from the dawn of our being, have the advantage of first possession, and get the start of their competitors in the race for supremacy. Lurking unobserved between the folds of nature's faculties, before the understanding is developed, they come away early and grow rapidly, and obtain a firm footing before the saving truth, the seed of the kingdom, has burst the kernel and broken through the ground. Crucify the flesh with its affections and lusts; begin that work early, and persevere in that work to the end.

2. As long as the weeds live they grow. Every moment, until they are cast out of the field, they spread themselves more widely over its surface and drain away more of its nutritive juice. Delay is dangerous. If it be painful to pull out the root of bitterness from your heart to-day, it will be more painful to-morrow. Take for example the love of money: we know well that though money is a useful servant it is a hard master; be assured if it get and keep the mastery of a soul, its little finger in the end will be thicker than its loins were at the beginning. Avarice chastises its slave in middle life with whips; but if he abide its slave, it will chastise him when he is old with scorpions.

3. The thorn is a prickly thing; it tears the husbandman's flesh, as well as destroys the fruit of his field. In like manner the care of the world and the deceitfulness of riches lacerate the man who permits them to grow rank in his heart. The vain man is continually meeting with slights, or suspecting that his neighbours are about to offer them. The miser is always losing money, or

trembling lest he should lose it in the next transaction. The world itself knows, and in its proverbs confesses, that around the most coveted pleasures are set sharp thorns, which wound the hand that tries to pluck the rose.

4. It was where the seed and the thorns grew together that the mischief was done. If the grain is permitted to occupy alone the heart of the field, the thorns that grow outside and around it may constitute a hedge of defence, not only harmless but useful. There is a place for cares, and for riches too,—a place in which they help and do not hinder the kingdom of God. Kept in its own sphere, the lawful business of life becomes a protecting fence round the tender plant of grace in a Christian's heart. Permit not the thorns to occupy the position which is due to the good seed. Not as rivals within the field, but as guards around it, earthly affairs are innocent and safe. "Seek first the kingdom of God and his righteousness, and all these things shall be added unto you."

5. When the husbandman perceives a huge prickly weed in the midst of his field robbing and overshadowing the corn, he sends his servant to cast out the intruder. In such a case, a bare spot is left where the thistle grew; but at this stage experiences diverge and travel on different lines towards opposite results. In some cases the blank is soon made up again, and the corn waves level like a lake over all the field, so that none could tell where the thistle stood: in others, the blank caused by the removal of a rank weed remains a blank throughout the summer, presenting to the reapers in harvest only a spot of bare ground. Why do opposite effects proceed from similar operations? Time was the turning point. In

the one case the weed was torn out at an early period of the summer ; in the other case it was torn out too late.

We have often seen a soul placed in imminent danger by the overgrowth of cares or pleasures that threatened by their rankness to choke the seed of the word; and we have afterwards seen that soul delivered from the danger, by a stroke of God's providence that plucked out the weeds in time. Many of the saved both in earth and in heaven now praise the Lord, because he tore the idols from their hearts and spared not for their crying. The love of Christ that had been planted in their youth, and had, though hard pressed, still kept hold, soon spread again and occupied all the empty space, whence the fortune, or fame, or living treasures dearer still, had been plucked. When he came to himself, that disciple, afflicted sore but comforted again, clearly saw and gladly sang the mercy and judgment joined together that had cleared the room for Christ in his heart. But examples of an opposite experience, here and there one, stand on the edge of life's crowded highway, ghastly as the pillar of salt on the plain of Sodom, burning into the soul of the passenger the warning word, " Be in time." An old man has, by the hand of the Lord in providence, been stripped of all his treasures. These treasures, whether they were in themselves the noblest or the meanest,—for when a man made in the likeness of God abandons himself to the worship of an idol, it matters little whether the idol be made of fine gold or of dull clay,—these treasures possessed and filled his heart. Round them his understanding and affections had closely clasped, so that his whole nature had taken the mould of the object which it grasped. In this attitude the man grew old: the faculties of his mind became hard and rigid like the members of his body. The bosom, no longer pliable to open by gentle pressure, was rudely rent, and its portion in one lump wrenched away. A deep, broad, dark chasm, like the valley of the shadow of death, was left: and the chasm remained dark and empty to the end; for neither the affections of the old man's soul nor the joints of the old man's frame would fold round another portion now. Ah! the cares and pleasures that drove Christ from the heart may be cast out too late for letting Christ come in again to occupy the empty room. "Now is the accepted time; now is the day of salvation." "To-day, if ye will hear his voice, harden not your hearts."

IV. THE GOOD GROUND.—Guided by the Great Teacher's own interpretation, we have travelled through the series of successive obstacles which hinder the growth and mar the fruitfulness of God's word in the hearts of men,—travelled through, weeping as we went. At the close of this sad but instructive journey, a beauteous sight bursts into view: it is a field of ripe grain on a sunny harvest day. The ground was ploughed, and the seed sank beneath it from the sower's hand in spring; the earth was soft and sapful to a sufficient depth, and the roots of the springing corn found ample room to range in; the soil was clean, and its fatness, not shared by usurping weeds, went all to the nourishment of the sown seed: therefore in the balmy air and under the beaming sun it is ripe to-day, and ready to fill the reaper's bosom. It is a refreshing, satisfying sight; but, fair though it be, we shall not now linger long to gaze upon it. By the parable the Master meant mainly to teach us what things are adverse to his kingdom. Having learned this lesson from his lips, we go away grateful for his pungent, deeply-traced, and memorable warnings, without pausing to examine minutely the glad prospect to which our thorny path has led.   The traveller who has come safely through many dangers by flood and field, narrates at large, with burning lips and throbbing heart, the varied toils of the journey; but his home,—he does not describe, he enjoys it.*

---

* It is not intimated by the parable that our Father the Husbandman finds any of the good ground in us : the ground, like the tree in another analogical lesson of the Lord, is not good until it is *made* good.   It is beyond the scope of this parable to explain how the ground is rendered soft and kept free from thorns.   The Teacher was content in this lesson to tell us what the good ground produces; we must discover elsewhere in the Scriptures whence its goodness is derived.   " . . . . The similitude from nature is no longer applicable to the mystery of the kingdom of heaven ; as a parable, it has already reached its limits, when the truth goes beyond the similitude.   There is a *miraculous seed* superior indeed to all natural seed, so powerful that by its growth it can and will choke all thorns.   Nay more, it can also break through the rock in striking its root down into the earth, and can make that to be again a field of God which was a way for the feet of the prince of this world."—*Stier in loc.*

Among the many incidental and collateral applications of which this parable is susceptible, one of the most interesting and instructive is—That every man has within himself the elements of all the four kinds of ground. The conception is thus presented by Fred. Arndt : " At the outset, the word of God finds all in the first unreceptive condition ; we go away without experiencing its power, and remain in a state of nature, unconverted. Next, the word begins to take effect upon us, and we are awakened.   Oh now the word of the Lord burns with a holy glow in our hearts !   We give ourselves over with our whole souls in those first days of love.   We have found heaven ; we have seen it opened, and the angels of God ascending and descending on the Son of man.   But this condition does not endure. The fightings begin from within and from without, and the flame is quenched. The heart becomes cold and empty.   The life of faith becomes silent and slow in its course.   We become languid in watching and prayer ; the love of the world and its sinful pleasures awakes again ; and before we are aware, we are trying to serve both God and the world.   Then the war bursts out : this moment God is above us, the next beneath us, and we get no rest until we have renounced the world, and surrendered our heart and life to God wholly, and to God alone.   Thus we pass, in the faith-school of the Holy Spirit, through all the four classes, deceiving ourselves and being deceived, until at last, after many a bitter experience, we strike upon the narrow way, and through the strait gate."—*Die Gleichniss-reden. Jes. Chr.*

While all the ground that was broken, deep, and clean in spring and summer, bears fruit in harvest, some portions produce a larger return than others. The picture in this feature is true to nature; and the fact in the spiritual sphere also corresponds. There are diversities in the Spirit's operation; diversities in natural gifts bestowed on men at first; diversities in the amount of energy exerted by believers as fellow-workers with God in their own sanctification; and diversities, accordingly, in the fruitfulness which results in the life of Christians. While all believers are safe in Christ, each should covet the best gifts. No true disciple will be contented with a thirty-fold increase of faith, and patience, and humility, and love, and usefulness in his heart and life for the Lord, if through prayer and watching—if by denying ungodliness and worldly lusts—if by sternly crucifying the flesh and trustfully walking with God, he may rise from thirty to sixty, and from sixty to an hundredfold in that holy obedience which grows on living faith.

The Tares
(Matthew 13:24-30, 36-43)

" Another parable put he forth unto them, saying, The kingdom of heaven is likened unto a man which sowed good seed in his field : but while men slept, his enemy came and sowed tares among the wheat, and went his way. But when the blade was sprung up, and brought forth fruit, then appeared the tares also. So the servants of the house-holder came and said unto him, Sir, didst not thou sow good seed in thy field? from whence then hath it tares? He said unto them, An enemy hath done this. The servants said unto him, Wilt thou then that we go and gather them up? But he said, Nay ; lest while ye gather up the tares, ye root up also the wheat with them. Let both grow together until the harvest : and in the time of harvest I will say to the reapers, Gather ye together first the tares, and bind them in bundles to burn them : but gather the wheat into my barn. . . . . Then Jesus sent the multitude away, and went into the house : and his disciples came unto him, saying, Declare unto us the parable of the tares of the field. He answered and said unto them, He that soweth the good seed is the Son of man ; the field is the world ; the good seed are the children of the kingdom ; but the tares are the children of the wicked one ; the enemy that sowed them is the devil ; the harvest is the end of the world ; and the reapers are the angels. As therefore the tares are gathered and burned in the fire ; so shall it be in the end of this world. The Son of man shall send forth his angels, and they shall gather out of his kingdom all things that offend, and them which do iniquity ; and shall cast them into a furnace of fire : there shall be wailing and gnashing of teeth. Then shall the righteous shine forth as the sun in the kingdom of their Father. Who hath ears to hear, let him hear."

A S the main design of the first parable is to exhibit the kingdom in its relation to unbelieving men, who, in various forms and with various measures of aggravation, ultimately reject it ; the main design of the second is to exhibit the kingdom in its relation to the wicked one, who endeavours, by cunning stratagem, to destroy it. In either case there is a conflict : in the first, the conflict is waged chiefly between the word, which is the seed of the kingdom, and the various evil dispositions which impede its growth in the hearts of men; in the second, the conflict is waged chiefly, as in the mysterious temptation in the wilderness, between Christ, man's Redeemer, and the devil, the adversary of man. In the first parable the obstacles to the progress of the kingdom lay in the heedlessness, the hardness, and the worldliness of men; in the second, the old serpent is the opposer, and wicked men are wielded as instruments in his hands.

The picture is sketched from nature; the lines are very few, but each contributes a feature, and all, together, make the likeness complete.

A Galilean countryman, after having fenced and ploughed and cleaned his field, has watched the condition of the soil and the appearance of the sky, until he has found a day on which both were suitable for the grand decisive operation of the season, the sowing of the seed. With anxiety, but in hope, this critical and cardinal act is performed; the seed is committed to the ground.

It was "good seed" that the careful husbandman cast among the clods. If the last season's crop was of inferior quality, he and his children have cheerfully lived upon the worst, that the best might be reserved for sowing; if the last crop was scanty, the family were content with a less plentiful meal; and if none of the previous year's produce was well ripened, better grain has been bought in a distant market, that at all hazards a sufficient quantity of good seed may be secured for the coming season. Those only who have lived among them, and shared their lot, know how much the poor but intelligent and industrious cultivators of the soil will do and bear in order to preserve or obtain plenty of "good seed."

The great crisis of the season is now past; and the husbandman, wiping his brow as he glances backward upon his completed work, goes home at sunset with limbs somewhat weary, but a heart full of hope. The next portion of the picture is of a dark and dismal hue. When the farmer and his family, innocent and unsuspicious, are fast asleep, a neighbour, too full of envy for enjoying rest, stalks forth into the same field under cover of night, and with much labour scatters something broadcast over its surface. He is secretly sowing tares, with the malicious design of damaging or destroying the wheat. As soon as the deed of darkness is done, he creeps stealthily back to his own bed, and in the morning, when he meets his fellow-villagers, does his best to put on the air of an innocent man.

Weeks pass ; showers fall ; the seed springs and covers all the ground with beautiful green. The owner visited his field from time to time in spring, and thought it promised well. But at that period of the summer, still a good while before harvest, when the ears of the grain begin to appear, some of the farmer's servants, looking narrowly into the quality of the crop, discovered that a large proportion of it was darnel. Forthwith they reported the sad intelligence to their master, and requested permission to pluck out the intruders. It was agreed among them that good seed had been sown, and the darnel or false wheat was by common consent and without hesitation set down as the work of an enemy. As to the treatment of the disaster now that it had occurred, the master's judgment was clear, and his order explicit : to pull out the darnel at this stage, as the servants proposed, would hurt the wheat more than help it ; both must be permitted to grow together till the harvest ; they may be safely and effectually separated then.

Some interesting questions connected with the natural

objects claim our regard in the first instance, before we proceed to investigate the spiritual significance of the parable.

What are the tares? The original term does not elsewhere occur in Scripture, and in the total absence of examples for comparison, it is somewhat difficult to ascertain its precise signification. The word and the thing which it signifies have exercised the learning and ingenuity of expositors both in ancient and in modern times. On such a subject as this it is on the line of natural history rather than philology that the investigation should mainly proceed ; there, from the nature of the case, surer results may be obtained. Through the increased facility of making local inquiries which has of late years been enjoyed, it is now known, and apparently with one consent acknowledged by intelligent inquirers, that the seed which the malicious neighbour sowed in order to injure the produce of the field was *Lolium temulentum,* or darnel, a kind of false wheat to which the Arabs of Palestine at this day apply a name (zowan) which bears some resemblance to (ζιζανια) the original word in the Greek text.* It has long narrow leaves and an upright stalk, and is indeed in all respects so like the wheat, that even an experienced eye cannot distinguish the two plants until they are in ear : the distinction then is manifest, and any one may observe it. The grains of the darnel are not so heavy as the wheat, and not so compactly set upon the stalk. They are poisonous, their specific effect both in man and in beast being nausea and giddiness. The remark of Schubert in his " Natural History," quoted by Stier, that "this is the only poisonous grass," is deeply significant in relation to the spiritual meaning of the

---

* "The Land and the Book." by Dr. Thomson. T. Nelson & Sons.

parable ; it suggests the reason why the Healer selected this plant as the symbol of sin.

But another question meets us here, more obscure and difficult than either the appearance or the characteristic effects of the darnel,—the question whether it is originally a specifically different plant, or only wheat degenerated. Some maintain that it is wheat which, by some mysterious causes in the processes of nature, has fallen, as it were, into a lower type. This view imparts additional fulness to the parable in its spiritual application. So interpreted, the picture exhibits not only the low estate of the sinful, but also the fact that they have fallen from a higher. In such cases, however, there is some danger lest the beauty and appropriateness of the conception should entice us to receive it on insufficient evidence. The fact that some plants in certain adverse circumstances tend to degenerate, and in certain favourable circumstances to attain a higher type, is well known in natural history; but it seems questionable whether these changes ever take place to such an extent, and in such a uniform method, as must be assumed if we take darnel for degenerated wheat. Agriculturists in Palestine believe and declare, that, when the season is wet, the wheat which they sow in certain fields in spring grows as zowan in harvest. It is difficult for one who is accustomed to observe the uniformity of nature in the reproduction of each species from its own seed, to believe that transformations so great are accomplished at a single step. An American writer, one of the latest authorities, and, in respect to his abundant opportunities of observation, one of the best, bears witness that he has often seen the wheat and barley fields overrun with darnel, and that the native owners stoutly declare that the good wheat which they sowed has been changed into the false in the process of growth during a single season; but he intimates at the same time that he believes the men are mistaken, and that the presence of the darnel must be attributed to some other cause, and accounted for in some other way.* The suggestion that the same peculiarities of season which destroy the sown wheat may favour the springing of the darnel, that had lain in the ground dormant before, may possibly account for the present experience of the Syrian cultivators; or the effects may be in whole or in part due to other causes of which we are not cognizant; but the solution of this question is by no means essential to the right interpretation of the parable, and therefore we shall not prosecute the investigation further in this direction.

Dr. Thomson gives unequivocal testimony, at the same time, that at the present day no instance is known of the growth of darnel among the wheat being caused by the malicious act of an enemy. This, however, as he distinctly owns, does not prove that the transaction depicted in the parable had no foundation in fact. It must have happened substantially in history, otherwise it would not have been introduced as a supposition into these lessons of the Lord. Some travellers have stated that this species of crime is known in India; but I do not set much value on the discovery of precisely identical facts in modern times. The existence of the representation in this parable is, simply as a matter of rational evidence, a tenfold stronger proof that the facts in their essential features actually happened, than any quantity of analogous cases drawn from other countries in later times. It is of greater importance to note that the malice which endured the

* "The Land and the Book." Note by Principal Fairbairn in translation of "Lisco on the Parables."

toil of sowing tares in a neighbour's field grows yet, and grows rankly in human breasts. In different ages and regions, that spiritual wickedness may clothe itself in bodies of diverse mould and hue, but it is in all times and places the same foul and malignant spirit, acting according to its kind. The same spirit that sowed darnel among wheat at night in a corn field of Galilee, two thousand years ago, will set fire to a stackyard, or hamstring the horses, or shoot the overseer from behind a hedge in our own day, and, alas! in some parts of our own land. As in the highest good, so in the deepest evil, there are diversities of operation by the same spirit. When we take into account the changes of fashion which occur both in clothing and in crime, we have no reason to be sceptical as to the ancient fact, and no difficulty in obtaining a modern specimen.

From the results already gained, it appears obvious that the translation "tares" in our English version is unfortunate: it not only fails to represent clearly the state of the fact, but leads the reader's mind away in a wrong direction. To an English reader the term suggests a species of legume, which bears no resemblance to wheat at any stage of its progress. By the use of this word the characteristic feature of the picture is greatly obscured. Had the plant which sprung from the envious neighbour's seed been a legume, its presence would have been detected at the first, and it could have been separated at any stage. The darnel, on the contrary, cannot be distinguished from wheat until both are nearly ripe, and the process of separation, whether in the field or on the threshing-floor, is much more difficult.

Again the Lord becomes his own interpreter: at the

request of the disciples he explained to them in private the meaning of his allegory. The points are great, few, and clearly defined. In this journey the Master has kindly gone before us; reverently, trustfully, we shall follow his steps. " He that soweth the good seed is the Son of man; the field is the world." It is in connection with the "field" that the greatest difficulty has occurred, the greatest mistakes have been made, and the deepest injury has been done. Few words of Scripture are more plain; and yet few have been more grievously misunderstood and wrested. At the entrance of the inspired explanation, the expositor, bent on the defence of his own foregone conclusion, takes his stand, like a pointsman on a railway, and by one jerk turns the whole train into the wrong line. " The field is the world," said the Lord: " The field is the Church," say the interpreters. It is wearisome to read the reasonings by which they endeavour to fortify their assumption. Having determined that the field is the Church, they are compelled immediately to address themselves to the great practical question of discipline. If they were prepared to admit that there should be absolutely no discipline—that no man should be shut out from communion, however heretical his opinions or vicious his practice might be, their task under the general principle of interpretation which they have adopted would be very easy. The command is clear, cast none out of the "field," however fully developed their wickedness may be, until the angels make the separation between good and evil at the consummation of all things. If the field means the Church, the exclusion of the unworthy by a human ministry is absolutely forbidden. But the expositors are not willing altogether to abandon discipline. They maintain, on the one hand, that this parable deals with and settles the question of the right to eject unworthy members from the communion of the Church; and on the other hand, that while it condemns excessive and puritanical strictness, it permits and justifies the ejection of those who are manifestly unworthy. Most of the commentaries that have come under my notice betray on this point weakness and inconsistency. If by this feature of the parable the Lord gives a decision on Church discipline, he forbids it out and out, in all its forms, and in all its degrees. The separation suggested, he permits not to be attempted at all, until he shall charge his angels to accomplish it at the end of the world. In my judgment, to contend for the right of excluding some of the ranker tares, after admitting that this parable bears upon the subject of ecclesiastical discipline, tends not only to perplex the student, but to throw a reflection on the authority of the Word. I see only two doors open: either cease to hold that the field is the Church, or cease to claim the right of excluding any from communion.

Good old Benjamin Keach, in a portly volume on the parables, addressed "to the impartial reader," and sent "from my house in Horsley Down, Southwark, August 20. 1701," indicates with clearness and simplicity his own judgment; but, overawed by authority, seems afraid at the sound of his own words: "The field is the world; though it may, as some think, also refer to the Church. Marlorate saith by a synecdoche, a part for the whole, it signifies the Church; though this seems doubtful to me, and I rather believe it means the world." The second of two reasons which he submits as the grounds of his opinion is,—" Because tares, when discovered to be such, must not grow among the wheat in the Church, but ought to be cast out, though they ought to live together in the world." Here Keach reasons most naturally, and indeed irrefragably, against the interpretation that the world is the Church, from the monstrous consequence to which it necessarily leads. I am beyond measure amazed to find the general stream of interpretation, as far as I have had an opportunity of examining it, ancient and modern, German and Anglican, flowing in this channel. When I find the great and venerated name of Calvin contributing to swell this tide, I am compelled to pause and examine the subject anew; but my judgment remains the same. We must call no man master on earth; one is our master in heaven. It is not necessarily presumption in one of us to oppose the judgment of the great and good of a former age, especially on such a subject as this. In regard to all the relations between the Church and the civil power, we are in a better position for judging than either the early Reformers or the Continental and Anglican theologians of the present day. The general progress made since the time of Calvin in the historical development of the Christian Church, and the particular experience through which Christians in Scotland have in later times been led, greatly contribute to elevate our stand-point in relation to the discipline of the Church, and its right to freedom from civil control. As a child on the house-top can scan a wider landscape than a man on the ground, although the child may have been indebted to that man for his elevation; so we may own the Reformers as in a right sense our teachers, and yet on some subjects form a sounder judgment than they. Although no new revelation has been made since the Lord's apostles were removed from the earth, the Church does under the government of her Head, advance from age to age; and the principle embodied in the declaration, "The least in the kingdom of heaven is greater than he" (Matt. xi. 11), emerges still in manifold subordinate fulfilments. As to the greatest modern scholars of Germany and England, the accepted and even lauded Erastianism in which they are steeped is a beam in their eye, which dims and distorts their sight when they look in the direction of the Church with its constitution and discipline. While on other subjects their insight is such that we may be content to sit at their feet, the view on this side is from their stand-point cut off short, as if by a mountain in the foreground, and they can afford us no help.

"The field is the world:" in the prevailing confusion we hold to this, as the ship to her anchor in a storm. Men should remember when they explain away the meaning of the term "world," and teach that it signifies the Church, that they are dealing not with a parable, but with the explanation of a parable given by the Lord. The parable is professedly a metaphor; but when the Lord undertook to tell his disciples what the metaphor meant, he did not give them another metaphor more difficult than the first. I venture to affirm that the expositors would have found it easier to show that the "field" is the Church than to show that the "world" is the Church. According to their view, it results that the Lord proposed to interpret his own allegory, but only gave on this point another allegory somewhat more obscure. The outrageousness of the conclusion proves the premises false. In affectionate tenderness to the twelve, the Lord Jesus undertook to translate a figurative expression which puzzled them into a literal expression which the feeblest might be able to comprehend. The "field" is the metaphor, and that metaphor interpreted is the "world;" it does not need to be interpreted over again. This Teacher means what he says. He points to this globe, man's habitation, and mankind its inhabitants in all places and all times.

Into this world Christ, the Son of man, the Son of God, cast good seed. The children of the kingdom are the good seed: in the beginning men were made in God's likeness, and placed in his world. Thereafter and thereupon an enemy stealthily and maliciously sowed tares in the same field. The enemy is the devil; and the tares which he by his sowing caused to spring in the field are the children of the wicked one. In the first instance, the Day in which the sower spread good seed in his field was the day in which God made man upright: the Night in which the enemy sowed tares was the period of the temptation and the fall. Both these antagonistic processes are carried on still. The Son of man sows the good seed day by day in the world, and night by night the enemy sows his tares. Especially and signally in the fulness of time the good seed, more completely developed, was again committed to the ground in the ministry and sacrifice of Christ; and again the wicked one renewed and increased his efforts to counteract and destroy it. These two, opposite in origin and in nature, are commingled and interwoven in all the ordinary relations of life. The children of the wicked one and the children of the kingdom live together in the world, eat of the same bread, and breathe the same air, and look upon the same light.

In the Galilean field, which the Lord employed as a type with which to print his lesson, portions might be seen where, owing perhaps to peculiar wetness and sourness in the soil, the wheat had wholly disappeared, and the darnel grew alone; in other parts, probably where the soil was warm and dry, the good seed had gained the mastery, and the false scarcely showed its head; and in a third quarter the good and bad might appear in equal numbers and equal strength. Such precisely is the aspect of the world. Large portions of it have been heathen from a higher date than that to which history ascends; large portions, which were Christian long after the apostolic age, have been overrun and laid waste by the blind but strong system of Mahomet; while in other parts a vigorous Christian life appears, although even there the good seed must maintain a struggle against bitter roots below and poisonous fruit rearing its head on high.

I accept, therefore, in all simplicity, the Master's own definition: I see in the field of the injured husbandman a picture, not of the Church in the world, but of the world in which the Church must for the present live and labour. The ingenious effort made by a recent Swiss expositor* to find a middle path only serves to show how heavily the difficulties of the common interpretation press on those who maintain it. Having confessed, according to the terms of the text, that the field or ground is not the Church, but the world, he proceeds, with a very strong animus against what he calls puritanism or separatism,† to argue in the usual way against every attempt to purify the visible Church except by the exclusion of persons who are notoriously heretical or vicious. The grounds on which he pleads against separation from the impure, in

---

* Die Parabeln des Herrn, für Kirche, Schule, und Haus, erklärt von Dr. De Valenti. Basel, 1841.

† It is quite possible that the separatists whom De Valenti scolds, with more warmth than elegance, may deserve his censure; for severe restrictive measures adopted by governments to suppress religious dissent have frequently the effect of deteriorating its character, on the principle that oppression makes a wise man mad.

as far as this parable is concerned, are—(1.) That there was no need of a revelation to make known the universally acknowledged maxim that bad people should be tolerated in the world ; (2.) That, according to the terms of the parable, the farmer sowed wheat in his ground, but did not sow the whole of his ground—so that the ground may be the world, and the portion sown, or the wheat field, may still represent the Church; (3.) That the parable of the fishing-net confirms this interpretation ; and (4.) That in the world there was no wheat until the preaching of the gospel reached it, and consequently the mixture is in the Church, and not in the world.

The first of these grounds seems most unfortunate; for corrupt ecclesiastics, from an early age to the present day, have ever shown themselves ready to cast those whom they call heretics, not out of the Church only, but out of the world :* the second is a refinement too narrow for building any conclusion upon : the third applies a mistaken view of one parable to support a mistaken view of another : and the fourth is the second in another form. After having in effect explained away his own admission, that the field is the world, and not the Church, he freely concedes in the close that the openly heretical and vicious should not be tolerated within the Church. But I ask what right has he to exclude those whom, according to

---

* Lange (*in loc.*), having quoted Gerlach to the effect that this prohibition refers to extremes of ecclesiastical discipline, for the purpose of excluding all unbelievers and hypocrites, and constituting a perfectly pure Church, timidly replies : " We can scarcely agree with him that it contains no allusion to the punishment of death for heresy. . . . . . It is well known that Novatianism, on the one hand, and the Papal hierarchy, on the other, have addressed themselves to this work of uprooting despite the prohibition of the Lord, and that the Romish Church has at last ended by condemning to the flames only the best wheat. . . . . . The *auto da fés* of the middle ages were only a humble caricature and anticipation of that fiery judgment."

his exegesis, the Lord commanded his ministers to tolerate
in the Church?

In the intimation that it was while men slept that the
mischief was done, I cannot find any covert reproof of an
indolent ministry in the Church. It was night: all the
community had retired to rest. The species of criminal
which the parable depicts was not numerous,—the crime
was not of daily occurrence. It was neither the practice
nor the duty of the people, after they had toiled all day
in their fields, to watch their work by night, to protect it
from possible injury. The expression, "while men slept,"
is intended merely to indicate that the evil-doer took
advantage of the darkness to cover his deed: accordingly,
in the interpretation no specific meaning is attached to
this feature of the parable.

In regard to the servants, and their proposal instantly
to pull up the tares, the interpretation is attended with
difficulty. With some eminent ancient expositors I am
convinced that, if not exclusively, yet primarily and chiefly,
the servants who offered to make the separation are the
angels. The parable stretches far into both time and
space: it comprehends the world, and the successive dispensations of God there. Morning stars sang together
when they saw beautiful worlds starting into being at
their Maker's word: the same high intelligences must
have been surprised and grieved when they saw God's
fairest work marred by sin. It is like the impulse of
beings perfect in holiness, but limited in knowledge, to
offer themselves on the instant as willing instruments to
cast the defilers out. Pleased, doubtless, with their instinctive zeal for holiness, but comprehending his own
purposes better than they, the Lord declined the proffered
ministry. At the same time he intimated that the separa-

tion which the servants suggested was not refused, but only postponed. His plan required that good and evil, now that evil had begun, should mingle in the world till the end. At the close of the dispensation, when the Son of man shall come in his glory, he will give the commission for a final separation to the angels who shall constitute his train.

It seems to be generally assumed by modern expositors, that while the reapers who shall separate the tares from the wheat in harvest are angels, the servants who offered to weed out the tares while they were yet green are the human ministers of the visible Church. Archbishop Trench, for example, says: "These servants are not, as Theophylact suggests, the angels (they are the reapers, ver. 30); but men, zealous, indeed, for the Lord's honour, but zealous with the same zeal as animated those two disciples who would fain have commanded fire to come down from heaven on the inhospitable Samaritan village" (Luke ix. 54). I think the learned author is mistaken here, and that the preponderance of evidence lies on the other side. The subject is interesting, and will repay the labour of investigation.

Here two questions, distinct, yet closely connected, constitute the case: on the answer which may be given to them the decision will turn. One relates to the persons, and the other to their acts: Are the "servants" who propose to pull up the tares in summer, and the "reapers" who are commanded to make the separation in harvest, the same, or different persons? and is the separation proposed by the servants substantially the same in kind with that which is ultimately effected by the reapers, or is it different?

I think the servants and the reapers are substantially identical. The troop of servants who haunt a rich man's house, and the band of labourers who reap his patrimonial fields, stand far apart in our land and our day. Not so, however, in the establishment of a Galilean householder eighteen hundred years ago. When you take into view the habits of society at the date and on the scene of the parable, it will appear certain and obvious that the servants who proposed to weed the fields in summer were, in part at least, the same persons who would be sent to reap the fields in autumn. The reapers might be a more numerous band than the servants who were employed throughout the year, but to a large extent the constituents must have been the same. In another parable (Luke xvii. 7–10), a servant, who has been ploughing or feeding cattle, is obliged, after he returns from the field, to gird himself and wait on his master at table. This shows conclusively that the division of labour which obtains among us was unknown then in Galilee. The master does not, indeed, say to the servants who made the proposal, I will employ you in harvest to accomplish the separation: the form of expression is, "I will say to the reapers;" but reapers and servants were of the self-same class, and in all probability to some extent the same individuals.

The second question can be more easily answered. The separation which the reapers ultimately effected is essentially the same with that which the servants at an earlier period proposed. It is an actual, material, final separation of the tares from the wheat.

It results that there is no solid ground in the parable for the assumption that those who proposed to make the separation at an earlier date represent men, while those who were employed to accomplish it afterwards represent angels; and that the separation which the Lord prohibited was spiritual, while that which he permitted was physical

In regard to the separation which he sanctioned, the Lord interprets what the operation is, and who are the operators ; whereas, in regard to the separation at an earlier date proposed, he gives no interpretation. Instead of beginning by giving my own assumption as to the meaning of the uninterpreted part, I go first to the part that is interpreted to my hand, and from the point which is illuminated I get light thrown back on the point which was left in the shade. The reapers, I know, are the angels ; and the servants were the same, or at least the same class of ministers, proposing to accomplish the work at an earlier date. The separation which was actually effected in the harvest represents, we know, the personal and local as well as moral and spiritual separation of the good and the evil ; thence I conclude that the separation which the same ministers, or the same class of ministers, had previously offered to make was personal and local as well as moral and spiritual. The proposed and the accepted separations were precisely the same in kind and degree ; they differed only in their dates : while, therefore, one of the two is interpreted to my hand, I have no right to attach to the other an interpretation totally different. The assumption that the separation which the Lord prohibited was only a spiritual sentence, while the separation which he permitted was actual, local, complete, and final, derives countenance neither from the parable nor its interpretation.

It appears to me, then, that the Lord's direct and immediate design in this parable is, not to prescribe the conduct of his disciples in regard to the conflict between good and evil in the world, but to explain his own. Knowing that their Master possessed all power in heaven and in earth, it was natural that Christians of the first age should expect an immediate paradise. Nothing was more necessary, for the support of their faith in subsequent trials, than distinct warnings from the Lord, that even to his own people the world would remain a wilderness. Accordingly, both in plain terms and by symbols, he faithfully, frequently intimated that in the world they should have tribulation, but that all should be set right at last. On both sides they needed, and on both sides he gave, the instruction, that in this life they must lay their account with a mixture, but that after this life they would escape. Left to their own imagination, they would readily have expected that their omnipotent Head would so rule over the world, and so instruct his ministers, whether stormy winds or flaming fires, that evil, as soon as it showed its head, would be weeded out of his people's way: but with this parable and other cognate lessons in their hands, they would not be surprised at any amount of success which the enemy might be permitted to obtain ; they would possess their souls in patience, and wait for the end of the Lord.

The parable condemns persecution, but it seems not to bear upon discipline at all. In its secondary sense, or by implication, it protects the wicked from any attempt on the part of the Church to cast them out of the world by violence; but it does not, in any form or measure, vindicate a place for the impure within the communion of the Church of Christ. Arguments against the exclusion of unworthy members, founded on this parable, are nothing else than perversions of Scripture. Elsewhere Christians may clearly read their duty in regard to any brother who walks disorderly ; elsewhere they may learn how to counsel, exhort, and rebuke the erring, and, if he remain impenitent, how to cast him out of communion by a spiritual sentence; but in this parable regarding these matters no judgment is given.

While the "Notes" of Dr. Trench on the parables are generally judicious and valuable, his exposition of this and one or two others that are cognate is injured by a secret bias towards the forms in which he has been educated,—a bias that is natural and human, but not on that account less hurtful. The body of the vast and venerable institution of which he is at once a chief and an ornament, stands so near, and bulks so largely, that where it is concerned his usual acuteness fails him. The general announcement at the commencement of the parable, that it concerns the kingdom of heaven, he seems to think is sufficient proof that the "field" must mean the kingdom of heaven or the Church. It does, indeed, concern the kingdom of heaven, for it shows that when that kingdom has, by the Son of man, been introduced into the world, many things spring up and mingle with it there to mar its fruitfulness; but it betrays an unaccountable confusion to argue formally that because the parable concerns the kingdom of heaven, therefore, of all the features which the parable contains, "the field" must specifically represent that kingdom, in the face of the express testimony of Scripture that the field represents a totally different thing. The parable of the mustard-seed concerns the kingdom too, but does the "field" in that parable therefore mean the Church? No. The mustard-seed that grew in the field means the Church, and the field means the world in which the Church is planted. So in this parable the only thing that represents the Church, or aggregate of individual believers, is the mass of the wheat stalks that sprang from the good seed: the good seed are the children of the kingdom, and the field is the world in which these children live and labour. Looking minutely to the phraseology employed, we find that the kingdom of heaven is not said to be likened unto a field, but unto a man that sowed seed; pointing to the Lord himself as the head, and the good seed as his members, and the wide world as their place of sojourn, till he take them to himself.

Dr. Trench remarks further on this point, that the use of the term "world" need not perplex us in the least; and perhaps he was led to make that assertion because the use of the term did perplex him much. His solution of the difficulty is this: "It *was* the world, and therefore was rightly called so, till this seed was sown in it; but thenceforth was the world no longer." If it has any meaning at all, this sentence must mean that what was the world yesterday becomes the Church to-day, when some seed is sown, when some children of the kingdom are in it. Does the whole world become the Church when one country is christianized? or is it only the portion christianized that becomes the Church? If so, how many Christians must be in a given portion of the world, to constitute that portion the Church? If there were three of the true seed in Sodom, was Sodom the Church? or did not the three constitute the Church in Lot's house, while the world raged around it like the troubled sea?

Some of Stier's remarks are good: "The parable moves in quite a different sphere from that of the question concerning Church discipline." "The householder forbids and will not allow what the servants wish. These would have all the tares removed entirely from their place among the wheat, from the kingdom of Christ (ver. 41). But because the field is the world, that were equivalent to removing the bad out of the world (slaying the heretics)," &c.

The conclusion of the whole matter is, that whatever separation the parable forbids, it forbids entirely: if it speaks of discipline, it says there shall be none; so that they are wholly out of their reckoning who lean on it for the condemnation of what they consider excessive strictness while they would retain the power of excluding the worst from communion. But, in truth, the parable has nothing to say on the subject.

When we have made our way through the discussions that have accumulated round it, we return to the text in its simplicity, and grasp its plain positive truth, " The field is the world." It was all empty; nothing good grew there, until the seed was brought from heaven and sown. The nation, the family, the soul that has not Christ, is poor, and wretched, and miserable, and blind, and naked.

" The good seed are the children of the kingdom." They are bought with a price and born of the Spirit; they are new creatures in Christ and heirs of eternal life. Expressly it is written in reference to Christ's disciples, " All things are for your sakes" (2 Cor. iv. 15). For their sakes the world is preserved now, and for their sakes it will be destroyed when the set time has come. The darnel is permitted to grow in summer, and in harvest is cast into the fire,—both for the sake of the wheat. Because Christ loves his own he permits the wicked to run their course in time; but because Christ loves his own he will separate the wicked from the good at last.

The tares are the children of the wicked, and " the enemy that sowed them is the devil." Some people doubt, and some positively deny, the existence of the devil; but one thing is clear, the Lord Jesus Christ, the eternal Son of the Father, has no doubt on that point. He believes in that doctrine and teaches it: he teaches it to the multitude on the margin of the lake, and to the select circle of his followers in a private dwelling.

Lively and energetic are the remarks of Fred. Arndt on this subject: "Yes, Jesus says, in dry, clear words, 'The enemy that soweth them is the devil.' But surely there is not any devil? Who says that? The Son of God, the mouth of eternal truth, who knows the realm of spirits even as he knows this visible world,—who is the highest reason and the deepest wisdom, yea, even Omniscience itself,—he believes it. He holds it reasonable to believe in it. He teaches what he believes. Dost thou know it better than he, thou short-sighted being, thou dust of yesterday, thou child of error and ignorance? He says it, and therefore it is eternal truth. 'But is it not intended to be taken figuratively?' Well, suppose it were meant figuratively, we can only comprehend the figures of actually existing things, and the figurative representation of the devil would imply his real being: but here in the text the speech is not figurative ; the expression stands not among pictures and parables, but in the interpretation of a picture and a parable."* Whence hath it tares? inquired the servants. Already in those days they had begun to probe the question around which the conflict of ages has been waged—the origin of evil. One thing in the answer of the Lord is fitted to pour a flood of comfort into our hearts when they are agitated by the difficulties of this tremendous problem,—" an enemy hath done this." Evil does not belong originally to the constitution of man, nor has God, his maker, introduced it. Our case is sad, indeed; for we learn that an enemy whom we cannot overcome is ever lying in wait seeking how he may devour us. But what would our case have been, if evil, instead of being injected by an enemy from without, had been of the essence of the creature, or the act of the Creator? Our

* *Die Gleichniss-reden Jesu Christi*, von Fried. Arndt.

condition would have been one of absolute and irremediable despair. What a strong one, who is our enemy, has brought in, a stronger, who is our friend, can cast out—will cast out. Be of good cheer; believe on the Lord Jesus Christ, and thou shalt be saved.

How grand is the view which this picture discloses, when in the interpretation of it we closely follow the Master's steps! It is, indeed, a parable concerning the kingdom of heaven. The whole world belongs to the King; he has placed his children in it, and commanded them to multiply till they people all its borders. The enemy has introduced among them evil persons, and within them evil thoughts. It is not a part of the omniscient Ruler's plan to remove, by the ministry of either angels or men, all the wicked at once from his world. For his own purposes, which are only in part discernible by us, he permits the good and the evil to mingle and contend with each other until the fulness of time, as he left the Canaanites in the land to chastise and exercise his chosen people. When the tares prosper, the wheat languishes : when the wheat prospers, the tares languish. Evil men have lived in God's world ever since sin began : evil thoughts and deeds will be found in God's children as long as they remain in the body. The angels are not sent to-day to make such a separation as would leave the children of the kingdom nothing to do, or to bear.

If you desire the heavenly to prosper within you and around you, fight with the proper weapons against the devilish : if you desire the devilish within and around you to languish and decay, cherish the heavenly. As David's house waxes stronger, Saul's house will wax weaker. When Christ gets more of the world and of our hearts, the devil will get less.

Introduction: Mustard-seed
and the Leaven

IN the first two parables the kingdom of heaven is represented in conflict with its enemies ; in the next two it stands alone, putting forth its inherent life and power. There we learn the strength of its adversaries, and here we learn its own. There we saw the efforts made to check the progress of the kingdom; and here we see the progress which, in spite of these efforts, the kingdom makes. There the combat is exhibited, and here the victory. Devils and men, conscious conspirators or unconscious tools, did their utmost, as explained in the first pair of parables, to strangle the kingdom in its infancy, or to overpower it at a later stage ; but the kingdom, as we learn from the second pair, shakes its assailants off, emerges unhurt from the strife, and goes forward from strength to strength, until it has subdued and absorbed all the world. I have seen clouds gathering at dawn on the eastern horizon, with dark visage and a multitudinous threatening array, as if they had bound themselves by a great oath either to prevent the sun from rising or afterwards to quench his light ; but through them, beyond them, above them, slowly, steadily, majestically rose the sun, nor quivered from his path, nor halted in his progress, until by the power of his mid-day light he had utterly driven those clouds away, so that not a shred of their tumultuous assemblage could any more be seen on the clear blue sky. Such and so impotent in

Christ's hands are the adversaries of Christ's kingdom, although they seem formidable to men of little faith : such and so glorious will be the final victory of the King, although even his true subjects may fret and fear over his incomprehensible delay. The coming of the kingdom is like the morning, as slow, but as sure. As smoke is driven before the wind, so shall the Redeemer in the day of his power drive away all those adversaries, whether within his people or without, that now impiously say, " We will not have this man to reign over us." Christ's disciples are on the winning side, whatever may be the present aspect of the world. " He that believeth shall not make haste."

The two parables which now claim our attention, although closely allied, are not in meaning and application precisely identical. Both show the progress of the kingdom from a small beginning to a glorious consummation; and both indicate that this growth, as to cause, is due to its own inherent unquenchable life, and as to manner, is silent, secret, unobserved. Thus far these two are in the main coincident ; but besides teaching the same lesson in different forms, they teach also different lessons. The parable of the mustard-seed exhibits the kingdom in its own independent existence, inherent life, and irresistible power ; the parable of the leaven exhibits the kingdom in contact with the world, gradually overcoming and assimilating and absorbing that world into itself. Both alike show that the kingdom increases from small to great ; the first points to the essential, and the second to the instrumental cause of that increase : in the mustard-seed we see it growing great because of its own omnipotent vitality; in the leaven we see it growing great because it uses up all its adversaries as the material of its own enlargement.

The Mustard Seed
(Matthew 13:31-32)

" Another parable put he forth unto them, saying, The kingdom of heaven is like to a
grain of mustard-seed, which a man took, and sowed in his field : which indeed is the
least of all seeds : but when it is grown, it is the greatest among herbs, and becometh
a tree, so that the birds of the air come and lodge in the branches thereof."

WE are familiar with the mustard-plant both in a
wild and in a cultivated state in our own
country. Although not the smallest, it is by
no means the largest of our herbs. On this
point it is necessary to recall and keep in mind the
fact that when a given plant is indigenous in a southern
climate, the corresponding species or variety that may
be found in more northerly latitudes is generally of a
comparatively diminutive size. I have seen a maho-
gany-plant cultivated in a flower-pot, the best representative that could be obtained here of those forest
patriarchs in tropical America which constitute the
mahogany of commerce. The diminutive proportions of
our mustard-plant prove nothing regarding the magnitude
of the herb which bears the corresponding name in Syria.
We know, in point of fact, that it grows there to a great
size at the present day. "I have seen it," says Dr. Thomson, "on the rich plain of Akkar as tall as the horse
and his rider."* Irby and Mangles found a tree grow-

* The Land and the Book, p. 64.

ing in great abundance near the Dead Sea possessing many of the properties of mustard, which they suppose must be the mustard of the parable ; but this suggestion seems incompatible with the main scope of the representation, for its turning-point lies in this, that a culinary herb became great like a tree. That a forest tree should be large enough to afford shelter to the birds, is nothing wonderful; the parable is hinged on the fact that the garden herb ($\lambda\alpha\chi\alpha\nu o\nu$) became a tree ($\delta\epsilon\nu\delta\rho o\nu$).

But in this case an investigation exact and minute into the natural history of the plant is by no means necessary to the appreciation and explanation of the parable. It is not needful to determine what amount of credit is due to the witness who declared that he had seen a man climbing into the branches of a mustard-plant, or how far the fact, if real, was uncommon and exceptional. This plant obviously was chosen by the Lord, not on account of its absolute magnitude, but because it was, and was recognised to be, a striking instance of increase from very small to very great. It seems to have been in Palestine, at that time, the smallest seed from which so large a plant was known to grow. There were, perhaps, smaller seeds, but the plants which sprung from them were not so great ; and there were greater plants, but the seeds from which they sprung were not so small.

But the circumstance that most clearly exhibits and indicates the appropriateness of the choice, is the fact that the magnitude of the mustard-plant, in connection with the minuteness of its seed, was employed at that day among the Jews as a proverbial similitude, to indicate that great results may spring from causes that are apparently diminutive, but secretly powerful. The expression, " If ye had faith as a grain of mustard-seed," employed by the Lord on another occasion, is sufficient to show that both the conception and its use were familiar to his audience.

The spiritual lesson of the parable diverges into two lines, distinct but harmonious. By the kingdom of heaven, as it is represented in the growth of the mustard-plant, we may understand either saving truth living and growing great in the world, or saving truth living and growing great in an individual human heart. In both, its progress from small beginnings to great issues is like the growth of a gigantic herb from the imperceptible germ that was dropped among the clods in spring.

I. The kingdom of heaven *in the world* is like a mustard-seed sown in the ground, both in the smallness of its beginning and the greatness of its increase. The first promise, given at the gate of Eden, contained the Gospel as a seed contains the tree. It fell among Adam's descendants as a mustard-seed falls between the furrows, and lay long unnoticed there. With the Lord, in the development of his kingdom, a thousand years are as one day in the growth of vegetation. A man who in his childhood observed the seed cast into the ground, may live long and die old before the plants have reached maturity; but the seed of the kingdom has not lost its life, the God of the covenant has not forgotten his own. At the appointed time he will visit his husbandry, and fill his bosom with its fruits.

Never to human eye did the seed seem smaller than at the coming of Christ. The infant in the manger at Bethlehem is like a mustard-seed—an atom scarcely perceptible in the hand, and lost to view when it falls into the earth. Yet there lay the seed of eternal life—thence

sprang the stem on which all the saved of mankind shall
grow as branches. Israel was feeble among the nations
—a little child writhing in the grasp of imperial Rome;
Judea and Galilee, with the heathenish Samaria between,
constituted his beat throughout the brief period of his
public ministry. The range was short in its utmost
length, narrow in its utmost breadth. In a map of the
world of ordinary size, the spot that indicates Palestine
can scarcely be seen; yet from that spot radiated a power
which is at this day actually paramount. The Christ
who seemed so small both in private life at Nazareth and
in the public judgment-hall of Pilate at Jerusalem, is
greatest now both in heaven and in earth. Christendom
and Christianity are both supreme, each in its own place
and according to its own kind. This world already
belongs to Christian nations, and the next to Christian
men. So great has the religion of Jesus grown, that its
body overshadows the earth, and its spirit reaches heaven.

As the leaves and branches of a tree tend to assume
the form and proportions of the tree itself, so subordinate
parts in the development of God's kingdom follow more
or less closely the law of the whole kingdom—a progress
secret, slow, and sure, from a diminutive beginning to an
unexpected and amazing greatness. Take, for example,
the history of Moses, which is a vigorous branch shooting
out from the mustard-tree under the ancient dispensation.
The branch, a part of the tree, is, like the tree itself, small
at first and great at last. A poor Hebrew slave-mother,
counting her own " a goodly child," as every true mother
will to the end of time, strove, by a strange mixture of
ingenuity and desperation, to preserve him from the cruel
executioners of Pharaoh. When she could no longer
hide him in the house, she laid him in a wicker basket

and set it afloat in an eddy of the Nile. How small the seed seemed that day! A slave's man-child, one of many thousands destined by their jealous owners to destruction, cast by his own mother into the river, that he might not fall into the more dreaded hands of man—how small that germ was, and yet how great it grew! From heaven the word had gone forth, "Destroy it not, for a blessing is in it." On the mighty stream, and the cruel men who frequented it, the Maker of them both had laid the command, Touch not mine anointed, and do my prophet no harm. From that small seed, accordingly, sprang the greatest tree that grew in those old days upon the earth. Moses, the terror of Pharaoh, the scourge of Egypt, the leader of the Exodus, the lawgiver of Israel—Moses in his manhood was to the foundling infant what the towering tree is to the imperceptible seed from which it springs.

The operation of the same law may be observed in later ages. In the Popish convent at Erfurt a studious young monk sits alone in his cell, earnestly examining an ancient record. The student is Luther, and the book the Bible. He has read many books before, but his reading had never made him wretched till now. In other books he saw other people; but in this book for the first time he saw himself. His own sin, when conscience was quickened and enlightened to discern it, became a burden heavier than he could bear. For a time he was in a horror of great darkness; but when at last he found "the righteousness which is of God by faith," he grew hopeful, happy, and strong. Here is a living seed, but it is very small; an awakened, exercised, conscientious, believing monk, is an imperceptible atom which superstitious multitudes, and despotic princes, and a persecuting priesthood will overlay and smother, as the heavy furrow covers the microscopic mustard-seed. But the living seed burst, and sprang, and pierced through all these coverings. How great it grew and how far it spread history tells to-day. We have cause to thank God for the greatness of the Reformation, and to rebuke ourselves for its smallness. Through the grace of God it made rapid progress at the first, and by the passions of men it was arrested before its work was done;—not arrested, but impeded; it is growing still, and growing more vigorously in our own day than it has done in any generation since its youth.

But the present time supplies examples of the kingdom's growth from small to great, as distinct and characteristic as any period since the apostles' days. The revivals of these times are vigorous off-shoots from the great stem of Christ's kingdom in the world, and the part observes the same law of increase that operates in the whole. Trace any one of the local awakenings back to its source, and you will discover that the interest in spiritual, personal religion, which now overtops and overshadows all other interests in the neighbourhood—which has led many wanderers back to Christ's fold—which has caused friends to sing aloud for joy, and enemies to stand mute in astonishment—which has emptied jails and filled prayer-meetings—which has changed the wilderness into a garden, and drawn wondering witnesses from distant lands—sprang from some upper or lower room in which two or three unnoticed and unknown believers were wont to meet at stated times for prayer. Many of those small but living seeds have burst through the ground and made themselves known by their magnitude; and many similar seeds are lying hid to-day under the capacious folds of our vast and earnest industry. May great trees spring from these small seeds in the Lord's good time!

Robert Haldane in Geneva, with his Bible in his hand and a group of students around him, is a modern example of the same law in the growth of the kingdom.

II. The kingdom of heaven *in a human heart* is like a mustard-seed, both in the smallness of its beginning and the greatness of its increase. In the grand design of God, moral qualities hold the first place; physical magnitude is subordinate and instrumental. We may safely accommodate and apply to space the principle which the Scripture expressly applies to time: One man—as a sphere on which his purposes may be accomplished and his glory displayed—one man is with the Lord as a thousand worlds, and a thousand worlds as one man. There is room, brother, for the whole kingdom of God "within you." In one sense, it is most true, we ought to abase, but in another we ought to exalt ourselves. We should reverence ourselves as the most wonderful work of God within the sphere of our observation. The King, as well as the kingdom, finds room in a regenerated man. Here the Lord of glory best loves to dwell.

In this inner and smaller, as well as in the outer and larger sphere, the kingdom of heaven, following the law of the mustard-plant, grows from the least to the greatest. All life, indeed, is, in its origin, invisible; and the new life of faith is not an exception to the rule. The Lord himself, in the lesson which he taught to Nicodemus, compared it in this respect to the wind. In its origin it is imperceptible; in its results it is manifest and great. To wash seven times in Jordan seemed a small thing to the Syrian soldier, and such it really was; but when his leprosy was cleansed, and his flesh restored like that of a little child, he perceived that a great effect had sprung from simple means. The little-child look unto Jesus which the Gospel prescribes for the saving of the soul seems to the wisdom of this world as inadequate to heal a leprosy as the waters of the Jordan seemed to Naaman; yet from that small seed springs the tree of life, with all its beautiful blossoms of hope, and all its precious fruits of righteousness.

The first true, deep check in the conscience because of sin; the first real question, "What must I do to be saved?" the first tender grief for having crucified Christ and grieved the Spirit; the first request for pardon and reconciliation made to God, as a child asks bread from his parents when he is hungry;—the kingdom, coming in any of these forms is small and scarcely perceptible; but it lives, and in due time will grow great. Be of good cheer, ye who have felt the word swelling and bursting like a seed in your hearts. That plant may not yet have attained maturity in your life, but greater is He who shields it than all who assail it: the enemy cannot in the end prevail. He who hath begun a good work in you, will perfect it until the day of Christ. You could not make a living seed; but God has given it. Thus far all is well, but you are as helpless at the second stage as you were at the first; you have no more power to make the seed grow than you had to make the seed. The Author and Finisher of this work keeps it from first to last in his own hands. It is He who gives rain from heaven and fruitful seasons. The small seed of the kingdom has fallen on your hearts, and been hidden in their folds; it has taken root, and sent up into your lives some tender shoots of faith, and hope, and love. It is well; thank God for the past, and take courage for the coming time. The plant is small now; it will be great hereafter. It is small on earth; it will be great in heaven. Weed it and water it, sun it and shelter it. Be diligent on your own side of this great business, and God will not withhold his power. Cultivate the kingdom in your own hearts, and count on the blessing from on high to make it prosper. From the tender, diminutive life of grace, the life of glory will in due time grow.

When painters have drawn their figures in light, they throw in dark shadows beside them, that the positive forms may thereby be more prominently displayed. So, beside the kingdom of heaven, under the aspect of its growth from small beginnings, let us throw in the outline of the kingdom of darkness, that thereby the glory of light may be better seen.

Although one kingdom differs from another in character and aim, all kingdoms are like each other in the method of their operation. The kingdom of darkness, like the kingdom of light, grows gradually from very small to very great. The kingdom of Satan hangs on and follows Christ's kingdom like a dark shadow, and the shadow depends upon the light. The first sin against God was a very small seed, but the tree which sprang from it was the fall of man. "Thou shalt not eat," is a small point—its smallness has sometimes supplied unbelievers with wit, if not with argument—but on that point a door was hung, which, turned this way, opened heaven and shut hell; turned that way, opened hell and shut heaven. In its beginning the kingdom of evil was small; but from that small seed a mighty tree has grown.*

---

* "Good is like the mustard-seed; from small it becomes great : evil resembles it not less. Here, too, the great springs from the small. An evil thought, when once it has made its way into a poor soul, may become mighty enough to cast it into hell."—*Dräseke vom Reich Gottes*, ii. 238.

As there is no sin so great that the blood of Christ cannot blot it out, so there is no sin so small that it cannot destroy a soul. A little sin is like a little fire: stand in awe of the spark, and rest not till it is quenched. As Christ our Lord is tenderly careful of spiritual life when it is feeble, and cherishes it into strength, we should sternly stamp out evil while it is yet young in our own hearts, lest it spread like a fire. He will not quench the smoking flax of beginning grace, and we should quench with all our might the smoking flax of sin. He commanded the Church in Sardis to "be watchful, and strengthen the things which remain, that are ready to die" (Rev. iii. 2). The counterpart and complement of that command is binding, too, upon his disciples: Be watchful, and weaken—if possible, kill outright—the germs of evil that are springing from unseen seeds within your own heart and around you in the world. "The God of peace will bruise Satan under your feet shortly:" He will bruise Satan, but Satan must be bruised under your feet.

The Leaven
(Matthew 13:33)

"Another parable spake he unto them; The kingdom of heaven is like unto leaven, which a woman took, and hid in three measures of meal, till the whole was leavened."

IN the mustard-seed we saw the kingdom growing great by its inherent vitality; in the leaven we see it growing great by a contagious influence. There, the increase was attained by development from within; here, by acquisitions from without. It is not that there are two distinct ways in which the Gospel may gain complete possession of a man, or Christianity gain complete possession of the world; but that the one way in which the work advances is characterized by both these features, and consequently two pictures are required to exhibit both sides of the same thing.

The thought which is peculiar to this parable, the specific lesson which it teaches, is, the power of the Gospel, acting like contagion, to penetrate, assimilate, and absorb the world in which it lies. The kingdom grows great by permeating in secret through the masses, changing them gradually into its own nature, and appropriating them to itself.

The material frame-work which contains the spiritual lesson here is, in its main features, easily understood. Immediately below the surface, indeed, lie some hard questions; but all that is necessary is easy, and the discussion of difficulties, although it may well repay the labour, is by no means essential.

The chief use of leaven in the preparation of bread is, as I understand, to produce a mechanical effect. A certain chemical change is caused in the first instance by fermentation in the nature of the fermented substance, and for the sake of that change the process is in certain other manufactures introduced; but along with the chemical change which takes place in the nature of the substance, a mechanical change is also effected in its form, and for the sake of this latter and secondary result fermentation is resorted to in the baking of bread. The moist, soft, yet dense mass of dough, is by fermentation thrown into the form of a sponge Owing to the consistence of the material, the openings made by the ferment remain open, and consequently the lump, which would otherwise have been solid, is penetrated in every direction by an innumerable multitude of small cavities. Through these the heat in the oven obtains equal access to every portion of the dough; and thus, though the loaf is of considerable thickness, it is not left raw in the heart. Other methods, essentially different from fermentation, are in modern practice adopted in the preparation of bread; but by whatever means channels may be opened for the admission of heat to every particle of the dough, the result is practically the same as that which is obtained by leavening. The operator converts the mass of solid dough into swollen, light, porous, spongy leaven, by introducing into it a small quantity of matter already in a state of fermentation. It is the nature of that substance or principle to infect the portion that lies next it; and thus, if the contiguous matter be a susceptible conductor like moistened flour, it spreads until it has converted the whole mass. The knowledge of this process is not so universal amongst us as it was then in Galilee, or is still in many countries, because baking by fermentation, especially in the northern division of the island, is not much practised in private families. In countries where bread is prepared by that method, and every family prepares its own, the process is, of course, universally familiar.

The three measures of meal, which together make an ephah, were the understood quantity of an ordinary batch in the economics of a family, and as such are several times incidentally mentioned in the Scriptures of the Old Testament. See, for example, the preparation of bread by Sarah, as it is narrated in Gen. xviii. The various suggestions which inquirers have made regarding the specific significance of the *three* measures of meal, are interesting and instructive. As they do not directly traverse the lines of the analogy, they are entitled to a respectful hearing; but the subject is subordinate, and the meaning must ever be comparatively obscure. Whether the three measures are understood to point to the three continents of the world then known, or to the three sons of Noah by whom the world was peopled, or to spirit, soul, and body, the constituent elements of human nature, an interesting and useful conception is obtained. Each of these suggestions contains a truth, and that, too, a truth which is germane to the main lesson of the parable.

The same historic incidents which show that three measures were the ordinary quantity, show also that the women of the house were the ordinary operators. Baking the bread of the household was accounted women's work; as men ploughed and sowed in the field, women kneaded and baked at the oven. An inversion of this order would

have been noticed as incongruous, and presented a difficulty. Exceptions may be found, both in ancient and
modern times, but the representation in the text proceeds obviously upon the ordinary habits of society. On
this account, although I willingly listen to interesting
and ingenious speculations regarding the significance of
the woman who hid the leaven among the meal, I cannot
accept them as the foundation of any positive doctrine.
I am jealous, not without cause, of ecclesiastical tenden-
cies and prepossessions in the interpretation of the
parables. It is quite true that both in the discourses of
the Lord and in the epistles of his followers, reference is
made sometimes to the community or communities of
believers constituted as a Church; but the Church in the
Scriptures is a much simpler affair than it is in ecclesiastical history. Moreover, in these lessons which were
taught by the Lord in the beginning of the Gospel, we
find much about the individual man, and about the
aggregate of mankind, but little about the Church in its
visible organization. Accordingly, while I endeavour to
keep my mind open for everything that the Scriptures
bring to the Church, I am disposed to shut the door hard
against anything that I suspect the Church is bringing to
the Scriptures. When the woman who kneaded the
dough, and the woman who lost and found the silver
coin, come forward, backed by much learned authority,
saying, We are the Church, I stand on my guard against
deception, and carefully examine their credentials. A
man took the mustard-seed and sowed it in his field; a
woman took the leaven and hid it in three measures of
meal. The two parables are in this respect strictly
parallel; in both alike an ordinary act in rural economy
is performed, and in either it is performed by a person of

the appropriate sex. The converse would have been
startling and inexplicable. Whatever the operator may
represent in the sowing of the seed, the operator in the
hiding of the leaven represents the same. To neglect
the strict parallelism between the two cases, and attribute
some meaning to the selection of a woman as the operator
in the one, which the selection of a man in the other does
not convey, is, as I apprehend the matter, to forsake the
main track of the analogy, and follow by-paths which
lead to no useful result. The same divine hand that
dropped the word of eternal life as a mustard-seed into
the ground, also hid the word of eternal life as leaven in
the ephah of flour. Looking to the spiritual significance
of the two parables, we have in both cases the same act,
and in both cases, therefore, the same actor.[*]

A question of deep interest and considerable difficulty
arises from the fact that here, and here only, the greatest
good—the kingdom of God in the world—is unequivocally
compared to leaven, whereas this similitude, in all other
places of Scripture where it occurs, either stands indefinitely for progress of any kind, or expressly represents
the energy of evil. I assume without argument that in
this parable the diffusion of leaven through the mass represents the diffusion of good in the world, although
here and there, both in ancient and modern times, an
inquirer appears who understands the leaven in this place
to predict the prevalence of false doctrines and practices
in the Church. This interpretation no man would volun-
tarily adopt in the first instance, for it is obviously incongruous with the signification of the kingdom in every
other parable of the group; but some have permitted

[*] To the question what the woman specially represents in the parable,
Dräseke answers, " The grace of God."—ii. 263.

themselves to be driven into it by a difficulty that threatens on the opposite side. Because in other portions of Scripture they find leaven employed as an emblem of evil, they think themselves obliged to take it as a representative of evil here. But the difficulty which is presented by the use of a type to denote good, which is elsewhere employed to denote evil, must be fairly met and explained: to escape an imaginary difficulty we must not plunge into a real mistake. I am convinced that here, as in many similar cases, that which at first sight and on the surface wears the appearance of harshness, will be found, on fuller consideration, to contain a new beauty, and impart additional power.

It is obvious, in the first place, from the references made to it both by the Lord and his apostles, and especially from the iteration of the same maxim by Paul in two distinct epistles, that the similitude was current and familiar among the people as a proverb. It is conceded, that apart from this parable, wherever its application is expressly indicated, it is employed to designate the progress of evil; but it ought to be borne in mind that Paul has twice, in the same words, enunciated the universal proposition, " A little leaven leaveneth the whole lump " (1 Cor. v. 6; Gal. v. 9). By expressly mentioning the leaven of malice and wickedness in connection with this proposition, he leaves room for the supposition that there may be also a leaven of truth and holiness. In like manner, the Lord in another place warns his followers to beware of the leaven of the Pharisees, which is hypocrisy; but he nowhere says that leaven is hypocrisy. Leaven does, indeed, illustrate the method in which falsehood spreads; but it may, for aught that is said in the Scriptures, illustrate also the manner in which truth advances,

when it has gotten a footing in the world or in a man.
If truth and error, though opposite in their nature, are
like each other in their tendency to advance, as if by contagion; and if error is in this respect like leaven, then
truth must be in this respect like leaven too. When two
things are in a certain aspect like each other, and one of
them is in the same aspect like a third thing, the other
must also be like that third thing, provided the point of
view remain unchanged. Leaven represents evil not in
its nature, but only in the manner of its progress; and in
this respect the symbol is equally applicable to the opposite good.

This argument, indeed, may be carried one step further.
It is not enough to show that no loss of meaning is sustained by the application of this analogy to a new and
opposite class of facts; a positive gain thereby accrues.
The circumstance that in all other places of Scripture in
which the symbolical meaning of leaven is specifically applied, it is, in point of fact, employed to designate the progress of evil, instead of obscuring, rather reflects additional
light on the comparison as it is used in this parable.
The Teacher who speaks here is sovereign. By him the
worlds were made, and by him redemption wrought. In
both departments he executes his own will: when he
speaks, he speaks with authority. Observing that the
principle which ordinarily enters and pervades human
hearts is evil, a leaven of hypocrisy, he does not submit
to that state of things as necessary and permanent: this
is, indeed, the condition of the world; but he has come to
change it. Such is the direction of the current, and the
proverb which compares moral evil to a leaven correctly
describes its insinuating and persevering course; but here
is one who has power to turn the river of water so that it

shall flow backward to its source. Corruption has, indeed, spread through the world as leaven spreads through the dough, but here is Truth incarnate, another leaven, introduced into the mass, having power to saturate all with good, and thereby ultimately to cast forth evil from the world. The kingdom of darkness, for example, comes secretly,—the wiles of the devil constitute his policy and secure his success; the kingdom of God, although opposite in essence, is similar in the method of its advance, for it " cometh not with observation." The wheat and the darnel were opposite in character and consequences as light and darkness, but they were precisely alike in the manner of their growth. The loyal army adopts the same tactics which the rebels employ, while it strives to defend the throne which they are leagued to overthrow.

Thus, it is not enough to say that although the diffusion of evil in God's intelligent creatures is like the diffusion of leaven in the dough, Jesus may notwithstanding employ the same analogy to indicate how grace grows: we may proceed further and affirm, as Stier has ingeniously suggested, that because evil has often been compared to leaven in the manner of its advance, Jesus adopts that similitude to illustrate the aggressive, pervasive power of the truth.

Boldly, as a sovereign may, this Teacher seizes a proverb which was current as an exponent of the adversaries' successful stratagems, and stamps the metal with the image and superscription of the rightful King. The evil spreads like leaven; you tremble before its stealthy advance and relentless grasp: but be of good cheer, disciples of Jesus, greater is He that is for you than all that are against you; the word of life which has been hidden in the world, hidden in believing hearts, is a leaven too. The unction of the Holy One is more subtle and penetrating and subduing than sin and Satan. Where sin abounded grace shall much more abound.

The appropriation by Christ and to his kingdom of a similitude which had previously been applied in an opposite sense may be illustrated by many parallel examples in the Scriptures.* Of these, as far as I know, the different and opposite figurative significations of the serpent are the most striking and appropriate. The conception of secret motion, followed in due time by a surely planted effectual stroke, which is associated with the faculties and habits of a serpent, Christ found appropriated as a type to express the power of evil: but he did not permit it to remain so appropriated; he spoiled the Egyptian of this jewel, and in as far as it possessed value, enriched with it his own Israel. The serpent, as a metaphor, was in practice as completely thirled to the indication of evil as leaven had been, but Jesus counselled his disciples to " be wise as serpents." A similar example occurs in the parable of the unjust steward: it teaches that the skill of the wicked in doing evil should be imitated by Christians in doing good. Christ acts as king and conqueror. He strips the slain enemy of his sharpest weapons, and therewith girds his own faithful followers. Whatever wisdom and power may have been employed against them, wisdom and power inconceivably greater are wielded on their side.

We shall be better prepared to appreciate for practical purposes the peculiar meaning which the symbol bears in this parable if we advert, in the first place, to its ordinary meaning in other parts of Scripture. Both in the typical

---

* " Thus in different passages the lion is used as a figure of Satan, but also of Christ; the serpent as a figure of the enemy, but also of the wisdom needful to the apostles; birds as a figure of believing trustfulness, but also of the devil catching away the word."—*Lange* in loc.

worship of the Old Testament and in the doctrinal teaching of the New, leaven is ordinarily employed to denote the insinuating, contagious advance of sin. When the Hebrews were instructed to cast all leaven out of their houses during the solemnities of the Passover, their lawgiver meant to teach them by type that in worshipping God through his ordinances they should cast all malice and wickedness out of their hearts. In like manner, when the great Teacher warned his followers to beware of the leaven of the Pharisees and of the Sadducees, he meant that they should eschew on the one hand the lie of self-righteous superstition, and on the other the lie of libertine unbelief. The Apostle Paul, too, while he does not forbid another use, employs the conception, in point of fact, to illustrate the presence and power of sin.

Evil is a mysterious, self-propagating principle, like leaven. In the fact of the fall a piece of this leaven was hidden in the mass, and all mankind have consequently become corrupted. The leaven of sin that touched humanity at the first has infected the whole. The fact of a universal corruption appears in all history, and its origin is explained in the beginning of Genesis. The whole lump has been leavened: break off a bit at any place, at any time, and you will find it tainted. "The innocence of childhood" is a fond, false phrase, employed to conceal the terrible reality: there is no innocence, no purity, except that which comes through the gift of God, the sacrifice of Christ, and the ministry of the Spirit.

Idolatry, for example, is a leaven that must have been small in its beginning, but at a very early date it had grown great. The world was idolatrous when Abraham was called out to become the nucleus of a religious nation; and even his descendants, though constituted as a commonwealth expressly for the purpose of maintaining the worship of the true God while all the world beside had sunk into idolatry, were, through contact with the contaminating leaven, frequently overrun by the same sin. It became necessary that they should be poured from vessel to vessel, and tried as by fire, in order to keep them separate.

Small and apparently harmless Popery began: with the power and perseverance of a principle in nature it spread and defiled the Church. How completely that leaven penetrated the lump may be seen everywhere throughout Europe, in the architecture, sculpture, paintings,—in the laws, habits, and language that have come down from the middle ages to our own day. The evil spirit of the Papacy has intruded into every place; into the councils of kings, into the laws of nations, into the births, marriages, and deaths of the people. Between ruler and subject, between husband and wife, between parent and child, comes the priest, gliding in like water through seamy walls, sapping their foundations. Into the inmost heart of maid, wife, mother, creeps the confessional, tainting, souring, defiling society in its springs,—a leaven of malice and wickedness, a leaven at once of Pharisee and Sadducee, a superstition that believes everything in alliance with a scepticism that believes nothing, and all combined to conceal the salvation of God and enslave the spirits of men. Beware of the leaven of the Papacy.

Other things of grosser and more material mould follow the law of leaven in their progress from small to great, until they obtain the mastery of a community or a man. Such, for example, are the use of ardent spirits in Scotland and the use of opium in China. A hundred years ago how small was either bit! but being a bit of leaven, when it is once introduced it creeps stealthily forward, the appetite growing by what it feeds on, until it dominates, and in some cases utterly destroys. These creeping leavens stain the beauty and waste the strength of nations. Some tribes of Indians in North America have been annihilated mainly by this process; and at this day the Canadian Parliament, through a benevolent law, sanctioned by the Sovereign, entirely prohibit the sale of spirits to the Indians, and thus save from extinction the remnants of the tribes that live under our protection. Those subtile and powerful material agents which create abnormal appetites and influence the moral habits of a whole people, afford ample room for gravest thought both to Christians and patriots.

The fact acknowledged in Scripture, and manifest in all experience, that evil has transfused itself through humanity like leaven, serves to bring out in deeper relief the comforting converse truth which Christ has embodied in this parable. The universal diffusion of corruption in the world becomes a dark ground whereon the Lord may more vividly portray the progress and final triumph of holiness. Good introduced among the good is not much noticed; but when good assails, overcomes, and transforms evil, its power and beauty are conspicuously displayed. Employing the sad facts already stated as shadows filled in to make the lines of light more visible, I shall proceed now to express and enforce positively some of the practical lessons which the parable contains.

1. Christ, the Son of God, became man and dwelt among us. Behold the piece of leaven that has been plunged into the dead mass of the world! " In him was life, and the life was the light of men" (John i. 4). The whole is not leavened yet, but the germ has been introduced. The

meaning of Immanuel is, "God with us:" the incarnation is the link that binds the fallen to the throne of God. One without sin and with omnipotence has become our brother,—has taken hold of our nature, and will keep hold of it to the end. He will not fail nor be discouraged. To him every knee shall bow, and every tongue confess: the prophecy has been written, and the history will follow. In the meantime, while we wait for the accomplishment of the promise, we may obtain from this parable some glimpses of the method by which the change will be effected at last.

Leaven consists in, or at least causes, fermentation. The name suggests the mechanical process of boiling. The most sublime and awful scenes which nature has ever presented have been produced in this way. When great masses are affected, a boiling becomes unspeakably grand and terrible. This earth, now so solid beneath, and so green on the surface, seems to have been once a boiling mass. Those mountains that cleave the clouds are the bubbles that rose to the surface and were congealed ere they had time to subside again: there they stand to-day, monuments of the fact. The moral government of God is like the natural. The Maker's method, when he would bring down the high things and exalt the low, is to throw in an ingredient which will produce fermentation. He can make the world of spirit fervid as well as this material globe. The earth is shaken by moral causes. The Gospel sends a sword before it brings peace. Wars and rumours of wars rend the nations, and make men's hearts melt within their breasts. In some cases it is obviously Christian truth plunged into the mass that agitates the nations; and if we were able to discern the links of cause and effect a few degrees further into the fringes of the cloud that encircles God's throne we would perhaps see the same central fact setting in motion more distant forces. Our life is so short, and our range of vision so contracted, that we cannot observe the progress which the kingdom makes. Sometimes, and in some places, it seems to recede; but when the end comes it will be seen that every step of apparent retreat was the couching in preparation for another spring. The kingdoms of this world shall become the kingdoms of our Lord and of his Christ. The captive's chains shall be broken, whether they bind more directly the body or the soul, although the ancient political organizations of Europe, and the more recent fabrics of America, should be torn asunder and tossed away in the process, as foam is tossed from the crest of a wave upon the shore. " Thou shalt break them with a rod of iron; thou shalt dash them in pieces like a potter's vessel. Be wise now therefore, O ye kings; be instructed, ye judges of the earth. Serve the Lord with fear, and rejoice with trembling. Kiss the Son, lest he be angry, and ye perish from the way, when his wrath is kindled but a little. Blessed are all they that put their trust in him" (Ps. ii. 9–12).

2. Converted men, women, and children are let into openings of corrupt humanity, and hidden in its heart. There they cannot lie still: they stir, and effervesce, and inoculate the portions with which they are in closest contact. In this respect the lesson is the same with that which is taught in those other short parables of Jesus,—" Ye are the light of the world. Ye are the salt of the earth."

Nor is the conception essentially different from that of Christ or his word dropped into the lump of humanity; for Christians have no life and no expansive power, except in as far as Christ dwells in their hearts by faith. They are vessels which contain the truth, and when these vessels are hidden under the folds of families and larger communities, the word of life, which is within them, touches and tells upon their neighbours.

The most recent experience of the Church exhibits the kingdom spreading like leaven, as vividly, perhaps, as any experience since apostolic times. By contact with one soul, already fervid with new life, other souls, hitherto dead, become fervid too. One sinner saved, his heart burning within his breast, as he consciously communes with his Saviour, touches a meeting and sets it all aglow; the prayer-meeting thus moved touches the congregation and throws its settled lees into an unwonted and violent commotion; this assembly, all throbbing with the cry, What must we do to be saved? infects a city; and the city so infected communicates its fervour to the land; and a nation thus on fire kindles another by its far-reaching sympathy beyond intervening seas. Thus some portions of the world have been thrown into such a state of effervescence, by the leaven of the Gospel hidden in their heart, that for a time the sound of praise for sin forgiven has risen in the highways and market-places, louder than that other old, strong cry, What shall we eat, and what shall we drink, and wherewithal shall we be clothed?

The leaven, like gravitation, follows the same law on smaller spheres that it follows on the larger. Brother infects sister, and sister brother; parent child, and child parent; shopman shopmate. We often lament the contagious influence of evil, and it is right that we should; but it is an unthankful, unhopeful spirit, that thinks and speaks of the dark side only. Oh, thou of little faith, wherefore didst thou doubt? The new life which Christ has brought into the world is a leaven too. Working on the same method, but backed by a mightier power, good will yet overcome evil,—life will destroy death. Life from the Lord and in the Lord, though small at first as to the number of persons whom it animates, will increase until it fill the world. It will absorb surrounding death, and in absorbing quicken it. He that sat upon the throne said, " Behold, I make all things new " (Rev. xxi. 5).

3. There is yet another branch of the practical lesson which ought not to be overlooked : The life of faith, when it is hidden in the heart, spreads like leaven through the man, occupying and assimilating all the faculties of his nature and all the course of his life. The whole lump of the individual must be leavened, as well as the whole lump of the world. Christ will not be satisfied until he get every man in the world for his own, and every part of each. Whatever amount of ground there may be for the judgment of some expositors that the three measures of meal in the parable represent spirit, soul, and body, the constituents of human nature, certain it is that if the leaven of the kingdom is deposited in the heart, it will not cease until it has interpenetrated the human trinity and conformed all to the likeness of Christ. In the new creature, as in the new world, " dwelleth righteousness." That which is now laid on the conscience of Christians as a law will yet emerge from their life as a fact,—" Whether therefore ye eat or drink, or whatsoever ye do, do all to the glory of God."

From a circumstance not expressly mentioned in the parable, but obviously contained in the nature of the case, springs a thought of tender and solemn import. The piece of leaven was hid in the meal, and the whole quantity, in consequence, was converted into leaven ; but the leaven will not spread through meal that is dry; the meal is not susceptible, receptive, until it is saturated with water.

Within some persons, some families, some congregations, some communities, the leaven of truth has been deposited for a long time, and yet they are not moved, they are not changed. The leaven remains as it came, a stranger; all around, notwithstanding its presence, is still, is dead. It is when the Spirit is poured out as floods that the leaven of the kingdom spreads with quickening, assimilating power. I will pour out my Spirit upon you, saith the Lord : the promise is sent to generate the prayer, as a sound calls forth an echo. Behold, I come quickly, says Christ : Even so, come, Lord Jesus, respond Christians. Catch the promise as it falls, and send it back like an echo to heaven. I will pour out my Spirit upon you : Pour out thy Spirit, Lord, on us, as floods on the dry ground ; so shall the word already lying in our Bibles and our memories run and be glorified in our life and through our land.

The Hidden Treasure
(Matthew 13:44)

" Again, the kingdom of heaven is like unto treasure hid in a field ; the which when a man
    hath found, he hideth, and for joy thereof goeth and selleth all that he hath, and
    buyeth that field."

THESE two parables, the hidden treasure and the
costly pearl, are even more closely allied to
each other than the two which precede them.
Generically they teach the same truth ; but
they teach it with distinct specific differences. It will be
most convenient to notice in connection with the first, the
lessons that are common to both ; and in connection with
the second, the points of distinction between them.

These twin parables, then, exhibit on the one hand the
intrinsic preciousness of the Gospel, and on the other the
high esteem in which that precious thing is held by a
spiritually quickened man. They set forth first how
valuable the kingdom of God is, and next how much it
is valued by those who know its worth.

These two, along with the concluding representation of
the general judgment, were spoken, not to the multitude
on the shore of the lake, but more privately to a smaller
audience in a neighbouring dwelling. Many expositors
believe that they can discern a difference in the nature
and treatment of the subjects between the first four and
the last three, corresponding to the different circumstances

in which the two portions of the group were severally delivered. It is thought that those which were addressed to the multitude in public represent the kingdom in its more general and external aspects, as was suitable in a miscellaneous audience ; while those which were addressed privately to the circle of disciples represent the kingdom more especially in its intrinsic nature and individual, personal application. I would not presume to affirm that there is no ground for this distinction ; but I think it is a mistake to make it the hinge on which our view of the whole group must turn. I suspect there are things in the parable of the sower which require, for their appreciation, the faith and experience of true disciples, as much as anything that the parable of the hidden treasure contains ; and, on the other hand, that the lessons suggested by the treasure were as necessary and appropriate to the mixed multitude as those which are taught by the sowing of the seed on different kinds of ground. The necessity of personal appreciation and acceptance of the Gospel, which is the main lesson of this parable spoken privately in the house, is pre-eminently a word in season to those that are without. That lesson, accordingly, the Lord and his apostles were wont to teach in promiscuous assemblies. While, therefore, I notice the fact that the three later similitudes of this group were given to a smaller circle after the crowd had dispersed, I am not able to say that the reason of the change is evident in the nature of the subjects. Had these three also been spoken from the fishing-boat to the promiscuous assemblage on shore, I would not have been able to affirm that the themes seemed less appropriate to the audience, or less in accordance with the Teacher's method at other times. I look with interest into the distinctions which some have drawn between the four *exoteric* parables addressed to a miscellaneous assembly, and the three *esoteric* parables spoken to a more select and more sympathizing few ; but to me they do not appear to be of substantial importance in the interpretation.

The treasure may have been gold or silver or precious stones, or a combination of all three : it may have been anything of great value that lies in small bulk, and is not liable to decay,—such a treasure as may lie buried under the earth for a long period without any diminution of its worth. In oriental countries and in ancient times treasures were hid in the ground more frequently than in our land and our day ; but it is probable that even there and then the subterranean wealth was tenfold greater in the popular belief than it was in reality.

Two distinct causes, or classes of causes, lead to the concealment of treasure under ground : the feeble bury their wealth when they are oppressed, and the guilty when they are scared. As a general rule, we may assume that the treasure which is found buried in the earth has been placed there either by honest men when the law was feeble, or by dishonest men when the law was strong. The two classes of persons who bury gold are the robbed and the robbers.

In both cases, the treasure which is intentionally and intelligently buried is liable to be lost through the removal or death of those who were in the secret. Such secreted and lost wealth is afterwards from time to time found by those who build houses or cultivate the soil. In all lands and ages some such hoards have been actually discovered, and many such have been imagined and expected by the credulous. The conditions of the treasure that may be buried under ground exist in substances widely different from gold and silver and precious stones. On the west coast of Scotland, a few years ago, some men, while engaged in digging fuel from a moss, found at a great depth large quantities of tallow carefully sewed up in raw ox-hides, and in good preservation. In troubled, lawless times, a clan had ravaged their neighbour's territory : not having had time to drive away the cattle, they had buried the only portion of the spoil that could be preserved, intending to return when the danger was past and carry it away. The opportunity of realizing the booty had never occurred, and the clansmen had carried the secret with themselves to the grave.

In modern times, treasures a thousand-fold more valuable than any that have ever been hidden by human hands are frequently discovered under the earth, and wealth correspondingly great obtained by purchasing the field in which they lie. The much disputed and now celebrated mineral at Torbanehill, near Bathgate, in the county of Linlithgow, affords a good example. A person discovered that a coal or other mineral substance of great value lay in the ground. Without revealing, perhaps not knowing to the full extent the value of his discovery, he forthwith concluded, not precisely a purchase, but a long lease of the ground for mining purposes. When his bargain was securely made, he began to bring up the precious substance. As a raw material for the manufacture of gas and oil, it was found precious beyond all precedent. The original proprietor then raised an action for the dissolution of the lease. The action has been several times renewed in various forms, and its fame has resounded through all Europe. Meantime the prudent discoverer of the treasure and purchaser of the field is reaping a rich harvest from his transaction.

In North America, both in the States and in Canada, similar facts have often of late years emerged, especially in connection with oil springs and copper mines. Some men have obtained enormous wealth by purchasing for a small price a piece of ground in which a seam of copper lay, and selling it again when the fact was verified.

A question has been raised and discussed at greater length, I think, than its importance warrants, regarding the conduct of the man who found the treasure and hid it again till he had secured the field—whether the act was fair or unfair. The parables of the Lord are allowed to flow like a mountain stream in its natural channel. In those at least that are metaphorical, the narrative does not undertake to prescribe what should be, but to represent what is probable in human history. The fact as narrated may or may not be an example worthy of imitation.* The moral lesson is found, not by looking directly at the story, but by looking at the shadow which the material case projects on the spiritual sphere. The conduct of the person in the picture may be good, bad, or indifferent ; the spiritual lesson is not affected by the moral character of the act which is employed as a leaden type to make it visible. As the lesson on a printed page is not affected by the baseness or the pureness of the metal which constituted the type, provided always that the form of the type were appropriate ; so the doctrine left for us after the parabolic picture has passed is not dependent for its purity on the material of which the type was formed. The shifty dishonest factor, and the in-

---

* It is otherwise, of course, in those that are directly moral, as the Good Samaritan; they are not metaphors to be translated, but examples to be imitated.

dolent unrighteous judge of subsequent parables, occur as conspicuous examples.

The picture is obviously true to nature. When a man became aware that a great treasure lay under ground at a certain spot, he concealed his knowledge of the fact, and took measures to obtain possession of the field. Believing that this hidden wealth was greater far than all that he possessed in the world, or could ever hope to acquire by the ordinary produce of his property, he sold all that he had without a grudge, in order to make sure of the prize. The love of his own possessions, whether hereditary or acquired, whether lands or money, was overbalanced and so destroyed by the estimate which he had formed of the hidden treasure. The new and stronger affection neutralized and blotted out all previous predilections for what was his own. He sold all that he had, and bought the field. The turning-point is here; and here, accordingly, the story is abruptly broken off. There is not a word regarding the subsequent steps of the important and critical transaction. How much he gained by his bargain ; whether the validity of the purchase was disputed in a court of justice by the former proprietor, on the ground of a concealment of facts by the buyer;—these and all similar points are designedly veiled off. If they had been introduced, they would have served only to lead the investigator into a wrong track, and the meaning of the Master would thereby have been lost. The story advances in broad and manifest accordance with nature, both in its main line and in its subordinate accessories, until it has reached and passed the point which marked its goal : then the curtain suddenly drops, resolutely concealing all the rest, and so compelling the reader to fix his regard on the great essential lesson, instead of dissipating his energies on a multitude of interesting but unnecessary speculations.

Such is the material framework which sustains the spiritual truth,—such the trellis which bears up the fruitful vine: having first gone round it to survey its construction and its form, we now approach it to gather for our own use the ripe fruit that hangs within reach on every side.

1. There is a treasure, placed within our reach in this world, rich beyond all comparison or conception,—a treasure incorruptible and undefiled and unfading. "God is love,"—behold the fountain-head, where an exhaustless supply is stored: in the Gospel of Christ a channel has been opened through which streams from that fountain flow down to this distant world. In the Son of God incarnate divine mercy reaches our nature, and supplies our wants. Through the ministry of the Spirit, in the earliest promise and in subsequent prophecy the refreshing water was brought into contact with parched lips. A heavenly treasure lies on this poverty-stricken, bankrupt, accursed world, sufficient to enrich every one of its poor and miserable and wretched and blind and naked inhabitants.

2. The treasure is hidden. In early ages it was concealed under certain veils, constructed of design in such a manner that through their half-transparent folds a halo of the unseen glory should excite the hopes and attract the steps of every generation. The promise given at the gate of Paradise contained the treasure, but contained it wrapped up in allegoric prophecy which nothing but subsequent fulfilment could completely unfold. Down through the patriarchal and prophetic ages it continued a hidden treasure, although the new life of the faithful

was secretly sustained by it all the while. Even when
Christ through these parables taught his disciples in
Galilee, his kingdom was still hidden. A few fishermen,
and here and there a ruler, had discovered the precious
deposit, and had drawn from it enough to enrich themselves for ever; but to the multitude it was still unknown. Under the form of a man—under the privacy
and poverty of a Nazarene, was the fulness of the Godhead hid that day from the wise and prudent of the world.
The light was near them, and yet they did not see; the
riches of divine grace were brought to their door, and yet
they continued poor and miserable.

But even after the Lord had fully declared his mission
and finished his work,—after he had died for our sin, and
risen again for our justification,—after his disciples
through the ministry of the Spirit had published the glad
tidings in many lands,—the treasure still lay hidden. It
was near, and yet out of sight. Those who find it, find
out at the same time that they have been almost treading on it for years, and yet ignorant of its existence and
its worth. Saul of Tarsus had been often near it, before
he found it for himself. When Gamaliel lectured on the
Mosaic sacrifices, the attentive, clear-headed and ardent
pupil, was on the very point of discovering where the
treasure lay; but though often near it, he never fell on it
until that day when he fell to the ground near Damascus.
Felix was near it when, shut in between his own sin and
God's righteousness, he trembled at the sight of the
judgment-seat, like an angel with a drawn sword right
before him on the narrow path. Agrippa was near it
when, caught and carried away ere he was well aware by
the close, clear reasoning of a true preacher, he was almost
persuaded to be a Christian. Still men may be walking

near the treasure of eternal life,—walking over it, and yet miss it : the treasure that they trod upon remains hidden, and they remain poor.

3. The hidden treasure is at last found. It is noticed by all students of the parables, that on this point there is a marked distinction between the experience of the man who found the hidden treasure, and that of the merchant who found the pearl of great price. It is probable that this man was not aware that there was any treasure in that field : he seems to have been neither looking for it nor expecting to find it. He was probably employed in some other work, and prosecuting some other object. He may have been a labourer toiling there for his daily bread ; or he may have been engaged in making a road or digging for the foundation of a house, when the treasure, concealed in a troubled time, was exposed to view. He found what he was not seeking : he was seeking a bit of bread, and stumbled upon a fortune. The merchant, on the contrary, who fell in with the precious pearl was travelling with the express purpose of discovering goodly pearls and buying them. He obtained what he was seeking ; but obtained a pearl of greater value than he had previously seen, or expected ever to see.

Outwardly at least, and on the surface, a similar distinction seems to obtain between one man's experience and another's, in regard to the manner of finding the treasures of divine grace. Some seem to find the Saviour when they are not seeking him ; and some, after deliberately and consciously seeking him long, are rewarded at length. It is the former of the two classes with whom we are more directly concerned in the exposition of this parable. Looking abroad upon the past history or the present experience of the Church, we observe that some suddenly stumble, as it were, upon salvation, when they neither expected nor desired to find it. Not a few have come to laugh, and remained to pray. Many authentic cases are recorded of persons who entered the house of God bent on making sport of the preacher, and who went away believing in the Saviour whom he preached. A youth has left his home in the country and plunged into a great capital to push his fortune, and has found there, what he did not seek, pardon of sin and peace with God through the Saviour. Another has gone to India as a soldier, dreaming of war and victory, and honour and wealth ; but has returned a meek disciple of Jesus, glory to God and peace with men radiating like sunlight from all his spirit and all his life. A young female, chafed and fretting under the enforced dulness of a sober home, has received and accepted an invitation which promises to set her free from restraint for a time, and permit her to flutter at will in the midst of a fashionable throng. At the threshold of the prepared festivities a message meets her,—a message charged with a mighty sorrow, which drives the crowd of joyful anticipations forth from her heart, as a swollen stream bears down the dry leaves of autumn. She is thrown aside in solitude, in emptiness, in agony. In the silent night, and in the aching emptiness of her soul, the knocking of Christ from without is for the first time heard. The weary heart opens at last, and lets the Stranger in. She has found a treasure which, though often near her before, had hitherto escaped her notice. From the peace of God in which she now dwells she looks out from time to time on the pleasures of sin which she formerly chased, and borrows from the experience of ancient Israel a phrase best fitted to express her mind,—"The Portion of Jacob is not like them."

The history of the Church is studded with such examples : the hearts of believers, when they are ready to
faint, are cheered from time to time by such good news
from countries far and near. It is a reproof to us, but a
glory to the Lord, that he is often found of those who
sought not after him. Perhaps the man in the parable
was digging for stones when he fell upon the treasure :
they who find the true riches meet often with a similar
surprise.

4. The next feature that claims attention is the instant
ardent effort of the discoverer to make the treasure his
own, now that he knows what it is and where it lies.

In the parable, the man conceals his discovery, because
he knows that if the secret leak out, the owner will not
part with his field at any price. One can easily imagine
the scene and the act that enlivened it. A labouring
man, digging for some purpose in a field alone, in the
progress of his hard and humble work lays open one side
of a glittering golden store. As soon as the first tumult
of emotion has subsided, he gathers his wits and goes
into action. First of all he throws some earth over the
exposed portion of the treasure; then he looks cautiously
round to ascertain whether any witness was near enough
to observe his motions. He proceeds next, probably, to
ply his ordinary task on another spot with an indifferent
air, that he may not attract attention. The place where
the treasure lies, the place that he loves best, he carefully
avoids : he comes not once near it again until he has
paid the price, and secured the titles of the property.

Too much has been made of the subordinate circumstances here. A person in the position of this man could
not do otherwise than he did, without abandoning all
hope of obtaining the prize. To blab it out, would

have been to throw it away. If he had talked about it, the fact would have proved that he did not care for it. The concealment is not an essential feature, but a subordinate circumstance of the parable. It was resorted to, not for its own sake, but as an obvious means of obtaining a desired end. The hiding of the treasure is introduced into the picture simply to mark the man's estimate of its worth and his determination at all hazards to obtain it.

In the spiritual department a similar end is pursued, but the adoption of similar means there would not tend to insure success. In the nature of the case it is not necessary to conceal the spiritual treasure from others in order to secure it for yourself. Although the world should discover it, by an intimation from you, and enrich themselves out of it, you would not therefore obtain less. It is thus a vain labour to search, as many do, for something in the spiritual sphere corresponding to the concealment by the discoverer in the story. The best way of interpreting that feature is to represent by it a soul's high appreciation of divine mercy and earnest desire to obtain it, and then allow the feature to drop out of sight, like the husk after the ripened grain has fallen from it and been secured. It has been said that one of the rarest kinds of knowledge is to know when to hold your peace. Many know well how to speak; few know when to be silent. A similar experience emerges here: many have an excellent faculty for opening up the parables, and tracing every feature up to all its springs, and down to all its consequences. The power of attributing a distinct spiritual import to every light and shadow of the picture is common; but the faculty of permitting a subordinate accessory to drop when it has fulfilled its office, and following stanchly on the main track, is comparatively rare.

You may, indeed, find instances in which a man, awakened and persuaded of the preciousness of Christ, has kept all silent within his own breast until he has made his own calling and election sure; but in these cases the secrecy is by no means prompted by a fear that to publish the secret were to lose the treasure; and in many other examples the discoverer, during the continuance of his efforts to obtain possession, publishes the secret to the world, and enters at last into his heritage in presence of many witnesses. The discoverer of Christ's preciousness is like the discoverer of hid treasure, in his ultimate aim, but not in his mediate methods. Concealment would not help him to possession, and therefore he does not uniformly or necessarily take pains to conceal.

5. He parts with all in order that he may acquire the treasure. This is the turning-point of the parable, and the turning-point too of that which the parable represents,—the conversion of sinners,—the saving of the lost. The picture, being framed of earthly materials, fails on one point to represent the idea of the Lord. When the man had converted all his property into money, and offered the net proceeds for the field, his offer was accepted as adequate, and the property was conveyed to him in return for value received. The transaction which takes place in redemption between a sinful man and God his Saviour is essentially different. Although it is true on the one side that in accepting pardon we must and do surrender all to Christ, pardon is, notwithstanding, bestowed as a free gift. Our self-surrender does not in any sense or measure give to God an equivalent for that which in the covenant he bestows on his own. The same two things occur, indeed, in the natural and in the spiritual spheres, but they occur in the reverse order.

The price which the buyer offers induces the possessor to give him the property; on the contrary, on the spiritual side it is the free gift of the treasure by the Proprietor that induces the receiver to part with all that he has to the Giver. In one aspect the acquisition of the treasure which enriches a soul is a purchase which a needy man makes by the surrender of all that he has, and in another aspect it is a free gift bestowed by God for Christ's sake upon him who had nothing to give in return. In as far forth as it is a purchase which a sinner makes, this parable represents its nature; but in as far forth as it is a gift given on the one side and accepted on the other, this parable is silent. It contains no feature capable of presenting salvation in that point of view.

6. Mark, now in the close yet another specific feature of the material fact which has its counterpart in full on the spiritual side. It is intimated that when the man had discovered the treasure, "for joy thereof" he went and sold all, in order to buy the field that contained it. This "joy" is an essential element in the case. If it is wanting the business will at some stage certainly miscarry, the transaction will never be completed. One love in a human heart cannot be overcome and destroyed except by another. Love, among the affections of our nature, is one of those high born nobles who refuse to be tried or superseded except by their peers. Love of the world will not yield to fear, even though the fear be a fear of God's anger. You cannot overcome and cast it out until you bring against it another and greater love.

A man has joy in his possession, and lives without God in the world: he is a god unto himself. He cannot and will not surrender his joy, such as it is, to any summons except to that which a greater joy sends in. When

the preciousness of peace with God through the blood
of Christ is revealed to him, the "joy thereof" becomes so great that all his gold becomes dross, and all
his fine gold dim in his own esteem.   This new joy is so
weighty that it tosses up the scale in which all his former
delights lay, as if they were only the small dust of the
balance.

A young rich man came running once to Jesus, as the
owner of the field that contained the treasure of eternal
life, and entered gravely into terms for the purchase.   He
would give so much for it, but the owner held it high :
"All that thou hast," this is the price, and there is no
abatement.   The young man did not close with that offer,
and did not complete the transaction.   He went away;
but what was the state of his mind as he departed ?   "He
went away sorrowful."   Ah ! the secret is out.   Although
he desired, in some sense, to obtain what he called eternal
life, the "joy thereof" had not been kindled in his cold,
calculating heart.   His love of earthly riches was too
strong to yield to the suggestions of prudence, or the fear
of a future judgment.   The love of the old portion will
yield to nothing but love of the new; and love of the new
he had never felt.

The case of Paul supplies an exact contrast.   A learned
Pharisee, conscious of a power that would one day place
the highest dignities at his disposal, he was a man of great
and manifold possessions.   A curious and interesting in-
ventory of his goods has been preserved like a fossil in
the Scriptures (Phil. iii. 5, 6).   These things he highly
valued and fondly loved; but another and opposing love
came against them, and the strong man succumbed to
the stronger.   "What things were gain to me, these I
counted loss for Christ:" he parted with all and purchased

the newly discovered treasure; but it was "for joy thereof." He went into the transaction not driven by dread, but drawn by the expectation of a greater joy.

It is thus that men buy an incorruptible treasure; it is thus that men win Christ. They deceive themselves who try how cheaply they may get to heaven,—how much of their idol they may retain and yet be safe in the judgment. The man who was "sorrowful" when the two portions were set before him for his choice, "went away." As long as peace with God in his Son, labelled with its price, "All that you have," makes us sorry that the boon is held so dear, we will never obtain the boon: when the sight of it, price and all, sends a flash of more than earthly joy into the soul, then we shall bound forward, leaving all behind, and win Christ.

The Pearl
(Matthew 13:45-46)

" Again, the kingdom of heaven is like unto a merchant man, seeking goodly pearls : who, when he had found one pearl of great price, went and sold all that he had, and bought it."

SO closely allied are these two parables, that if we had regarded repetition as a formidable blemish in our lessons, we would not have proposed to expound them separately and successively. The two lines are coincident throughout their whole length, except at one point; but there the diversity is broadly marked, amounting in one aspect to a specific contrast. In view of this difference on the one hand, and of the example of the Lord on the other, I think it right to open and apply the parable of the pearl as fully as if the parable of the hidden treasure had not gone before it. We need and get not only different pictures of the same objects, but also the same pictures repeated in different colours and on different grounds. One eye may be more touched and taken by this colour, and another by that, although the outline of the objects be in both cases essentially the same. Thus, the conception of a treasure found may convey the meaning more impressively to one mind, and the conception of a pearl purchased may convey it more impressively to another; and so, although the lesson of the second parable had been more nearly identical with that of the first than it is, it would not have been expedient to dismiss it with a cursory notice. By a full examination of the principle under the picture of a precious pearl, we shall obtain the advantage which in moral questions, as in material operations, is often unspeakably great, of a second stroke on the same spot. The usefulness, and even the necessity of this method is acknowledged by all teachers, in whatever department they may be called to exercise their office. The same reasons, moreover, which induced the Master to reduplicate his lesson demands that we should also reduplicate ours : it is our part both in matter and in method to follow his steps.

Pearls seem to have borne a higher value in ancient times than they bear now, both absolutely and in comparison with other kinds of jewels. Romantic ideas prevailed regarding their origin and their nature; but it is well worthy of remark that the parable passes in silence all that was false or fanciful in the ideas of the ancients regarding the production and the medicinal virtue of pearls. There is not a word about their origin in a drop of dew, or the colour imparted to them by the brightness or darkness of the heavens at the moment of their conception: the only circumstance regarding the pearl which the Lord employs in his instructions is its high price. He seizes the obvious and universally known fact, taking no notice of the fanciful theories with which it was connected.

This fact possesses a value in relation to Apologetics which intelligent students will readily appreciate. It is instructive and suggestive to compare the Scriptures on such subjects with other books both ancient and modern. Take, for example, a passage from the comment of Benjamin Keach, which gives both the conceit of the ancients and the endorsement of it at a comparatively recent era. "Pearls," naturalists tell us, "have a strange birth and original. Pliny saith, Shell fish is the wonderful geniture of a pearl congealed into a diaphanous stone, and the shell is called the mother of pearl. Now at a certain time of the year this shell fish opens itself, and takes in a certain moist dew, after which they grow big until they bring forth the pearl. By which it seems they have their birth from heaven in a marvellous manner." Planting his foot upon this story, the worthy expositor gravely and devoutly prosecutes the parallel; but already, although it is only a century and a half old, his speculation serves only to provoke a smile. The comment, written in England a hundred and sixty years ago, is antiquated and set aside by the light of the present day; but the parable, spoken in Galilee eighteen hundred years ago, stands in the middle of the nineteenth century, enduring in safety the scrutiny of adversaries, and ministering to the delight of friends, as fair and fresh as on the day of its birth. "Whence hath this man this wisdom?"*

---

* For the sake of its bearing on the divine authority of the Scriptures, and the questions that are agitated at the present time, I subjoin a similar example, extracted from a lecture which I contributed to the Exeter Hall series of 1860–61 :—

"A very remarkable expression occurs in the Apocalypse (xvi. 18) bearing on the work of preparing the earth for man, before man was made : 'And there was a great earthquake, such as was not since men were upon the earth, so mighty an earthquake and so great.' There the advent of man, as an inhabitant of the earth, is formally given as an epoch after which great earthquakes did not occur. It is well known now that earthquakes must have rent this globe before the birth of man, which make all that have occurred since sink into insignificance; but how was John, the fisherman of Galilee, led to employ, eighteen hundred years ago, a phraseology which the researches of our own day have now for the first time shown to be philosophically exact? Speaking of this verse, and quoting it freely, John Bunyan ("Reign of Antichrist,") says, 'For the earthquake, it is said to be *such as never was*, so mighty an earthquake and so great.' He thought the

Pearls are the product of certain species of shell-fish, both marine and fluvial. The cause and manner of their formation have not even yet been completely ascertained. They do not constitute any part or organ of the creature that contains them. They are not found in every shell, nor of the same size and shape in any two. They are eccentric and accidental, probably also morbid excrescences, thrown out by some individuals of the species in irregular forms and at uncertain times. They probably owe their origin to the presence of some minute foreign substance within the shell, which is distasteful to its occupant. Not being able to cast out the intruder, the feeble but diligent inhabitant covers it with a sort of saliva, which hardens over it into a substance similar in consistency and sheen to the interior surface of its own shell. The act of covering a base substance of any shape with gold or silver by the process of electrotype is in human art an analogous operation. When the material, distilled in imperceptibly minute portions from the living mollusc, has chemically agglomerated round the original kernel, the pearl is made. The creature having covered the irritant atom with a coating at once hard and smooth, can now endure with equanimity its presence within the shell. Thus unconsciously it manufactures those indestructible and much coveted jewels, for the sake of which its own life is sought and taken by man.

In modern times pearl fishing has become a business, and is prosecuted on a great scale in several far separated regions. Perhaps the increase of production, through superior methods and instruments, may, here as else-

------

phrase, 'since men were upon the earth,' was equivalent to 'never:' so he wrote and fell into the blunder. Who led John the Apostle safely past the mistake into which John Bunyan fell?"

where, have contributed to depreciate the value of the article.*

---

* I have been informed by a British merchant who, under license from the government of India, conducts the pearl fishing in the Bay of Kuratchee, that the method pursued is to bring the shells to shore as they are brought up from the bottom of the sea until a considerable quantity has been accumulated, disposed in a series of small contiguous heaps, and that then the men stand round the heaps, open the shells, and search for the pearls. So much loss accrues from the dishonesty of the men and the facility of secreting a treasure that lies in such a small bulk, that the proprietor of the fishing has had under consideration a suggestion to sell the heaps of shells by auction to the natives, and permit them then to make the best of their bargain. Whether this method of preventing peculation has been actually adopted, I have not learned.

Our own Scottish rivers are frequented by a large bivalve mollusc, which produces true pearls, although their size and number have never been sufficient to attract capitalists or sustain a steady trade. I do not know how others operate in other localities, but here is a method which I either invented for myself or borrowed from a neighbour, and practised with considerable success on the river Earn in Perthshire when I was a boy :—Provide a long straight rod, thin and broad and rounded at the point after the manner of a paper-cutter. Jump into a light fishing-boat, and bring it right over the oyster bed when the sun shines brightly and no ripple disturbs the surface of the water. Bring the boat into such a position with respect to the sun that your own body, bending over the gunwale, will throw a shadow on the immediately subjacent surface. Through that shaded spot you see the bottom with great distinctness, and can distinguish there the objects of your search lying invitingly still, and open, and unconscious. The depth may be from six to twelve feet. The molluscs lie bedded in the mud, with one edge above the ground, and that edge slightly open. Push your rod now gently down in a perpendicular direction,—for if you permit an angle the different degrees of refraction in the air and water will make your straight rod crooked, and you will egregiously miss your object at every stroke,—until its point is within an inch or two of the opening between the shells of the mollusc, and then quickly plunge it in. Hold it still there for a few seconds until the creature has time to close and bite the rod, you may then pull it up at your leisure. Throw your capture into the bottom of the boat, and proceed in the same manner with the next. When you have collected a sufficient store, sit down and open them one by one with a knife, feeling carefully with your thumbs for the little hard round knots among the velvet folds. These knots, when extricated from the fleshy lobes that cover them, turn out to be pearls, in form more or less globular, and in sheen more or less bright. You rejoice more or less, accordingly, in your capture. The day on which a good pearl was found became a day to be remembered in

I suppose diamonds occupy now the place that was held by pearls in ancient times. While a vast number of goodly diamonds are in circulation, affording occupation to many dealers, here and there one is found which alone constitutes a fortune of almost fabulous amount for its owner. One that was brought from India a few years ago, and is now in the possession of the Queen, has a history extending upward several generations. It passed, like provinces, from potentate to potentate by natural inheritance or the fortunes of war. If it had fallen into the hands of any private person, it would have made him an object of wonder on account of his wealth, even in presence of modern accumulations. The history and fame of the Kooh-i-noor supply the best illustration of this parable that I know.

Conceive a merchant with a moderate capital setting out on a journey with the view of collecting diamonds for sale in the home market. In the course of his travels, in the interior of India it may be, he discovers a diamond such as the Kooh-i-noor in the hands of a countryman.

---

the family group. The price of the finest never rose above a shilling or two; but as riches are relative, and must be estimated by comparison, these were treasures to us, and the sight of a large bright pearl suddenly shining out of the shell was enough to set a boy's heart a-beating in those early days.

During a drought in the summer of 1863 the small river Doon, in Ayrshire, fell so low that some pearl-beds in pools, that had not been noticed in other seasons, were exposed to view, and placed within reach : the consequence was that the people in the neighbourhood, old and young, betook themselves to pearl fishing, and that with considerable success. Among other facts circumstantially related in the local papers at the time, it was stated that one poor woman, during the sickness of her husband, gained as much by the sale of her pearls as made good the loss of her husband's wages for a whole month. In the course of this summer (1864), and since the preceding notes were written, a considerable amount of pearl fishing has been carried on in certain rivers in the northern districts of Scotland, and efforts have been made to organize a regular trade.

The possessor may know generally the value of diamonds, and know that this one in particular is of greater value than any that had ever come into his hands; yet, because it is unique, and he has nothing in his experience wherewith to compare it, he may dispose of it for a tenth of its value. If the best diamond that the seller had ever seen were worth twenty thousand pounds, he might value this one at forty thousand; and that price the buyer might cheerfully pay down, although it constituted all his property, knowing that at home the prize will command four hundred thousand. Thus, without supposing ignorance on the one side or dishonesty on the other, you have a transaction which will enrich the merchant at once and enable him to retire in affluence. This is the sort of transaction that is supposed in the parable. It was a natural and probable supposition at a time when information did not spread so quickly as in our time, and when pearls held as to value the place which diamonds occupy in modern merchandise.

It is true that the merchant went abroad expressly for the purpose of seeking goodly pearls; yet this pearl was to him an unexpected and surprising discovery. He had provided funds sufficient to purchase many pearls; but when he met with this one, its value was such that he could not make an offer for it until he had returned to his home and converted all his property, including the pearls that he had previously purchased, into money. In this parable as well as in that of the hidden treasure, an object is discovered of a value hitherto unknown and unsuspected. But the lesson here is in one important respect different from that of the preceding parable, and the point of distinction is, that there a man stumbled upon a treasure when he was in search of meaner things, while here the merchant finds in kind the very object which he sought, but finds it in measure far surpassing all his expectation or desire.

Well might the merchant return and convert all his estate into money that he might purchase this jewel; for if it were once in his possession, as there could be no rival, he might command his own price. None but monarchs could aspire to the possession of such a treasure, and these would compete with each other at his desk for a gem that could not elsewhere be obtained.*

The application of the parable is, intellectually at least, a short and easy process. It is not precisely the case of a man who finds the kingdom of God when he is seeking something else: neither is it the case of a man who first thoroughly knows the worth of that kingdom and then sets out in search of it. There is no such example: no man knows its worth before he obtains it. The merchant knew the value of pearls and set out in search of them, but such a pearl as that which he found he had never seen before, and never expected to see. So, although a man has some spiritual perceptions and spiritual desires: although by a deliberate judgment he determines to seek the life-eternal in preference to all the business and pleasures of the world, he does not at the outset understand how exceeding rich the forgiving grace of God is. Nay, he thinks, when he first begins his search for salva-

---

* Although their place is not the highest now, yet pearls even in our own day are sometimes found of a value so great that the history of an individual is recorded and its praises published through the world. The following, for example, are the terms of a paragraph taken from a British journal of last year:—" One of the finest pearls in the world has been found in the bay of Panama. It is of a perfect pear shape, and of the finest water."

tion, that it may be accomplished by the union of many attainments, such as men may possess. Precious pearls and a number of them indeed; but still such pearls as he has often seen in the possession of other merchants, and such as he has in former times had in his own store. He goes out with cash in hand to buy pearls, but he leaves his house and land still his own. He expects to acquire many excellent pearls and retain all his property besides. He did not conceive of one that should be worth all he had, until he saw it. It is thus that people under convictions set out in search of something that will make them right before God. They want to get righteousness and temperance, and a good case for the judgment to come. In their search they come to the Gospel; they get a glimpse beneath the surface; they see protruding from beneath the folds something that surprises them. Can that be a pearl? No; that is larger than any pearl ever was or can be, and brighter; surely that cannot be a true pearl. What? Pardon of sin to sinners without stipulating for a price in their own repentance and righteousness,—peace with God and sonship given free to the chief of sinners before he has done anything to deserve it,—all sin forgiven, and that now and that free, and no condemnation thenceforth, but the place and the favour of God's sons! and these not only to some who stand out from their fellows as great and good, but these to me,—from God to me to-day as surely as if there never had been a human being on the earth but myself, and the errand of Christ had been only and all for me! These glimpses stagger the man at first; he thinks they are too good to be true. It is as if some one should tell a skilful pearl merchant that under yon covering lay a pearl a thousand times more precious than any he had ever seen be-

fore: of course the merchant is incredulous, and demands
a sight of it. Then a portion of the covering is removed,
and a glittering disc is partially revealed, so vast and so
lustrous, that instantly and instinctively the merchant
feels, If that be a pearl it is more precious a thousand-fold
than any that I have ever seen: but at the same time he
secretly fears it is not a pearl, and that, not for want of
the true pearly lustre, which his eye has been well educated
to detect, but because of its very greatness and goodness.
The process in his mind is not that it does not seem a
genuine pearl, but that if it were a pearl it would be so
inconceivably great and precious that he must conclude
there is some deception. But when it is more fully
revealed and more thoroughly inspected, he finds that it
is indeed a true pearl. Instantly he determines to part
with all he has that he may obtain it: he parts with
all that he has, and makes it his own. He has not
only made a successful bargain, as other merchants may
do, or as himself may have done at other times: he has
in one moment enriched himself beyond all conception
that he formerly entertained. His merchandise has been
brought to an end. There is no need now for more buying
and selling in order to acquire wealth; his fortune is made.

This is really very like the process that goes on in a
human spirit when an anxious inquiry about salvation
terminates in finding and closing with Christ the Saviour.
The expectations with which the inquirer set out were
very low. If he could get his sense of guilt somewhat
lightened that he might begin anew and endeavour to
please God; if he could get the fear of wrath diminished,
and some assurance that the Judge would not visit him
to the full extent for all his sins;—he does not venture to
expect more. Expressly he had no conception of all in

one: he thought of a multitude of good religious attainments, which, when added together, would make him, if not rich enough, yet as good as any of his neighbours. Some low and little thing he went out to seek, and, lo! he came upon all the fulness of the Godhead bodily treasured up in Christ, and all that fulness offered in return for simple surrender of himself.

Surprised by the greatness of the treasure, he suspects at first that there must be some mistake; but when he becomes convinced of its reality, his resolution is instantly taken, and the transaction irrevocably closed. Like the merchant rejoicing in his fortune is a believer who has found peace with God: henceforth he is rich. He does not need now to huckster in small bargains between his conscience and the divine law every day, and struggle to diminish the ever-increasing amount of guilt by getting small entries of merit marked on the other side of the page. All this is past. He is in Christ Jesus, and to him, therefore, there is now no condemnation.

The treasurer of the Ethiopian Queen was precisely such a merchant. Before he left home he evidently counted himself poor, and longed to possess the true riches: before he left home he was aware that a man is not profited although he gain the whole world, if he lose his own soul. It was an oppressive sense of poverty that compelled him to travel. He occupied the highest office in a kingdom; he stood on the steps of the throne, and had charge of the royal treasury; but he counted himself poor notwithstanding. He must go in search of more precious pearls than these. Peace of conscience, righteousness, hope for eternity,—these are goodlier pearls than any that can be found in Ethiopia; and the man undertakes a journey to Jerusalem to try if he can find them there.

Disappointed there, he was on his way home, seeking still for the pearls, and seeking near the very spot in the Scriptures where the one priceless pearl lay, when Philip met him. By the Evangelist's skilful help he found it then and there; but when he found it at last, it was much more precious than he had ventured to expect. " He was led as a lamb to the slaughter." " Of whom speaketh the prophet this?" inquired the Ethiopian, " of himself, or of some other man?" Some subordinate benefit he was contemplating,—the suffering of some good man, perhaps, as an example to his brethren. Even that, as being something that might contribute to the peace of his soul, he was glad to hear of, and would gladly buy, that he might add it to his stock of goodly pearls. But when Philip, beginning from that scripture, " preached to him Jesus," he found that the lamb led to the slaughter is the " Lamb of God, who taketh away the sin of the world." The worth of the pearl turned out to be immeasurably greater than the merchant had previously been able to conceive. He exchanged all for it on the spot, and went on his way rejoicing. He did not require to go from country to country any more in search of goodly pearls He was rich,—rich toward God.*

---

* Das ist Philippus element,
    Er übt sein Predigtamt,
Lebendig wird das Pergament,
Des Mohrenfürsten Herze brennt,
    Sein dunkles Auge flammt.

Denn was er im Juwelenschrein
    Kandaces nimmer sah,
Die eine Perle, himmlischrein
Die köstlicher als Edelstein,
    Er fand am Weg sie da.

Kari Gerok.

I think all speculations about the whiteness and purity and lustre of the pearl as an ornament should be set aside, as being an attempt to bring a meaning out of the parable which its Author did not put into it. Obviously the merchant did not buy it in order to wear it. If after giving all that he had for the pearl, he had hung it on his neck, where could the poor man have found food and clothing? No; the pearl is presented here in one aspect only,—as being "of great price." It was worth much—it was a fortune to a merchant; but when you speak of it as an ornament on the wearer's brow, you turn aside from the line of the parable, and miss its meaning.

The true lessons of the parable, as I understand them, are briefly these:—

1. It represents the experience, not of a careless or a profane man, who stumbles suddenly upon the Gospel when he was in search of other things, but of one who is awakened, and has begun to seek the true religion, endeavouring to add attainment to attainment sincerely, according to his light. His conscience is uneasy. He has tried the old specific, " All these have I kept from my youth up;" but it no longer avails to soothe his spirit. "What lack I yet?" burst from his breast in broken sighs. There is truth in the man, though not wisdom. He is honestly seeking the way, and the Lord leads him. He is seeking; he shall find.

2. It represents the unparalleled, inconceivable richness of God's mercy in Christ, taking away all a sinner's sin, and bestowing on him freely the place and privileges of a dear child.

3. It represents that these riches lie, not in an accumulation of goodly attainments, such as men are wont to

traffic in, but in one undivided, indivisible, hitherto unknown and unimagined treasure.

4. It represents that the inquirer, the instant he discovers that this one incomparable, all-comprehending treasure exists and is offered to him, cheerfully, eagerly,
unhesitatingly gives away all that he possesses, in order
to acquire it. That is, he gives all for Christ, and then
enjoys all in Christ.

Let me suppose myself a merchant, travelling in a
foreign country in quest of pearls. I have found and
secured several lots that I count good. I have still capital
remaining sufficient to purchase many more; I therefore
continue my search. One day I meet a man who shows
me a pearl more precious than any that I had ever seen
before. At a glance I perceive that it is worth all I
possess twenty times told. I say to the owner, and say it
with a beating heart, fearing that he will despise my offer,
" I shall give you all I possess for this pearl." He accepts
my offer; he gives me the pearl into my own hands,
and I consign over to him all that I have in the world:
first, all the pearls that I have bought in my journey;
next, all my remaining capital; then houses, lands, books,
—all. I sign the deed with a throbbing heart, not from
fear, but from abounding joy. My act does not intimate that I value lightly my possessions and rights:
it intimates that my new portion is, in my esteem, so
greatly good, that it will repay all my outlay, and give
me a fortune beside.

So when I abandon my repentance, and my prayers,
and my services and gifts—when I sign away all my expectations on account of all religious attainments, and
accept Christ alone as my soul's portion—my act does
not intimate that I count little on the various graces of

the Spirit in a disciple's life : it means that in Christ and with him I have all good things in measure infinite, in duration eternal.

If our suggestion regarding the cause and manner of the pearl's growth is correct, the kingdom of God in the Gospel of his Son was generated in the same way: the pearl and the pearl of great price have the same natural history.

Some foreign, hurtful thing falls on the creature's life. Forthwith the irritation which that invader produces causes the creature to throw out and over the disturber that which forms a covering round it—hiding, smothering, annihilating the originating evil, and constituting over it and in place of it a gem of the ténderest, gentlest beauty —impenetrable, imperishable, glorious.

So sin, a corroding drop, a dark, deadly, vexing, torturing thing, fell upon God's fair creation, threatening to inoculate it with a poison that should leaven the whole lump, and change its beauty into corruption. But around the dark sin-spot, and because the sin-spot was there, divine love showered down, like the impalpable silver gathering on its object in the electrotype, embracing, surrounding, covering, killing the evil and bitter thing that threatened to destroy the works of God. Death was swallowed up in victory. The Son of God came into the world because sin was on it. He, the Holy One, took sin into his bosom, that he might quench it in his own embrace. It was sin that summoned the Saviour to the world, and gave shape to the Gospel of God. To the devil's wile in Eden, as the occasion, though not the cause, unfallen angels and ransomed men will for ever be indebted for that specific work of their Creator which will most attract their eyes and inspire their songs. On one side they behold mercy, in spotless, unmingled white; and on the other side they behold judgment, darker, indeed, yet equally resplendent. But here in the midst, in the person of God incarnate, they see mercy and judgment meeting—the pearl of great price—where two different and apparently opposite glories mysteriously and beauteously mingle and play. Death swallowed up in victory; sin embraced and so destroyed in the person of Immanuel; sin lost in the holiness and love that agglomerated round it;—this pearl will shine in heaven with a glory that excelleth, when the sun and stars shall have fallen like unripe figs from the sky.

The Draw-net
(Matthew 13:47-50)

" Again, the kingdom of heaven is like unto a net, that was cast into the sea, and gathered
of every kind : which, when it was full, they drew to shore, and sat down, and
gathered the good into vessels, but cast the bad away. So shall it be at the end of
the world : the angels shall come forth, and sever the wicked from among the just, and
shall cast them into the furnace of fire : there shall be wailing and gnashing of teeth."

GREAT variety obtains in the size and structure
of fishing-nets; and great variety, too, in the
manner of using them.   Some are stationary,
fixed to poles in the sea or the estuaries of
rivers; some are dropped in a straight line into the water,
and allowed to remain there suspended until a shoal of
fish, endeavouring to pass, become entangled one by one
in the meshes; others are shot in a semicircular form into
the sea, and immediately drawn back by both extremities
simultaneously to the shore.

It is this last mentioned species of net that is employed
in the parable.   Its depth is comparatively small, but its
length is great.   One side is kept close to the bottom by
weights, and the other side drawn towards the surface by
corks or bladders.   Thus when spread it stands erect like
a wall in the water, enclosing a large space.   As soon as
it has been spread, the fishermen begin to draw it at both
ends slowly and steadily towards the land.   As the enclosed semicircle gradually diminishes, the captured

fishes, having still room for motion, retire before the advancing prison wall, until they are at length confined within a very narrow space, and drawn into shallow water. There is then a violent flutter for a few moments, and the whole are laid helpless on the sand.

Then begins that operation on which the Master has here mainly fixed his eye, and to which exclusively he directs attention in his own exposition. When the fishermen have at last drawn the net wholly out of the water and secured its contents on dry land, they sit down to examine leisurely the worth of their capture, and to separate the precious from the vile. The good they gather into vessels for preservation; the bad they simply throw away. The net surrounded and brought to land every living creature that fell within its sweep, and was not small enough to escape through its meshes. Some of these are in their own nature and at all times unfit for food; others are useless at particular seasons. Every one who has watched the operations of fishermen on the shore is familiar with the appearance of star-fish and other low forms of marine life, which are drawn out by the nets, and cast away upon the sand. Large predatory fishes of a low type are also sometimes caught, when they venture too near in search of prey. In some instances, moreover, fishes that are dead and partially decayed are brought up in company with the living, and these are of course cast out as vile.

The central figure of the parable, round which the other features congregate only as fore or back ground accessories—the central figure is, A group of fishermen, panting from recent exertion, sitting on a knoll close by the sea-side, with the newly-drawn net lying in a soaking heap at their feet, picking up one by one the fishes that are fit for food, and putting them on one side into baskets, and casting the rest away. The men are skilful, experienced, and cool; they have no interest in forming an erroneous judgment, and they are not liable to fall into mistakes. The separation between good and bad is made without partiality and without hypocrisy; it is deliberate, accurate, inevitable. At the close, not one good fish has been cast away, and not a bad one has been admitted into the vessels.

It is of great importance to note that when the Lord undertakes to explain this parable, he determines for us the spiritual meaning of the last act only of the fishermen's labours, and passes in silence all the rest. I do not conclude from this fact that the earlier features of the scene possessed no spiritual significance, or that their meaning cannot be ascertained. But it is undeniable that when Christ himself gives the meaning of his own parable, the part that he leaves unexplained cannot be as surely and clearly understood as the part which he has explained: and further, the portion of a parable on which he maintained silence while he explained another part, is not for us in the same position as another parable of which he has not given an exposition at all. Some of them are so transparent that he did not count it needful to give the interpretation; in other cases, such as the sower, he gave the signification of the whole; in a third class of cases, to which this parable belongs, he explains one feature of the picture, and maintains silence regarding the rest. Now it is precisely the portions left without explanation in parables partially explained, that must in the nature of the case be to us most uncertain. It may be assumed regarding them that their spiritual meaning is either self-evident, and therefore required not a comment, or of subordinate importance, and therefore did not obtain one. In this case it is certain, from the diversity of opinion that prevails regarding them, that these portions are not easily understood : there remains only the other alternative, that they are not essential.

Our view of the grand lesson which the Master taught from the closing act of the fishermen, is very little affected by the opinion which we may form regarding the preparatory portions. Those who differ widely regarding the significance of trees and animals that occupy the background of a picture, may notwithstanding agree entirely regarding the meaning of the picture itself Although we entertain various views in respect to the spreading and drawing of the net, we come all, under the Master's guidance, to substantially the same view of the separation between good and evil which was accomplished when the net was brought to shore. Upon this point the Lord fixed his eye and expressed his mind. He has made it so plain that there is not room among Christians for serious diversity concerning it.

A river in Africa is known and navigated in its lower reaches near the sea. Ships from many nations frequent the estuary, and obtain cargoes of oil, and wax, and fruit from the inhabitants on its shores. But a question, meantime, arises among geographers regarding the source of this river in the interior of the continent, and the direction of its current before it reaches the navigable portion near the ocean. One believes the river rises in the north, and flows mainly southward ; another contends that it springs in a mountainous ridge far to the eastward, and flows in a westerly course to the Atlantic. In defect of an actual exploration, there is room for differences of opinion ; and differences have accordingly sprung up.

The right is better than the wrong even here; but the importance of the point is in a commercial point of view, secondary. Waiting till time shall afford the materials for decision, the disputants meanwhile frequent the deep estuary in company, and grow rich by the merchandise which it supplies. Thus we all understand, from the Lord's own transparent, decisive exposition, the last, the deepest, the most profitable portion of the parable. While we endeavour reverently to investigate the portions that are still uncertain, we should rejoice with thankfulness that where agreement was most necessary, the Great Teacher has made it impossible to differ.

After this explanation, I need not hesitate to admit that the view of the parable, in its earlier and unexplained portions, which on the whole most commends itself to my judgment, differs essentially from the expositions that are generally given. With modest, grave, watchful spirit should one student of the Scripture suggest and another receive, an interpretation of any portion different from that which has been given by the earnest, accomplished, and devout scholars, who in various countries and times have sought to discover the mind of the Spirit. On the other hand, to suppress a judgment, in deference to human authority, would be disloyal to the Lord and contrary to the principles of Protestants.

The view commonly entertained is, that the net is the Church, or, as some express it, the Bible and the ordinances of religion; while the fishermen who spread and draw it are the apostles in the first instance, and afterwards the ordinary ministers of the word. If the net is the Church, and its drawers the Church's ministers, the whole question of discipline is immediately raised. This parable, accordingly, like that of the tares, has been impressed into their own service by the opponents of discipline both in ancient and modern times. We emphatically repeat here, what we formerly stated in connection with the cognate parable, that no consistent argument can be maintained in regard to discipline from this scripture, except an absolute and entire repudiation of all effort, by a human ministry and in this present world, to keep any person or class of persons without the pale of the visible Church on account of their opinions or their conduct. Very few, however, venture to take this ground. The ordinary method is to contend for some measure of Church order—for the right and duty of excluding some of the worst—and then to lean on this parable for an argument in favour of a lax and against a stringent administration. We submit that to take your stand on this parable, and thence contend for the exclusion to some extent of the evil from the pale of the Church, is to trample all logical and critical laws under foot. This scripture manifestly either forbids all effort to discriminate in this world, or says nothing at all on the subject.

I shall now state, as distinctly and fairly as I can, some of the difficulties and inconsistencies which adhere to the common interpretation of the net and its drawers, and convince me that it is not the true interpretation.

1. It makes those who draw the net through the water, and those who separate between good and evil on the shore, not the same, but different persons, and persons of different classes,—the one representing men ministering to the Church in time, the other angels executing judgment in eternity ; whereas, both from the terms of the narrative and the ordinary practice of fishermen, we know that the same persons who draw the net to shore afterwards divide between the worthless and vile of its

contents. The net "was cast into the sea, and gathered of every kind: which, when it was full, they drew to shore, and sat down, and gathered the good into vessels, but cast the bad away." There is no ambiguity here; the drawers are also the dividers. I suppose none will take advantage of the impersonal form in which the casting of the net is expressed, and assume that while one class, representing a human ministry, cast the net into the water, another class, representing ministering angels, drew it to land and divided its contents; for it would be, contrary to all analogy and propriety, to assume that the Lord introduced into his picture a feature that is never found in fact. There is no such thing in reality as one set of men throwing the net into the water, and then retiring from the scene, while another set of men draw it out.

The ordinary interpretation assumes, contrary both to the letter of Scripture and the custom of men, that when ministers of flesh and blood have spread the net, and drawn it toward the shore, enclosing a multitude good and bad of their brethren, they disappear and take no part further in the transaction. Another party, representing the angels, now fasten on the net, and pick out the good from the bad. A late German expositor, learned, suggestive, and devout, Olshausen, yielding to the inexorable logic of the case, concedes that the drawers of the net and the dividers of the fish are not diverse, but the same. He turns, however, to the other side for a solution of the difficulty. Instead of simply proceeding to determine the unknown by the known ;—instead of owning that as angels separate the good from the evil on the shore, they must have also thrown and drawn the net, he explains away the specific signification of angels, and supposes that those who minister the Gospel in time are employed, under the general designation of angels, to separate between good and evil in the world to come. This solution will not readily commend itself to British students of the Scripture. The fact therefore remains, that the ordinary exposition of the parable, in this part of its progress, is palpably at variance with the structure of the parable itself, and the facts on which it is founded.

2. In the visible Church, the profession, at the very least, is to enclose the good within the communion of saints, or to rescue the evil by making them new in the act of entrance; whereas the net is let down at a certain spot to sweep indiscriminately all within its circle to the shore. It makes absolutely no distinction between good and bad; it can discriminate only between great and small. The net is laid down in the sea along a certain line: twelve inches beyond that line fishes good and bad are swimming, which it does not touch; while an inch within that line are fishes good and bad which it draws indiscriminately to the shore. I can perceive no likeness between this and the kingdom of heaven, if you understand thereby the visible Church and the efforts of the ministry.

3. One of the chief practical lessons which expositors ancient and modern have drawn from the parable, under this view of its meaning, is extremely incongruous, and even grotesque. Churchmen cling to it as a sheet anchor in controversy with Nonconformists. If this notion were adopted only by mediæval monks and modern Romanists, I would reckon it unworthy of notice; but it is received and uttered again as genuine at this day by grave and learned Protestant theologians of Germany, and notwithstanding the solidity and good sense which characterize

his "Notes" generally, is formally reproduced in its boldest form by Dr. Trench.*

The practical lesson, then, which these expositors draw from the parable is, that disciples of Christ are not justified in leaving an organized Church with which they were connected, and forming a Christian community beyond its pale, on the ground that unworthy members are tolerated within its communion. This is, indeed, not the true state of the question as between the Established Episcopal Church in England and the early Nonconformists ; the Puritans did not spontaneously retire, they were ejected by the hand of power because they refused to comply with new ordinances imposed upon the Church of Christ by human authority. But although the state of the question were conceded, the argument completely fails. If this lesson against separation is justly deduced from the parable, there must be in the natural object some parallel more or less distinct which suggests and supports it. What is that parallel, and where does it lie ? Translate the spiritual lesson, which men profess to find, back into the material facts, and observe the straits into which your mistake has brought you. The parallel obviously must be,—The good fishes that are enclosed

---

* "They [this and the parable of the tares] convey, too, the same further lesson, that this fact [the actual intermixture of evil in the visible Church] does not justify self-willed departure from the fellowship of the Church, and impatient leaping over or breaking through the nets, as here it has often been called; but the Lord's separation is patiently to be waited for, which shall surely arrive at the end of the present age."—*Dr. Trench, Notes on the Parables*, p. 133. This is a style far too loose for a critical exposition of Scripture. If the actual presence of tolerated impurity within the Church does not justify a "self-willed" departure from her communion, does it justify a departure that is not self-willed, but a solemn separation in order to carry out the will of the Lord? The assumption that the separation of the English Nonconformists was "self-willed," of course begs the whole question.

within the net, or those that count themselves good
should not leap out because star-fish and molluscs are enclosed along with them. Either this is the parallel on
which the lesson leans, or it has no foundation at all; but
there is no such thing in nature, and no such representation
in the parable. The fishes when they are once enclosed
within the net cannot break out; and even if they could,
they would break out not because they were confined in
low company, but because they were confined. The
good would fain be free; and the bad too. From first to
last the net is to all its inmates and to all alike a dreaded
prison. I do not descry a solitary feature of resemblance
between the parable at this stage and the doctrine regarding Church discipline which the expositors deduce
from it.*

4. The sea, according to the interpreters, being the
world, and the net being the Church, I want to know
what is meant by drawing the net to land. To be drawn
from the sea to the land must mean to be led, willing or
unwilling, from this life into eternity; for both good and
bad are brought to the shore; then and there the separation takes place which all acknowledge to be final. But
are the members of the visible Church alone drawn out
of this life into the other world? Do the ministers of the
Gospel occupy themselves in dragging their brethren away
from the world? Here, too, the interpretation is incon-

---

* While Stier and Trench seem to start with the same principle of interpretation on this subject, they are led ultimately to opposite practical results. Trench, as we have seen, gathers from the parable that the pure,
or those who consider themselves pure, are not justified in leaping out of
the net at their own pleasure; that is, the Nonconformists should not go
and constitute conventicles beyond the pale of the Establishment. Stier,
on the contrary, represents the evil as endeavouring to break out of the net,
but unable to accomplish their purpose: " Many a leviathan is caught, and
although he would fain get out, yet cannot break the net."—*Stier* in loc.

sistent with the facts of the case and the representations of the parable.

These difficulties in which the common interpretation is involved, go far to prove that it must be erroneous ; a true principle of exposition would surely not lead its adherents into such straits. The real key, if it were found, might be expected to open the lock without wrenching its parts asunder.

Although for my own part I would be content to take the plain and undoubted doctrine which the closing scene of the parable contains, and leave the earlier stages of it as the Lord left them, without attaching to them any definite and distinct significance, I am prepared at the same time to suggest a totally different interpretation of the net drawing the fishes to land, for the consideration of those who love to search the Scriptures. I shall state the principle of interpretation which commends itself to my judgment, and leave every one to judge for himself whether it will consistently and profitably explain all the facts.

The net is not the visible Church in the world, and the fishes good and bad within it do not represent the true and false members of the Church. The sea is the world. The net, almost or altogether invisible at first to those whom it surrounds, is that unseen bond which, by an invisible ministry, is stretched over the living, drawing them gradually, secretly, surely, towards the boundary of this life, and over it into another. As each portion, or generation of the human race, are drawn from their element in this world, ministering spirits, on the lip of eternity that lies nearest time, receive them and separate the good from the evil.

I shall enumerate here some of the reasons which commend this interpretation, and notice some of the objections which may be urged against it.

Among the reasons which commend it,—

1. It assumes, according to the facts of the case and the express terms of the scripture, that the same persons who draw the net also separate the worthy from the worthless of its contents on shore.

2. In owning this along with Olshausen, it owns also that the angels who separate the good from the evil at the end of the world are angels, and does not with him explain them away into the human ministry of the Gospel.

3. It is perfectly congruous with the habits of fishermen and the character of the instruments which they employ. As fishers drop the net over a certain space, and, without making any pretence of discriminating between good and bad, drag all within that space to shore; so the invisible agents whom God employs in his universal administration, whether laws or angelic spirits or both combined, make no distinction between good and bad, when by successive castings of the net, as it were, they enclose section after section, generation after generation of human kind, and draw them slowly, silently, but inevitably to the edge of this life, and over it into the unseen world. I scarcely know in the whole range of nature an analogy more true and touching than this. When you allow that the angels cast and draw the net as well as divide its contents, the incongruities disappear, and the picture starts into life, true to the original. The fishes, enclosed within the net when it is first thrown out, but still swimming in the sea, not aware that the net is round them, are intensely like a human generation, with the sentence of death hanging over them, yet living and moving freely, and looking for many days. As the circle of the net grows narrower

the fishes gently give way before it, and so enjoy for a little longer the sensation of floating at liberty in the water; and it is not until they touch the ground that they become thoroughly alarmed. The struggle then is sudden, earnest, short, unavailing. Thus are mankind, without respect to their vice or their virtue, indiscriminately drawn to the margin of this world's life, and, willing or unwilling, thrown into an unknown state beyond.

4. If any struggles are made against the encircling net during the slow, solemn process of drawing—any efforts on the part of the captives to leap out into freedom, they are made, not by one kind in displeasure at being shut up with another, but by every kind indifferently in displeasure at being shut up at all. Like the indefinite terror of mute fishes when they feel the net coming closer in, is the instinctive alarm of human beings when the hand of death is felt gradually contracting the space in which the pulses of life are permitted to play.

I shall now notice and endeavour to estimate the principal objections, as far as I am able to anticipate them, which may be urged against the interpretation that I have suggested.

1. The Lord at another time, in calling some of his apostles, said, " Follow me, and I will make you fishers of men" (Matt. iv. 19). He did; and I think it is by a mistake in instituting an analogy between that fact and this parable that interpreters have been led into a wrong track.

Some expositors have made a similar mistake in regard to the parable of the leaven, and the one error will throw light upon the origin and nature of the other. Observing that the Lord in another place represents the doctrines of the Pharisees and the Sadducees as a leaven, some have concluded that the leaven in the parable also must point to the spread of error, and have expounded it accordingly. All judicious critics, however, clearly see and distinctly explain in that case, that the leaven which was in other instances employed to represent the diffusion of evil, was in the parable employed to represent the prevalence of good. Although leaven in one of the Lord's discourses pointed to hypocrisy and unbelief, they teach, and teach correctly, that leaven in another of his discourses points to the progress of saving truth.

The same discrimination should be exercised here. It is quite true that the Lord at one time, and in one discourse, compared the ministry of apostles in winning souls to the labour of fishers in the ordinary exercise of their craft; but that does not prevent him from employing at another time the universal sweep of the draw-net to represent the silent, slow, and sure encompassing of human kind, which draws them, good and bad alike, by instruments and agencies which they do not see and cannot resist, from this troubled sea of time toward the shore of the unknown eternity. Because the conception of capturing fishes in the sea is at one time in the Lord's discourses employed to indicate the benevolent labour of the Gospel ministry, it does not follow that you are compelled to construe that conception in the same way wherever it occurs, although the circumstances manifestly render the application incongruous and contradictory.

Let it be observed, moreover, that when the apostles in respect of their work are called fishers of men, not one feature in the process of fishing is specified in detail. Nothing is introduced but the general conception of a fisherman catching fishes in the sea. This conception in the abstract contains nothing incongruous with the labour of the apostles. As long as you abide by the bare general term "fisher," the analogy, as applied to "apostle," is obvious and the meaning easily recognised; but the moment you descend into the details of a net, and the mixture of good and evil, you plunge into inextricable confusion, if you persist in maintaining an analogy between the detailed process of fishing and the labour of apostles for the kingdom of Christ.

The general conception of fishing, as it appeared to the mind of speaker and hearers on the margin of the Lake of Galilee, diverged into two dissimilar branches as soon as it descended into practical detail. The fishermen prosecuted their avocation sometimes with line and baited hooks, sometimes with boat and nets. Fishing with line and hook, a process of watching, selecting, discriminating, whereby the fishes are one by one enticed and taken, readily spontaneously leaps up before the imagination as a line parallel with the work of an evangelist, bent on winning souls; but fishing by the draw-net absolutely refuses to be fashioned into an analogue of the evangelistic work. The Lord in his teaching said that fishers were like apostles; but he never said that the process of fishing by the draw-net resembles the efforts of his ministers for the conversion of the world. Of the two methods of fishing which were familiar to the parties, one is in some of its main features analogous to the new employment into which Jesus called the twelve, and the other is totally dissimilar. When I read, therefore, that an apostle is a fisher of men, I shall think of the selecting, discriminating method of casting a hook into the water; and when I learn from this parable that the separation between the good and bad of the net's contents upon the shore represents the separation between good and bad men by the ministry of angels in the unseen world, I am not compelled—I am not permitted to believe, contrary to all analogy, that the Church encloses all, like the net, without an effort, a hope, a desire to discriminate, and that the ministers of the Church, like the fishermen, drag their brothers unwilling out of the world to the judgment-seat.

2. But has not the Lord said in this parable, as in all the rest of the group, the kingdom of heaven is like unto a net that was cast into the sea? He has; yet the fact does not prove that he meant to represent the Church by the net, and the labour of apostles by the spreading and drawing of the net. The formula, "The kingdom of heaven is like," relates to the parable as a whole, and not specifically to that feature of the parable which lies next to it in the record. For the evidence of this proposition it is not necessary to go further than the two immediately preceding parables. In one, "the kingdom of heaven is like unto treasure;" in the other, it "is like unto a merchant-man." If, instead of looking to the picture as a whole, you insist on finding the analogue of the kingdom or the Church specifically in the net, you must, in like manner, in the parable of the pearl, find that the Church is specifically compared to a man, whereas in the preceding example it was compared to a treasure. In these examples it is demonstrated that the analogy instituted refers to the picture as a whole, and not to the single feature that first occurs in the narrative.*

The Lord intimates in the introductory formula that

---

* The argument on this point is well stated by Limburg Brouwer. His conclusion is : "Accedit quod προμυθιον illud, (ὡμοιωθη ἡ βασιλεια, κ.τ.λ.) saepe ita comparatum est, ut proprie non conferendum sit cum solo illo subjecto, quocum ab auctore connectatur, sed potius cum universa re narrata."—*De Parabolis Jesu Christi*, 153.

he intends by this parable to give yet another lesson regarding the kingdom of heaven; and it must be determined otherwise than by the mere juxtaposition of the clauses, on what aspect or period of the kingdom he will by this similitude throw light. Six consecutive lessons on the subject have already been given. He has taught already what hinders the kingdom in the deceitfulness of human hearts, and the machinations of the wicked one; what its inherent power is, and what its contagious all-pervading influence; what is its value in the estimate of those who know it, and how much they willingly part with in order to obtain the treasure. What new and additional characteristic of the kingdom does the Master teach his disciples in the seventh and last parable of the group—the parable of the draw-net? The closing lesson about the kingdom relates to the closing scene of the kingdom—the separation of the wicked from the good on the great day. From the order of the subjects in the series you might expect this; from the picture actually presented you are logically led to infer this; but, especially, you know this from the spontaneous explanation then and there given by the Lord. Although, according to his usual method, he completed the parabolic picture, filling up the fore and back grounds with the objects that naturally lay there, yet when he comes to the interpretation, he passes in silence all these preparatory features, and tells the meaning of the last only—the separation of the wicked from the just through the ministry of angels at the end of the world. Yes, as the Lord said, this parable sheds light on the kingdom, but the portion of the kingdom on which the light falls is the close. It brings out in strong relief the final separation between those who remain distant and those who are brought nigh.

In view of the decisive fact that the Lord gives an interpretation, and does not interpret the casting and drawing of the net to mean the visible Church and its operations—does not interpret the casting and drawing of the net at all, I cannot assent to the demand that the general formula of introduction common to all the seven parables should be held to determine what specific portion of the extended picture, or whether any, represents the Church in relation to the character of its members and the duty of its ministers.

When God in his work of creation determined to give this globe a " lesser light," to mitigate the necessary darkness of its night in the absence of the sun, he provided an orb which serves that purpose, and more. Although only one of its sides is turned towards the earth, the moon has another side formed in full. For light to the earth the Creator needed only a disc ; but in order to provide it he made a sphere. In a similar manner the Lord has acted in the parable, when he desired to give his disciples a lesson upon the separation which takes place at the close of the dispensation; He made the orb full, although he illumined only one side of it by his own interpretation.

If any one is disposed to hold me to the letter of this similitude, and say that the uninterpreted portion of the parable is left, like the further hemisphere of the moon, deep in the shade, and beyond our view, I frankly consent to be so held. I agree that those portions of the parable should be considered to us of uncertain significance. We may lawfully and profitably examine them, and test every proposed explanation, and profit by every good lesson that may be obtained ; but we ought absolutely to abandon all attempts to find there an authority for any doctrine or any duty. I think when the Lord has explained a part of one of his own parables, the portion of it which he has left unexplained is in a different position from a parable which he has not explained at all. When he gives any interpretation, his silence has a meaning as well as his words. If he had meant to determine by a particular feature of this parable any important doctrine or duty, we may rest assured, when he did undertake to give an explanation, he would not have left that part altogether unexplained. On the whole, I think the earlier portion of the parable is debatable ground; it is left in the shade; there is room for difference of opinion in regard to it. In some aspects it may suggest useful reflections as a picture of the good and evil mingled in the Church; in other aspects it may suggest solemn thoughts as a picture of successive generations being gradually drawn from life's moving sea to eternity's stable unknown shore. I believe that profitable lessons may be obtained from it in both of these, and perhaps in other aspects; I believe that the disciples do not sin, and the Master is not displeased, when to one inquirer it suggests this lesson, and to another it suggests that, as long as all is done in charity, and according to the analogy of the faith. I have suggested a line of thought, which I believe to be relevant and profitable; but I would not dare to plant my foot on this exposition as the ground of any doctrine or any duty. It is because others, both in ancient and modern times, have pretended to find on the unillumined side of this parable a light to guide Christians authoritatively in points that vitally affect the kingdom of Christ, that I have entered at so great length into the inquiry.

I confess frankly that I count it a good and necessary work to wrench this scripture from the hands of those who, whether in ignorance or conscious partiality, use it as an instrument practically to blot out the line which the Lord has elsewhere drawn between the Church and the world.

It is not necessary now to refute formally the fond, feeble notion, that this parable proves the sinfulness of dissenting from the Church of England, established by the State and prelatic in its government. Even although we should concede that the visible Church and the character of its constituents are the subjects with which the parable deals, it would be childish trifling on the part of a Churchman to quote it as of authority against Nonconformists. In the same Bible stands the precept, "Come out from among them and be ye separate;" and the Nonconformist has as good a right, that is, no right at all, to quote it as of authority by itself against a Churchman. The matter cannot be settled, on either side, by general announcements like these, although they are selected from the Scriptures. Every case must be judged upon its own merits. The question whether a dissenter has separated from a corrupt community in order to obey his Lord, or has rent the Church to gratify his own pride, must be determined in each case by an appeal to the facts : no solution satisfactory to intelligent Christians, or to grown men, can be reached by superciliously throwing a text in your neighbour's face. This remark is made upon the supposition that the parable bears upon the point, which I think is more than doubtful. Those who gravely counsel the fishes to abide peacefully within the net, and not to leap out pharisaically and schismatically because foul fish abound within the same enclosure, certainly show themselves incapable of appreciating the analogies of nature, whatever may be their familiarity with ecclesiastical affairs.

We subjoin two practical lessons; the first, though in itself self-evidently true, depending for its suggestion here on the special view of the net which we have submitted; the second founded directly on the word and enforced by the authority of the Lord.

1. We of this generation, a miscellaneous multitude of old and young, good and evil, move about at liberty in the wide expanse of life, as fishes move about in the deep broad sea; but certain mysterious, invisible lines, have been let down into the water, and are silently, slowly creeping near, and winding round us. The net at first has a vast compass: a fish within its circle has as much room as it needs, and cares not for distant danger. Even when the cords begin to come near, he moves out of their way, and for his own comfort embraces warmly the opinion that these cords do not constitute a net. They are some loose things,—certain species of sea-weed, such as he has often seen before. He has gone round them or through them often and easily: he will do so again. But these approach persistently, and still from the same side: they lie between him and the open sea: to avoid them he must move in-shore. Getting now a nearer view, he descries some new features of the danger. These lines are crossed and knitted in a manner all unlike the sea-weed threads that streamed so long and straight and loose in the tide-way. A secret foreboding of some unknown doom arises: the alarmed captive, having now no further room to retire, darts wildly sea-ward, and is caught in the inevitable meshes of the encircling net. After a moment of violent but feeble struggle, he is laid still and dumb on the shore.

It is a picture touchingly, terribly exact of our own state. The net has been spread around us: the sharp knitted lines gradually approach and touch us. Shrinking from the clammy contact as we would from living snakes, we retire before them, and still find room. But the lines appear again, always on the same side. Our space grows narrower as we recede, from year to year, from week to week, from day to day, until at length we graze the ground and strike upon the eternal world.

That net cannot be removed or evaded; but it may be changed, so that you would not fear its approach. When we become new creatures in Christ, death approaching us becomes a new creature too, as the image in a mirror changes with the object that stands before it. This dreaded net becomes like a warm, soft, encircling arm, pressing a frightened infant closer to a mother's breast.

2. Good and bad alike are drawn in company toward the shore, but the good and bad are separated when they reach it.

No lesson can be addressed to men more touching, more piercing than this. Nor is its penetrating power diminished by any deficiency of authority in the word that presses it home. It is the word of the Lord; not spoken in parables, but expressly given as the meaning of the parable that had been spoken. Its force is not weakened by any quiver of doubt in the Christian brotherhood as to the Master's mind. All Christians hear this word and understand it alike: the whole assembly, when they hear it, bow the head and worship. On the authority of our Redeemer, and in terms so transparent that they afford no room for doubt, we learn that on the shore to which we are silently, surely moving, a separation infallibly exact and irrevocably final will be made between the evil and the good. As to the positive punishment into which the impenitent will be cast, while I simply receive all the words of the Lord, I shall take care not to obtrude many of my own. He spoke of matters beyond the cognizance of sense, and beyond even the range of imagination, and therefore in the nature of the case we cannot fully understand his words. But He who utters this solemn warning knows what we understand by " a furnace of fire," and by "wailing and gnashing of teeth :" he intends to convey to us, regarding sufferings that are not only unknown, but in our present condition to us unknowable, as clear and deep and awe-inspiring an impression as our minds are capable of receiving. He leads our minds in that direction as far as they can follow ; and, for the rest, darkness will cover it until "that day." In the direction downward unto death, as well as upward unto life, the word holds good, " What thou knowest not now, thou shalt know hereafter." Either line, when it crosses the border of this life, " passeth all understanding." I suppose it is as completely impossible for a human heart to conceive what God hath prepared for them that hate him, as to conceive what he hath prepared for them that love him.

It is eminently noteworthy here, that the clearest, most articulate, and most emphatic announcements regarding the positive punishment of the wicked in a future world which the Scriptures contain, were spoken, and spoken repeatedly, by the lips of the Lord Jesus. Wherefore ? Did the love of the Redeemer sometimes wax cold ? Did even he, through the provocations that he met in his ministry, sometimes forget to be gracious ? No ; never at any time did his heart melt more with tenderness for men than when he proclaimed that the wicked shall be cast into outer darkness. He not only intimated, as in this parable, that such sentence would be pronounced but declared that himself would pronounce it: "When the Son of man shall come in his glory.... then shall he say unto them on the left hand, Depart from me, ye cursed, into everlasting fire, prepared for the devil and his angels" (Matt. xxv. 31–41). He who uttered these words pitied and loved sinners; he loved them while he spoke these words; he loved them although he spoke these words;—*because* he loved them, he spoke these words. The thing which these words declare is true: Christ did not change the eternal law of God that evil shall not dwell in his presence: since this law remains beyond the line of the present world to meet every man as he enters eternity, it was kind to give us warning. It would have been unkind, and therefore unlike the Lord, to conceal the dreadful fact, and leave unwarned sinners to learn it first by feeling it. It was love, overflowing love in the heart of our Brother, that drew these warnings repeatedly from his lips. The reason why he tells us that the wicked shall be cast away, is that we may never be cast away. The good Shepherd would compel the sheep to flee to the fold by sending out his terrors, when they refused to be more gently led.

There is a machine in the Bank of England which receives sovereigns, as a mill receives grain, for the purpose of determining wholesale whether all are of full weight. As they pass through, the machinery, by unerring laws, throws all that are light to one side, and all that are of full weight to another. That process is a silent but solemn parable for me. Founded as it is upon the laws of nature, it affords the most vivid similitude of the certainty which characterizes the judgment of the great day. There are no mistakes or partialities to which the light may trust : the only hope lies in being of standard weight before they go in.

I gratefully recognise tender, overflowing love, in the faithful testimony of Christ regarding the punishment of the wicked : it is meant to compel sinners now to take refuge in his righteousness.*

---

* Arndt closes his exposition of this parable with a hymn, which I subjoin, not only for the sake of the doctrinal statement regarding the ground of a sinner's hope contained in the first verse, but also, and still more, for the union of simplicity and solemnity in the conception of future punishment contained in the second :—

> Christi Blut und Gerechtigkeit,
> Das ist mein Schmuck und Ehrenkleid ;
> Damit will ich vor Gott besteh'n
> Und zu der Himmelsfreud' eingeh'n.

> Hilf, Gott, dass yeder kommen mag,
> Wo tausend Yahr' ist wie ein Tag :
> Vor dem Ort uns, O Gott, bewahr',
> Wo ein Tag ist wie tausend Yahr' !

> Christ's blood and righteousness
> Shall be the marriage-dress,
> In which I'll stand
> At God's right hand
> Forgiven,
> And enter rest
> Among the blest
> In heaven.

> Help, Lord, that we may come
> To thy saints' happy home,
> Where a thousand years
> As one day appears,
> Nor go,
> Where one day appears
> As a thousand years
> For woe.

The Unmerciful Servant
(Matthew 18:23-35)

" Therefore is the kingdom of heaven likened unto a certain king, which would take account of his servants. And when he had begun to reckon, one was brought unto him, which owed him ten thousand talents. But forasmuch as he had not to pay, his lord commanded him to be sold, and his wife, and children, and all that he had, and payment to be made. The servant therefore fell down, and worshipped him, saying, Lord, have patience with me, and I will pay thee all. Then the lord of that servant was moved with compassion, and loosed him, and forgave him the debt. But the same servant went out, and found one of his fellow-servants, which owed him an hundred pence : and he laid hands on him, and took him by the throat, saying, Pay me that thou owest. And his fellow-servant fell down at his feet, and besought him, saying, Have patience with me, and I will pay thee all. And he would not : but went and cast him into prison, till he should pay the debt. So when his fellow-servants saw what was done, they were very sorry, and came and told unto their lord all that was done. Then his lord, after that he had called him, said unto him, O thou wicked servant, I forgave thee all that debt, because thou desiredst me : shouldest not thou also have had compassion on thy fellow-servant, even as I had pity on thee ? And his lord was wroth, and delivered him to the tormentors, till he should pay all that was due unto him. So likewise shall my heavenly Father do also unto you, if ye from your hearts forgive not every one his brother their trespasses."

THIS parable, and that of the Good Samaritan, as has been justly suggested by Fred. Arndt, although historically separate, are logically related, like two branches that spring from one stem : together they express a Christian's duty to his brother in respect of injuries. When a brother inflicts an injury on you, forgive him ; when a brother suffers an injury from another, help him. Forgiving love is taught in this parable ; helpful love in the parable of the Good Samaritan.

The immediate occasion of this parable is obviously Peter's question, " How oft shall my brother sin against me and I forgive him ?" but how Peter's question springs from the preceding context does not so readily appear. The Natural History of the process in that apostle's. mind was probably something of this sort : The Master had instructed his disciples how they should act in the event of a brother doing them an injury : three distinct steps are indicated, rising one above another like courts of appeal ; first, a private remonstrance ; if that prove unavailing, then a remonstrance in the presence of one or two witnesses ; and lastly, an appeal to the Church. These rules are very specific, and together constitute a complete code on the branch of the subject to which they refer. In the matter of dealing with an offending brother with the view of bringing him to a better mind, you can no further go : if all these efforts fail, you must separate yourself from the offender, lest by continued intimacy you should seem indifferent to his sin. After this the Lord proceeds to give instruction on other subjects, and especially on united prayer. Peter, I suppose, had allowed his mind to be so completely occupied with the question of forgiving injuries, that he failed to follow his Teacher when the lesson glided into another theme. I could suppose him to have been so busy with the thought of injuries received, and the difficulty of forgiving them, all the time that the Lord was discoursing on united prayer, that he scarcely observed his Master's words. All the more readily might this happen, if the impetuous fisherman had a quarrel with some of his neighbours on hand at the very time, and was exercised in conscience about the duty of bringing it to a close. At the first pause, the current which had been for a time flowing under ground, burst out on the surface. Taking up and again abruptly introducing the subject which had been for some time dismissed, he asked, as if unconscious that the theme had been changed during his reverie, "Lord, how often shall my brother sin against me, and I forgive him ? Till seven times ?" He wanted to have a number specified, beyond which he should not be bound to forgive repeated offences. In suggesting seven he seems to have had in his mind some Pharisaical formula : probably he thought the allowance was liberal, and expected to be approved for his magnanimity.

The formula, seventy times seven, while it serves to intimate that there is in the law no limit to the exercise of a forgiving spirit, seizes upon Peter's narrow proposal and makes a show of it openly. It is possible that he may have fallen into a mistake here through the misapprehension of a lesson on the same subject given by the Lord. He may have heard the Master teach, as at Luke xvii. 4, —" If he trespass against thee seven times in a day, and seven times in a day turn again to thee, saying, I repent, thou shalt forgive him." But evidently the number seven in that discourse has substantially the same meaning with seventy times seven here : seven times a day, even when literally understood, includes as much as the absolute seventy times seven. The doctrine in both cases is that it is not lawful to set any limit to the principle and the practice of forgiving injuries.

To repeat, expand, and enforce this lesson, the parable is introduced. The kingdom of heaven is like a man king —$\alpha\nu\theta\rho\omega\pi\omega$ $\beta\alpha\sigma\iota\lambda\epsilon\iota$. Expressly the divine is in this respect analogous to the human. This ruler proposed to take account of his servants. It was not the final reckoning, but a periodical balance. A king 'is in this respect like a merchant: he takes account from time to time of his own affairs, and the intromissions of his servants. " Short counts make long friends."

These servants were not slaves, the property of their master ; for afterwards it is assumed that he may sell them, not as an ordinary right, but as the special penalty incurred by an insolvent debtor. A king, in ancient times and oriental regions, entered into pecuniary transactions with his servants on a great scale. One man, who owes all to the personal favour of the sovereign, is the governor of a wealthy province. Bound by no written law, and living at a distance from the seat of government, that servant possesses always the power, and too frequently seizes the opportunity of oppressing the people on the one hand, and defrauding the royal treasury on the other. In many cases fortunate or powerful dependants farmed the taxes of a district, paying, or at least promising to pay, a certain sum yearly to the supreme government, and obtaining authority in return to levy contributions on the inhabitants for their own behoof, sometimes almost according to their own pleasure. Vast sums passed through the hands of these great officers, and vast sums also remained in their hands that should have passed through them.

The amount specified in the parable—ten thousand talents—is very great, of whatever species you may suppose the talent to be. The inquiry which has been prosecuted with a view to determine precisely the value of the talent in this case is difficult, and does not lead to any certain or important result. The question is interesting to Biblical scholars and antiquarians, but the solution of it is by no means necessary to the perception or the application of our Lord's meaning in the parable. The sense is completely obtained by taking the ten thousand talents as a vast but indefinite sum. A hundred talents of silver constituted the hire of a great army, 2 Chron. xxv. 6 ; and notwithstanding the lavish use of gold in the construction of the Tent-Temple in the wilderness, only twenty-nine talents were employed in all (Ex. xxxviii. 24) Besides the distinction between gold and silver, other variations occur in the value of a talent, depending upon time, place, and other circumstances. In any view of its worth, however, the disparity between the sum which this servant owed to the master, and the trifling amount which a fellow-servant owed to him, is as great as the imagination can effectually grasp; larger numbers would not sensibly intensify the impression.

" One was brought to him :" this servant would not have come to the king of his own accord ; but he could not escape the interview and the reckoning. Aware of his enormous debt, he would fain have kept out of his master's way, but could not. God looks on the heart, and grasps the conscience, whether the man will or be unwilling.

The punishment is very severe, but in accordance with law and custom. No complaint is made against the sentence as if it were unjust in principle, or excessive in degree: the culprit appeals only to the mercy of the judge, and thus the righteousness of the verdict is tacitly acknowledged.

His promise to pay means nothing more than his desire to escape. He made the promise, not in the expectation of being able to perform it, but as the most likely means of escaping from punishment. His worship was prompted by selfish fear, not by filial love. He did not know his master's heart: he thought he would gain his object most readily by leading the king to expect payment in full.

The king did not grant his servant's request: he did more; he forgave that servant all. The absolved debtor, as soon as he obtained his liberty, went out, and met a fellow-servant, who owed him an hundred pence. I suppose, if that fellow-servant had come to him while yet he was in his master's presence, he would not have dared to act the tyrant; but "out of sight, out of mind." He forgot his own prayer, and his lord's compassion. He grasped the fellow-servant by the throat and threw him into prison, until he should pay.* The amount is comparatively small, as is fit between servant and servant: the smallness of the debt brings the cruelty of the creditor out in high relief. His neighbour's pleading is expressed in the same terms as his own: the sound should have reminded him of his duty.

Fellow-servants observing the outrage were at once indignant and compassionate. They informed their master. The master displeased, pronounced his condemnation in full. He who showed no mercy to his brother received judgment without mercy for himself.

Before proceeding to the exposition of the parable in its spiritual meaning and application, I shall submit a remark of a general character, bearing on the parables at large, as well as on this in particular, which can be made more conveniently now than at the close.

The more I examine the structure and use of the parable in the teaching of the Lord, the more I am convinced that men make a great mistake when they betake themselves to a single feature of the natural scene as a defence of

---

* Die am meisten geschont sind erweisen sich als die Schonungslosesten. Unter den Flügeln der Zärtlichkeit wird die Grausamkeit ausgebrütet. (Those who get most mercy give least; and cruelty is hatched under the wings of tenderness).—*Dräseke vom Reich Gottes*, ii. 141.

some specific and controverted dogma. The rule may be made absolute, or if there are exceptions they are few that the parables are intended to expand, illustrate, and enforce what is elsewhere clearly taught in the Scriptures, and not themselves to constitute the grounds or evidences of the doctrines. But to whatever extent such a general rule may be applicable, it is most certain that those who run to a corner of a parable and take their stand on it, as impregnable evidence of some doctrine which they hold, are in all cases egregiously mistaken. The controversies, for example, on the question of Church discipline, which were made to turn on the tares among the wheat, and the net that caught all kinds of fishes, are a mere waste of words. Those parables do not afford material for the decision of the question ; they do not speak to the point.

In like manner, when theologians gravely refer to this parable in order to prove that after a man's sins have been all freely forgiven by God, he may yet fall from grace, and the guilt of all his sins be laid upon him at the last, they waste their own time, and trifle with the scripture. True, in this picture you see one whose great debt was all freely forgiven by the master brought back into judgment, and made answerable for the whole amount ; but this incidental feature of a human procedure will not bear the weight which men would fain lay on it. This king, whose conduct is represented in the parable, is expressly called a *man* king. No doubt his procedure in that case is employed to illustrate some laws of the kingdom of heaven ; but this is done by analogy. Analogy is not identity; the very essence of it lies in coincidence in some points, with diversity in others; if the two were identical, there were no longer an analogy. Take two pictures of a person printed from the same negative photograph ; you do not say they are like each other, they are the same. It is most dangerous to fasten on any point of the depicted human procedure, and found on it the affirmation that the divine must be precisely the same.

But besides this general consideration demanding caution, there is enough in the parable itself absolutely to refute the notion, that God may forgive a man all his sins, and thereafter lay these very sins all to his charge. It is indeed said in the earlier portion of the parable that the lord of that servant forgave him the debt; but it is as clearly indicated in the close that the debt was not forgiven. The man was cast into prison until he should pay it all; he was held bound for all the original debt, and was punished accordingly. If he was forgiven all that debt, not one penny of it can afterwards be placed to his account; and if it is afterwards placed to his account, the fact proves that it had not been forgiven.

The meaning of the phraseology must be determined by the necessary conditions of the fact. That word of the king, "I forgive thee," was not a discharge; if it had been, mere justice demanded that the debt discharged should not be charged again. The fact that it was all charged again, proves irrefragably that it was not discharged. The meaning in the light of the facts must be that these terms were offered by the king. His terms are free forgiveness, bestowed in sovereign love by the giver, and accepted in grateful love by the receiver. The servant, as is shown by his conduct, did not accept these terms, and so there was no transaction.

The key-notes of the parable are found at the beginning and the end. It was spoken in order to show that a man should set no limit to the forgiveness of injuries;

and in order to show this, the parable goes into the deep things of God. It shows that the motive power which can produce in man an unlimited forgiveness of his brother, is God's mercy forgiving himself. At the close it lays down the law, that the act or habit of extending forgiveness to a brother, is a necessary effect of receiving forgiveness from God. If you get pardon from God, you will give it to your brother; if you withhold it from your brother, you thereby make it manifest that you have not gotten it from God.

As the king determined to take account of his servants during the currency of their work, and before the final winding up of their engagement, so the King Eternal in various ways and at various periods takes account of men, especially of those who know his word, and belong externally to his Church. One by one the servants are brought into their Lord's presence. The messenger that brings them may be a commercial crisis, a personal affliction, or a revival in the neighbourhood. The King has many messengers at his command, and he employs now one and now another to bring a professing Christian forward to his presence. When one who has contrived to keep out of the way, both of his own conscience and of God, is at length compelled to open his heart to the Omniscient, and fairly look into it himself, he discovers that his debt is unspeakably, inconceivably great. The sum of ten thousand talents in the picture is not an exaggeration; it does not indicate all the guilt which God detects in the conscience, and which the awakened conscience detects in itself. It is a dreadful moment when a sinner is brought face to face with God, and charged with his guilt; it is then that the law performs its terrible yet merciful work of conviction.

The first purpose that springs in the heart of the alarmed transgressor is to satisfy the demand: Give me time, and I will pay all. Whether he deliberately expects to be able to pay it may be doubted; but one thing is clear, he thinks that nothing else will appease the Master, and he makes the promise accordingly. This is, in point of fact, the first proposal of an alarmed conscience, " I will pay thee all." The natural history of the process is here.

God does not hold the convicted transgressor to his own rash promise. Treating the criminal, not according to his desert, but according to his need, the Judge announces the terms of his own covenant—a pardon immediate, complete, and free.

"The same servant went out:" the moment of close dealing between God and the soul has passed: the man who has trembled at the sight of his sin, and the prospect of judgment, has heard the Gospel, and gotten a respite. He goes out from that solemn and searching communion: he is released for the moment from the presence of the Judge, and from the sense of his sin. He glides again into the world. He has not been converted; he has only been frightened. He has not been forgiven; he has only been respited. He has not accepted God's grace, and therefore is not under law to God. The fright is past, and faith has not taken its place. The heart, after terror had driven the evil spirits out, does not open to the Lord, and therefore the evil spirits come back, and possess the empty room in sevenfold power. As soon as he comes in the way of temptation, the unsubdued carnality of his soul asserts its life and power. A fellow-servant who has in small matters offended him, begs for pardon, as he had done from God, and begs in vain. He shows no mercy; the fact proves that he has not himself accepted the mercy that was offered by God. If the channel of his heart had really been inserted into the fountain-head of mercy for receiving, mercy would infallibly have flowed in the way of giving, wherever the need of a brother made an opening; if the vessel had been charged, it would certainly have discharged. No compassion flowed from that heart to refresh a fellow-creature in distress, because that heart had never truly opened to accept mercy from God; the reservoir was empty, and therefore the outbranching channels remained dry. *

Beyond all question, the design of the Lord in this parable is to enforce the duty of forgiving one another. In teaching this lesson, he touches matters greater than itself; but these occupy here only a secondary place. The drift of the parable is to take off the artificial limit laid by Peter, and by the Pharisees before him, on the disposition to forgive an offending brother, and to leave it limitless,—infinite, as far as the faculties and the time of men can reach.

I think the substance of the lesson may be expressed in these two words, the *practice* and the *principle* of forgiving injuries. These two are in effect the *ultimate act* and the *secret power* that produced it. They are at once distinguished and united in that new commandment which Jesus gave to his disciples,—" That ye love one another, as I have loved you" (John xiii. 34). The first

---

* Dräseke expresses the same conception in his own peculiarly terse and antithetic way :—So gewiss kein Gottesreich ohne die Schulderlassung die wir empfangen ; so gewiss kein Gottesreich ohne die Schulderlassung die wir leisten. (As certainly as there is no kingdom of God without the forgiveness which we receive, so certainly there is no kingdom of God without the forgiveness which we bestow.)—ii. 147.

part of that commandment tells what they ought to do and the second part tells what will make them do it. It is when they place themselves under the power of Christ's forgiving love to themselves, that they are impelled in turn to forgive each his brother. The duty corresponds to the moving machinery, and the motive to the stream of living water which makes the machinery go.

1. The PRACTICE of forgiving injuries. The terms employed indicate clearly enough that the injuries which man suffers from his fellow are trifling in amount, especially in comparison of each man's guilt in the sight of God. There is a meaning in the vast and startling difference between ten thousand talents and a hundred pence. Even when the injury is the greatest that human beings are capable of inflicting on the one side, and enduring on the other; even when an enemy has killed the body and ceased then, because he has no more that he can do, it is still a measurable thing. Love in a finite being's heart may swell high over it, and exult in bestowing forgiveness on the murderer with the victim's dying breath. In the beginning of the Gospel a vivid example of that very thing stands recorded: " Lord," said Stephen with fainting heart and failing breath, " Lord, lay not this sin to their charge." Great as the injury was, according to earthly measurements, the imperfect love that lived in a man's heart was more than a match for it, and the martyr with his dying breath forgave his murderers. But how rare are those injuries that rise to this extreme height! Most of the injuries with which we are called to deal are small, even in relation to human capacity: they are very often precisely of the size that our own temper makes them. Some people possess the art of esteeming great injuries small, and some the art of esteeming small

injuries great. The first is like a traveller who throws a great many stones out of the burden which he carries, and so walks with ease along the road; the other is like a traveller who gathers a great many stones on the way-side, and adds them to his burden, and is therefore soon crushed by the load.

But more than this: the foolish man who made his burden heavier, retains the redoubled weight upon his back; while the wise man who made his burden lighter, contrives to throw off even the smaller weight that remained. The same spirit that induced the suffering Christian to diminish his estimate of the injury, induces him to forgive even that which remains, and thus he gets quit of it altogether; for to forgive it, is equivalent to throwing it away, in as far as it had power to burden or irritate you. On the other hand, the same spirit which in an irritable man magnified and multiplied the actual injury which he received, prevents him from forgiving the great and exaggerated mass; thus in effect he is crushed under the accumulated weight of all the real injury he has sustained, and all the imaginary injury he has added. The compassionate, loving man, who counted the great injury small, was relieved even of that small remnant by forgiving it: the selfish, unloving man, who counted a small injury great, could not forgive his neighbour, and so was compelled to bear the heavy burden on his heart. In this case that sublime rule of the Scripture takes effect: "To him that hath shall be given, and he shall have abundance; but from him that hath not shall be taken even that which he hath." *

* Fred. Arndt puts the lesson warmly and well; his appeal is in substance this:—"A man without compassion has all against him, God and the world; and meets as many adversaries in judgment as he had associates

But we must carefully discriminate here, and ascertain what the Lord means by forgiving a brother. There should not be a little, narrow, grudging forgiveness; it should be large, loving, and free. But parallel with forgiveness there must be faithfulness. Faithfulness to the evil-doer himself, and to the community, comes in here to modify, not the nature, but the outward form of forgiving.

For example, there is no virtue in simply permitting a man to wrong you as often as he chooses,—forgiving him and doing nothing more. In the immediately preceding context the Lord has taught that the injured should tell the injurer his fault. Tell him faithfully in secret his sin: if he repent, thou hast gained thy brother: if he do not listen, tell it in the presence of two or three witnesses: if he is

in life. Woe to him who is arraigned in secret by the tears of the feeble and oppressed! The sighs which he has pressed out, the plaints which he has generated, cry up to heaven against him, and their echo clangs horrid from heaven down again upon the life of the loveless and revengeful. . . . . And can we sleep in peace another hour, as long as there are men upon the earth with whom we live in unpeace and enmity? Cannot be written the happiness, the inward bliss of the peaceful and peace-making. Revenge, indeed, seems often sweet to men; but, oh, it is only sugared poison, only sweetened gall, and its after taste is bitter as hell. Forgiving, enduring love alone is sweet and blissful; it enjoys peace and the consciousness of God's favour. By forgiving, it gives away and annihilates the injury. It treats the injurer as if he had not injured, and therefore feels no more the smart and sting that he had inflicted. Forgiveness is a shield from which all the fiery darts of the wicked one harmless rebound. Forgiveness brings heaven to earth, and heaven's peace into the sinful heart. Forgiveness is the image of God, the forgiving Father, and an advancement of Christ's kingdom in the world. Your unalterable duty is clear: as surely as we are Christians, men who have experienced great compassion, who see in every man a brother in Christ, and are going forward to God's righteous judgment, so surely we must forgive. Of no commandment will the fulfilment be demanded of us with such stringency, no divine rule so strictly enforced as this, without the slightest exception to leave a loop-hole of hope to the transgressor. If we forgive not those who injure us, neither will our heavenly Father forgive us; and this would be the greatest calamity that could befall us in time and in eternity."—*Die vergebende Liebe; oder Gleichniss vom Schalksknecht.*

still obdurate, tell it to the Church : and if he refuse to hear the Church withdraw from his company; let him and all the world know that you do not make light of his sin.

Again, in some kinds of injury, it becomes your duty for the sake of the community to aid in bringing the criminal to justice. To bring the discipline of the righteous law upon the criminal, is not revenge : to shield him from its stroke is not love. So far from being necessarily inconsistent with forgiveness, such faithfulness in action may be associated with a Christ-like love to the sinner, and a thorough forgiveness of his sin, as an injury inflicted upon you.

Here is a side on which there is much room for advancement: let us forget the things that lie behind us on this path, and reach forward to higher attainments. In as far as Christians unite faithfulness and tenderness in their treatment of evil-doers, they become "imitators of God, as dear children."

2. The PRINCIPLE of forgiving injuries. Suppose that the methods for practice are accurately laid down, where shall we find a sufficient motive ? Suppose that an unexceptionable machinery has been constructed, whence shall we obtain an adequate force to set it in motion ? From an upper spring in heaven the motive power must flow; it can be supplied only by God's forgiving love, on us bestowed and by us accepted. When, like little closed vessels, we are charged by union with the fountainhead, forgiving love to erring brothers will burst spontaneously from our hearts at every opportunity that opens in the intercourse of life.

The express command of Him who redeemed us is, " Love one another, as I have loved you." In teaching his disciples how to pray, he linked their promise to forgive with their plea for forgiveness, so that no prayer of theirs should rise to heaven for receiving pardon unless it were accompanied by an engagement expressed or implied to bestow pardon: " Forgive us our debts, as we forgive our debtors."

But there is much more in the connection between receiving and bestowing forgiveness than can be expressed by the conception of yielding to the pressure of a motive. It is not only obedience to a command enjoined ; it is the exercise of an instinct that has been generated in the new nature. The method in which this and other graces operate is expressed by an apostle thus : " It is no more I that live, but Christ that liveth in me." When Christ is in you, he is in you not only the hope of glory, but also the forgiving of an erring brother.

A traveller in Burmah, after fording a certain river, found his body covered all over by a swarm of small leeches, busily sucking his blood. His first impulse was to tear the tormentors from his flesh: but his servant warned him that to pull them off by mechanical violence would expose his life to danger. They must not be torn off, lest portions remain in the wounds and become a poison; they must drop off spontaneously, and so they will be harmless. The native forthwith prepared a bath for his master, by the decoction of some herbs, and directed him to lie down in it. As soon as he had bathed in the balsam the leeches dropped off.

Each unforgiven injury rankling in the heart is like a leech sucking the life-blood. Mere human determination to have done with it, will not cast the evil thing away. You must bathe your whole being in God's pardoning mercy ; and these venomous creatures will instantly let go their hold. You will stand up free.

Two wheels protrude from a factory, and are seen in motion on the outer wall by every passenger. They move into each other. The upper wheel is large, the under small. From without and at a distance, you cannot tell whether the upper is impelling the under, or the under moving the upper. This question, however, might be settled by an inspection of the interior. By such an inspection it would be found that the larger and higher wheel communicates motion to the lower and smaller. If the upper wheel, which communicates the motion, should stand still, so also would the lower : but more than this,— if the lower wheel, which receives the motion, should by some impediment be stopped, the upper wheel also would stand still.

It is in some such way that God's goodness in forgiving freely for Christ's sake our sins, impels us to forgive from the heart those that have trespassed against us. The power is all from above ; yet, though we by our goodness do not set the beneficent machinery in motion, we may by our badness cause it all to stand still. It is not our forgiveness accorded to an evil-doer that procures forgiveness to ourselves from God ; the opposite is the truth : yet our refusal of forgiveness to a brother prevents the flow of pardon down from God to our guilty hearts. Such is the structure of the covenant. It is only a small part of that covenant that we can comprehend ; but, as far as we are able to perceive its provisions, behold, they are very good !

While a few acres of cold barren moorland constitute all your heritage, if a neighbour encroaches on it by a hair's-breadth, you assert your right and repel the aggression : possibly you may, in your zeal, accuse him of an intention to trespass, if you see him digging his own ground near your border. While your property is very small, you are afraid of losing any of it; and perhaps you cry out before you are hurt. But if you become heir to a broad estate in a fertile valley, you will no longer be disposed to watch the motions of your neighbour, and go to law with him for a spadeful of moss that he may have taken from a disputed spot.

Thus, while a human soul has no other portion than an uncertain shred of this uncertain world, he is kept in terror lest an atom of his property should be lost; he will do battle with all his might against any one who is, or seems to be, encroaching on his honour, or business, or property: but when he becomes a child of God, and an heir of an incorruptible inheritance—when he is a prince on the steps of a throne, he can afford to overlook small deductions from a possession that is insignificant in itself, and liable to be taken away at any time without an hour's warning.

In this aspect it is eminently worthy of notice that the disciples, when their Master on another occasion (Luke xvii. 3–5), taught them a similar doctrine on the forgiveness of injuries, immediately exclaimed, "Increase our faith." They seem to have been surprised by the extent of the demand, and conscious of their inability to meet it. As soon as the duty of forgiving injuries was laid before them in its true magnitude, they were brought to a stand; but they had sense to know wherein their weakness lay, and simplicity to seek in the proper quarter for renewed strength. It was a true instinct that led them, then and there, to plead for an increase of faith. A wider, freer channel for the inflow of God's compassion into their own hearts,—this is what they need in the emergency, and this is what they get from the Lord.

The miller, finding that some of the lumps are large and hard, and that the mill-stones are consequently almost standing still, goes quietly out and lets more water on. Go you, and do likewise. When injuries that seem large and hard are accumulated on your head, and the process of forgiving them begins to choke and go slow under the pressure, as if it would soon stop altogether; when the demand for forgiveness grows great, and the forgiving power in the heart is unable to meet it; —then, enter into your closet and shut your door, and pray to your Father specifically for more experience of his forgiving love; so shall your forgiving love grow stronger, and overcome every obstacle that stands in its way. Your heart, under the fresh impulse of pardon to you through the blood of the covenant, will toss off with ease the load of impediments that obstructed for a time its movements, and you will forgive even as you have been forgiven.

The Vineyard Laborers
(Matthew 20:1-16)

" For the kingdom of heaven is like unto a man that is an householder, which went out
early in the morning to hire labourers into his vineyard.   And when he had agreed
with the labourers for a penny a day, he sent them into his vineyard.   And he went
out about the third hour, and saw others standing idle in the market-place, and said
unto them; Go ye also into the vineyard, and whatsoever is right I will give you.
And they went their way.   Again he went out about the sixth and ninth hour, and did
likewise.   And about the eleventh hour he went out, and found others standing idle,
and saith unto them, Why stand ye here all the day idle?   They say unto him,
Because no man hath hired us.   He saith unto them, Go ye also into the vineyard;
and whatsoever is right, that shall ye receive.   So when even was come, the lord of the
vineyard saith unto his steward, Call the labourers, and give them their hire, beginning from the last unto the first.   And when they came that were hired about the
eleventh hour, they received every man a penny.   But when the first came, they supposed that they should have received more ; and they likewise received every man a
penny.   And when they had received it, they murmured against the goodman of the
house, saying, These last have wrought but one hour, and thou hast made them equal
unto us, which have borne the burden and heat of the day.   But he answered one of
them, and said, Friend, I do thee no wrong : didst not thou agree with me for a penny?
Take that thine is, and go thy way : I will give unto this last, even as unto thee.   Is
it not lawful for me to do what I will with mine own ?   Is thine eye evil, because I am
good ?   So the last shall be first, and the first last : for many be called, but few chosen.

AGAIN the heavenly kingdom is compared to the
proceedings of a human householder.   While
in fertile plains, like Esdraelon, the grain-field
was the Hebrew husbandman's chief care, on
the mountain sides, the vineyards were the most valuable
property, and required the greatest amount of labour.
The steepness of the slopes on which the vine grows best,
greatly increases the owner's toil.   In many cases the
terraces must be supported by strong stone walls; and

not only must the manure be carried on men's shoulders up the steep, but in some cases even the soil itself is carried up in the same way, and laid upon the bare rocks.

Different kinds of work are required in vineyards at different seasons. In spring they prepare the soil ; in summer they prune and tie up the vine branches; and in autumn all the joyous labour of the vintage comes suddenly on. Looking to the circumstance in the parable, that the labourers who began early counted much on having borne the heat of the day, we might be inclined to suppose that the scene is laid in the middle of summer; but the fact that the householder required so many labourers and hired all that he could find, points rather to the vintage in the end of autumn.

The master went out early in the morning to hire labourers. There was some spot, doubtless, recognised both by masters and men, as the common meeting-place for those who needed work, and those who needed workmen,—the Cross or the Buchts * of that place and day. This husbandman at once engaged all the men that he found, and sent them into his vineyard to begin work at six in the morning,—the first hour of the Jewish day. The terms were arranged beforehand,—a penny a day. The Roman denarius is reckoned equal to sevenpence half-penny of our money; but obviously it was considered the ordinary rate of a labourer's wages at the time.

Again at nine o'clock the husbandman went to the market-place, and finding some unemployed men, sent them also to work in his vineyard. Again at mid-day,

---

* The name of a great trysting place for selling cattle and hiring men and women on the eastern outskirts of the city of Glasgow, where the two operations resemble each other too closely for the credit of our institutions or the safety of society.

and yet once more at five o'clock in the afternoon he went out, and finding men on each occasion loitering about the market-place, he sent them also into the vineyard. In these cases, however, as was meet when the day was broken, the master did not promise any specific rate of wages; and the men, thankful for an opportunity of turning to some profitable account a day which would otherwise have been wholly lost, were content to accept whatever he might be pleased to give.

About six o'clock in the evening,—earlier or later according to the season of the year and the consequent duration of daylight at the time,—work in the vineyard ceased for the day, and each labourer, called forward in turn by the steward, received his wages in the master's presence.* The steward, acting doubtless under special instructions, called first the men who had entered the vineyard at five, and quitted it at six, and gave each a penny for his hour's work. Surprised by the munificence of their employer, these men retire towards their homes with silent gratitude. Afterwards those who had laboured one-half, and those who had laboured three-fourths of the day, were called in succession, and each received also a penny. Last of all came the men who had laboured from morning till night. They had been standing near, and had observed that all their fellow-labourers, not excepting even those who had been employed only an hour, received the same uniform reward, each man a penny. As this process was going on, they cherished in silence the expectation that when their turn should come, they would receive more of the master's money, because they had done more of his work. But the steward, evidently acting

---

* By law, wages for the work of the day must be paid the same evening (Deut. xxiv. 15).

on precise orders, gave each of these men also a penny, and no more. No longer able to conceal their disappointment, although they were well aware that they had no legal claim for more than they had received, they broke out into murmurs against their employer. Of course, he closed their mouths in a moment: he had completely fulfilled his agreement with them, and they had no right to interfere with his spontaneous generosity, whenever and towards whomsoever he might choose to exercise it.

Here, again, the key-notes of the parable are found at the beginning and at the end. The direct and immediate occasion of the discourse lies in Peter's question at the 27th verse of the nineteenth chapter, "We have forsaken all and followed thee: what shall we have therefore?" But as the parable sprang from Peter's question, so Peter's question sprang from an antecedent fact. To that fact, accordingly, we must look as the true ultimate root on which the parable grows.

As Jesus was going about in the Father's business, attended by the twelve, a young man came running forward to him, bending the knee in token of reverence (Mark x. 17), and asking, "Good master, what good thing shall I do that I may inherit eternal life?" Accommodating his lesson to the condition of the learner's heart, the Lord saw meet, at the close of his discourse, to lay a specific cross on this promising disciple, in order at once to reach and eradicate the specific disease that threatened the life of his soul,—"Sell all that thou hast, and come, follow me." The young man loved the world more than Christ: compelled to make his choice, he cleaved to the portion that he loved best. When by the sovereign act of the Lord he was placed in such a position that he could not enjoy both portions, he parted with the Saviour and clung to his wealth. Peter and the rest of the apostles listened and looked on, during this decisive interview : they gazed after the youth, perhaps with tears, as he slowly and sorrowfully withdrew. But their Lord did not leave the impressive fact to sink into their minds in silence : He interposed at the moment, to print the lesson permanently on their hearts, " How hardly shall they that have riches enter into the kingdom of heaven!" " Then answered Peter ;"—as usual this impetuous man burst suddenly into a speech upon the point in hand, before he had well considered what he was about to say. For one thing, there is no deceit in Peter's question ; he thinks aloud, and his thought is one of intense and undisguised self-conceit. The spirit of the Pharisee was there, " Lord, I thank thee that I am not as other men." His heart at this moment was undisguisedly mercenary ; his eye was on the main chance. We have done and suffered so much for God ; what return may we expect for our services ? That young rich man would not part with his portion in this world, in order to follow Christ : Peter, thereupon, made a most comfortable comparison between himself and the undecided youth, and expressed a hope that his own great devotion would not be overlooked in the day of reward.

I sometimes think the Papists acted wisely in making Peter the first Pope. He serves better as a type for them than any one of the twelve, unless they had gone all the way and chosen Judas. None of the true men were so forward as Peter in giving their judgment, or so frequently wrong.

The reply of our Lord to Peter's self-righteous demand is twofold. First, he owns and reiterates the truth that all labourers in his kingdom will be rewarded ; and next corrects the abuse of that principle into which a self-pleasing human heart is apt to fall. In the discourse recorded at the close of the nineteenth chapter, he teaches the cheering truth that the Lord will richly reward the services of his people, and in the subsequent parable gives to them and us a solemn admonition against the error into which Peter had been for the moment betrayed.

The positive doctrine regarding compensation for all sacrifices and wages for all work needs only to be read in the memorable words of Jesus, as the evangelist has recorded them here. Notwithstanding the incrustations of ignorant self-righteousness that now and then covered and disfigured their faith, these Galileans have in very deed left all for Christ, and shall all in very deed receive from Christ a hundred-fold. Even Peter's own decisive life-act,—his consecration to Jesus, was a higher and purer thing than his own foolish words at this time would represent it to have been. It was not with a mercenary eye to a subsequent equivalent that he left his nets and followed Jesus. That self-devotion in the simplicity of faith will be gloriously recompensed, notwithstanding the subsequent slips that dishonour the disciple and grieve the Master; but Peter, and through him all men, must be clearly taught that work done for the sake of the reward is not owned in the kingdom of heaven.*

---

* These two are thus united and distinguished by Dräseke,—" Although the kingdom of God is God's gift in the souls of men, yet without a worthiness in men it can neither begin nor continue, neither reveal nor develop itself. And again, although our worthiness is necessary, we nevertheless obtain the kingdom, not through the merit of works, but from the fulness of grace, yea, from that alone. In short, the kingdom demands workers ; hirelings it disdains (das Reich verlangt Arbeiter; Söldlinge verschmäht es). . . . . Thus it stands shut against the hireling, open to the worker. Not as though the kingdom needed thy labour. He who makes the winds his mes-

Every one that hath forsaken earthly possessions for Christ's sake shall receive an hundred-fold, and shall inherit everlasting life,—" *But* many that are first shall be last, and the last first."

This short antithetic sentence is the very gate by which we enter into the meaning of the parable; if we rightly comprehend it, we rightly comprehend all. It is necessary to determine here the connection between this sentence and the doctrine which is taught in the immediately preceding verses. While the Lord undertakes that service and sacrifice in his cause will be rewarded, he warns his disciples in the next breath that those who labour longest, or produce the greatest quantity of work, do not in every case, and necessarily, receive the highest reward. In his kingdom the reward is not measured only and always by the length of the service or the quantity of work ; many who are first as to the amount of work done will be last as to the amount of recompense received.

A lesson drawn from this scriptural principle may be legitimately addressed to those who are not within the kingdom, but I think the Master in this parable primarily intends to draw distinctions, not between those who are within and those who are without, but between two classes

sengers and the flames his servants, can do without thy hand-work, O little man. Thy labour avails not; but that thou shouldest be a labourer, that thou shouldest have a mind for God, and through that mind shouldest elevate thy life into a free and joyful service of him—that avails."—*Vom Reich Gottes*, ii. 40, 42.

Remarkable is the construction of the chain by which this writer connects the poor unemployed men who were standing idle in the market-place with the ever-during, ever-increasing satisfaction of their souls in eternity. So verlangt das Reich Arbeiter, nicht Söldlinge. Es beruft die Arbeitlosen. Es stellt die Berufenen an. Es beschäftigt die Angestelleten. Es übt die Beschäftigten. Es belohnt die Geübten. Es genügt den Belohnten. Und Gnüge währt ewig; wächst ewig.—ii. 51.

of genuine disciples,—between those who simply trust in the Lord and serve him in love, and those who, although also in the main believers, allow the leaven of self-righteousness to creep in and mar the simplicity of their faith.*

It is not said that those who are first in the quantity of work shall all or uniformly be last in the measure of reward, but "many" that are first shall be last. Some who are foremost in the amount of service may also be most free from the self-righteous spirit, and some who have laboured least may also receive least if they do their little under the influence of a hireling's selfishness. The meaning is, that although you be first as to length of time and quantity of labour, if the leaven of self-righteousness mingle in your offering, you will be lowest in the Master's esteem, and least in the day of reward; whereas, although you be last in point of time, and least in point of service, if you receive all from Christ's mercy, and render all in love to Christ, you will be higher in the end than some who seemed more energetic and successful workers.

" For the kingdom of heaven is like unto a man that is a householder," &c. This picture will illustrate the truth which has been declared; the householder represents Christ, the vineyard his kingdom, and the labourers his servants. The main lesson of the parable concerns, not the way of redemption, but the service which the redeemed render to their Lord. The wages of the labourer represent the rewards which Christ confers upon his servants, but this must be taken with certain

---

* On the other hand the text, Luke xiii. 30, although precisely similar to this in form, distinguishes, as may be seen from the context, between those who are within and those who are without.

explanations and limitations, especially these two.—
(1.) That the reward is partly a thing now begun, and
partly something that is completed in heaven; (2.) That
the value of the reward depends essentially on the disposition of heart with which the workman receives it.

It is not necessary to determine whether the labourers
who were first hired, and who laboured all the day,
represent the Jews under the first dispensation, or those
in the Christian Church who individually are converted
in early youth, and continue in Christ's service throughout
a long life, or those who, from special talent, or zeal, or opportunity, do and suffer most for the Lord and his cause.
The all-day labourers may represent all these classes,
each in turn, and especially the last. We must not understand exclusively by "the first" those who began first
in point of time. The term indicates rather those who
are first in the sense of being chief or greatest; it points
especially to those who were first in rank as having
endured the greatest amount of loss, and done the
greatest amount of work in Christ's cause. In the
parable it is true those who were first sent into the vineyard, in point of time, were chief among the labourers as
to the quantity of labour contributed, but the time is
only an accident. The matter truly brought into view is
not the time, but the quantity of work. Time is here
employed simply as a measure of quantity, for it is obviously assumed throughout that all the men performed
equal amounts of labour in equal times. It conduces
greatly to a clear conception of the whole lesson when
you think of the first and last as indicating those who
did and suffered most in Christ's cause and those who
did and suffered least.

Those who toiled only one hour or other larger fraction

of a working day had no contract as to amount of wages; they entered the vineyard and laboured without a bargain. They did not know what wages they would be paid with, but they knew what master they were working for; they were prepared to accept whatever he might be pleased to bestow. In this respect they correctly represent the truest of Christ's disciples—those little-child Christians whom he sets up as a pattern for others. Those, on the other hand, who were first in point of time, and therefore first in point of quantity, made their bargain before they began. This is like disciples who slide back in some measure from the simplicity of faith and allow a mercenary motive to mingle in their devotions. Especially is it like Peter when, contrasting his own large sacrifices with the refusal of the young man to sacrifice anything, and counting himself first, while he looked down on others as last, he cunningly inquired,—Lord, what shall we get for leaving all and following thee? In answer to his egotistical inquiry, he is informed in plain terms that he is one of those first who shall be last. This, however, according to all the analogy of Scripture, is not, in regard to Peter or any individual disciple, an absolute prediction of what shall be, but a warning of what may be if the same spirit remain.

Our Scottish forefathers at the period of the Reformation suffered much for Christ; some pined long in prison, some died at the stake. These were first, and we who contribute a few pounds to a missionary society, or teach a Sabbath school, or visit some poor families, are last in respect to the quantity of our doing and suffering in the Saviour's cause. But if any of those first were proud of their sufferings, they will be last in the reward; and whosoever of these last give their mite in simple love to the Lord that bought them, will be first when he comes to bring home his own.

Such is the structure of the parable that it must express the difference by giving one labourer not an absolutely but a comparatively greater amount of wages than another. The last are recompensed at a higher rate than the first, yet all go home with the same sum of money. But although the labourers are all equal in the absolute amount of wages received, the last are made higher than the first by a distinct addition to the pecuniary recompence—that is, a contented, loving, thankful mind.

See the two groups of labourers as they severally wend their way home that evening. As to amount of money in their pockets, they are all equal : but as to amount of content in their spirits there is a great difference. The last go home each with a penny in his pocket, and astonished glad gratitude in his heart : their reward accordingly is a penny, and *more*. The first, on the contrary, go home, each with a penny in his pocket, and corroding discontent in his soul: their reward accordingly is *less* than a penny. Those who know how great a gain is godliness with contentment, and how small a gain is even godliness, when discontent is eating into it like rust, will allow that, while the labourers first and last alike had each his penny, yet the last were first and the first last in the real value of their reward.

Considering that Peter is evidently designated as one of the first who shall be last, I cannot understand the parable otherwise than as showing differences among the disciples of Christ,—differences in simplicity of spirit while the labour lasts, and consequently in the value of the reward when the labour is done. As all the labourers get the wages of a day, so all who are represented by them, inherit the kingdom: but as one star differeth from another star in glory, so shall it be when Christ comes to gather all his own. They will wear the brightest crowns who thought most of their Redeemer's goodness, and least of their own sacrifice and work.

The latter clause of the 16th verse, "for many be called, but few chosen," being evidently attached to the parable as its application by the Lord, demands our earnest attention.* If we should understand by it, that many hear the call of the Gospel, but few are chosen by God and admitted through regeneration into his family, it would not be possible, as far as I can perceive, to assign to it any proper connection with the lesson of the parable. But by the terms in which this sentence is introduced, it is clearly intimated that it is the very conclusion and kernel, so to speak, of the doctrine which the parable was intended to convey. Whether we shall be able to understand it or not, it certainly must be something precisely in the line of the preceding instructions. In that direction we must seek for its meaning; for it is manifestly introduced as a gathering up in short and condensed form of all that the parable contained.

The exposition suggested by Bengel is simple, consistent, and clear; and it is, I think, correct. Taking the

---

* While in some cases the application of the parable which the Lord himself makes at the moment is full and perspicuous, it is in other cases like the parables themselves, and doubtless for good reasons, short, sententious, and partially veiled. In some cases the subjoined doctrine must be read in the light of the parable itself ere it can be understood. "Majus vero et certius auxilium interpreti paratur in illis locis, in quibus ipse Jesus sensum parabolarum explicat, quod quidem modo luculentius, ut in orationibus Mat. XIII. modo paucis tantum verbis fit. Saepe enim praemittitur vel subjungitur ab eo doctrina per parabolam prolata, quae tamen ipsa interdum paulo obscurius exprimitur, ita ut nisi per parabolam ipsam intelligi non possit."—*Schultze de par.* 86.

term "called" as signifying not all to whom the call of
the Gospel is addressed, but those only who are effectually
called,—not those who only hear, but those who also
obey the call,—taking the term in this sense, which is a
sober and scriptural view, he finds that this is not a distinction between saved and lost, but between two classes
of the saved. The called and the chosen are both true
disciples of Christ, and heirs of eternal life, and yet
there is some distinction between them. Chosen must
here therefore mean, what it did sometimes mean in
ancient times, and does often mean still, the best of their
kind. We constantly speak of choice or select articles,
meaning the most excellent. The phrase, whether used
proverbially before Christ's time or not, is in nature and
structure proverbial. He either found it a proverb and
used it, or he made it a proverb there and then, for such
it essentially is. It seems to have been employed by the
Lord on more than one occasion, and differently applied
at different times. As we might say among a great
number of manufactured articles, all true and genuine,
"few are first-rate;" so, among a great number of real
disciples, few stand out unselfish, unworldly, and Christ-
like, honouring their Lord, and making the world wonder.
Most, even of those who are disciples indeed, and shall
inherit eternal life, are so marred by self-righteous ad-
mixtures, and unsanctified temper, and conformity to the
world, that their light is dim and their witness inarticulate.
Peter, for example, was one of the called, in that he heard
and obeyed Christ, and was saved; but he was not a
chosen or choice disciple, when he demanded of his
Saviour what he should get for what he had done; or
when in the hour and power of darkness, he denied all
connection with Jesus of Nazareth. Alas! though there

are many Christians, how few there are who forget the things behind, and press forward till they reach the high calling of God in Christ Jesus.*

Some obvious practical lessons may be appended to the exposition.

1. Judge not. Let a man examine himself rather than his neighbour. When Peter saw the young man refusing to make a sacrifice for Christ, he complacently remembered his own sacrifices, and thought he had done remarkably well. Ah, Peter, Satan desires to have thee that he may sift thee as wheat; but what by the Master's rebukes addressed to him, and what by prayers poured out for him, he will be saved; yet so as by fire. You left all,

---

* In the transaction with the young man from which this parable remotely springs, an analogous expression is employed to indicate a chosen or choice disciple; "Jesus said unto him, If thou wilt be perfect, go and sell that thou hast," &c. (xix. 21.) The term "perfect" in that text seems to be entirely parallel with "chosen." The meaning of both is determined by the main drift of the parable; and the meaning thus given accords with the analogy of faith.

Another remarkable confirmation of this exposition is found in the use of the same term, ἐκλεκτοί, in Rev. xvii. 14. The word in that passage must have the same meaning that we have attributed to it in the parable. Two reasons, a supreme and subordinate, are given to account for the victory of the Lamb,—his own omnipotence, and the trustworthy character of the instruments whom he employs. "The Lamb shall overcome them: for he is Lord of lords and King of kings: and they that are with him are called, and chosen, and faithful;" κλητοὶ καὶ ἐκλεκτοὶ καὶ πιστοί. If you understand here by ἐκλεκτοί, chosen by God in the eternal covenant, the logical arrangement becomes obscure. It would be strange if, in enumerating the qualifications of soldiers, one should represent first that they were summoned to the warfare, next that they were chosen for that purpose before, and last that they were stanch in the battlefield. If this had been the meaning of ἐκλεκτοί it must have stood first in order. The fact that it stands second suggests another explanation. Take it, in the sense which it readily assumes and frequently bears, and the order of the series becomes at once transparent. The soldiers were "called, and choice, and faithful." They were enlisted in the cause, excellent in character, and found unflinching when the fight began.

you say, to follow Jesus; and how much was that? a share in a boat and some nets, both probably the worse for wear. Ah, Peter, if you had been as rich as this young man, I am not sure whether you would not have done as he did,—gone away, sorrowful indeed, but away from Jesus!

Disciples of Christ that are poor, should beware of judging the disciples who are rich. You were enabled to break the tie that bound you to the earth; and you see a neighbour struggling with the yoke still on his neck. Be not high-minded but fear. The line that bound you was a slender cord; the line that binds that brother is a cart rope. He, if he is set free at a later day, may be first in the day of reward, and you last.

2. All whom the Lord meets and calls are sent to work, and all go. From the moment they meet the Master till the evening of life's labour-day, they work for him. They not only labour for the Lord, they labour "in the Lord." Thus it is not a pain but a pleasure; it is their meat and their drink.

God needs not our work, but we, for our own sakes, need work in his kingdom. He can find other servants; but if we refuse his call we shall never find a "good Master."

3. The true spirit of a worker is love to the Master, and to the work for the Master's sake. The moment that a thought of merit glides into the servant's heart, it brings him down, not indeed from the number of true disciples, but from the highest to the lowest class there.

Among the motives that, in these matters, sway a human heart, there are two forces equal and opposite: one is a humble, broken-hearted consciousness that you deserve nothing, and receive all free; the other is a self-righteous conceit that your valuable services deserve a great reward. If this latter spirit is the main spring of your activity, it determines your position to be altogether outside of the circle of true believers ; if it intrudes more or less as a temptation, and tinges with self-righteous blemishes a substantial faith in Christ, it reduces you from the highest to the lowest rank of disciples, and from the first to the last in the final award of those who serve the Lord.

In one of its aspects the lesson of this parable is parallel with that which is taught by the experience of the penitent thief. Both greatly magnify the patience and long-suffering of God : they record and proclaim, each in its own way, that there is hope at the eleventh hour. But in such a case, a perverse carnal mind frequently turns the grace of God into lasciviousness. Because the mercy of our Redeemer is stretched to the furthest verge of safety to leave room for the outcast to enter, when on the darkening evening of the day of grace he flees at last from the wrath to come; souls cleaving to the dust, take the liberty of stretching their expectations a little further than Christ stretched his offer, and find the door shut, when they come too late. Ah, when the tender Saviour of sinners, by his parable, and the experience of the thief, gives you encouragement to come, although you are late; beware lest you take from his words wrested an encouragement to be late in coming.

Introduction: Two Sons, Wicked Husbandmen and Marriage of the King's Son
(Matthew 21:28-22:14)

THE natural history of a parable is like the (probable) natural history of a pearl. Something alien and irritating has alighted upon life, and forthwith a covering of pure and precious matter is thrown over it. After this manner, indeed, as we have already noted, a greater than the parable came. In this way redemption began, and grew. Sin entered Eden and fastened upon that image of God which had appeared on earth in the person of primeval man; forthwith holy promises from heaven began to cluster round the sin-spot. As age suceeeded age these promises distilled like dew and crystallized around the original nucleus, until redemption was completed in the sacrifice of Christ and the ministry of the Spirit: that glorious gospel on which we now fondly look, gathered round the fall. The sin of man, though not the cause of God's salvation, became its occasion and determined its form.

The particular lessons which Jesus taught in the course of his ministry, followed in this respect the analogy of his redeeming work as a whole; in most cases his instructions were called forth and fashioned by hard, bold outstanding sins. Some of the brightest jewels which shine in the life of Christ are the pure pearly coverings

which he threw around Pharisaic pride, or Sadducean unbelief, or the self-righteous stumbles of his own disciples.
Thus he made the wrath, and the malice, and the deceit
of men to show forth his own praise; thus rust-spots were
converted into shining pearls; thus human errors, as they
sprung up, were seized and choked and buried under a
mantle of glorious grace.

Here in Matthew's Gospel, we encounter a group of three
parables, the two sons, the wicked husbandmen, and the
marriage of the king's son, connected with each other
historically in a consecutive report, and logically as successive steps in the development of one argument. The
portion, chapters xxi. xxii. xxiii., is the compact record of
a single scene. Approaching by the Mount of Olives, Jesus
entered Jerusalem in a simple but significant triumphal
procession, heralded by the hosannahs of the multitude,
which, if for the most part neither intelligent nor permanent, were sincere and spontaneous. Arrived in the city
he at once made his way to the Temple, and there assumed
an unwonted and severe authority. The mercenary pro-
faners of the temple he cast out; the blind and lame he
healed. On the way to and from Bethany, where he lodged
for the night, the fruitless fig tree withered under his word.
Next morning as he was teaching in the temple, the heads
of the Jewish external theocracy, stung to rage by his
words and deeds on the preceding day, formally demanded
the exhibition of his authority, as a preliminary step to
the violent suppression of his work. Jesus knew the hearts
of these men; he knew that while, in virtue of their office,
they affected to expound and apply the divine law, and
to rule the people in accordance with it, they were at once
ignorant of God's word and tamely subservient to the
passions of the people. To tear off, or rather to compel

them with their own hands to tear off their cloak of
hypocrisy, he addressed to them that question of wonderful simplicity but wonderful power, The baptism of John,
whence was it? from heaven or of men? Knowing that
if they should confess the divine origin of John's mission
they would thereby establish the Messiahship of Jesus to
whom John had borne witness, and that if they should
deny it they would forfeit the favour of the people, they
answered, We cannot tell, meaning, It is inconvenient to
express an opinion. As they could not venture to pronounce whether a ministry which had left its impress deep
on the whole land, was a human usurpation or a divine
mission, they had obviously no right to sit in judgment
on the credentials of Jesus. When on this point they
were condemned out of their own lips the Lord, rising
now more into the stern dignity of judge when his
ministry was drawing to a close, advances against the
discomfited and stunned hierarchs, with another, another,
and yet another stroke, unveiling the hypocrisy of their
religious profession, predicting the consummation of the
crime, the murder of the Father's well beloved, which
they were already cherishing in their hearts, and denounc-
ing finally the doom which in the righteous government
of God should fall upon themselves and their city.* Such
are the occasion, the places, the object, and the nature of
the three parables which Jesus spoke that day in the
Temple, and the Evangelist Matthew has recorded in
this portion of the word. The first is the parable of—

---

* " He now constrains them, in the first parable, to declare their own
guilt; and, in the second, to declare their own punishment; and as they
had now decided to put Him to death, He describes to them, in the third
parable, the consequences of their great violation of the covenant and ingra-
titude,—the destruction of their ancient priesthood, and the triumphant establishment of his new kingdom of heaven among the Gentiles."—*Lange in loc.*

The Two Sons
(Matthew 21:28-32)

" But what think ye ? A certain man had two sons; and he came to the first, and said, Son, go work to-day in my vineyard. He answered and said, I will not : but afterward he repented, and went. And he came to the second, and said likewise. And he answered and said, I go, sir : and went not. Whether of them twain did the will of his father? They say unto him, The first. Jesus saith unto them, Verily I say unto you, That the publicans and the harlots go into the kingdom of God before you. For John came unto you in the way of righteousness, and ye believed him not : but the publicans and the harlots believed him : and ye, when ye had seen it, repented not afterward, that ye might believe him."

FROM this parable, in connection with that of the labourers in the vineyard, we incidentally learn that among the cultivators of Palestine in those days there was the same admixture of large and small farms which prevails in our own land. In order to provide for the structure of the preceding parable, an agriculturist is introduced who cultivates on a large scale. Group after group of labourers are hired wholesale, and sent successively into the vineyard ; in the evening a steward pays each labourer under the general instructions of his chief. There in a few strokes you have the picture of an ancient Israelitish magnate, owning a broad estate and affording employment to a multitude of dependants. In the parable which is now under review, we have a picture equally distinct, but representing another class of countrymen. This is neither on the one hand a great proprietor, nor on the other a landless labourer. Here is a man who has a stake in the country, a portion of ground of size sufficient to provide for the wants of his family; but his farm cannot afford employment and remuneration to a gang of labourers; the work must be all done by the owner himself and his children. This is a desirable condition of life, and the class who occupy it are valuable to society. There, in the middle, they are sheltered from many dangers to which their countrymen on either extreme of social condition are exposed. Woe to the country in which there are only two classes,—the greatest and the smallest,—the large proprietors and the floating sea of labourers. The strong fixed few and the feeble surging many are to each other reciprocally dangerous. Give me a country dotted all over with homesteads, where father and mother, sons and daughters, till their own ground and eat the fruit of their own labour.

"To the first he said, Son, go work to-day in my vineyard." The first was none other than the one whom the father first met that morning. To have intimated whether he was the elder or the younger, would have introduced a disturbing element, and obscured the meaning of the lesson. There is no question here between elder and younger, or between Jews and Gentiles. At all events, if those who maintained a place within the theocracy are distinguished from those who stood without its pale, we must conceive of the Father approaching on this occasion from without towards the centre, coming in contact first with those who were excluded as aliens, and afterwards reaching the inner circle, who counted themselves the seed of Abraham.

This son, rebellious in heart, and not trained to cover his disobedience under a smooth profession, meets his father's command with a rude, blunt refusal. I think the humble husbandman had received a similar answer from the same quarter more than once before. This is not the first unseemly word which the young man had spoken to his father: neither himself nor his wickedness has grown to maturity in a day. The habit of dishonouring his parents had sprung from a seed of evil in his infancy, and grown with his growth until he and it had reached full stature together. The father seems not to have spoken a word in reply. Probably he knew by experience that an altercation on the spot would only have made matters worse: perhaps he sighed, perhaps he wept as he turned gently round and went away. I do not know how often and how long he had meditated on the grand practical question for a father, when he should be severe, and when he should show indulgence. May God guide and help parents who have disobedient sons; they need much patience for bearing, and much wisdom for acting aright.

"But afterward he repented and went." There is much in these few simple words. He repented; perhaps his father's silent grief went to his heart at length and melted it. He saw himself in his true colours, and loathed himself for his sin. The son, who probably obtained a glimpse of his father's tears, wept himself in turn, and, as the best amends he could make, went silently into the vineyard, and did a good day's work there. Thus, when Jesus, suffering, bearing reproach before Pilate's judgment-seat, looked on Peter sinning, Peter went out and wept. When he was called to suffer for Christ, he had rudely answered, "I will not;" but afterwards he repented and went—to work, to witness, to suffer, to die for the Lord whom he loved.

Perhaps the father, from beneath the cottage eaves, saw the son on the brow of the hill toiling in the noonday heat,—saw and was glad. The value of a day's labour was something; but it was as the small dust of the balance in comparison with the price he set on the repentance and obedience of his child. I suppose there was a happy meeting at night when the son came home. I suppose the father was a happy man as he saw the robust youth wiping the sweat from his brow, and sitting down to his evening meal.

"He came to the second, and said likewise." The second son had an answer ready, sound in substance and smooth in form. It was a model answer from a son to his parent: " I go, sir," said the youth, without hesitation or complaint. I am not sure that the father was over-joyed at the promptness and politeness of this reply: probably he had received as fair promises from the same quarter before, and seen them broken. At all events, this young man's fair word was a whited sepulchre; he did not obey his father. Whether he fell in with trivial com-panions on his way to the vineyard, and was induced to go with them in another direction, or thought the day too hot and postponed the labour till the morrow, I know not; but he said, and did not. It was profession without practice. The tender vine-shoots might trail on the ground for him till their fruit-buds were blackened; he would not put himself to the trouble of tying them up to the stakes, although the food of the family should be imperilled by his neglect.

Now comes the sharp question, "Whether of them twain did the will of his father?" The answer is all too easy. The light is stronger than is comfortable for those owl-eyed Pharisees, who were prowling about like night-birds on the scent of their prey. The sudden glance of this sunbeam dazzles and confounds them. In utter helplessness, they confess the truth that condemns themselves; they say unto him "The first."*

In the first example the Lord represents chief sinners repenting; and in the second, the form of godliness without its power. The publicans and harlots, who had forsaken their sins and followed the Saviour, sat for the first picture; the chief priests and elders, who concealed their thirst for innocent blood under a mantle of long prayers and broad phylacteries, sat for the second.

Let us look first to the two distinct and opposite answers, and next to the two distinct and opposite acts.

The answers.—That of the first son, " I will not," was evil, and only evil. It is of first-rate practical importance to make this plain and prominent. Looking to the son in the story, we see clearly that the answer was outrageously wicked: it was an evil word flowing from its native spring in an evil heart. Looking next to the class of persons whom that son represents, we find they are the openly and daringly ungodly of every rank in every age. This son, when he rudely refused to obey his father, meant what he said; he was not willing to obey, and he plainly said so. This represents those who have neither the profession nor the practice of true religion; they neither fear God nor pretend to fear him.

At this point, among certain classes, a subtle temptation insinuates itself. In certain circumstances, ungodly

---

* At an earlier stage of the same interview, when a question regarding the ministry of the Baptist was addressed to them, fearing the consequences which an answer might involve, they had sought shelter under the plea of ignorance. As they gained nothing by their duplicity on that occasion, they may have been unwilling to try the same policy again ; and, accordingly, they give frankly the obvious answers to the questions that resulted both from this and the succeeding parable.

men take credit for the distinct avowal of their ungodli٠ ness, and count on it as a merit. They are not, indeed, submissive in heart and life to the will of God; but they do not tell a lie about the matter; they make no pretension. The frank confession, that they are not good, seems to serve some men as a substitute for goodness. By comparing themselves complacently with fellow-sinners of a different class, they contrive to rivet the fatal error more firmly on their own hearts. Observing among their neighbours here and there a rank hypocrite, they compare his sanctimonious profession with his indifferent sense of honesty, and congratulate themselves that they are not hypocrites.

Well, brother, suppose it were conceded that you are not a hypocrite; what then? If you have lived unrepenting, unforgiven, unchanged; if with your whole heart and habits you have departed from the living God, and not returned to him through the Mediator,—will all be atoned for and made up by the single fact that to all your other sins you did not add the cant of a hypocrite? It is true, a hypocrite is a loathsome creature; but his badness will not make a profane man good. When he is cast away for his hypocrisy, it will be no comfort to you as you keep him company that it is for open ungodliness, and not for lying pretensions to piety, that you are condemned. Hypocrites are, indeed, excluded from the kingdom of God; but it is a fatal mistake to assume that, provided you are not a hypocrite, you will be welcomed into heaven with all your vices on your back.

I scarcely know a more subtle or more successful wile of the devil than this. Many strong men are cast down by it. You don't pretend to be good; well, and will that save you? What comfort will it afford to the lost to reflect that they went openly to perdition, in broad day-light, before all men, and did not skulk through by-ways under pretence that they were going to heaven?

The answer of the other son was evil too, if you look not to its body, but to its spirit. There is no reason to suppose that it was, even at the moment, an act of true obedience to his father. " He said, I go, sir; and went not:" he said one thing, and did another, an opposite; but there is no ground for believing that he meant to go when he promised, and afterwards changed his mind. His smooth language was a lie; and his subsequent conduct showed, not that he had changed his mind when his father was out of sight, but that he concealed it while his father was present. It is worthy of notice, that although the first son changed his mind after he had given his answer, there is no intimation of any change having passed on the second son, between his answer and his act. By its silence on this point, the narrative leads us to infer that the purpose of the disobedient son was the same while he was promising well as when he acted ill. The course of the life flowing full in the direction of disobedience, proves that the expression of the lips which ran in the opposite direction, was a lie; it was like a glittering ripple caused by a fitful breeze, running upward on the surface of the river, while the whole volume of its water rolls, notwithstanding, the other way.

Thus is even the worship of hypocrites worthless: Not every one that *saith* unto me, Lord, Lord ; but he that *doeth* the will of my Father which is in heaven. The want of the subsequent obedience shows that the promise was not true.

Thus at first both these sons were in a false and unsafe position. Their characters were not the same,—were not similar: they differed in thought and word; but the difference, in as far as their answers were concerned, indicated only varieties of sin. Legion is the name of the spirits that possess and pollute the fallen; but all the legion do not dwell in every man. Different temptations tinge different persons with different hues of guilt. At the time when the father uttered his command, the character of the first son was bold, unblushing rebellion; the character of the second was cowardly, false pretence. The one son neither promised nor meant to obey; the other son promised obedience, but intended not to keep his word.

In the first instance, therefore, there is no ground for preferring the one to the other. While they stood severally in their father's presence, and before either had repented of his sin, they were both, and both alike evil. The blasphemer has no right to boast over the hypocrite and the hypocrite has no right to boast over the blasphemer. In either case it is a body of sin, but there is a shade of difference in the colour of the garments. The one pretends to a goodness which he does not possess; and the other confesses, or rather boasts, that he is destitute of goodness. They measure themselves by themselves; and therein they are not wise. The one thinks his smooth tongue will save him; and the other counts himself safe because he has not a smooth tongue.

We come now to the ultimate *act* of either son. The first, after flinging a blunt refusal in his father's face, repented of his sin. The turning-point is here. A change came over the spirit of the man, and a consequent change emerged in his conduct: his heart was first turned, and then his history. The honesty of his declaration—the absence of duplicity in giving his answer, would not have

justified him before either God or man. He repented;
he turned round. He grieved over his sin; he was sorry
that he had disobeyed his father. Repentance immediately brought forth fruit after its kind. He went into
the vineyard, and laboured there with a will all day at
the kind of work which he knew would please his father.
These two things go always in company, and together
make up the new man—they are the new heart and the
new life.

The grieved father would weep for joy, as he looked
up the precipitous hill-side on which the terraced vineyard hung, and saw there the head and hands of his son
glancing quickly from place to place among the vine
plants. Thus there is joy in heaven—deep in the heart
of heaven's Lord—over one sinner that repenteth. Among
the vines that day work was worship: the resulting act
of obedience—fruit of repentance in the soul, was an offering of a sweet-smelling savour unto God.

The other son promptly promised, but failed to perform. The first was changed from bad to good, but the
second was not changed from good to bad. No change
took place in this case, and none is recorded. It is not
written, that having promised, he afterwards repented and
did not go. His promise was not true; at the moment
when it was made, the youth did not intend to work, and
therefore it required no change of mind to induce him
afterwards to spend the day in idleness.

This son represents, in the first instance, those Pharisees
who were then and there compassing the death of Jesus.
They ostentatiously professed that they were doing God
service; yet they were spreading a net for the feet of the
innocent, and preparing to shed his blood. Wearing
broad phylacteries, making long prayers, and offering

many sacrifices, they were, notwithstanding, living in malice and envy, hateful, and hating one another. With their lips they honoured God; but in works they denied him. These, in as far as they are here represented, were evil first and last. In the second son we have an example, not of a man who meant to do good changing his mind and ultimately doing evil, but of a man who, notwithstanding his fair profession, meant evil at the beginning and perpetrated it in the end.

Nor are these lessons of the Lord limited to one private interpretation : the lesson of this parable was not exhausted when the Pharisees died out. As surely as the thorns, and the tares, and the lilies to which Jesus on various occasions alluded in his lectures, grow on the ground at this day, and have grown there through all the intervening generations—so surely the various classes of human character which he rebuked, warned, or encouraged in his ministry, have their representatives going out and in amongst us in the present day. It is meant that in this glass all the self-righteous to the end of the world should see themselves ; their profession is fair, but their life is for self, and not for God.

In the stratified rocks many species and genera of plants and animals are found in a fossil state which are not found in the flora or fauna of our present earth ; but the human characters that were fixed and stamped as by photograph in the Scriptures are not so far removed from the men and women who now live on the earth. No species has become extinct ; and even the minuter characteristics of distinct varieties remain legible still.

Here spring two distinct warnings to two distinct classes, with corresponding encouragements attached, as shadows follow solid bodies in the sunlight ;—to the Publicans and Harlots first, and next to the Pharisees of the day.

1. There is a class amongst us answering to those publicans and sinners to whom Jesus was wont to address the message of his mercy. Alas, they may be counted by thousands and tens of thousands in the land! They are the drunkards, the licentious, the profane, the false, the cruel,—those who abandon themselves to a vicious life, and do not take the trouble of attempting to hide their sin under a cloak of sanctity. They gratify every lust, and crucify none. They live without God in the world. The key-note of their being is, Let us eat and drink, for to-morrow we die.

To all this class the parable proclaims a warning. A rank, soporific superstition has crept over these free and easy spirits,—a superstition as dark and deceitful as any of the inventions of Rome. Men seem actually to persuade themselves that their very wickedness will supply them with a passport into heaven. They seem to expect that they will be made pets in the great day, because they made no pretension to saintship ; and that they will be fondled by the Judge as they have been by their boon companions, because hypocrisy cannot be reckoned among their sins. It is a false hope. Free thinking, free living brother, if I saw you about to put to sea in a ship which I knew to be affected with dry-rot in the timbers of the bottom, I would warn you with all my energy, that I might save your life : when I see you preparing to launch into eternity leaning on a lie, I cry vehemently, Beware, lest you be lost for ever! Without holiness no man shall see God. The absence of a hypocritical pretension to holiness will not be accepted instead of holiness. All who go away to the judgment-seat without holiness will be shut out of heaven—alike those who thought they had it, and those who confessed that they had it not. It was all right at last with the profane son in the parable; but mark, he repented and obeyed. God's invitation to the wicked is, Turn and live; but the promise contains in its bosom the counterpart threatening, If you turn not you shall die. It was not the bold, frank declaration of disobedience that made the first son all right: it made him all wrong. It was his change,—his passing out of that state, as if he had passed from death unto life, that saved him.

But to this class the parable speaks encouragement as well as warning. So great is God's mercy in Christ that even you are welcome when you come; the gate stands open; the Redeemer from within is calling chief sinners in; He has pledged himself to cast no comer out because of his worthlessness. Nor does the freeness of his grace prove that the prodigal's sins are small; it proves only that the forgiving love of Christ is great.

2. There is still a class corresponding to the Pharisees, and to these the Lord in this parable conveys both warning and encouragement.

The essence of the Pharisaic character, under every variety of form, consists of these two things,—an exact and laborious observance of external religious duties, and a heart satisfied with itself while it is devoted to the world. The species is described for all times and places in the Apocalyptic Epistle to the Church in Sardis: "Thou hast a name that thou livest, and art dead" (Rev. iii. 1). There is a profession of godliness wanting its power; Christ's name comes readily to the lip, but the god of this world possesses the heart and controls the life.

There is encouragement to the Pharisee as well as to

the publican to turn and live. There is no respect of persons with God; the Pharisee was as welcome to Christ as the publican, if he would come. A Pharisee and a publican went up to the temple at the same hour to pray; the publican returned to his own house pardoned and at peace with God, while the Pharisee went home still unreconciled and under condemnation: but wherefore? Not that God was more willing to forgive the publican than to forgive the Pharisee; but because the Pharisee did not ask forgiveness. He would have obtained it if he had asked it: his self-righteousness was his ruin.

Thus in the end of this parable, the Lord intimates to the Pharisees that the outcasts whom they despised are entering the kingdom of heaven before them. This does not mean that the way is made more easy, the gate more wide, to the licentious and profane than to the hypocrite, —it intimates merely that in point of fact the profane were then and there hastening in through the gate which stood open alike for all, while the self-righteous were standing aloof. The intimation, moreover, is made, not in order to keep these Pharisees back, but to urge them forward. The Lord desires to provoke them to jealousy by them that were no people. These despised outcasts are going in before you; arise and press in now, lest the door be shut. It was not because they were publicans and harlots that they were saved, but because they believed and repented under the preaching of John; and it was not because the others were Pharisees that they were still unsaved, but because even with the example of fellow-sinners repenting and believing before their eyes, they, thinking themselves righteous, would not repent and believe.

God delights as much to receive a Pharisee as to receive a publican. When a self-righteous man discovers himself at last to be a whited sepulchre, and counting his own righteousness filthy rags, flees to Christ as his righteousness, he is instantly accepted in the beloved.

If I could be admitted, in the body or out of the body, to a vision of the saints in rest, I would like to creep near the spot where two saved sinners chance to meet,—the man who wrote this narrative of Christ's ministry, and the man who preached Christ to the Gentiles. I would fain listen for an hour to the conversation of Matthew the publican and Saul the Pharisee when they meet in the mansions of the Father's house. Their loving argument, I could imagine, would sometimes run high. Matthew will contend that the grace of their common Lord has been most conspicuously glorified in his own redemption, "for," he pleads, " I was all evil and had nothing good, I had neither inside purity nor outside whitening. I had neither the seemly profession without nor the holy heart within. I was altogether vile ; and in me therefore is the grace of God glorified most." Paul, on the other side, will contend, with his keen intellect perfect at last, that he was the chief sinner, and that consequently in his redemption a more decisive testimony is given to the abundance of the Saviour's grace. After describing his own hardness and blindness and unbelief, he will add, as the crowning sin of man, the crowning glory of God, —While I was thus the chief of sinners, I gave myself out as one of the greatest of saints.

It may be hard to tell whether of the two mountains is the more elevated ; but one thing is clear,—both are covered by the flood. The blood of Jesus Christ, God's Son, cleanseth us,—the profane and the self-righteous alike,—cleanseth us from all sin.

The Wicked Husbandmen
(Matthew 21:33-46)

" Hear another parable : There was a certain householder, which planted a vineyard, and hedged it round about, and digged a winepress in it, and built a tower, and let it out to husbandmen, and went into a far country : and when the time of the fruit drew near, he sent his servants to the husbandmen, that they might receive the fruits of it. And the husbandmen took his servants, and beat one, and killed another, and stoned another. Again, he sent other servants more than the first : and they did unto them likewise. But last of all he sent unto them his son, saying, They will reverence my son. But when the husbandmen saw the son, they said among themselves, This is the heir : come, let us kill him, and let us seize on his inheritance. And they caught him, and cast him out of the vineyard, and slew him. When the lord therefore of the vineyard cometh, what will he do unto those husbandmen? They say unto him, He will miserably destroy those wicked men, and will let out his vineyard unto other hus- bandmen, which shall render him the fruits in their seasons. Jesus saith unto them, Did ye never read in the scriptures, The stone which the builders rejected, the same is become the head of the corner : this is the Lord's doing, and it is marvellous in our eyes? Therefore say I unto you, The kingdom of God shall be taken from you, and given to a nation bringing forth the fruits thereof. And whosoever shall fall on this stone shall be broken : but on whomsoever it shall fall, it will grind him to powder. And when the chief priests and Pharisees had heard his parables, they per- ceived that he spake of them. But when they sought to lay hands on him, they feared the multitude, because they took him for a prophet."

WHEN a proprietor has determined to appropriate as a vineyard a portion of ground which had previously lain waste, or been employed for some other purpose, his first care is to plant the vines. As some time must necessarily elapse before the young plants begin to bear fruit, he may prosecute the other departments of his undertaking at leisure. In due time, accordingly, he constructs a fence around the field to keep out depredators, whether men or beasts; digs a vat for receiving the juice, and prepares an appa·

ratus above it for squeezing the clusters quickly in the hurry of the vintage; builds a tower as at once a shelter for the keeper and an elevated stand-point for the watcher by night or day.

In the case which this parable represents, the owner did not continue to reside on the spot and cultivate his own vineyard; "he let it out to husbandmen, and went into a far country." This lease, granted by a non-resident proprietor, throws an interesting light on the habits of the place and the time. In regard both to the tenants and the terms, the information, though very brief, is very definite. The vineyard was let not to one capitalist, who might employ labourers to do the necessary work, but to a kind of joint-stock company of labourers who proposed to cultivate the property with their own hands for the common benefit. It was stipulated, moreover, that the rent should be paid not in money but in kind. It is the system known in India at this day as ryot-rent; the cultivator undertakes to give the owner a certain fixed quantity yearly from the produce of the farm, and all that is over belongs to himself.

The structure of the parable in its later stages presupposes a country in which the central government is paralyzed, and the will of the strongest has usurped the place of law. With us it requires an exercise of imagination to conjure up a scene in which these events could possibly occur; but in those regions such anarchy was not uncommon then,—is not uncommon now. It is probable that the annals of our own empire in India could supply some parallel conflicts between the privileged superiors and the actual cultivators of the soil.

The proprietor, being personally absent from the country, employed agents to demand his stipulated share of the produce at the proper season from the tenants in possession. The tenants, presuming on the distance of the superior, and the difficulty which he must necessarily encounter in any attempt to enforce his rights, not only refused to fulfil the conditions of their lease, but also assaulted the messengers who made the demand; they beat one, and killed another, and stoned a third. Obviously, they determined from the first to retain the whole produce of the vineyard for themselves. They do not seem to have laid their plans with much care: there is more of passion than of policy in their conduct. It is the ordinary practice of those who break the laws of God or of man, to grasp madly a present pleasure, and refuse to think of coming vengeance. Having heard of the treatment which his agents had received, the proprietor despatched another party more numerous, with the view probably of overawing the refractory peasants by a display of strength; but the second mission was as cruelly and contemptuously rejected as the first. The proprietor, still unwilling to bring matters to an extremity, adopted next an expedient which he hoped would subdue the rebellion, without imposing on him the necessity of punishing the rebels. Keeping out of sight for the moment his rights and his power, he appealed confidingly to their hereditary reverence for the family of their chief; he sent his son, and sent him unarmed, unattended.

The conduct of the husbandmen at this point is unintelligible, if you suppose that the country enjoyed a regular government, and that the men had deliberately adopted a plan. In order to account for the circumstances, you must suppose that the central government was paralyzed, and that these men were as stupid as they were wicked. Great criminals are often blind to their own interests: their blunders generally lead to their conviction.

The murder of the heir by these greedy tenants, in the vague hope of obtaining the property, is a probable event. To show that the scheme was not skilfully devised, does not by any means prove that the crime was not actually perpetrated. The owner was absent; no display of irresistible power was made to their senses; they were not in the habit of nicely considering the remote consequences of an act, and an overmastering passion completely paralyzed at that moment a judgment which was feeble at the best.

From this point the close of the tragedy is self-evident; the Lord accordingly does not further prosecute the narrative. Here the Pharisees are invited to pronounce judgment upon themselves; nor do they hesitate to accept the challenge. Whether in simplicity, as unconscious of the Teacher's drift, or in exasperation as knowing that by this time his drift appeared to the whole company all too plain, may not be certain; but in point of fact they gave the answer without abatement and without ambiguity: "He will miserably destroy those wicked men, and will let out his vineyard to other husbandmen which will render him the fruits in their season."

No serious difficulty occurs in the interpretation of this parable, and, consequently, no considerable differences of opinion have arisen among interpreters regarding it. The main lines of the lesson cannot be mistaken; but there is need of careful discrimination in some of the details.

Frequently in the Scriptures the seed of Abraham, called by God and endowed with many peculiar privileges, are compared to a vine, or to the aggregate of vines in a vineyard. I shall here point to three examples of this usage, in order to show that, notwithstanding an obvious general resemblance, they differ from each other and from this parable in the specific purposes to which they severally adapt and apply the analogy:—

1. Isa. v. 1–7: "Now will I sing to my well-beloved a song of my beloved touching his vineyard. My well-beloved hath a vineyard in a very fruitful hill. And he fenced it, and gathered out the stones thereof, and planted it with the choicest vine, and built a tower in the midst of it, and also made a winepress therein: and he looked that it should bring forth grapes, and it brought forth wild grapes. And now, O inhabitants of Jerusalem, and men of Judah, judge, I pray you, betwixt me and my vineyard. What could have been done more to my vineyard, that I have not done in it? wherefore, when I looked that it should bring forth grapes, brought it forth wild grapes? And now go to; I will tell you what I will do to my vineyard: I will take away the hedge thereof, and it shall be eaten up; and break down the wall thereof, and it shall be trodden down. And I will lay it waste: it shall not be pruned nor digged; but there shall come up briers and thorns: I will also command the clouds that they rain no rain upon it. For the vineyard of the Lord of hosts is the house of Israel, and the men of Judah his pleasant plant: and he looked for judgment, but behold oppression; for righteousness, but behold a cry."

The vineyard, with its slope to the southward, and rich soil, and careful cultivation, and secure defences, and convenient apparatus, represents the people whom God chose and cherished. The drift of Isaiah's parable is to show the exaggerated wickedness of that

favoured nation. The vineyard brought forth wild grapes,
—those sour grapes which set on edge the teeth of him
who tastes them (Ezek. xviii. 2). Israel lived like the
heathen, and thus the care bestowed upon them was
thrown away. As a punishment for its ungrateful return,
the vineyard was laid waste; the kingdom and polity of
Israel were destroyed by the decree of God, and through
the instrumentality of the king of Babylon.

2. Ezek. xv. 2–5: "Son of man, What is the vine
tree more than any tree, or than a branch which is
among the trees of the forest? Shall wood be taken
thereof to do any work? or will men take a pin of it to
hang any vessel thereon? Behold, it is cast into the fire
for fuel; the fire devoureth both the ends of it, and the
midst of it is burnt. Is it meet for any work? Behold,
when it was whole, it was meet for no work: how much
less shall it be meet yet for any work, when the fire hath
devoured it, and it is burned?"

Here Israel is compared, not to a vineyard, but to a
single vine; and the special characteristic selected for
purposes of instruction is the uselessness of the vine
tree as timber. Cultivated only for the sake of its fruit,
if it prove barren, it is not only no better than the
trees of the forest, but much worse. Forest trees are
useful in their own place, and for certain purposes; but a
vine, if it do not bear fruit, is of no use at all. No man
can make a piece of furniture from its small, supple,
gnarled stem and branches. The wood of the vine is fit
for nothing but to be cast into the fire, and, therefore, a
fruitless vine takes rank far beneath a forest-tree; thus an
apostate and corrupt Church is a viler thing than the
ordinary secular governments of the world. Such
obviously and notoriously is ecclesiastical Rome to-day.

3. Ps. lxxx. 8–15: "Thou hast brought a vine out of Egypt; thou hast cast out the heathen, and planted it. Thou preparedst room before it, and didst cause it to take deep root, and it filled the land. The hills were covered with the shadow of it, and the boughs thereof were like the goodly cedars. She sent out her boughs unto the sea, and her branches unto the river. Why hast thou then broken down her hedges, so that all they which pass by the way do pluck her? The boar out of the wood doth waste it, and the wild beast of the field doth devour it. Return, we beseech thee, O God of hosts: look down from heaven, and behold, and visit this vine ; and the vineyard which thy right hand hath planted, and the branch that thou madest strong for thyself."

Again Israel is represented as a vine ; but in this case the features brought into prominence are its former flourishing condition and great extent compared with its present desolation. By the removal of the protecting fence, the wild beasts of the forest were permitted to trample at will on its feeble and lowly boughs. The picture sets forth the ruin of Jerusalem through the with-drawal of God's protecting hand, and the consequent irruption of hostile nations.

In all these cases the vine, or aggregate of vines, repre-sents the privileged persons who constituted the kingdom of Israel or Church of God, as it then existed in the world. In the first example, the *wickedness* of Israel is represented by the bitterness of the fruit which the vineyard produced ; in the second, the *unprofitableness* of Israel is represented by the want of fruit on the vine; and in the third, the *sufferings* of Israel are represented by the inroads of the wild beasts upon the wide spread, tender, unprotected vine.

Our parable differs from all three as to the point where

its lesson lies. It is not a case in which a favoured vineyard produces bad fruit; it is not a case in which a vine
bears no fruit ; it is not a case in which a vine that might
otherwise have been fruitful is trampled down by wild
beasts for want of a fence. It is a case in which, after the
vineyard has brought forth its fruit, the cultivators who
have charge refuse to render to the owner the portion of
the produce which is his due. The difference is important : it determines clearly the main line in which the interpretation of the parable should proceed.

By the vineyard with all its privileges, I understand
the ordinances of Israel as appointed by God, and the
people of Israel in as far as they were necessarily passive
in the hands of their priests and rulers. The husbandmen manifestly represent the leaders, who at various
periods had usurped a lordship over God's heritage.
Extraordinary ambassadors were sent from time to time
in the owner's name, to demand the stipulated tribute,—
prophets such as Elijah, Elisha, Isaiah, Jeremiah, and
Ezekiel, men not of the number, or in the confidence of
the ordinary rulers, but specially commissioned by the
Supreme, to approach them with reproof and instruction.
The established authorities of the nation, exercising their
office for their own pleasure or profit, rejected the counsel
and assaulted the persons of the messengers. Some were
imprisoned, some driven into exile, and some put to death.
Successive embassies, sent in successive ages, met with
similar treatment, until, in the fulness of time, Christ the
Son became the messenger of the covenant. He came
unto his own, and his own received him not. Already
those Jewish rulers who listened to this parable, were
laying their plans to cast this greatest prophet out of the
city, and to crucify him.

The owner of the vineyard said, "They will reverence my son." The expression is natural and appropriate in the lips of a human proprietor; but obviously when it represents the purpose of God, it means only that such reverence was claimed, and such reverence was due. The omniscient knew beforehand that the Jewish rulers would not yield even to this last and tenderest appeal. The expectation of the husbandmen that when they should have murdered the heir, the property should become their own, does not point to any definite, well considered plan by which the wicked expect to gain a permanent portion by rejecting the Gospel; it indicates merely the blunt determination of the carnal mind to grasp and enjoy God's bounties while it despises and rejects his grace. To crucify Christ by the hands of the Romans, or to crucify him afresh through unbelief, was and is a short-sighted policy.

When the Lord of the vineyard cometh he will destroy those wicked men, and will let out the vineyard unto others. The interpretation of this turning-point is given to the Jewish rulers in full, and without concealment. "The kingdom of God shall be taken from you and given to a nation bringing forth the fruits thereof" (ver. 43). The polity of the Jews was crushed by the Romans, and the charge of the Church fell into other hands. The "nation" that has succeeded to the kingdom is constituted on a different principle, and held together by different bonds. It is not after the flesh, but after the spirit that citizenship is obtained in the Christian commonwealth; henceforth, the partakers of Abraham's faith are the seed of Abraham to whom the covenant of promise pertains The worship and ordinances of God's house were transferred to the apostles and their followers, neither as Jews nor as Gentiles, but as the disciples of Christ. A new nation ($\epsilon\theta\nu o\varsigma$) is constituted of those who are born again; of those the kingdom consists, and under their charge its affairs will be carried on until the Lord come again.

The personal and permanent application of the lesson is obvious.

A rich vineyard, planted and fenced to our hand, has been let out to us by the Maker and Owner of the world. Civil and religious liberty, the Bible and the Sabbath, the Church and its ministry, have been provided and preserved for us by our Father's care. We are permitted to enjoy all for our own benefit, under deduction of a tribute to the Giver. Our offerings cannot directly reach him, but he has made them payable to the poor.

When Christ the messenger of the covenant stands at the door and knocks, a worldly heart within refuses to admit him. The carnal mind is enmity against God, and therefore resists the claim which the Mediator bears: its language is, "We will not have this man to reign over us."

The lesson bears also upon the gradual corruption of the Christian Church in the first centuries, and the absolute apostasy of the lordly hierarchy at Rome. At the Reformation the kingdom was in part taken from that faithless priesthood; but they retain vast multitudes in bondage still. The Lord reigneth; and the time will come when every yoke shall be broken, and the Church set free to serve the Lord alone. The vineyard will one day be delivered from the tyranny of usurping tenants, and its fruit fully rendered to its rightful Lord.

Ah, my country, I dread the punishment of thy unfaithfulness! The same righteous God, who cast out the Jews and admitted the Gentiles, reigneth still. On the same principle he has taken the kingdom from Asia Minor and

Greece, and given it to this island of the sea. Alas, if we render not to him the fruits of his vineyard, he may take our privileges in judgment away, and give them to another nation, perhaps to Italy—emancipated, regenerated Italy (Rom. xi. 19).

This parable is remarkable for the codicil taken from the Old Testament and attached to it by the Lord on the spot and at the moment. The picture of the tenant vine-dressers usurping possession—driving off the owner's servants and slaying his son, although transparent in its meaning and pungent in its reproof, does not contain all that the Lord then desired to address to the Pharisees. It pleased him to employ that similitude as far as it reached; but when its line had all run out, he seized another line that lay ready in the Scriptures to his hand, and attached it to the first, that by the union of the two he might make the reproof complete. The first type taken from human affairs is not broad enough to represent the kingdom of God at a crisis of its conflict. The son whom the proprietor sends on an embassy to the vine-dressers, points to Christ sent by the Father to his own Israel. The terrestrial fact serves to show that the son was put to death by the rebels in possession, but there its power is exhausted ; it has no means of exhibiting the other side of the scene,—that this son rose from the dead, and now reigns over all. The parable, when it came to its natural conclusion, left the lesson which it had begun to teach abruptly broken off in the midst,—left a glory of the Lord unrevealed, and a terror to wicked men un-spoken. That he might proclaim the whole truth, and leave his unrepenting hearers without excuse, the Lord proceeded then and there to demand of them, " Did ye never read in the Scriptures, The stone which the builders rejected, the same is become the head of the corner ?"

The parable of the husbandmen has already shown that the Son was rejected by the favoured people to whom he was sent ; and this grand text from the Old Testament Scriptures, which the Scribes well knew, shows further that he whom the official but false builders rejected and cast down, was accepted and raised up by God. Whom they refused, dishonoured, and slew, him God raised up and made King upon his holy hill of Zion.* It is a dreadful discovery for those husbandmen to make, that the Son whom they murdered lives, and has become their Lord. Nothing is more appalling to criminals than to be confronted with their victim,—living and reigning. Hence the agony of Joseph's faithless brothers when they discovered that Joseph was their judge. Herod beheaded the Baptist in the intemperate excitement of a licentious feast, that he might keep before his nobles the word which he had rashly pledged to a fair, false woman : but Herod was not done with John when John's body, tenderly buried by his disciples, lay silent in the grave. Many times by night and day the king saw that gory head again lying on the charger—it would not go out of his sight. The creaking of a door, or the sighing of the wind among the trees, seemed the footfall of the Baptist stalking forth to reprove him. When an attendant reported to Herod the miracles of Christ, reporting at the same time that some took Jesus of Nazareth for Elias, and some for another prophet, he had his own opinion on the point ; he knew better, and

* What wise one of this world,—what human reason would have conceived, under the cross, that this man suspended between two malefactors, and despised by all, would one day receive the worship of the whole world ? This is the Lord's doing, and it is marvellous in our eyes.—*Heubner in Lange.*

in a whisper, with pale face, and starting eye-balls, and trembling limbs, he said to his informant,—"It is John the Baptist whom I beheaded" (Mark vi. 14).

It is a fearful thing for his murderers to fall into the hands of this *living God*. It is a fearful thing to see him whom you have crucified afresh coming in the clouds to judge the world in righteousness.

Further expanding this conception regarding the chief corner stone, the Lord transfers from another scripture (Isa. viii. 14, 15), the prophecy spoken of old on this very point,—"And whosoever shall fall on this stone shall be broken; but on whomsoever it shall fall, it will grind him to powder." We seem to mark here a change in the character of Jesus. Sterner and more stern he becomes, as in his prophetic office he approaches the subject of his own kingly judgment. His eyes pierce these hypocrites, and they quail before him. As his witnessing approaches its close, he draws the two-edged sword from its sheath and holds it before the time over the naked heads of his enemies, if so be they may even yet fear and sin not. For his own holy purposes he lays aside for a moment his gentleness, and appears as the Lion of the tribe of Judah. The last days of the Mediator's ministry on earth are now running: it must now be decided whether his own will receive or reject him. The leaders of Israel stood before him, with all their crooked purposes revealed to his eye; the plot was ripening to take his life away. Laying aside the style of a meek Beseecher, he assumes the aspect of a just Avenger; already we seem to see the wrath of the Lamb gathering on his brow. Kiss the Son, lest he be angry; as yet, his wrath is kindled but a little; in that day, it will burn like fire. Why has it been kindled a little before the time? Mercy has lighted this premonitory fire. This terror of the Lord, like all the others that he sends in the day of salvation, is employed as the means of persuading men. He not only receives all who come at his invitation, but sends out foreshadowings of judgment to drive from their unbelief those who refuse to yield to gentler means. Many of the forgiven, on earth and in heaven, are ready to tell that after they had long resisted his tender invitations, they were overcome at last by gracious terrors launched against them by a loving Saviour.

The Jews were familiar with these ideas connected with the corner stone. The prophecy in the aspect of a promise they readily understood, but here the other and opposite side of it also is displayed.

The picture—for it is by itself a short parable—represents a great stone at rest. In Alpine valleys, close by the root of rent, rugged, precipitous mountains, you may often see a rock of vast dimensions lying on the plain. In magnitude, it is itself a little hill; and yet it is only a stone that has fallen from the neighbouring mountain. Suppose a band of living men should rush with all their might against that stone, they would be broken and it would not be moved. If they retire and repeat the onset, the rock lies still in majestic repose, while their feeble limbs are mangled on its sides, and their life-blood sinks into the soil at its base.

The next part of the conception, which the imagination can easily form at will, is precisely the reverse of the first. The rock rises now into mid-heaven, hovers over the assailants for a while, and then falls upon their heads. Here, as in the other case, the human adversaries of this rock are destroyed, but their destruction is wholly different in degree and kind. In the first case, they were broken;

in the second, they are grinded to powder.* The words in the original are very specific, and the translation is remarkably accurate. The term employed to indicate the injury which men inflict upon themselves when they resist the Redeemer in the day of grace, conveys the idea of the crushing which takes place when a man strikes swiftly with all his force against a great immoveable rock; the term which indicates the overwhelming of Christ's enemies by his own power put forth in the day of judgment, conveys the idea of the crushing which takes place when a great rock falls from a height upon a living man. The one calamity is great in proportion to the weight and impetus of a man; the other calamity is great in proportion to the weight and impetus of a falling rock. Both the rejection of Christ by the unbelieving in the time of grace, and the rejection of the unbelieving by Christ when he comes for judgment, are bruisings; but the second is to the first, as the power of a great rock is to the power of a man. The first bruising, caused by a man's unbelieving opposition to Christ under the Gospel, may be cured; but the grinding accomplished by the wrath of the Judge when the day of grace is done can never be healed. There remaineth no more sacrifice for sin.

There are only two ways. This stone lies across our path from edge to edge. It is not possible to be neutral, so as to be neither for Christ nor against him: we must either accept or reject the Son of God. In the prophecy to which the text refers (Isa. viii. 14, 15,) it is intimated that "He shall be for a sanctuary, but for a stone of

---

* The expression is chosen with reference to the mysterious stone in Daniel ii. 34, 35, which grinds to powder the image of the monarchies; that is, to Christ who unfolds his life in the kingdom of God and grinds the kingdom of this world to powder.—*Lange.*

stumbling." The mighty one stands on our life path, and we cannot pass without coming into contact with him. If we flee to him for refuge, he is the sanctuary in which we shall be safe; if we fall on him, in a vain effort to escape, we shall stumble, and fall, and perish.

As a general rule, it is in the present life that he bears the weight of sinners striking against him; and in the life to come that those who rejected him here, must bear the weight of his judgment.

But some do not relish this doctrine; those who heard it directly from the lips of the Lord resented it keenly, and many resent it still when it is taught from the Scriptures. In our day men do not often expressly find fault with the teaching of Jesus as it is recorded by the Evangelists: they prefer to blame the ministers who take up and echo their Master's words. People fondly grasp one side of God's revealed character and use it as a veil to hide the other from themselves. The tenderness of God our Father is employed to blot out from view the wrath of God our righteous Judge. Since the fathers fell asleep, all things continue as they were; where, therefore, is the promise of his coming?

A great rock is lying on the plain: the cultivators have ploughed and the cattle have grazed round it since the flood. Standing beside it, and reverting to its possible history, you give scope to your imagination and ask, What if it had fallen, or should yet fall on me? The bare conception makes you shudder: you are fain to shake off the reverie and compose yourself by the reflection that the rock, fixed to the spot by the laws of nature, cannot move to harm you.

But the Judge of the quick and the dead, though likened to a stone as to crushing power, is not like a stone in its silent still inertia. He liveth and abideth for ever. He bears now,—has borne long. The Almighty God does not move himself to hurt those who are his enemies, any more than the rock which has slept half buried in the valley many thousand years. But he will not thus bear for ever : he will come to judge the world. He will come as the lightning comes : then blessed will all be who shall have put their trust in him, while he waited, through the Gospel, to be gracious. "When the Son of man cometh" the second time, "shall he find faith on the earth ?" He will then *find* only the faith which his first coming generated ; for his second coming *creates* no new faith. Then, it is not "believe in the Lord Jesus Christ and thou shalt be saved ;" but "a fearful looking for of judgment."

The Royal Marriage Feast
(Matthew 22:1-14)

Part 1 — The Wedding Guests

" And Jesus answered, and spake unto them again by parables, and said, The kingdom of
heaven is like unto a certain king, which made a marriage for his son, and sent forth
his servants to call them that were bidden to the wedding: and they would not come.
Again, he sent forth other servants, saying, Tell them which are bidden, Behold, I
have prepared my dinner: my oxen and my fatlings are killed, and all things are
ready: come unto the marriage. But they made light of it, and went their ways, one
to his farm, another to his merchandise: and the remnant took his servants, and entreated them spitefully, and slew them. But when the king heard thereof, he was
wroth: and he sent forth his armies, and destroyed those murderers, and burned up
their city. Then saith he to his servants, The wedding is ready, but they which were
bidden were not worthy. Go ye therefore into the highways, and as many as ye shall
find, bid to the marriage. So those servants went out into the highways, and
gathered together all, as many as they found, both bad and good: and the wedding
was furnished with guests. And when the king came in to see the guests, he saw there
a man which had not on a wedding-garment: And he saith unto him, Friend, how
camest thou in hither not having a wedding-garment? And he was speechless. Then
said the king to the servants, Bind him hand and foot, and take him away, and cast
him into outer darkness; there shall be weeping and gnashing of teeth. For many are
called, but few are chosen."

THIS parable stands connected both historically
and logically with the two which immediately
precede it: especially between the guests
here invited to the feast and the husbandmen
to whom the vineyard was entrusted, there is a close
resemblance in privileges enjoyed, in perversity manifested, and in judgment incurred. Yet the lessons, though
in some respects parallel, are to a great extent distinct;
and though both traverse partially the same ground, the

latter carries the argument some steps further forward than the former parable.

A question has arisen and been largely canvassed, on the relation between the parable and one* recorded in Luke xiv. 16–24 regarding a certain man who made a great supper and bade many. Around this subject much useless and some mischievous debate has accumulated The criticism which assumes that only one discourse on the subject was spoken by Jesus, and that consequently two reports of it differing from each other, cannot be both correct, is impertinent and trifling. It is a pedantic literalism contrary to experience and to common sense. It rests upon the assumption that a public Teacher who taught the common people daily, on the margin of the lake and in private dwellings, in the Temple at Jerusalem and in the sequestered villages around, never repeated with variations in one place the substance of a lesson which he had given in another. Even in the immense profusion of nature every plant is not in all its features different from all others; two individuals or species are found in some respects the same and in some respects different. The two walk together as far as they are going the same way, and separate when each approaches his own peculiar and specific terminus. This combination of identity and difference pervades creation; and you may observe the same characteristics in the scheme of Providence. Two men during a portion of their life-course suffer the same troubles and taste the same joys; but at a certain point in their progress their paths diverge, and they never meet again in a common experience. Look even to the history of any citizen whose life is public, and you will find that by speech, or writing, or act, he prosecutes

*Number 21 of this series, p. 387.

his objects by a mixture of sameness and diversity. His address in the high court of the nation, and his address to his rustic constituents in a distant province, will be found in some features similar and in some different: yet the address in either case will be found an independent and consistent whole, corresponding to the character of the speaker and the circumstances of his audience.

This "Teacher sent from God" was wont in later lessons to walk sometimes over his own former footsteps, as far as that track best suited his purpose, and to diverge into a new path at the point where a diversity in the circumstances demanded a variety in the treatment. This is the method followed both in nature and revelation,—the method both of God and of men.

" A certain king made a marriage for his son," the two important features here are the royal state of the father, and the specific designation of the supper as the nuptial feast of his son. It may be quite true, as some critics say, that because the greatest feasts were usually connected with marriages, the epithet "marriage" was some times applied to any sumptuous banquet ; if in the Scriptures or elsewhere we should find a banquet denominated a marriage feast, while from the circumstances it appeared that no marriage had taken place, we should experience no difficulty in explaining the apparent incongruity. But in this case there is no reason for adopting the exceptional, and the strongest reason for retaining what is confessedly the ordinary and natural signification of the term. The conception of the Redeemer as the bridegroom, and his redeemed people as the bride, lies too deep in Scripture and protrudes too frequently from its surface to leave any doubt concerning the allusion in the parable. The feast, introduced into the story for the sake of its spiritual significance, is the marriage supper of the king's son.

The king sent forth his servants, not on this occasion to give the first invitation, but to warn those who had been previously invited that the time had come, and the preparations been completed. It is obviously assumed, and analogies are not wanting to justify the assumption, that those whom the king desired to honour were informed of that desire before the day of the feast, and that another message was sent to each, after everything was ready, requesting his immediate attendance in the palace of the king. This feature of the transaction is not explained or defended in the narrative ; it is silently taken for granted as at least sufficiently common to be well understood.*

This peculiarity of the invitation is important in con- nection with the severity of the punishment which was subsequently inflicted on the recusants. They did not repudiate the invitation when it was first addressed to them. By retaining it, and enjoying the advantage of being accounted the king's guests during the interval, they pledged themselves to attend the marriage festival, and honour their sovereign by their presence. Their abrupt refusal at the eleventh hour, after all was ready to receive them, partook of the nature both of breach of engagement and disloyalty. "They would not come."

---

* I have witnessed a process closely analogous, in a small detached island of the Shetland group in which the message sent was an invitation, not figurative but literal, to come and hear the word of the kingdom. It had been previously intimated to the islanders that a minister of the Gospel from the south would preach to them on the occasion of his visit to the neighbour- ing mainland, as the largest island of the group is styled. When the minister and his friends succeeded at length in crossing the Channel, several children were dispatched as messengers in different directions to inform the people that public worship would immediately begin. In a very short time a con- gregation was assembled consisting of the whole population of the island.

A second message was sent, more specific and more urgent: but the men met the importunate kindness of the king with contemptuous mockery: "they made light of it, and went their ways, one to his farm, another to his merchandise." A portion of them carried their opposition beyond supercilious neglect into blood-thirsty enmity ; "the remnant took his servants and entreated them spitefully and slew them."

"But when the king heard thereof, he was wroth : and he sent forth his armies, and destroyed those murderers, and burned up their city." As far as appears from the narrative, those who affronted the king by neglect, and those who put his messengers to death, received the same punishment. Although the cruelty perpetrated by some of the conspirators was an aggravation of their guilt, the crime for which they suffered was one of which all alike were guilty,—the crime of despising the king's invitation, and pouring contempt upon his authority.

The transaction may have had great political significance. It was a combination among the aristocracy to thwart the king and dictate to nim a line of policy. They meant by their absence in mass to leave him without support, that he might be compelled to court them on their own terms. In such a case only two alternatives are open to the supreme magistrate : he must either submit to the aristocracy and buy them back at their own price, or supersede them by a bold appeal to the common people. Suppose that in this country the Lords should by compact refuse to attend Parliament, for the express purpose of extorting concessions in favour of themselves by bringing the process of legislation to a stand : the sovereign, in that case, must either submit to the terms of the refractory nobles, or by prerogative create a new peerage from the plebean ranks. Such, on a minute scale and in a simple form, was the course adopted by the king in this ancient oriental drama.

He destroyed their city: it was the king's own city, but he loathed it because of the rebellion of its inhabitants. He took no pleasure in its streets and palaces when their moral glory had departed. The loss of so much property was a small loss; the gain for the discipline of unborn generations was unspeakably great. The overthrow of the city in which the rebels dwelt would make children's children shudder at the thought of apostasy. The sacrifice of a material interest in order to afford sanction to moral laws is the highest wisdom of government, both human and divine. This principle was adopted on the largest scale after the first rebellion, when the earth was cursed for man's sake.

The king took his servants into his counsel. They had suffered in his cause, and he will not conceal from them what he is about to do. "Go ye therefore into the highways,"—the public places of resort, as well the city's streets as the roads that traverse the country,—"and as many as ye shall find, bid to the marriage." In the first instance the invitation was limited to the class who had a prescriptive right to appear at court; when these by their perversity had excluded themselves, the king in his sovereignty extended the invitation generally to the common people,—to persons who previously possessed no right of admission, but who obtained the right then and there by the free act of the sovereign.

The servants did as they were instructed. They understood and executed their commission according to its letter: they brought in "bad and good." As they were not instructed to institute an inquiry into the character or social position of the persons whom they should invite, they made no distinction ; they swept the streets to fill the royal halls.

At this point the parable becomes logically complete, and its lesson may be exhibited apart from the addition regarding the wedding garment which immediately follows. It will be more convenient, accordingly, to prosecute the exposition of the earlier portion by itself, and leave the latter portion to be treated afterwards as substantially a separate lesson.

The parable, as far as we have hitherto read it, repeats and extends the warnings previously given regarding the spiritual privileges which the Jews enjoyed and abused, the judgments which had been and still would be poured out upon the nation, and the successful proclamation of the Gospel to the Gentiles, when the natural seed of Abraham should have in rebellious unbelief rejected the offers of their Lord.

The marriage festival made by the king in honour of his son, points manifestly to redemption completed in the incarnation, ministry, death, and resurrection of Christ. Banquets had before this period been provided by the king, and enjoyed by the favoured circle of his guests ; much advantage was possessed by the Jews over the Gentiles in every way, but especially in that to them were committed the oracles of God. But the feast depicted in this parable was the last and best; it was the way of salvation in its completed state. As the king made known his intention before it was carried into effect, and intimated to the guests that they would be summoned as soon as the preparations were complete; so a period of preparation, and promise, and expectation intervened between the incarnation and the sacrifice of Christ. To the Jewish commonwealth the promise was made in the birth of the babe at Bethlehem, and they were invited to be upon the watch for the moment when the kingdom should come in its power.

When the fulness of time had come, the Lord himself undertaking the work as well as assuming the form of a servant, carried to the chosen people the message, " Come, for all things are now ready." His immediate followers and their successors repeated and pressed the invitation. It is worthy of notice that the servants, when they went out with the commission of the king, did not announce the feast as a new thing, then for the first time made known; they spoke of it as that which was promised before, and actually offered them; they summoned those who had previously been fully informed that the feast was provided for their use. These favoured but unthankful people were not taken at their word ; after the first refusal, another and more urgent invitation is sent. The successive reiterated mission of the servants to the class who were orignally invited, may be understood to point to the ministry of the Lord and the seventy until the time of the crucifixion, and the second mission of the apostles after the Pentecost, and under the ministration of the spirit. Both invitations were neglected and rejected by the people to whom they were sent; Christ came unto his own, and his own received him not.

Significant are the differences in the treatment which the message and the messengers received from different classes within the privileged circle of the first invited. We learn here the solemn lesson that though there is much diversity in the degrees of aggravation with which men accompany their rejection of the Saviour, all who do not receive him perish in the same condemnation. At

262 / Parables of Our Lord

first no distinction is made between class and class
of unbelievers; of all, and of all alike it is recorded,
"they would not come." But when the offer became
more pressing and more searching, a difference began to
appear, not as yet the difference between the believing
and the unbelieving, but a difference in the manner of
refusing, and in the degrees of courage or of cowardice
that accompanied the act. The greater number treated
the message lightly, and preferred their own business to
the life eternal which was offered to them in Christ; while
a portion, not content with spurning away the offer, persecuted to the death the ambassadors who bore it. The
fault of those who are first mentioned takes the form of
indolent, frivolous neglect, rather than of active opposition.
They were occupied with many other things, and therefore could not attend to this one; they were bent on prosecuting their own gains, and therefore set no value on
God's favour.*

These two, ungodliness and worldliness, are always
found in company; but it is sometimes difficult to determine which of the two goes first, and draws the other
after it. You seldom meet a man who neglects this great
salvation, and neglects also the gains and the pleasures
of life. Those who forget God follow hard after another lord,
although they may be unable to detect or unwilling to
confess their own idolatry. No man can serve two
masters; but every man practically serves one. It may
not, however, be easy in any given case to discover
whether a man pursues some particular pleasure because

---

* A melancholy interest adheres to the contrast between man's heedlessness of God as expressed in this parable, ἀμελήσαντες, made light of it, did
not care for it ; and God's regard for men as expressed in 1 Peter v. 7, αὐτῷ
μέλει περι ὑμων, he careth for you.

he is determined to abide far from Christ, or is kept far from Christ because his heart is pre-engaged to some worldly lust. In the case which the parable exhibits, this point has not been expressly determined. When the second and more urgent message arrived, demanding their immediate attendance on the king at the marriage of his son, those men departed in an opposite direction, each to his own business; but it remains an open question whether their hearts were first so glued to the farm and the merchandise, that they could not be persuaded to take from these engrossing pursuits as much time as would suffice to attend upon their sovereign; or whether there was first a determination to resist the sovereign's call, and that they then introduced the business as an excuse, and fled to it as a welcome occupation.

It may have been either or both; but in the circumstances I think it was primarily the latter of the two. In the hearts of those men lay a deep design against the authority of the king; but it would have involved serious risk to have flatly refused his reiterated invitation. They had actually incurred a grave responsibility, and they were disposed to lighten it somewhat by interposing a plausible excuse. Troubled, moreover, by the gravity of their step they were fain to seek refuge from reflection by plunging into the ordinary avocations of life. I think it was not an excessive zeal for agriculture and trade that really prevented them from attending on the king that day; but a consciousness of having conclusively offended the king that drove them for relief into agriculture and trade. On the spiritual side of the parable, in like manner, the excessive devotion to business which occupies some men, and leaves not a shred either of their hearts or lives for Christ, may be in many cases not a primary affection.

but the secondary result of another and deeper passion. When Christ has often knocked at the door, and the inhabitant soul within has as often refused to open, there is no longer peace in the dwelling that has been barred against its Lord. He who has rejected the merciful offers of a merciful God, does not afterwards sit at ease; every sound that in moments of solitude falls upon his ear, seems the footstep of an angry God, returning to inflict deserved punishment. When one has distinctly heard the Saviour's call, and deliberately refused to comply with it, he thenceforth experiences a craving for company and employment. He cannot endure silence or solitude. When he stands still, he seems to hear the throbbings of his own conscience terrible as the ticking of the clock in the chamber of death. To be alone is unendurable, because it is to be with God. To escape from this fiery furnace, he hastens to plough in his field or sell in his shop. In such a case, the worldliness, even when it runs to the greatest excess, is not the primary passion, but a secondary refuge,—the trees of the garden among which the fallen would fain hide from the Lord God.

But in some cases the disease may first approach by the other side: love of the world may be the earlier matured and more imperious passion. The farm and the merchandise may become the soul's first and fondest love; and that love possessing all the soul's faculties, may cast or keep out Christ and his redemption. If you suppose those invited guests to have been previously wedded to the idolatry of covetousness, worshipping gain in secret as their god, you can easily comprehend how they should grudge a day taken from traffic in order to honour their king; so in the interpretation of the parable, when riches or pleasures increase, and the possessor sets his heart upon them, he has already obtained his portion, and will not cast it away for Christ; he will mock the messengers who bring the distasteful proposal.

Among the invited guests, however, there is another class who treat the king's servants in another way. The first class made light of the message; the second murdered the messengers. It is intimated that while the bulk of those to whom the Gospel was preached, neglected the offer and busied themselves with earthly gains, some rose against the preachers and persecuted them unto the death. These last, however, seem to have been in point of numbers an inconsiderable minority,—" the remnant entreated them spitefully and slew them."

There were persecutors in the earliest days of the Gospel, and there have been persecutors in every generation since. The Pharisees plotted that they might put Jesus to death: Saul of Tarsus at a later date was their willing tool in a desperate effort to quench the life of the infant Church in the blood of its members. After he was turned, and the mighty stream of his life compelled to flow like a river of water in the opposite direction, a constant succession of cruel men has been kept up in this restless, sin-stained world, whose life-work is to crucify Christ in his members. The unchanged, unrepenting hierarchy of Rome, successor not of Peter the apostle, but of Saul the persecutor, does yet all that it can and dare to treat spitefully and slay those servants of the king who invite them and the world to the marriage-supper of the King's Son.

But the crucifiers of Christ are not all shedders of human blood. Deadly emnity to the truth and its publishers may be manifested where stakes and fagots are out of fashion and inconvenient. The soul of the persecution which the parable represents lies in entreating spitefully the king's messengers, because they loathed the invitation, and were irritated by the urgency wherewith the servants, remembering their sovereign's command, felt themselves constrained to press it on every man they met. In our own day, it does not require extraordinary sagacity to perceive the same spirit in the relish and readiness with which certain classes catch up a cry against any one who, not ashamed of the Gospel of Christ, has discharged his commission in full.

But when you add together both classes of open antagonists,—those who shed the blood of Christians, and those who merely calumniate them, you have only a very small company before you. On the one side I see a little flock,—those who meekly receive Christ ; on the other and opposite side I see also a little flock,—those who loudly proclaim by word and deed, " We will not have this man to reign over us:" but there is a multitude, whom no man can number, in the midst, who neither accept the king's message nor persecute the servants of the king. The character of the company on either extreme is distinctly marked, and easily seen. Those have manifestly closed with Christ's offer, and are accepted through faith ; these, on the other hand, have considered the offer, and proved their rejection of it by killing its bearers. But the multitude in the middle have not taken a decisive part ; they have remained apparently in a state of equilibrium. As yet they have not indeed actually and personally closed with the Redeemer as their own ; but neither on the other hand have they determined and proclaimed that they will not accept him. They have not moved to either side to take a decisive part for or against the Lord.* This feature of

* These three different methods of treating the message were all exhibited

their condition and their history helps to deceive and so to destroy them. If the condition of the world and the law of God were such that all would be safe in the great day who did not blaspheme Christ's name, and mock his Gospel, and put to death his ministers, this multitude in the middle might remain where they are at ease. But this is not the state of the case; life and death for us depend on our knowing and not mistaking the state of the case here.

To all the multitude in the middle the word of a merciful and faithful God proclaims, In order to be saved, it is necessary that you should arise, and turn to the right hand, and join the company there who have gladly welcomed the Son of God as their Saviour; but, correspondingly, in order to be lost, it is not necessary that you should arise from your state of indifference, and join the scoffer's ranks. To be saved you must flee to the refuge; but to be lost, it is enough that you remain where you are.

In the Theocracy, the Hebrew nation were the hereditary nobles. It is said of them in the Scriptures that they are a people near unto God (Ps. cxlviii. 14). They enjoyed a right of entry into the king's presence. Having, in virtue of their birth-right, a perennial invitation to the royal festivals, they needed only a message as a matter of course, demanding their presence when the feast was prepared. The Gospel of grace complete in Christ is obviously the feast to which the house of Israel were in the fulness of time specially summoned. When they refused to come to the banquet, the Provider was displeased,

---

simultaneously at Athens when Paul preached there: "Some mocked, others said, We will hear thee again of this matter. . . . . Howbeit, certain men clave unto him and believed" (Acts xvii. 32–34).

but not put about: the Omniscient knows his way. He never permits his purposes to be thwarted: He makes the wrath of man to praise himself, and the remainder of that wrath he restrains.

In the beginning of human life and of God's moral government on earth, the enemy seemed to triumph. Creation was thrown out of joint; the being made in God's image was defiled by sin. But although the garden of Eden was emptied, God was not left without a witness in the world : sin abounded, but grace did much more abound. In like manner, at a later stage of the divine administration when the favoured vine became barren, another was brought out of Egypt and planted in its stead. When Israel rejected Christ, God rejected Israel, and called another people to be his own. "We have Abraham to our father," said the Jewish leaders to the Baptist when his lessons began to gall them, "We have Abraham to our father," meaning thereby to intimate that they alone were the chosen people, and that failing them God would have no children on the earth. How did John answer this boast? "Think not to say within yourselves, We have Abraham to our father; for I say unto you that God is able of these stones to raise up children unto Abraham" (Matt. iii. 9, 10).

Although those privileged Hebrews rejected him, Christ did not remain a king without subjects, a shepherd without a flock. In the exercise of the same sovereignty through which he chose Abraham at first, he passed over Abraham's degenerate posterity and called another family. This family was Abraham's seed, not by natural genera- tion, but in the regeneration through faith. Of these stones he raised up children to Abraham, when the natural children of the family had through unbelief shut them- selves out. "Go to the highways " Christ commanded his

apostles to begin at Jerusalem indeed, but he did not en-
join,—did not permit them to continue holding out their
hands to a disobedient and gainsaying people; the alternative was embodied in their commission, If the Jews do
not receive you, go to the Gentiles.

It becomes us to stand in awe before these deep things of
God: their fall became our rising. In the channel through
which a running stream is directed upon a mill wheel the
same turning of a valve that shuts the water out of one
course throws it into another, that had previously been
dry; thus the Jews by rejecting the counsel of God shut
themselves out, and at the same moment opened a way
whereby mercy might flow to us who were afar off.

The servants went out and did as they were bidden.
Peter went to the house of Cornelius, and in that lane of
the world's great city found a whole household willing to
follow him to the feast his royal master had prepared.
Soon thereafter Paul and Barnabas, Silas, Titus, Timothy,
and others traversed the continents of Europe and Asia,
bringing multitudes of neglected outcasts into the presence
and the favour of the king.

"They brought in good and bad." This is a cardinal
point in the method of divine mercy, and therefore it is
articulately inserted in the picture. The scene is taken
from life in the world; the conceptions accordingly, and
the phraseology correspond with the circumstances. In
society at large, and in every section of society such as
the rich or the poor, two classes are found distinguished
by their moral character, and in ordinary language designated the good and the bad. The thought and the style
of ordinary life are adopted in the parable, and every reader
understands easily what is meant. Every great community
has its virtuous poor and its vicious poor. The invitations

of the Gospel come to fallen human kind, and to all without respect either of persons or of characters. Apart from Christ and prior to regeneration the distinction between bad and good is only an earthly thing: in God's sight and in prospect of the judgment, there is none good, no not one. There are not two roads from earth to heaven: there is only one gate open, and by it all the saved enter. It is not the man's goodness that recommends him to God's favour: the worst is welcome through the blood of Christ, and the best is rejected if he approach by any other way. Nor does it follow thence that the Judge is indifferent to righteousness; that which the unreconciled offer to him as righteousness is in his sight sin; and the fact of offering it as a ground of justification aggravates the offerer's guilt.

Part 2 — The Wedding Garments

We have here two parables in one. In their union and relations they resemble the two seed-stones which are sometimes found within one fruit, attached to each other, and wrapped in the same envelope, but possessing each its own separate organization, and its own independent germ of life. The parable of the prepared, offered, and rejected feast, and the parable of the wedding garment, although actually united in the Lord's ministry and the evangelic record, are in their own nature distinct, whether you consider the secular scenes delineated or the spiritual lessons which they convey.

When the wedding was furnished with guests the king came in to see them. The representation is in strict accordance with the relations of the parties and the customs of society both in ancient and modern times. When a citizen entertains his equals he must himself be first in the festal hall to welcome the guests as they successively arrive; but when a sovereign invites subjects to his palace he appears among them only when the company have all assembled.

The instant that he entered the festive hall the king saw there a man who had not on a wedding-garment. Although this is the turning point of the parable, it is represented with extreme brevity. The great central facts are recorded with the utmost distinctness, but all the surrounding circumstances are in silence assumed: no explanation is given, and the reason doubtless is that no explanation is needed. Some customs and allusions connected with the scene remain obscure to us, after all that modern research has done to illustrate them, but the lesson which our Lord intended to teach stands relieved in clearest light and sharpest outline, like distant mountain tops when the sun has newly set behind them. Some points regarding which we might desire information are left in the shade, but in as far as the story is necessary to unfold and perpetuate the spiritual lesson, it is accompanied with no doubt and with very little difficulty.

1. The wedding garment was something conspicuous and distinctive. As soon as the king entered the room he detected the single man who wanted it in a great company of guests.

2. It was not a necessary part of a man's clothing, but rather a significant badge of his loyalty. The primary use of the symbol was neither to keep the wearer warm nor to make him elegant, but to manifest his faithfulness.

3. The want of it was, and was understood to be, a decisive mark of disloyalty. The man who came to the feast without a wedding-garment endorsed substantially the act of those who had proudly refused to comply with

the king's invitation.   It was the same heart-disobedience
accompanied by a hypocrisy that would fain commit the
sin and yet escape the consequences.

4. The question whether a wedding-garment was proffered to every guest as he entered, out of the royal store,
is attended with some difficulty.   The preponderance of
probability seems to lie with those who think that these
decorations were freely distributed in the vestibule to every
entrant, in some such way as certain badges are sometimes given to every one of a wedding party amongst ourselves in the present day.   But the point is not of primary
importance.   From what is tacitly assumed in the narrative it may be held as demonstrated alternatively that either
the king gave every guest the necessary garment, or it
was such that every guest, even the poorest, could on the
shortest warning easily obtain it for himself.   Two silences
become the two witnesses out of whose mouths this conclusion is established,—the silence of the king as to the
grounds of his sentence, and the silence of the culprit
when judgment was pronounced.   The judge does not
give any reason why sentence should be executed, and
the criminal does not give any reason why it should not.
On both sides it is confessed and silently assumed that
the guest had not, but might have had, the wedding-garment on.   If there had been any hardship in the case the
king would have vindicated his own procedure, and the
condemned guest would not have remained speechless
when he heard his doom.*

---

* "It should be assumed that the guests were not instantly hurried into the
festal hall, but that an opportunity was afforded to them of changing their
dress.   This, however, is not expressly asserted in the narrative, but may
be gathered from the term εφιμωθη (he was speechless) in ver. 12; and must be
understood on this account also, that, otherwise the sentence in ver. 13 would
stand exposed to the charge of injustice."—*Storr, de parabolis Christi*, p. 113.

From the circumstances in which that motley company was collected and introduced into the palace, we may safely conclude that no kind of clothing, however torn and mean, would have been counted a disqualification. Over the whole surface of the scene is spread the proof that nothing in the character or condition of the attire which a street porter or a field labourer might happen to wear, when he was intercepted on the highway by the king's messengers, and hurried away to the palace without an opportunity of visiting his own home, could possibly have been a ground of exclusion. When such persons in such circumstances were invited to the banquet, assuredly the king was prepared to welcome them, as far as dress was concerned, precisely as his servants had found them. No man forfeited his place at that table on account of any defect in the quality or condition of the clothing which he wore when he unexpectedly met the messengers and was suddenly hurried away to the feast. Thus far, treading on firm ground, we tread surely.

Alike from the facts of the case, from the analogy of others, and from the corresponding spiritual lesson as elsewhere declared in Scripture, we conclude with confidence that the wedding garment was a well understood distinctive badge, expressive generally of loyalty, and specifically constituting and declaring the wearer's fitness for sitting as a guest at the marriage supper of the king's son. In appearance it must have been conspicuous ; but its value may not have been great. It was not the inherent worth of the material but the meaning of the symbol that bulked in the estimation of both the entertainer and his guests. It may from analagous cases be shown to be probable that a loyal heart could have easily extemporized the appropriate symbol out of any material that lay next at hand. Where there is a will there is a way. Italian patriots at the crisis of their conflict with multiform oppression, and while the strong yoke of the despot was still upon their necks, contrived to display their darling tricolor by a seemingly accidental arrangement of red, white, and green among the vegetables which they exhibited in the market or carried to their homes. Nay more, the loyalty of a loyal man may in certain circumstances be more emphatically expressed by a rude, extemporaneous symbol, hastily constructed of intractible materials, than by the most elaborate and leisurely products of the needle or the loom. In such cases, the will of the man is everything; the wealth of the man nothing. The meanest rag suddenly thrown across the shoulders, arranged so as unequivocally to express the wearer's faith may be a better evidence of loyalty than the richest silks of the East.*

Let us now endeavour to appreciate and express the spiritual lesson. True to nature on the earthly sphere the parable represents the invitation, the assembling of the guests, and the entrance of the king, as three several and successive acts ; but in the processes of the spiritual kingdom these three operations advance simultaneously. Some are in the act of hearing the invitation,—some are accepting it and going to the feast,—some are sitting at the

---

* A custom connected with funerals, which prevails in some districts of England, if not in all, approaches closely in some of its essential features to that which occupies the most conspicuous place in this parable. A scarf of black silk, large, conspicuous, and expensive, yet constituting no part of the proper garments of the wearer, is given by the person who invites, and worn by every one who accepts the invitation. A single person without the badge in the procession would be instantly detected, and the omission would, in the circumstances, be taken as proof of disrespect.

table under the inspection of the king,—all at the same moment. The process is like the habit of some species of fruit trees, on which flowers, green berries, and ripe fruit may be seen at the same time ; the flowers of this season become the green berries of the next, and the green berries of this season become the ripened fruit of the next ; and thus a constant succession is maintained. In like manner, as the generations pass, all the processes of Christ's kingdom are simultaneously carried forward.

The guests who have come at the call of the servants, and taken their places at the table of the king, are those who hear the Gospel and fall in with its terms,—who adopt Christ's name and enrol themselves among his people,—who hope in his mercy and commemorate his death. Herein they are broadly distinguished from those who made light of the message, and those who persecuted the messengers ; but it is not yet certain whether they are forgiven and renewed. The profession which they have made distinguishes them from those Jews who refused the invitation, and those Gentiles who have not yet heard it ; but among those who thus far comply with the call, another distinction must still be made. That goodly heap must be tossed up and winnowed yet again, that the chaff may be driven before the wind, and only the wheat gathered into the husbandman's garner.

As in the parable, we are not informed what were the shape, size, colour, or material of the wedding garment, but only that it was necessary that every guest should wear it ; so we do not find here any specific doctrinal instruction as to the method of redemption and the decisive characteristics of believers. We learn from the parable that every sinner must simply comply with God's terms in order that he may be saved ; and elsewhere in Scripture we are fully taught what these terms are. An abundant answer to the question, " What must I do to be saved ?" is recorded by the Spirit : the only point regarding it which this parable teaches, is that a sinner must abandon his own method, and fall in with Christ's. The meaning of the man who sat at the feast without a wedding garment seems to have been, " I am my own master, and I shall work my own way to heaven :" the meaning of the men who meekly wore it was, " We are not our own ; we are bought with a price; our righteousnesses are as filthy rags, but the Lord is our righteousness."

Thus the lesson of the parable concentrates itself at last upon a point ; but that point is the turning-point of life or death to men. Is any one disposed to complain that it stakes all upon an opinion ? It does, and why not ? One man's opinion is that his own righteousness, especially when he has gotten time to improve it, may be safely presented in the judgment, and ought to satisfy the judge. Another man counts all his efforts vile, as lacking the vital element of love, and at God's command places his trust wholly in Christ his substitute : the first does deepest dishonour, the second gives highest glory to God. A man's opinion on a trifling subject, may be of trifling import ; but a man's opinion—his mind on how he may be just with God, is the greatest and most pregnant fact in creation. Opinion here is nothing less and nothing else than the attitude of a fallen creature towards his Maker and Judge : one opinion is the alienated heart of a rebel, another is the glad trustfulness of a dear child.

If the head of a Hebrew family, on the dread night of the Exodus, had said within himself, What shall I gain by sprinkling a lamb's blood upon my door-posts ? Or, if a conspicuous mark be necessary, may not the blood of this animal suffice, that was killed for the use of my family in the ordinary way ? If moved by some self-confident speculations regarding the constancy of nature, he had entered through the portals of the twilight into that awful night, he would have perished while his neighbours were preserved : not that a lamb's blood had power to save, but because this man refused to take God's way of being saved, and trusted in his own.*

The rest may be expressed in few words. He saw there a man which had not on a wedding garment. Here, first of all, it is not intimated that ordinarily there is only one hypocrite in a large company of professors : it is no part of the Lord's design in this parable to tell us whether the false members of the visible Church are many or few. The single point on which the Master has fixed his eye is the certainty that the false will be detected: the parable does not reveal their numbers, but it assures us that none of them shall escape in the crowd. If the re-presentation had been that a large proportion, say a half or three-fourths of the guests, had been detected at the table without the appropriate symbol of loving loyalty to the king, the omniscience of the visitor, and the certainty of the criminal's doom would not have been so clearly and strongly expressed. That the king's eye instantly

---

* I do not attach much value to the question which has been much can-vassed here, whether the wedding garment specifically signifies Faith or Charity,—whether it points to what the saved get from God, or what they do in his service. To wear the garment at the feast means that the wearer takes God's way of salvation and not his own ; to want it, means that the wanter takes his own way of salvation and not God's. This is the conclusion of the whole matter. If you suppose that the garment means evangelical obedience, you must assume that faith in Christ is the root on which obedience grows ; if, on the other hand, you suppose that the garment means faith in Christ, you must assume that it is a living not a dead faith,—a faith that will work by love and overcome the world.

detects the undecorated guest, although he is only one in a multitude, is the most emphatic warning that could possibly be conveyed to the unbelieving. None who live without Christ in the world shall be permitted to glide into heaven with the crowd in the great day. The constancy of nature is sometimes wielded as a weapon of assault against revealed religion : it will one day strike a heavy blow on the other side. When a mixture of wheat and chaff is thrown up in the wind, the solid grains drop down on the spot, and the light chaff is driven away. You never expect, in such a case, that to please some fancy of yours, the solid grain will fly away on the wings of the blast, and the chaff drop down at your feet. The constancy of nature prevents. Well; by a law as constant and changeless—a law of the same God, reigning over the world of spirit, "the wicked is driven away in his wickedness, but the righteous hath hope in his death" (Prov. xiv. 32).

He was speechless. The judgment will be so conducted that the condemned will be compelled to own the justice of their sentence. Conscience, brought again into contact with God, will be awakened and restored to the exercise of its functions; like a mirror it will receive and repeat the decree of the Judge. Persecutors were wont to gag their victims while they burnt them; it was found necessary to put iron on the tongues of the witnesses, to make them silent while they suffered. No such clumsy device is needed in the assize which the righteous God will hold upon the world. Conscience swelling within will stifle the complaint of the guilty. The courage of the despiser will fail : the last poor comfort of the blasphemer, to hurl against the judgment seat the last despairing, defiant word, will be taken away. The history of the fact written by divine prescience before the time, makes no mention of what the condemned will say. The record simply runs, "These shall go away into everlasting punishment."

" Outer darkness:" tell us in detail what the condition the outcast will be, and what will be the constituents of their suffering ? We cannot. Rome has impiously traded upon this weakness of humanity. She has parcelled out her purgatory, as we delineate this upper world on a map. This is the machinery whereby she is enabled to traffic in the souls of men. No ; that condition lies in outer darkness ; I cannot see through the veil, and tell the specific sufferings that lie beneath it. My Lord has told me that it is in outer darkness ; but he has covered it from my sight. He hath done all things well. He often warns us that the wicked shall be cast away; but he never tells us the particulars of their torments. For teaching about this terror let me listen to his word; for safety from it, let me hide in his bosom.

Introduction: Ten Virgins and Entrusted Talents
(Matthew 25:1-30)

BOTH historically and logically the two parables, of the ten virgins and of the talents, are connected and constitute a group: in place they are contiguous, and in nature they are reciprocally complements of each other, making together a complete whole. De Valenti has by a happy generalization placed their relations in an interesting and instructive light. He points out that there are two kinds of almost-Christians, the bustling labourers, and the mystic dreamers. One class tries to live on works without faith, and the other on faith without works. From opposite causes both efforts fail. The parable of the ten virgins addresses its warning to the Almost-Christianity which is all body with no spirit; and the parable of the talents addresses its warning to the Almost-Christianity which is all spirit with no body.

These constitute a pair; or rather they are the right and left sides of one living lesson. Both represent the character and condition of the Church and its members, while they wait for the coming of the Lord; both apply decisive tests to a seemly profession, and thereby separate between the true and the false: but they differ in that the first searches the heart, and the second examines the life. The first test detects the want of secret faith; the second the want of active obedience. The parable of the ten virgins prepares and throws into the mass of Christian profession a solvent which serves to determine whether and where there is life *in* the Lord ; the parable of the entrusted talents prepares and throws into the mass of Christian profession a solvent which serves to determine whether and where there is life *for* the Lord.

These two,—the inward grace of faith and the outward life of obedience, constitute the two sides,—the right and left of the new man. To that new man as a whole both parables alike refer ; but the one touches him for testing on the right side, and the other on the left. The first tests his works by his faith, and the second tests his faith by his works. The first goes directly to the root and inquires whether the tree is good or bad; thus determining what the character of the fruit must be ; the second goes first to the fruit, and by its sweetness or bitterness ascertains the character of the tree. The parable of the ten virgins speaketh on this wise,—If there be true faith in the heart, there will be active obedience in the life: the parable of the talents speaketh on this wise,—If there be active obedience in the life, there must be a root of faith unseen whereon that good fruit grows.

The Ten Virgins
(Matthew 25:1-12)

" Then shall the kingdom of heaven be likened unto ten virgins, which took their lamps,
and went forth to meet the bridegroom.   And five of them were wise, and five were
foolish.   They that were foolish took their lamps, and took no oil with them: but the
wise took oil in their vessels with their lamps.   While the bridegroom tarried, they all
slumbered and slept.   And at midnight there was a cry made, Behold, the bridegroom
cometh; go ye out to meet him.   Then all those virgins arose, and trimmed their
lamps.   And the foolish said unto the wise, Give us of your oil; for our lamps are
gone out.   But the wise answered, saying, Not so; lest there be not enough for us and
you: but go ye rather to them that sell, and buy for yourselves.   And while they went
to buy, the bridegroom came; and they that were ready went in with him to the marriage: and the door was shut.   Afterward came also the other virgins, saying, Lord,
Lord, open to us.   But he answered and said, Verily I say unto you, I know
you not."

HERE is one of the larger and grander pictures
in this gallery of various glory.   It is sublime
in its ample outline, and exquisitely tender in
its details.   It is charged with many precious
lessons, which flow freely at the gentlest touch; and it is
cruel to put it to the torture to compel it to give meanings which it never received from its author.

The painful search for precisely identical customs in
eastern countries and ancient times is here, for the most
part, unnecessary and unprofitable.   The usages incidentally photographed in such a parable as this are indeed
true sections of the place and the time, but others, agree-
ing in general character though differing in detail, might
have been substituted in perfect consistency with the
circumstances.   There is some elasticity even in Oriental

manners. It is not probable that all marriages were conducted on precisely the same plan. There might, for aught I know, be a difference between a wedding among the rich and a wedding among the poor, and another difference between the method of celebrating a marriage in the city and the country,—in Galilee and Judea. In examining analogous cases, I would look for similarity of style rather than identity of individual features. Looking on the parable of the ten virgins as a grand original, I don't trouble myself with the work of hunting for corroboration of its truth or explanations of its meaning in the form of identical observances recorded in other books.

The more important portion of the nuptial ceremonies were performed at night. They consisted in a great measure of processions along the road and festivals within the dwelling. The out-door part of the pageant is of course conducted by torch-light. A small cup, filled with rags and resin, is affixed to a rod, that it may be held aloft. At the proper time the rags are lighted, and the flame is fed from time to time by pouring oil into the cup. Each processionist carries such a lamp, and the many separate lights dancing and crossing each other, and changing places as the bearers advance on the undulating and tortuous path, impart great liveliness to the joyful nocturnal scene.

From the nature of the case there must be two successive processions, one in which the bridegroom with his friends goes for the bride to her father's house, and another in which bride and bridegroom, together with the friends of both families, march to the future home of the married pair. There was more or less of ceremonial and feasting in either mansion. It is not certainly known, and the knowledge would not be important although it were obtained, whether the principal feast was held in the home of the bride's father or in that of the bridegroom. It is probable that the practice in this matter varied according to the wealth of the parties and the capacities of the several mansions. In one case the father of the bride, and in another the bridegroom, might possess the more commodious dwelling, and be more able, in virtue of ampler resources, to entertain the company. I am not aware that there is any ascertained law or habit of the places and times demanding that the principal feast should be always given by the father or by the bridegroom.

In this case there is nothing in the narrative that determines with certainty whether the bridegroom, when the ten virgins waited for him, was on his way for the bride to her father's house or with her to his own. On the whole, the balance of probability inclines to the side of those who think that this is the procession coming for the bride rather than the procession returning with her. The particular expression, "The bridegroom cometh," among other circumstances, points in this direction. Lange's conception commends itself as probable that the virgins are in some sense representatives of the bride, that they go forth to meet the bridegroom, that he has come from afar, and that some unexpected delays have occurred on the journey.

The house whose door was shut ere the foolish five came up was obviously the house in which the grand marriage festival was held: to be shut out of that house was to be shut out from the marriage.

When the curtain rises and the scene is first displayed, we behold ten young women, adorned according to the fashion of the time, lingering in a group by the wayside at night in the warm climate of Palestine.

They may have been the young companions of the bride, a selected ten, specially invited to meet the bridegroom on the way, and enter with him into the festal hall,—a group in character and constituents closely corresponding to the bridesmaids at our marriage feasts,— or they may have been the daughters of neighbouring families, sent by their parents, or going of their own accord, in compliance with the custom of the place, to offer a tribute of respect and affection to the bride and bridegroom on their marriage-day.

This feature of the scene, although in itself subordinate and incidental, derives great importance from the subsequent development of the parable: it becomes the hinge on which the lesson turns. From the circumstance that a portion of the company neither came with the bridegroom nor waited in the house for his arrival, but went out to meet him, all the tender and solemn teaching of this parable has sprung.*

---

* The closest analogue that I know of the fact which plays so great a part in the structure of this scriptural lesson may be found in a custom which prevails at funerals in the rural districts of Scotland. When the distance between the house of the deceased and the cemetery is considerable, a common, perhaps I should say a uniform, practice is, that those friends of the mourning family who reside in the neighbourhood of the burying place assemble in a group at a convenient turning of the road, and wait till the funeral procession reaches the spot; they then silently fall into their places and follow the corpse to the grave. I like the analogy none the less that it is taken, not from a time of mirth, but from a time of weeping. The two cases coincide in all their features except one. In either example we have an occasion of absorbing interest to one family, and the sympathy of neighbours expressed by means of large assemblies and public processions. In a minor but characteristic feature there is an exact coincidence,—a portion of the sympathizing neighbours wait for the main body at a point on the path and fall into the line of march from that spot to the terminus. That the one is a joyful and the other a mournful group enhances rather than diminishes the value of the comparison.

Waiting long without employment, the group of maidens would stand, and sit, and recline by turns. Each holds a tiny torch in her hand, or has laid it on the ground by her side. As the night wears on, the conversation that had at first been animated, gradually dies away, and one by one the wearied damsels drop over into snatches of slumber. Before midnight they have all sunk into a continuous sleep. At midnight a cry arose, apparently from some more wakeful watcher in the neighbourhood, "Behold the Bridegroom cometh; go ye out to meet him." At this alarm the whole band awake simultaneously and spring to their feet. Each maiden hastily snatches up her torch; not one of them burns brightly now; some are flickering low, and some are altogether extinguished. In a moment, all those nimble young hands begin to ply the work of trimming the expired or expiring lamps. All alike are able to touch them skilfully, but the main want with every lamp is a new supply of oil. Some can supply that want at the moment on the spot, while others cannot. Those who had brought from home a supply of oil in separate vessels, found it easy to make the flame of their torches burn up as brightly as ever; but those who had neglected to provide such a supply could not with all their efforts revive the dead or dying light. "Give us," said the five improvident maidens, "give us of your oil, for our lamps are gone out." The more thoughtful, and therefore more fortunate watchers, while they pitied their sisters, were afraid to part with any portion of their own stores, lest they should be left in the same hapless condition ere the procession should close: "Go to them that sell, and buy for yourselves." Alas, this was now the only alternative! Away went those foolish virgins at the dead of night on the hopeless errand of buying oil for immediate use in the shops of the neighbouring town. The folly, however, lay not in this latest act; this was now their only resource. The foolish deed was done in the day time, and before the cry arose, Behold the bridegroom cometh.

As soon as the foolish five had gone, the procession came up, and they that were ready fell into their places. The new accession, each bearing a flaming torch aloft, increased the grandeur of the scene. When the company reached the house, they all entered with the bridegroom, and the door was shut. Some time afterwards the five who had gone away in search of oil, returned and pleaded for admission ; but they pleaded in vain. Within the house the glad festival went forward ; but those who came too late were not admitted.

The story at its close is indebted for its deep pathos, not to anything inherent in itself, but to the sublime lesson which it conveys. The Lord's great parable, like the Lord's great apostle, is " weak and contemptible " in its bodily presence ; but the letters in which it writes its meaning are like his, " weighty and powerful." A few country girls arriving too late for a marriage, and being therefore excluded from the festival, is not in itself a great event : but I know not any words in human language that teach a more piercing lesson than the conclusion of this similitude. The frame is constructed of common materials ; the sublimity lies in the spiritual truth which that frame sustains. This conception, like that of the hen gathering her chickens under her wing, seems so common and so common-place, that we would not have ventured in dignified discourse to employ it; in the hands of Jesus the similitude becomes at once tender and terrible in the highest degree. At his word the world sprang from nothing; we need not be surprised to find that under his touch small things become great.

I think no symbolic character should be attributed to the virgins, as such, in the interpretation of the parable; it is when they take their lamps and go forth to meet the bridegroom that they first acquire a spiritual significance. The whole group represent that portion of any community who hear the Gospel, accept its terms, and profess to be the disciples of Christ. The sincerity and depth of their profession will be tested afterwards; but in the meantime, both in their own opinion and that of their neighbours, they are all alike Christians. The structure of the parable required virgins in this place, in order that the picture might be true to nature; in the customs apparently of all times and all countries, this position at a marriage feast is assigned to young unmarried women. The ancient practice of the East is, in its essential features, reproduced among ourselves from day to day in the troop of virgins, dressed in white, who attend the bride on her bridal day. I cannot acquiesce in the view of those who see in the special condition of these watchers a symbol of the purity which becomes the followers of Christ, for I find, as I read onward in the parable, that while the ten were in respect to condition all equal, in as far as they represent spiritual relations, five are symbols of sincerity, and five are symbols of deceit. The condition of virgins which was common to all, cannot, without complete confusion of ideas, be made, within the compass of the same allegory, to signify both the true and the false. From the procession of virgins, therefore, I obtain no more than I would have obtained from a procession of men or matrons, if the habits of society had permitted such a representation to have been made.*

They took their lamps and went forth to meet the bridegroom; this represents an open, intelligent, and seemly profession of faith in Christ. As all the lamps burned at first with equal brightness, and no suspicion of a defect occurred either to the wise or the unwise, we learn that the profession which never had life may appear so well favoured for a time, that neither the false professor nor his converted neighbour may be aware of its shallowness.

"To meet the bridegroom;" the parable and the discourse which precedes it, bear upon Christ's second coming, and the attitude, which becomes his disciples in prospect of that decisive event. They who have been washed in his blood love his appearing.

No difference between class and class was as yet manifest; but already the causes which subsequently wrought the separation had begun to operate in secret, and here accordingly they are recorded by the Lord; "five of them were wise, and five of them were foolish." I stand in awe of this dividing word. While the whole band take part in the loyal exodus, and all seem equal in zeal and love, the Searcher of hearts already perceives and pronounces that some of them are wise unto salvation, and some are so foolish that they are throwing away their souls. That same Lord looks on the ten thousand times ten thousand who in our times go out to meet the bridegroom. There is not a more grand or a more beautiful spectacle on earth than a great assembly reverently

---

* Lange's view on this point seems sound and consistent; while both Olshausen and Stier endeavour with much pain but little fruit, to prove that the foolish represent true but defective disciples. "One part of the Church is living, while the other lives only *in* appearance, because it lives only *to* appearance."—*Lange.*

worshipping God together.   No line visible to human eye divides into two parts the goodly company; yet the goodly company is divided into two parts.   The Lord reads our character, and marks our place.   The Lord knoweth them that are his, and them also that are not his, in every assembly of worshippers.

The distinguishing feature is now specifically set down, —the wise carried each a separate vessel containing a supply of oil, that they might keep the flame of their lamps alive, however long the bridegroom might tarry: the foolish, satisfied that their lamps were burning at the moment, laid in no supply for future need.   This is the turning-point of the parable, and in the light of subsequent events its spiritual import may be determined with precision and certainty.   The oil in the lamp, and the flame which it sustained, indicate a seemly Christian profession; this the virgins all possessed, and all alike.   The quality that tested and divided them, lay not in the burning lamps but in the supply vessels.   The oil, whether employed to anoint a person or to feed a flame, represents, in Old Testament typology, the Holy Spirit.   That which the wise virgins carried in their vessels, as distinguished from that which burned in their lamps, points to the Spirit as a spirit of grace and supplication dwelling in a believer's heart.   All experienced convictions, and made profession, as is indicated by the lamps lighted and borne aloft; but some had nothing more than convictions and professions, while others had passed from death unto life and had gotten their life, through the Spirit's ministry, "hid with Christ in God." This will more fully appear as we proceed stage by stage with the interpretation.

"The bridegroom tarried."   For a special purpose, the Lord represents that the bridegroom lingered till a much later hour than that at which the virgins expected him. The disciples, during their Master's ministry and long afterwards, cherished a belief that the coming of the Lord and the end of the world would take place in their own generation. This expectation was, in its literal sense, incorrect; but it could not be corrected by an explicit announcement that for more than a thousand years all things should continue as they were; for such an intimation would have destroyed the expectant watchfulness which in the circumstances was salutary and even necessary. By that watchfulness the Christians of the immediately succeeding generation escaped the disasters which befell the Jews at the destruction of Jerusalem, and by it believers in subsequent times were kept more loose to the world and more close to Christ. In this parable, however, and elsewhere in the Scriptures, prophecies are recorded, which events subsequently explained,—prophecies which showed the Christians of a later age that while their Lord desires to keep them in an expectant attitude through all generations, his intention from the beginning was to permit a long period to intervene between his ascension and his return. The preparation which Christ desires and true Christians attain, pertains more to the inner spirit than to the anticipation of the external advent.

While the bridegroom tarried, they all slumbered and slept. At this point many interpreters endeavour to grasp a lesson regarding the tendency of even true disciples to slumber sinfully at their post, like their worldly neighbours. The lesson is in itself good, and comes readily to hand, but it is not taught in this text. Calvin has correctly conceived and clearly expressed the meaning of the sleep that oppressed the waiting virgins; it intimates the necessity that lies on all of going down into the ordinary affairs of this life.   Disciples in the body cannot be occupied always and only with the expectation of their Lord's appearing.   Sleep and food, family and business, make demands on them as well as on others,—demands which they cannot and should not resist.   If the coming of the bridegroom be delayed till midnight, the virgins must slumber; this is not a special weakness of individuals, it is the common necessity of nature.   So, when life is lengthened in the body, we must attend to the affairs of this world.

The coming of the Son of man may surprise one at his farm and another at his merchandise, but it does not follow, on that account, that it will surprise them unprepared. Now and then in the history of the Church a Christian has been found dead in his closet and on his knees.   A few years ago, in a rural district of Scotland, an elder who was leading the devotions of a district prayer-meeting suddenly ceased to speak,—ceased in the middle of a sentence, in the middle of a prayer.   The worshippers opened their eyes, and observed that his head and breast leant heavily on the desk; they approached and found him dead. At the moment when the bridegroom came this watcher was wide awake, standing on tiptoe, and straining forward to catch the first glimpse of the glory that should herald his approach.   When the bridegroom came this watcher went out to meet him, and went in with him to the feast: safe and happy he, but not he only.

On the other side we hear sometimes of a merchant who died in his counting-house, his ledger, not the Bible, the last book he had read; of a miner killed in an instant by an explosion while he was picking coals in the bowels of the earth; of a soldier falling on a battle-field, while his right hand raised the sword to strike a foe; these were all slumbering and off guard when the bridegroom came What of them? were they all shut out? Nay, verily Some of them were shut out, and some were let in, according as they were carnal or spiritual when the decisive moment came. The new creature in Christ, who is surprised amid the toils of his daily calling, goes as safely into rest as his brother of the same family who is summoned over in the very act of prayer. The five wise virgins were stretched on the ground asleep, with their lamp fires dead or dying, when the cry arose, Behold the bridegroom cometh, and yet there was no surprise, and no damage. Although they were only awakened by his coming, they were ready to meet him when he came, and to enter with him into his rest.

When the cry was heard all those virgins arose and trimmed their lamps. When life is closing behind, and eternity opening before us, we are all aroused. Every one who has a lamp hastens then to examine its condition and stimulate its flame: all who have borne Christ's name search themselves to see whether they are ready for his presence. There is no visible distinction at this stage between those who have only a name that they live, and those who have attained also the new nature: all bestir themselves to examine the ground of their hope, and the state of their preparation.

At this point the decisive difference which existed in secret long before emerges into view. The foolish virgins, having no oil in separate vessels, could not keep the flame of their lamps any longer alive. Both classes had a profession; the formalists had a profession and nothing more. Finding in the hour of their extremity that they had neglected their souls while the day of grace was running, they make a piteous appeal to believing neighbours for

help. "Give us of your oil, for our lamps are gone out"
How true to nature is this picture! He who draws it
knows "what is in man." How fondly the empty, in such
a crisis, lean on the full. Alas, even the full is but a little
vessel filled by Christ. That vessel is not a spring; this
saved sinner is not a saviour of sinners. He has gotten from
his Lord all that himself needs; but he cannot supply a
neighbour's want. Brother, if the call come to you while
you are not in Christ reconciled and renewed, though all the
saints in heaven and earth stood weeping at your bedside
they could not save you. If you neglect the Son of God
while he stands at the door and knocks, in vain will you apply to a godly neighbour, after the day of grace is done.

Taking into view generally the intimate relations which
subsisted among that group of maidens, and in particular
the unselfish tenderness which must have characterized
the wiser five, we should expect to learn that they had
generously resolved, at all hazards, to share their oil to
the last drop with their unfortunate companions. But
this, though consonant with nature in the external body
of the parable, would have been incongruous with the
spiritual truth which the parable has been framed to convey. In the structure of the parable provision is made
for defining sharply the spiritual lesson, even at the expense of some measure of harshness left on one feature of
the story. True Christians cannot impart a share of the
grace that dwells in their own hearts to deluded formalists in their departing hour. On the spiritual side such
a distinction cannot be made, and therefore the Master
represents the wise virgins as distinctly and peremptorily
refusing to share their store of oil with their improvident
companions.*

* They turn themselves to the wise. whom, perhaps, they had lately

"Go to them that sell, and buy for yourselves." The advice was the best that in the circumstances could be given. The mention of "them that sell" calls up all the scene of the preceding day. Oil was plentiful in the town; the five wise virgins having gone by daylight to the stores with their vessels, had experienced no difficulty in obtaining a supply. The same method was open to the rest: they failed to secure a store in the daytime, and then they tried in vain to make good the deficiency at midnight, after the merchants had retired to rest. This feature of the parable intimates that those who are found destitute at the coming of the Lord, enjoyed their day and their opportunity, but neglected them: they allowed the day of mercy to run out, and cried frantically for mercy after the merciful Saviour had wearied waiting and gone away.

While the foolish virgins are absent on this errand, the bridegroom comes up. They that are ready go in with him to the wedding, and the door is shut. Christ calls away his own at some midnight hour when they are off their guard; but though surprised, they are not hurt. The five wise virgins were asleep when the approach of the bridegroom was announced, and yet they were ready to meet him. Their safety resulted not from their fluttering activity at that moment in the trimming of the lamps, but from their wise foresight on the preceding

---

laughed at, with the prayer: "Give us of your oil, for our lamps are gone out." They betake themselves, if they are Catholics, to the dead saints, if they are Protestants, to the living, whom they have been accustomed to revere as their guides on account of their wisdom and grace, and plead, Help us, comfort us, pray for us, that we may be brought into a state of grace. In vain. They answer: Not so, lest there be not enough for us and you. What you desire is impossible. None of us has any surplus merit out of which he could give a portion to another.—*Arndt*, ii. 177.

day. The salvation of a soul depends not on frightened earnestness in the moment of departure, but on faith's calm closing with Christ, before the moment of departure comes. In the vessels of the wise there was store of oil, and it was easy for them at any time or place to refresh the fading fire of the torches which they bore. Deep in the hearts of those disciples dwelt the spirit of Christ, and the light of their profession which had shone brightly in a time of ease, burst into greater brightness in the hour of their extremity. An abundant entrance was administered to them,—an entrance into the joy of their Lord. The door was shut! Suffering, sorrowing believers, do you hear the clang of that closing gate! Be of good cheer, disciples; when your Lord and you go in, the door is shut behind you, and nothing shall enter that defileth. Heaven is for the holy, and for them alone; if it were open for all it would not be heaven.

The foolish virgins went away after midnight to seek a supply of oil; but we are not informed whether or not they obtained it. The omission is significant; this word of Jesus gives no encouragement to delay in the matter of the soul's salvation; not a ray of hope is permitted to burst through the gloom that shrouds these hapless wanderers. The sole lesson of the parable is a simple, sublime warning that sinners should close with Christ now, lest they should be left to invoke his name in vain at the hour of their departure. This parable is a voice from an open heaven promising all grace now, but refusing to promise any then.

They came afterwards to the door and cried bitterly for admission, but the Lord answered from within, I know you not. As the omniscient he knew them; he was acquainted with all their ways. He knew them, for they had crucified him afresh by their neglect. But he did not know them, as he knew the poor bashful woman who crept near in the crowd and by her touch drew saving grace from his overflowing heart; he did not know them by feeling their weight, like John's, leaning on his breast.*

After the parable is finished the marrow of its meaning is given in one short sentence by the Lord: "Watch therefore, for ye know neither the day nor the hour wherein the Son of man cometh." Let us take heed here, lest after all the pains we have bestowed on this scripture, we should miss the portion for ourselves with which it is charged. This parable was not spoken for the purpose of kindling an agony of repentance in the hour of death. It describes a sudden call, and an eager upstarting, and a fruitless effort, and a right prayer uttered too late, and a final rejection, and a fearful doom,—but it reveals this dreadful close of a life, in order to show us what we should be and do before the close of life comes on. The end of the foolish five is unveiled in order that we may be wise

---

* The concluding application is well expressed by Arndt:—"Perhaps the breaking heart grasps at the Bible; it has only spikes and nails, but no balm of consolation. Perhaps the dying man calls in those who have the care of souls; the words of comfort slide over the ears, while the Holy Spirit seals none of them upon the heart. Perhaps he partakes of the Holy Supper: ah, the feast is to him not a feast of blessings, but an eating of judgment. Perhaps he prays to the Lord himself: the Lord answers, I know you not.

Oh, it is sad to be so near heaven, and yet to be lost—to be almost saved, and yet altogether lost. Were it not the Lord who speaks here, Jesus Christ, the Life Eternal, the Judge of the living and the dead, our feeling would be mightily to resist the terrible conclusion of this parable, which cuts all and every hope clean away, and leaves not an If or a But behind, nor any other possible interpretation. But he speaks; and before his words every mouth is silent in fear and adoration. He writes into our breast, with a glowing iron pen, the warning word—therefore watch, &c.

Short is life; fleeting is time; quick is death; long is eternity. Therefore what thou desirest to do, do it quickly."—*Gleichnisse.*

unto salvation in the beginning of our days. The light-house reared on a sunken reef flings its lurid glare far through a stormy air and over a stormy sea, not to teach the mariner how to act with vigour when he is among the breakers, but to warn him back, so that he may never fall among the breakers at all. Even so, the end of the lost is revealed in the word of God, not to urge us to utter a very loud cry when the door is shut, but to compel us to enter now while the door is open.

"Behold I stand at the door and knock." His word to-day runs, Soul, soul, open for me: if that tender plea is echoed back from your closed heart in a beseeching Saviour's face to-day, your cry, "Lord, Lord, open to me" will come back to you in empty echoes from a closed heaven.

The foolish five came to the door only a little too late, but it was not a little damage that they suffered thereby. In the matter of fleeing to take refuge in Christ, to be late by a little is the loss of all.

The Entrusted Talents
(Matthew 25:14-30)

" For the kingdom of heaven is as a man travelling into a far country, who called his own servants, and delivered unto them his goods. And unto one he gave five talents, to another two, and to another one; to every man according to his several ability; and straightway took his journey. Then he that had received the five talents went and traded with the same, and made them other five talents. And likewise he that had received two, he also gained other two. But he that had received one went and digged in the earth, and hid his lord's money. After a long time the lord of those servants cometh, and reckoneth with them. And so he that had received five talents came and brought other five talents, saying, Lord, thou deliveredst unto me five talents: behold, I have gained beside them five talents more. His lord said unto him, Well done, thou good and faithful servant; thou hast been faithful over a few things, I will make thee ruler over many things: enter thou into the joy of thy lord. He also that had received two talents came and said, Lord, thou deliveredst unto me two talents: behold, I have gained two other talents beside them. His lord said unto him, Well done, good and faithful servant; thou hast been faithful over a few things, I will make thee ruler over many things: enter thou into the joy of thy lord. Then he which had received the one talent came and said, Lord, I knew thee that thou art an hard man, reaping where thou hast not sown, and gathering where thou hast not strawed: and I was afraid, and went and hid thy talent in the earth: lo, there thou hast that is thine. His lord answered and said unto him, Thou wicked and slothful servant, thou knewest that I reap where I sowed not, and gather where I have not strawed: thou oughtest therefore to have put my money to the exchangers, and then at my coming I should have received mine own with usury. Take therefore the talent from him, and give it unto him which hath ten talents. For unto every one that hath shall be given, and he shall have abundance: but from him that hath not shall be taken away even that which he hath. And cast ye the unprofitable servant into outer darkness : there shall be weeping and gnashing of teeth."

THE owner of a large property has occasion to leave the country for a time and reside in a foreign land. His possessions, consisting of " his own servants" and " his goods," must necessarily be left in the country, and naturally he considers how he may so dispose of them during the interval that they may yield to him the largest profit at his return. Two distinct principles were open to his choice corresponding to the methods of day's-wages and piece-work in modern social economics; he might either confide to his servants generally the management of his estate, and give them wages according to time, or give each a certain amount of capital, to be exclusively at his own disposal, promising to reward him according to his diligence and success. The latter method is obviously the one which contains a spring within itself constantly urging to diligence. With a set of slaves who are ignorant, degraded, and suspicious, this plan would not be practicable, but if the men possess a certain amount of moral principle, self-reliance, and intelligence, it is safest and best.

The master accordingly, counting on the good-will and honesty of his dependants, frankly entrusts each with a certain amount of capital, graduated according to their capacity for business. Nothing is said in the record regarding the terms of the compact, but it is implied that these were clearly understood between the parties. The money was given in order that it might be laid out to the best advantage, primarily for the owner's interest, and secondarily for the due remuneration of the faithful servant. This practice was carried to a great extent among the Romans; the owner of a skilful slave could make a greater profit by giving scope to the man's energies than by confining him forcibly to menial occupation.

It is by no means necessary to determine the precise character of the bond which united the servant to his master in this case. The circumstances of the parable will suit equally the supposition of absolute right on the part of the master and a voluntary contract between him and his servant for a limited time. Whatever may have been the amount of service due to the master at the time of his departure,—whether the whole life and energy of a slave, or a limited quantity of work from a servant,—that service was his property, and he desired to turn it to the best account.

Two of the servants traded with the capital entrusted to their charge and doubled it ere the master returned; one from a morbid dread of his master's severity, coupled with indolence in his personal habits, hid the money in the ground, thereby deliberately sacrificing his master's profit in order that himself might incur no risk. The two who had successfully traded were commended and rewarded; the one who allowed his talent to lie idle was condemned and punished for his unfruitfulness, although no positive dishonesty was laid to his charge.*

We are now ready to proceed with the exposition. The proprietor who went abroad represents Christ at the close of his ministry on earth leaving his disciples and ascending to heaven. His continued presence spiritually with his people is not inconsistent with this representation, for our parable deals with the bodily and the visible. His own servants, whom he called, like the ten virgins who went out to meet the bridegroom, represent the whole number of those who are called by his name and seem to be his disciples. The delivery of the master's goods to these servants intimates that the Lord gives to every member of the visible Church all his faculties and opportunities.

In this distribution different amounts are consigned to

---

* For the relation between the talents and the pounds, see the exposition of the latter parable.—the last of the series.

different persons. Here the representation obviously accords with the fact: of time, of intellect, of health, of learning, of wealth, scarcely any two persons possess a precisely equal portion. There is a clause here generally overlooked by expositors, but which must be intended to express some feature of importance,—" to every one according to his several ability." We can easily understand it as it occurs in the story: the master, at the moment of his departure, graduated his gifts according to the abilities and acquirements of the servants that he might not throw a great responsibility on a weak man, or leave a man of vigour only half employed. What doctrine does this feature represent? Probably that, while all the gifts that a man possesses are bestowed by God, some, such as bodily constitution and mental capacity are conferred by God as governor of the world; while others are subsequently conferred by the Lord Jesus as the king and head of the Church. I am inclined to understand these latter gifts by the goods which the master bestowed on the eve of his departure; these gifts are in some way proportioned to the faculties of the receiver, so that one may not be oppressed and another left with inadequate occupation.

The one who received most and the one who received a medium amount of gifts and opportunities proved both faithful, and both faithful alike. Although the first did absolutely more for Christ and the world than the second, both were equally diligent and faithful according to their means. Examples both of the likeness and the difference occur by hundreds day by day before our eyes. A disciple with greater and a disciple with smaller endowments labour in the Lord's work with equal love, but the amount of fruit is greater where greater gifts and graces have been received and employed. We shall learn soon how the two cases are treated at the master's return, but in the meantime we have observed what the two cases are.

The servant who had received one talent went and digged in the earth, and hid his lord's money. The meaning of his conduct and its result we shall discover more fully when we reach the record of the reckoning ; at present, and in general, we may understand that this man made no effort to serve his lord, but devoted himself exclusively to one aim,—that he might be able to stand at last on the plea that he had at least done his lord no harm.

These three examples are obviously given in order to cover all cases : they represent an indefinite and all but infinite variety in the measure of the gifts.

Two are represented to have been diligent and only one indolent, but no information is thereby given regarding the proportions of mankind in general or within the Church who shall be found faithful in the great day. Two cases were required in order to show that, where the diligence of the workers is equal, the result may, in quantity, be unequal; and a third case was required to show that, besides some who lack the power to do much, there are some who lack the will to do anything at all; the numbers have no other meaning.

Another very important question is suggested here,— What is meant by the representation that the person who possessed only one talent became unfaithful, rather than the person who possessed two, or the person who possessed five ? It is precisely analogous to the representation contained in another parable that one man, and not ten or twenty, came to the marriage-feast without a marriage garment. Most certainly it does not mean that

those who have few talents are more liable to be unfaithful than those who have many ; and yet something
is gained by making the servant who had received one
talent rather than the servant who had received five, the
example of unfaithfulness. It does not mean, If you
have only one talent you will be unfaithful ; but it does
mean, Although you have only one talent, you will be
condemned for unfaithfulness if you do not employ it.
The lesson is much more emphatically given than if the
servant who received five talents had proved unfaithful.
Much of the master's property was entrusted to him : if
he had permitted it to lie waste, and been punished accordingly, it might have been supposed that the essence
of the guilt lay in the largeness of the loss. As it is
faithfulness, without regard to the amount of capital at
stake, that determines the sentence of approval ; so it is
unfaithfulness, without regard to the amount involved,
that determines the sentence of condemnation. He who
has least is bound to serve the Lord with what he has ;
and if he serve the Lord faithfully with little, he will be
honoured and rewarded, while those who had greater
gifts, but less diligence, will be cast out.

Every one possesses some talents. He who has bestowed them expects that we shall diligently improve
them. He has departed, but he desires that we should
act as in his presence. In this respect he is never absent
—" Lo, I am with you alway." Now is the time for laying out our gifts in the Lord's service ; for it will be too
late to begin, in terror, when he comes to judgment.

" After a long time the Lord of those servants cometh
and reckoneth with them " (ver. 19). The time is not
long in the account of the Lord himself: his latest warning to the Church is, " Behold I come quickly ;" and with

him a thousand years are as one day. Nor is the time long to ungodly men; for in such an hour as they think not, the Son of man cometh. At whatever time he comes, he comes too soon for them who would give all the world, if it were theirs, that he should not come at all. But to the true disciples of Christ, especially in times of persecution, the period of his absence has often appeared long: they have often borrowed the unbeliever's cry, " Where is the promise of his coming?" and used it with a new significance. But to saints and sinners, whether they long for his presence or loathe it, he certainly will come at length.

The two who had received from their Lord unequal gifts, and had laid them out with equal faithfulness, give in their account with joy. They are equally approved; and either is rewarded with the fruit of his own diligence.

The case of the unfaithful one, in accordance with the obvious design of the parable, is given with much greater fulness of detail than those of the faithful two. Permitting our comment on this point to mould itself after the proportions of the text, we shall look more narrowly into this man's character and conduct. All the more willingly shall we devote the most of our attention to the darker side of the picture, that the evangelical obedience of the faithful servants may be most distinctly seen in the dark mirror of the opposite unfruitfulness.

In the case of the unprofitable servant, as it emerges in the latter portion of the parable, three points demand our attention separately and successively,—the Reason, the Nature, and the Reward of his unfaithfulness.

1. The reason of his unfaithfulness, as explained by himself, is, " I knew thee that thou art an hard man," &c. The naive confession of this man is a very interesting

feature of the story, and a very precious lesson to us regarding the deep things of God. Through this opening light is thrown at once upon the spring of continued disobedience in human hearts, and upon the nature of the remedy which the ailment needs.

Some persons take much pains to extol a good life at the expense of the mysteries of grace. They know not that they are endeavouring to break the upper links of a chain, while themselves are suspended on the lower. All the value of service rendered by intellectual and moral beings depends on the thoughts of God which they entertain ; and the thoughts which they entertain of God depend on the attitude in which he presents himself to them—that is, upon the revelation of the Father in the person and work of the Son.

Obviously the conception which this man had formed of his master's character, was the direct efficient cause of his unprofitable idleness. The picture, at this point, represents a human heart secretly conscious of guilt, not reconciled through the Gospel, and dreading the wrath of the righteous Judge. When one is at peace with God in the Redeemer, perfect love casteth out fear ; but here, in the absence of this reconciliation, perfect fear casteth out love. Love is the fulfilling of the law ; and without love there can, in God's sight, be no obedience. Thus, by a few links which can neither be obscured nor broken, active obedience is bound to faith in Christ. Where faith in the Mediator is wanting, God, as shown in a guilty conscience, is dreaded as an enemy ; and such fear produces no obedience. You might as well sow stones in your field, and expect them to produce bread.

It is not necessary to examine in detail the continuation of the unfaithful servant's answer. When he had

taken his ground on a sullen plea of not guilty which
threw the blame upon his Lord, it was natural that he
should endeavour to justify himself and fortify his position by specific averments of hard treatment; but the
essence of his answer lies all in his first words, "I knew
thee hard." The meaning cannot be mistaken here.
These words do not make known to us what the master's
character really was: the only thing which they determine is the servant's conception of the master's character.
The servant's conduct is, in point of fact, regulated not
by what the master absolutely is, but by what he is in
the belief and regard of the servant.

The parable represents at once, with rich pictorial
effect and strict logical exactness, the legal relation of
sinful men to a righteous God, apart from the peace that
comes through the Gospel. While you think of the
Judge, recording now your thoughts, words, and actions,
in order to render unto you what you deserve in
the great day, you cannot love him, and you do not like
to retain the knowledge of him in your mind. The Bible
calls him good, and perhaps your lips have pronounced
him good in your prayers and hymns; but what you
really know of him in your heart is his hardness. This
hard measure expected, haunts you like a spectre, and
casts a dark shadow over your path. Whatever your
ears may hear or your lips may speak, you know God
only as the disturber of your joy in life, and the inexorable exactor of impossible penalties at last.

The natural and necessary, as well as actual result of
this knowledge or conception of the master, is the utter
idleness of the servant. Tell a criminal in chains that by
his own hands he must remove yonder mountain into the
sea in the space of one year, on pain of death when the

year is done, and the certain result will be that the wretched man will permit the appointed time to expire without removing a single atom of its mass; but on the other hand, let it be gently intimated to some emancipated slaves that their service in removing earth from that mountain to the sea will please their deliverer, and forthwith they will carry with all their might, their burden meanwhile being their delight, because they have thereby an opportunity of serving the Lord that bought them. Thus the idleness of one servant is explained, and the activity of others.

2. As to its nature, the disobedience was not active but passive; he did not positively injure his master's property; he simply failed to turn it to profitable account. The terror of this servant was too lively to admit of his enjoying a debauch purchased by the treasure which had been placed under his charge. Fear is a powerful motive in certain directions and for certain effects; it makes itself felt in the heart, and leaves its mark on the life of a man. Like frost it has power to arrest the stream of energy, and fix it cold, stiff, montionless; only love can, like the sun of summer, break the chains and set the prisoner free to run his race rejoicing.

The passive character of the servant's fault greatly extends the sphere of the lesson, and increases the weight of its rebuke. If only positive activity in evil had been condemned, a multitude of the unfaithful would have escaped, or at least would have thought themselves exempted from the indictment. The bearers of poisonous fruit constitute a comparatively small class in the vegetable creation; the plants that bear no good fruit are much more numerous. Unfruitfulness includes both those that bear bad fruit and those that bear no fruit. The idleness of the servant who knew his master only as a hard man, reproves all except those who obey the Lord whom they love, and love the Lord whom they obey.

3. The reward of unfaithfulness is, "Take the talent from him and cast him out. In both parts the sentence of condemnation corresponds to its opposite in the reception of those who had been faithful to their trust. These retain their employed gifts; from him the unused talent is taken away. These are received into their master's favour; he is cast out of his master's sight.

It is worthy of remark that the execution of the sentence begins in time, and in its first stages lies within the reach of our observation. The portion of the sentence, moreover, which is inflicted in our sight, comes through the regular operation of law. The disuse of any personal faculty, surely, though gradually, takes the faculty away. Those who explain away the positive doctrines and facts of the Gospel, delight in representing that God does everything by the instrumentality of law. It is superstition, they say, to suppose that he will put forth his hand to arrest the mighty machinery of nature, with a view either to punish your guilt or reward your obedience. Here at least we can meet them on their own ground, and accept their rule. Let any member of the body, or any faculty of the mind lie dormant for a time, and by the very fact, its power is diminished or destroyed. It is a law of life that a talent becomes feeble in proportion as it has been left in idleness. It is not only true in point of fact that when we do not diligently lay out our gifts, the Giver recalls them; it is further true, that he recalls them in our sight by the silent operation of an inexorable law.

To waste life in the hope of getting all made right by

an energetic repentance at the close, is a very foolish and mischievous species of superstition; it is the exercise of a very strong faith, without any promise from God on which it may lean. You seem to expect that God will arrest the operation of his own laws in order to afford you every facility for living in sin. In the Scriptures we read of an interference with the natural laws—the sun standing still—in order that the enemies of the Lord and his people might be destroyed; but you expect a greater miracle; —you expect the Omnipotent to arrest the operation of his own laws, in order that his enemies may prosper now and escape at last. You expect that Jesus will work a miracle not to cast out the unclean spirit, but to maintain him in possession of a human heart. The disuse of the talent takes the talent away; this is the law of the kingdom; and it will not be changed in order to encourage the sinner in his sin.

"For unto every one that hath shall be given," &c. Obviously from the whole circumstances of the case, "to have" in this connection, means to possess and use aright. He who received only one talent was distinguished from him who received five, not by not having, but by not using. The law announced here is that they who employ well what they have, shall retain it all and receive more in addition; whereas they who do not rightly employ what they have, will be deprived of that which they possess but do not use.

Fearing lest I should darken counsel by words without knowledge, I leave the positive penal infliction, which takes effect beyond the precincts of this life, without one word of comment, in the short and solemn words of the Scripture, "Cast ye the unprofitable servant into outer darkness: there shall be weeping and gnashing of teeth"

The sentence " Take it from him," goes before the sentence, " Cast him out." A sinner is given over to himself, before he is given up to judgment. The first prepares the way for the second death; the process is now going on by which the destiny is decided. Now is the accepted time; now either salvation or condemnation is wrought out.

See the process and the path of death; the steps are few and well marked. I knew thee hard, and I hid thy talent; take it from him, and cast him out. The corresponding steps on the other side are, I tasted thy tender mercy, and lovingly laid thy talent out; give the faithful servant more, and lead him into the joy of his Lord.

The stumbling-block at the outset that turned the unfaithful servant aside was his conception of the Lord as a hard master: it is the experience of the master's love that impels the servant forward in the path of duty. When we know God in Christ, we know him reconciled to ourselves. Christ, therefore, is the way; by him we go *in* to the Father for acceptance, and by him we go *out* for needful work upon the world. Without me ye can get nothing from God; "Without me ye can do nothing" for God.

The Seed Growing Secretly
(Mark 4:26-29)

" And he said, So is the kingdom of God, as if a man should cast seed into the ground ;
and should sleep, and rise night and day, and the seed should spring and grow up, he
knoweth not how. For the earth bringeth forth fruit of herself ; first the blade, then
the ear, after that the full corn in the ear. But when the fruit is brought forth, immediately he putteth in the sickle, because the harvest is come."

THIS is the only parable that is peculiar to Mark.
The subjects contained in the fourth chapter
of Mark are obviously the same, in the main,
as those which occupy the thirteenth chapter
of Matthew. The parable of the sower occurs in both at
the beginning ; and at several other parts they coincide.
The parable of the seed growing secretly holds in Mark
the place that the parable of the leaven holds in Matthew.
We might, therefore, expect a close analogy between
these two parables: and accordingly we find in point of
fact that they exhibit the same characteristics of the
kingdom, and convey the same lessons to its subjects.

When a man has cast the seed into prepared ground
at the proper season, he thenceforth leaves it to itself.
He sleeps by night, and attends to other affairs by day,
often looking to it indeed, and oftener thinking of it, but
never touching it till harvest. By its own vitality it grows
secretly, gradually until it arrives at maturity. Man interferes only at the beginning and at the end; in spring
he sows, and in autumn he reaps, but throughout the

interval between these extremes he lets it alone. The point on which the parable concentrates our regard is, that the growth of the plant, from the time of sowing to the time of reaping, proceeds according to its own laws, and in virtue of its own inherent power, neither visible to the owner's eye nor dependent on his hand.

In the interpretation of the parable certain great leading points must first be determined, and then all the rest will be safe and easy.

There are two such points, one at the beginning and one at the end, which are in themselves uncertain; and one in the middle which, being itself determined by circumstances, serves to determine the other two. The question at the beginning is, Who is the sower? And the question at the end, What is the reaping? The point in the centre already fixed, on which the two extremities depend, is the growth of the seed without the aid, and even beyond the cognisance, of the sower.

Look first to the question which meets an inquirer at the outset, Who is the sower? Obviously it has two sides and two only; the sower represents either the Lord himself, or the human ministry that he employs from age to age. Both representations are in themselves true and scriptural; it is by means of other features less ambiguous that we shall be able to determine whether of the two is adopted in this parable. Try first the supposition that the sower is the Lord himself; of him, in that case, it is immediately said that he sleeps, and rises night and day, and that the seed meanwhile springs up, he knows not how. This representation is palpably incongruous with the attributes and character of the Lord. The things that are hidden from us, both in the natural and spiritual growth, are open in his sight. Expressly it is said of Jesus.

" he knew what was in man;" and we learn, from many circumstances in the evangelic history, that he knew the thoughts alike of plotting enemies and of fainting friends. The suggestion made by some that this part of the parable may be understood to represent the Lord's ascension into heaven, after having sown the word in his own ministry, does not satisfy the demands of the case. We cannot, without doing extreme violence to the analogy, find a sense in which the divine Redeemer does not help and does not know the growth of his own grace in believing hearts. The germination and increase of vegetation without the intervention of the sower and beyond his ken, represent a helplessness and an ignorance so definite and complete, that we cannot, on any rule of sober interpretation, apply it to the omniscient and omnipotent Redeemer.

The impossibility of accepting the first suggestion throws us necessarily back on the only other supposition that remains ;—the sower in the parable must represent the earthen vessel to which the ministry of the Gospel has been entrusted,—the human agent employed in the work of the Lord. This will, of course, accord perfectly with the representation in the heart of the parable that he who sows the seed neither helps the growth nor understands its secrets; but does it accord also with the representation, in the end of the parable, that he who in spring sowed the seed, thrusts in his sickle and reaps the ripened harvest? Some, assuming that the reaping means the closing of all accounts in the great day,* conclude that to represent the sowing as the ministry of men is incongruous with the

---

* Dr Trench takes for granted, without a word of proof, or any evidence that he has even considered the question, that the reaping is the consummation of all things, the exclusive prerogative of the Lord.

reaping, which must, as they suppose, be the work of the Lord at his second coming. In this way they become involved between two impossibilities. If the Lord himself is represented as the sower the representation is inconsistent with the middle of the parable, in which it is declared that he neither aids nor understands the growth of the grain; if, on the other hand, men are represented as the sowers, the representation is inconsistent with the end of the parable, in which it is declared that they thrust in the sickle at the close of the dispensation and reap the harvest of the world.

Now in order to escape from this double difficulty it is not necessary to put to the rack either the words or the thoughts of the parable. The path out of the difficulty is broad and straight; it is the path into it that is crooked and narrow.

The question which demands solution here, and which, when solved, will solve all the rest, is, What is meant by thrusting in the sickle and reaping the ripened grain when the harvest has come? Apart from this parable two distinct significations may be attributed to the analogy, both alike true in fact, and both alike adopted in the Scriptures. In some cases the harvest and the reaping point to the end of the world and the awards of the judgment; expressly in the Lord's own interpretation of the parable of the tares, it is said, " The harvest is the end of the world, and the reapers are the angels" (Matt. xiii. 39). But in other cases the reaping of the ripened grain is employed to represent that success in the winning of souls which human ministers of the word may obtain and enjoy. Such is its meaning in Ps. cxxvi. 6, " He that goeth forth and reapeth, bearing precious seed, shall doubtless come again with rejoicing, bringing his sheaves with him." In the same sense it is employed by the Lord (John iv. 35, 36), "Say not ye, There are yet four months, and then cometh harvest? behold I say unto you, Lift up your eyes, and look on the fields; for they are white already unto harvest. And he that reapeth receiveth wages, and gathereth fruit unto life eternal: that both he that soweth and he that reapeth may rejoice together." The same idea is expressed in terms, if possible, still more articulate, in Matt. ix. 37, 38. "The harvest truly is plenteous, but the labourers are few; pray ye therefore the Lord of the harvest, that he will send forth labourers unto his harvest."*

But while the symbol taken from the reaping of ripened grain represents alternately in Scripture, these two distinct though analogous conceptions, it is the latter and not the former which this parable adopts and employs. The reapers are the human ministers of the word, and the reaping is their successful ingathering in conversion here, not the admission of the redeemed into glory at the end of the world.

No other conclusion is compatible, either with the scope of the lesson or the facts of the case. The sower in this story neither helps the seed to grow nor understands how the growth proceeds. The parable is spoken in order to

---

* Bengel's suggestion is ingenious and interesting, but contributes nothing towards the solution. "Sermo concisus. Mittet falce preditos, nam αποσ-τελλεσθαι est viventis cujuspiam." He would understand the phrase "he putteth in the sickle" as a curt form of expression, intended to intimate that he sends out reapers with sickles to reap the grain; fortifying his opinion by the remark that the term "putteth in," (αποστελλει, "sends out,") refers to a living person, and not an inanimate instrument. Countenance for this view might be found in Matt. ix. 37 where εκβαλειν equivalent to αποστελ-λεσθαι is employed to indicate the sending forth of reapers. On the other hand, however, the passage, Rev. xiv. 15, 16, goes decidedly against it; for there both πεμμπειν and βαλλειν, "thrust in" (the sickle) are certainly applied to the instrument itself, and not to the men who wield it.

show that, while men are employed at first to preach the word and at last to gather the fruits in the conversion of their brethren, they can neither perform the converting work nor trace the footsteps of the quickening Spirit in the secrets of a human heart. By this similitude the Lord represents the extent and the limits of human agency in the progress of his kingdom.

Having made our way through the difficulties of the parable, and found the key-note of its interpretation, we turn again to its terms for the sake of observing and applying the practical lessons which it contains.

The sower sows the seed ; the seed is the word ; the hearts of those who hear it are the field. Parents make known the Gospel in their families, ministers in the congregations, teachers in the schools. These sowers lose sight of the seed from the moment that it drops into the ground. It sinks and disappears; they must go away and leave it. They sleep by night,* and attend to other matters by day ; they cannot see how it fares with the Gospel in a neighbour's soul. They cannot put their hand to the work at this stage to help it : the seed must be left to itself in the soil.

At this point the likeness between the natural and the spiritual is exact and obvious. When you have made the Gospel of Christ known to some in whom you are interested, you are precisely in the position of the agriculturist who has committed his seed to the ground. If you think of the matter when you lie down, or when you awake, you discover, perhaps with pain, that you do not

---

* Here, as in the case of the tares, the sleep of the husbandman implies no culpable negligence either in the natural or spiritual sphere. "Sind wir am Tage recht wach ; dann, mögen wir Nachts ruhig schlafen."—
Dräseke, vom Reich G.

know whether the seed is swelling and springing or not : and that though you knew its condition you could not reach it, to stimulate the process. It is out of your hands, and out of your sight. It is not, however, out of mind, when it is out of sight ; and your own helplessness may draw forth a more eager prayer to the Almighty Helper. In this way it is when we are weak that we become strong ; it is when we are made most keenly sensible of our own weakness that we cast our care most fully on the Lord. The law that shuts the sown seed out from us, shuts it in with God. One door closes ; but the closing that hides the seed in its seed-bed from our eyes and separates it from our hands, leaves it open to His sight, and pliant to his power. The moment that the seed is sown, he takes it out of our sight, but then and thereby he brings it into his own. It is away from us, and with God.*

The parable shows, with great perspicuity and certainty, both the extent and the limits of this withdrawal from human cognizance and help. In the main concern the exclusion is complete ; but in some subordinate and incidental matters, it is only partial. As to the power of germination, and the knowledge of it, the sower is entirely shut out from the seed, both in the natural and spiritual departments. But as he may continue his care in nature, with much profit to the seed ; so he may, in a subordinate capacity and in an indirect manner, do much to promote the growth of grace in the heart, after the Word has been addressed to the understanding. The exclusion of a minister, a teacher, a

---

* Like the seed, is the Word himself. He became flesh and dwelt among us ; but he has ascended out of our sight. At the beginning he came into the world ; and at the close he will return ;—a spring and a harvest, but all the space between, he is out of sight.

parent, from knowing and helping the growth of grace after the Gospel has been published, is like the exclusion of the farmer from his seed after it has been committed to the ground. He can help it, and does help it much by his care. He keeps the fences up, that the field may not be trampled by stray cattle: he keeps the drains open and the furrows clear, that water may not stand on the field, but run off as soon as it falls: he gathers off the stones, that they may not crush the seed, and pulls out the weeds that they may not choke it.

In a similar way and with similar profit, ministers and teachers of the word may remove obstructions which would prevent its growth. Not only have we permission to do this: we are bound positively to do it. The parable excludes us indeed from further knowledge or power, after the word is made known, but it excludes as the farmer is excluded from his sown seed. We know the nature and extent of that exclusion. While the lesson relieves us from the responsibility of that which is beyond our power, it lays upon us the responsibility of that which is within our power.

You may have seen a sown field in spring immediately after a great rain-fall; and you may have observed that a large portion of it, on its lower side, was smooth, and run together and caked, bearing all the marks of having been for some days under water. On the higher portions the wheat was springing, but on this portion, sown at the same time, the ground was bare. You examine the matter more minutely and discover that the drains that had been made for carrying off the surplus moisture, had been choked in the operations of the seed-time, and not cleared out again; and that consequently when rain fell heavily, it accumulated on the lower ground;

and having soaked and soured it for several days, had killed the germinating seed beneath the ground. You go to the farmer and ask why he had allowed a large portion of his crop to be lost. Suppose he should say, My work was done, as soon as the seed fell from my hand into the soil ; I can neither make it grow, nor understand how it grows ; it was not in my province that the failure took place, and therefore the failure could not be my fault. No such specimen of hypocrisy is found in the kingdom of nature : no man could hold up his face before his fellow and cover his indolence by such an impudent plea.

We must see to it, that we be not guilty of the same inconsistency in matters of greater moment. A parent or minister or teacher has committed the good seed of the word to the hearts of his young people, with all due solemnity and care ; and thereafter permits them to be steeped in a flood of folly, which he could easily have drained away. The good seed is drowned in that deluge ; but it is the sower's fault. It is true he cannot make it grow by his care ; but he can make it not grow by his carelessness. We cannot do the saving ; but we can do the destroying. Many pains and many prayers are competent to the sower, although he cannot directly control the growth of the seed. When it grows, it grows independently of him ; but when it fails, the failure may in part be due to his unfaithfulness.

Further, when it is said that the earth bringeth forth fruit of herself, the influences of heaven are not excluded, any more than the collateral care of the husbandman. We know how and in what sense the earth brings forth spontaneously, after it has received the seed into its bosom : if the sun were kept from shining, or the rain from falling on it, the earth would produce nothing. It is thus also with grace in the heart : the Spirit ministering the things of Christ is as necessary in the kingdom of grace, as rain and sunshine are in the kingdom of nature.

Surrounding circumstances, morever, tend powerfully to help or to hinder the growth of the new life. The seed grows indeed by its own vitality : the most favourable circumstances that are possible on earth could not produce a harvest of grace without the seed of the Word ; but these circumstances go far instrumentally to help or to hinder the growth and ripening of the seed. The family of which you are a member, either as child or servant,—the Church with which you worship,—the companions with whom you associate,—the tone of the society in which your social life moves on,—the business that occupies your day,—and the amusements that refresh you when you are wearied ;—these and many others affect for good or evil the growth of grace in Christians, as wet or dry, cold or warm seasons, affect the growth of the seed after it has been committed to the ground. Watch and pray ; one of these small points may be the turning-point of your destiny.

The seed grows gradually from stage to stage. Three stages are specified ; first the blade, then the ear, then the full corn in the ear. This does not determine the time occupied in the spiritual process. In this respect there is not uniformity: the spiritual growth from spring to maturity sometimes requires more than one natural season, and sometimes is accomplished in less.

In the first stage of growth, it is not easy to distinguish with certainty between the wheat and common grass ; it is when the ear is formed and filled, that you know at a glance, which is the fruitful and which the fruitless plant.

There is a similar ambiguity, in as far as appearance is concerned, in the earliest outgrowth of convictions from the hearing of the word. Not that there is any uncertainty in the nature of the things: the wheat is wheat, and the grass is grass from the first: but an observer cannot so surely at first determine which is wheat, and which is merely grass.

Thus, many hopeful impressions that appear for a while in the young, die away, and bring forth no fruit; but at later stages, a judgment may be formed with greater confidence. The plant assumes by degrees a more definite form, and a more substantial fulness: the fruits of the Spirit, green at first, but growing gradually more and more mellow, crown the profession of a Christian.

Let us not deceive ourselves, in connection with the acknowledged secresy of the Spirit's work. The growing is an unseen thing; but the grown ripened grain is visible. It is the inner power that is hid; the fruit may be seen by all. There is indeed an invisible Christ, who is already within his people the resurrection and the life; but there is no invisible Christianity. How grace in the heart grows is an inscrutable mystery; when it is grown, it is known and read of all men. Your life, as to its source and supply, is hid with Christ in God: but your life, as to its practical effects, is a city set on a hill. There is a great difference between the light that you get and the light that you give. The Lord in heaven is the light of Christians; but Christians are the light of the world.

The source of the mighty Ganges is secret; and that secret the superstition of the Hindus has converted into a religious mystery. But the Ganges is not a secret unseen thing, as it flows through the plains of India, fertilizing a continent.

" The harvest is come." It is not the end of the world; it is not even the close of a Christian life in the world. There is a ripening and a fruit-bearing while life in the body lasts : there is also a reaping and an enjoying of the harvest by those who sow the seed, or their successors. The announcement, "one soweth and another reapeth," clearly implies that the same one who sows may also to some extent reap. There is part of both : a sower gathers some of the fruit of his labour in his own lifetime; and some of it is gathered by others after he has departed.

Here is a lesson for ministers and teachers. The Lord, who sends them out to sow, expects that they will look and long for fruit, and be disappointed if it does not appear. When the case occurs, as occur it may, in which the sower is not permitted to reap, the delay, although not a ground of despair, should be a source of disappointment : the stroke will be felt painful, if there is life where the stroke falls. The giver of the seed expects that the sower, if he lives to see it ripening, will reap it joyfully. It is like the joy of harvest to see the Lord's work prospering under our own hand. The Master seems to chide the inertness of his servants when he says, "the fields are white already to harvest." If it were their meat, as it was his, to do the Father's will, they would bound more quickly into the field, whenever they saw it whitening.

Some lessons, partly encouraging, partly reproving, which lie in the parable, but have hitherto been either omitted or only incidentally touched in the course of exposition, may be now conveniently enumerated in the close.

1. The work of sowing and the joy of reaping advance simultaneously on the spiritual field. The labour of the

husbandman in the natural sphere is all and only sowing at one season, all and only reaping at another: the seed of the word affords a different experience; in the kingdom of God there is no period of the year when you must not sow, or may not reap. These two processes are in experience very closely linked together. They become alternately and reciprocally cause and effect: if we were not permitted at an early period to reap a little, the work of sowing would proceed languidly or altogether cease; on the other hand if we cease to sow, we shall not long continue to reap. When the workmen are introduced into this circle, it carries them continuously round.

2. In any given spot of the field there may be sowing in spring, and yet no reaping in harvest. If there is no sowing, there will be no reaping; but the converse does not hold good; you cannot say, wherever there has been sowing, it will be followed by a reaping. The seed may be carried away by wild birds, or wither on stony ground, or be choked by thorns. "Watch and pray that ye enter not into temptation."

3. The growth of the sown seed is secret; secret also is its failure. It is quite true, there may be grace in the heart of a neighbour unseen, unsuspected by me; but the heart of my neighbour may be graceless while I am in its earlier stages ignorant of the fact. The gnawing of a worm at the root of one plant is for a time as secret as the healthful growth of another. "Lord, is it I?" I must not too lightly assume either in the natural or the spiritual husbandry, that everything is prospering that is out of sight.

4. Though the sower is helpless after he has cast the seed into the ground, he should not be hopeless; we know that the seed is a living thing, and will grow except

where it is impeded by extraneous obstacles. " The word of God is quick (living) and powerful."

5. In every case the harvest, in one sense, will come; on every spot of all the field there will be a reaping. If one set of ministers do not reap there, another will. Where there is not conversion, there will be condemnation. The regeneration is one harvest; the judgment is another. The angels are not sowers, but they are reapers. Where the men who sowed the seed find nothing to reap during the day of grace, those ministering spirits to whom no seed has been intrusted will be sent with a sickle to cut down and cast away. The first harvest is like the first resurrection; blessed are they who have part in it. In the ministry of the Baptist, the appointed preparer of his way, Christ comes from heaven to earth on the blessed errand of gathering his wheat into the garner : rejoice therefore, Christians; he has prepared for you a place, and he will bring you safely to it; but take heed and beware of hypocrisy; for see, while he comes to bring home the wheat, he carries a "fan in his hand " (Matt. iii. 12).

The Two Debtors
(Luke 7:36-50)

"And one of the Pharisees desired him that he would eat with him. And he went into the Pharisee's house, and sat down to meat. And, behold, a woman in the city, which was a sinner, when she knew that Jesus sat at meat in the Pharisee's house, brought an alabaster box of ointment, and stood at his feet behind him weeping, and began to wash his feet with tears, and did wipe them with the hairs of her head, and kissed his feet, and anointed them with the ointment. Now when the Pharisee which had bidden him saw it, he spake within himself, saying, This man, if he were a prophet, would have known who and what manner of woman this is that toucheth him; for she is a sinner. And Jesus answering said unto him, Simon, I have somewhat to say unto thee. And he saith, Master, say on. There was a certain creditor which had two debtors: the one owed five hundred pence, and the other fifty. And when they had nothing to pay, he frankly forgave them both. Tell me therefore, which of them will love him most? Simon answered and said, I suppose that he, to whom he forgave most. And he said unto him, Thou hast rightly judged. And he turned to the woman, and said unto Simon, Seest thou this woman? I entered into thine house, thou gavest me no water for my feet: but she hath washed my feet with tears, and wiped them with the hairs of her head. Thou gavest me no kiss: but this woman since the time I came in hath not ceased to kiss my feet. My head with oil thou didst not anoint: but this woman hath anointed my feet with ointment. Wherefore I say unto thee, Her sins, which are many, are forgiven; for she loved much: but to whom little is forgiven, the same loveth little. And he said unto her, Thy sins are forgiven. And they that sat at meat with him began to say within themselves, Who is this that forgiveth sins also? And he said to the woman, Thy faith hath saved thee; go in peace."

AN interesting and difficult question regarding the harmony of the Gospels generally attaches itself to the exposition of this parable. Each of the four Evangelists narrates that a woman anointed Jesus while he sat at table; and it becomes difficult to determine with certainty whether they refer all to the same event, or some to one event, and some to another. In the narratives features of similarity occur, leading to the one conclusion, and features of dissimilarity leading to the other. The prevailing opinion now is that Matthew, Mark, and John, speak all of the same fact, and that Luke speaks of another. I have thought it right to mention, that this question has been often discussed in connection with our parable; but I shall do no more. The decision of it here and now is by no means necessary: the interpretation of the parable does not in any measure depend upon it. It is an inquiry belonging to a different branch of Scripture exposition, and to discuss it here would tend to distract attention from the subject in hand.

Assuming then without argument that Luke here records an event which is not mentioned by any of the other Evangelists, I shall proceed at once to examine its substance as the ground from which the parable directly springs. The husbandman at one time operates directly on the tree, and at another time directly on the ground in the neighbourhood; in both cases however, and in both alike, his aim is to increase the fruitfulness of the tree; it is thus that an expositor must in some instances turn his attention in the first place to the surrounding context which suggests and sustains the parable, as the best means of ascertaining the import of the parable itself.

A Pharisee invited Jesus to a feast: he accepted the invitation and joined the company at the appointed place and time. A woman who had been of bad character in the town, as soon as she learned that he was there, entered the apartment where the guests reclined at meat, and stood at his feet behind him weeping. Her tears rained down on his feet; she wiped them off with her hair, and then anointed them with precious ointment.

Let us endeavour to determine precisely the character of the several actors and the meaning of their acts.

The Pharisee, having formed, on the whole, a favourable opinion of Jesus as a prophet in Israel, and being, as he supposed, in a position to act the patron, with benevolent intent, but with a high estimate of his own character and position, invited to his house and table the remarkable Nazarene, whose miracles and doctrines were in every one's mouth. Doubtless he expected, also, that by closer contact, and by means of his own shrewd observation, he should be able definitely to make up his mind on the character of the new prophet, and so to favour or frown on him according to the result.

While her actions only are recorded in the narrative, we may, by the light of the Lord's subsequent declarations, also read without danger of mistake the emotions that were working in this woman's heart. She had fallen into a course of vice, and consequently lost caste in the community. Knowing that she had lost the respect of her neighbours, she had lost respect for herself. From a sinful act she had glided into sinful habits. Perhaps remorse from time to time made her inwardly sorrowful; but she put on a bold countenance, and tried to laugh down rebuke.

This woman, while in this state, crept one day to the outer edge of a crowd in the neighbourhood of the city, to satisfy her curiosity as to the cause of the concourse. In the centre stood Jesus of Nazareth preaching; and all the people in solemn silence hung upon his lips. She listened too, and heard some wonderful words ; God loved the world; God pardons sin—pardons freely, pardons it all; pardons chief sinners; loves to pardon; has given his Son to seek and save; this is the Son, revealing the

Father, and inviting the prodigal to return to the Father's bosom. Hark; he says, " Come unto me all that labour and are heavy laden, and I will give you rest." Peeping through openings in the crowd, she might see the love that beamed in the preacher's countenance, as well as hear the gracious words that came from his mouth.

The woman's heart is touched and taken ; the woman is won. By that still small voice the devil's chains are broken, the rocky heart is rent. When the congregation dissolves, she steals away to her house alone. There her eye falls on some gaudy ornaments, the instruments of her sin, and the badges of her shame. Whence this sudden strong loathing ? Perhaps she grasps them convulsively and flings them on the fire, shutting her eyes that she may not see her tormentors. She sits down, and searches her own heart,—her own life. She discovers that it is altogether vile. Her own heart is the darkest, deepest pit out of hell ; she is the chief of sinners. She never knew this before. She had often experienced twitches of conscience for particular acts of evil ; but now her whole life and her whole being seem one dark, deep, crimson sin. What has done this ? It was that word of Jesus; it was the pardon that he offered; it was the divine compassion that beamed on his countenance and glowed on his lips. She was melted. The old stony heart flowed down like water, and went away ; and a new, tender, trustful, loving heart came up in its place. She is not the same woman that she was yesterday. She is a new creature in Christ Jesus; but she could not yet tell the name and describe the nature of the change that had taken place in her being, as a new-born child could not announce the fact and explain the nature of its birth. The infant will manifest its birth and life, by seeking sustenance from its mother's breast; and when the child has grown, the grown man will reflect on his birth, and perhaps understand in some measure its nature and importance. Such was the passing from death into life in the experience of that woman. Conversion in our own day often takes place as secretly, and as soon. The word of the Lord that proved itself quick and powerful then, liveth and abideth the same for ever; and this is the word which by the Gospel is preached unto us still.

The natural history of conversion does not change with the lapse of centuries, any more than natural history in other departments ; there were doubtless examples of secret regeneration in the time of our Lord and his apostles, as well as in our own time. He knew this woman's case as well as he knew the case of the woman who pressed through the crowd to touch the hem of his garment. That woman, when she was healed, would have kept her case secret at the time if she could ; she was put about and ashamed when she was called in public, and her experience proclaimed in the crowd. It suited the purpose of the Lord to make known her experience on the spot; that method he saw would do most for his kingdom. But in the case of this woman who was a sinner, he did not act in the same way. There are diversities in his operation. He foresaw an occasion when her repentance and faith could be turned to greater account; accordingly he postponed the public announcement of her forgiveness till then. True to the new instinct that had been planted in her heart, this saved sinner, as soon as she heard that Jesus sat at meat in the Pharisee's house, grasped the richest offering she possessed and hastened to the spot. Her plans, I think, were not fully laid. The impulses of a bursting heart drew her to the place where her Redeemer was; but she had not foreseen all the difficulties, and consequently had not prepared the means of overcoming them.

Arrived at the house, she entered the open door; and passing through the attendants, penetrated into the apartment where the company reclined at meat. The table stood in the middle of the hall, and sofas in a continuous line were placed near it on either side. On these sofas were the guests, not sitting as we do with their feet on the floor beneath the table, but reclining with their feet projecting a little behind, the sandals having previously been drawn off by servants, for coolness and comfort. Thus it was easy for one who entered the room, to walk up to any individual of the company and converse with him during the meal; and, so far from being out of the way and unnatural, it was the easiest and most natural of all things, that the woman, when she came to Jesus, should touch his feet. This was precisely the part of his body which she could most easily reach, and which she might bathe and anoint, while the meal proceeded, without difficulty to herself or inconvenience to him.

We shall fall into a mistake if we think either that the act as here narrated was altogether accordant with the habits of the time and place, or altogether contrary to them; it was partly the one and partly the other.

In the first place it was an act radically diverse from the intrusion of a stranger to anoint the feet of a guest sitting at dinner with his friend in our country and our day. Such an act among us would be so unprecedented, so difficult, so awkward, that it would shock every observer, if it were attempted, and bring the whole business to a stand. There and then, in as far as the entrance of a person unbidden is concerned, there was nothing to attract attention. There is abundant evidence that even at this day, it is common in the East for persons not of the party to enter the feast chamber during the progress of the meal, and sitting on seats by the wall, converse on business or politics with the guests that recline beside the table ; and, further, from the position of the guests, it was not difficult, but easy to reach his feet. Thus far, all was accordant with use and wont. But as to the person who entered on that occasion, and the act which she performed, there was something strange and out of the way. It was fitted to attract attention, and to excite suspicion; and so indeed it did. A woman, coming in while the company sat at meat, and such a woman, habit and repute disreputable ; and besides all this, the ardency of her emotions, and the familiarity of her acts, surprised the onlookers.

I think it important to notice these two sides of the case; so much of it was according to use and wont, that the entrance of the woman by itself did not surprise and shock the company; and yet so much of it was strange, that the curiosity of the company was aroused, and their attention arrested. The circumstances of the incident on both sides, were thus calculated to promote the design of Jesus, to instruct and reprove. There was as much of the ordinary in the act as prevented it from shocking the feelings ; and as much of the extraordinary as awakened the interest of the spectators.

When she reached the feet of the Redeemer with the intention of anointing them in token of her adoring gratitude, her plan seems to have been deranged for the moment, by a sudden and uncontrollable flood of tears, as if the fountains of the great deep within her being had been opened, and grief and gladness, both at their height, had met and caused an overflow. From the position she had assumed those tears wet the feet of Jesus; and having no other towel, she, with a woman's sudden instinct, dried them again with her long flowing hair.*

" Now, when the Pharisee which had bidden him saw it, he spake within himself, This man, if he were a prophet, would have known who and what manner of woman this is that toucheth him." It was an acknowledged sign of a true prophet to be a discerner of hearts. Simon had this test before his mind, and was secretly applying it to determine the claims of Jesus. But another principle lay deep in the heart of the Pharisee, which he considered applicable to the case in hand: he counted, as a matter of course, that a prophet, while he might sit at table on terms of equality with himself, a good man, would not accept any mark of homage from a bad one. He believed that, by his knowledge of the town, he had gained advantage over the prophet of Nazareth, who was a stranger, and had found a ground on which he might reject his claims. Simon knew the character of this woman. Believing that Jesus, as a righteous man,

---

* " She was forgiven much ; therefore she loved much. As soon as she had learned that Jesus was at table in Simon the Pharisee's house, her heart drew her thither to him, that she might offer him the expression of her gratitude and love,—of her adoration and her joy. She took with her a phial of ointment, the costliest that she possessed, found an entrance into the Pharisee's house, and walked behind backs to the feet of Jesus, as he reclined at table on an elevated cushion. Arrived there, she is incapable of accomplishing her purpose. The thought of the greatness of her sin, and the greatness of the compassion of Jesus, broke her heart. She wept, and so unwittingly wet the feet of Jesus with her tears. Oh, salt, salutary tears! They are tears at once of repentance and gratitude. Now, she must first dry the Lord's feet again. But for this she had not prepared herself; for this she had nothing but her hair. So she wiped them with her hair ; and kissed the feet of Jesus, and then anointed them with ointment. All this was the manifestation of her inward burning love to the Lord."—*Arndt.* ii. 85, 86.

would have spurned her away if he had known what she was, he thought he saw in the fact of his bearing with her an evidence that he was ignorant of her character.

The reasoning was this. Either he knows what sort of a woman this is, or he does not. If he does not know, he is not a prophet, because he cannot discern spirits ; if he knows, he is not a prophet, for he does not cast the disreputable person away. On either alternative, therefore, he is not a prophet.*

I proceed now, under the direction of the Lord's own words, to consider the spiritual meaning and the practical use of the narrative. The creditor is God, in whom we live, and move, and have our being—from whom we derive all, and to whom we must account for all ; the debtors sinful men ; and the debts the sins which they have severally done.

Of the two, while both are in debt, one owes ten times as much as the other. A comparison of this proportion, with that which appears in the parable of the unmerciful servant, is interesting. Between the debt which the servant owed to his master, and the debt which a fellow-servant owed to him, there is no assignable proportion: so vast is the difference that we cannot form a definite conception of the relation. This is precisely what we should expect in order to show the disproportion, or want of all proportion, between sins against God and sins against a neighbour. In this parable, on the other hand, the debt in both cases is due to the master, and not in either due by one servant to another. We accordingly do not expect, and do not find a disproportion so vast; and yet, there is a great difference between the two sums. In

---

* The dilemma is well put by Dr. Trench.

the one case the debt is five hundred pence, and in the other fifty : the less is only one-tenth of the larger sum Although there are aggravations in one case, and alleviations in another, I think the disproportion would not have been so great as in the parable it actually is, if it had been the design of the Lord here to teach us how much the guilt of one man may exceed that of another in the sight of God. From the circumstances of this case we may safely gather that these sums represent not the absolute quantity of sin-debt that stood against these men severally in the book of divine justice, but the estimate which they severally made of their own shortcomings. The fifty and the five hundred pence indicate the amounts which the debtors severally acknowledged, rather than those which the creditor might have claimed.

The plan of providence in the present life permits every man to keep his own accounts of debt to God : no neighbour is empowered to record the items, and sum them up, and keep a record of their amount against you. The Romish priesthood attempt to usurp this prerogative, but in its purpose it is boldly unjust, and in its results miserably ineffectual. They ought not, in point of principle, to make the attempt ; and they are not able, in point of fact, to accomplish their object. Every man keeps his own account book ; and no other man dare or can look into it, except in as far as the owner opens it of his own accord for the inspection of his neighbour.

Some teachers adopt this principle, with good effect, in the discipline of children at school. Each child has a book in which he marks, from day to day and from hour to hour, his own successes and his own failures ; and according to this record the prizes are awarded or with-

held. When the child is put upon his honour, it is expected that he will be honourable. Probably a large
balance of advantage results from this contrivance where
it is judiciously managed ; but it is capable of telling
two ways, and does tell in opposite ways with different
persons. If the child deal fairly, the principle of truth
within him will be strengthened by habit; but if he cheat,
all of the sense of honesty that remained within him will
soon be worn away. "To him that hath shall be given,
and he shall have abundance ; but from him that hath
not shall be taken, even that which he hath."

But while each man is permitted to keep the account
of his own sins against God, and no human being can
rightfully possess a duplicate, there is a duplicate : another record is kept in the Book of God. That record is
true ; and woe to the self-deceiver who made false entries
in his own favour all his life, when it is found that the
two accounts will not tally in the great day.

Simon the entertainer kept account of his own debt to
God—his sins of omission and commission—and balanced
them from time to time against a column of merits which
he possessed. The balance, he confesses, was against
himself, and the difference he set down as the amount
due : it is expressed by fifty. The woman, on the other
hand, had during a course of wickedness lost all reckoning, both of her own sins and of God's mercies. Lately
she had obtained a copy of the missing documents. A
reflection of the charge had been suddenly thrown down
from the archives of the Judge, upon the tablet of her own
conscience. Without attempting to tax the account in
her own favour, she accepted it in full, and expressed it by
five hundred—ten times as much as the Pharisee had laid
to his own charge. He, taking his own reckoning for

authority, counted his liability light : she, taking her data from God's law, counted her liability heavy.

In the story, as it is constructed by the Lord for the instruction and reproof of Simon, the love of both servants to their master is caused, and consequently measured by, the forgiveness which they had received : one having obtained the remission of a small debt, loved the forgiver a little ; the other, having obtained the remission of a great debt, loved the forgiver much. In any such case, however, love springs up strong in proportion, not to the absolute amount of the debt remitted, but to the estimate of its amount which the debtor himself has formed. This principle must be kept in view when we apply the lesson of the parable to Simon. The Scripture does not concede that the amount of forgiveness that he needed and obtained was in respect to that of the poor woman as fifty to five hundred : the Scripture does not even determine that Simon was, in point of fact, forgiven at all. In its application to the case in hand, the Lord's instruction is equivalent to the conditional formula, If you have been forgiven fifty pence, and she five hundred, whether will she or you experience the more fervent gratitude to your common benefactor ? This, I think, is the only true and consistent method of applying the parable to the experience of the woman and the Pharisee. The point on which all the weight should lean is not the absolute amount of guilt incurred by the sinner and forgiven by God, but the estimate made by the sinner of his own sin, and his consequent appreciation of the boon he receives when it is unconditionally blotted out. This view, besides being in itself right, possesses this practical advantage, that it steers entirely clear of the entangling question, If the greatest sinner, when forgiven, loves his

Forgiver most, will not he be happiest at last who is the guiltiest now? There is no place here or elsewhere in the Scriptures for such a speculation : it is not admissable in any form. The conception which the parable produces when legitimately applied is at once beautiful and beneficent : love to the Saviour rises in the heart of a saved man in proportion to the sense which he entertains of his own sinfulness on the one hand, and the mercy of God on the other. Thus the height of a saint's love to the Lord is as the depth of his own humility : as this root strikes down unseen in the ground, that blossoming branch rises higher in the sky.

The woman did not speak of her own acts, either within herself or to her neighbours; but her acts are, notwithstanding, proclaimed and recorded. They are minutely catalogued (ver. 44–46), by the Lord himself. Nothing is lost on him; his ear is open, and his eye. As in providence not a sparrow falls to the ground without our Father's permission and regard, so in the new covenant not a tear falls for sin indulged, not a sigh rises for deliverance from its pollution, without attracting the notice and obtaining the approval of the Sinner's Friend. Love, burning as a night lamp silently in a penitent's breast, or bursting forth in impetuous praise, or calmly supplying the motive power of a useful life—love in the heart of the forgiven sinner, serves and pleases the forgiving Redeemer.

One point still remains unnoticed, needing indeed some notes of explanation, but capable of being easily and fully explained; it lies in these words of Jesus : "Wherefore I say unto thee, Her sins which are many are forgiven; for she loved much." A question has been raised here, Did the woman's love to the Lord cause him to forgive her, or did his pardon freely bestowed cause the forgiven woman to love him? To state the question is in effect to answer it. This announcement which Jesus makes in the close of his exposition is obviously meant to run in the line of the parable; but if you understand it to represent the woman's love as the procuring cause of pardon from the Lord, it runs right in the face of the parable from first to last. The love of the servants, the lesser as well as the larger love, is not the cause but the effect of the Master's kindness; and it would not only be out of harmony with the parable, but in sheer opposition to it in letter and in spirit, to understand it as countenancing the doctrine that the sinner's spontaneous love to God merits and obtains forgiveness.

Although, in sentences of this form, it is more common to express the effect in the first clause, and the cause, introduced by a For in the latter; yet the converse method is frequently employed and perfectly correct. You may say, Tan-waste is strewn on the street opposite this mansion, for a member of the family lies within it sick; or, A member of the family lies sick within this mansion, for tan-waste is strewn on the contiguous street. In the first instance you place the cause last, and in the second instance the effect, using precisely the same formula in both. Nor is it difficult to perceive why Jesus places the effect of forgiveness in the prominent position here, for it is the only thing that is visible to the Pharisee whom he desires to instruct. The pardon which this woman had obtained Simon did not and could not see; but her love being embodied in action was palpable to his senses. The energetic act of adoration was evidence of the heart-love from which it sprang. To this love accordingly Jesus points, and thence infers the existence of the great forgiveness which prompted it. In the end, He confirms and seals, by his own lips, the pardon which the repenting sinner had already secretly received. The Redeemer's forgiving love to sinners is the only cause of all their love to him. "We love him because he first loved us." Have you seen a broad, straight path of silver brightness lying by night upon a smooth sea, and stretching from your feet away until it was lost in the distance—a path that seemed to have been trodden by the feet of all the saints who have ever passed through a shifting world to their eternal home. Oh that silver path by night across the sea,—it glittered much: but it was not its brightness that lighted up the moon in the sky. Neither was it the love to Jesus trembling in a believer's heart, that kindled forgiving love in him. We love him because he first loved us; the love that makes bright a forgiven sinner's path across the world was kindled by the light of life in the face of Jesus; from him and to him are all things.

There is a peculiarly wise and tender adaptation to our need in that feature of our Lord's character, which consists in his desiring and appreciating our love. He is not a distant, cold, omnipotence. He lavishes love on the world, but he is disappointed when the world does not throw back a reflection of his own love, as the rippling sea throws up to heaven again, the light it got from heaven. When the ten lepers were cleansed, and one returned to lavish love on his healer, that healer, while he enjoyed the single penitent's devotion, permitted a sigh to escape his lips, articulated in the sad pensive question, "Where are the nine?" I love the Lord for uttering that complaint. It proves to me that he counts it no intrusion when we burst in upon him with our glad thanksgiving. In the bold inbursting of this woman; in her premeditated anointing, and unpremeditated tears, the Lord Jesus sees—tastes of the travail of his soul and is satisfied.

The Good Samaritan
(Luke 10:30-37)

" And Jesus answering said, A certain man went down from Jerusalem to Jericho, and fell among thieves, which stripped him of his raiment, and wounded him, and departed, leaving him half dead. And by chance there came down a certain priest that way: and when he saw him, he passed by on the other side. And likewise a Levite, when he was at the place, came and looked on him, and passed by on the other side. But a certain Samaritan, as he journeyed, came where he was: and when he saw him, he had compassion on him, and went to him, and bound up his wounds, pouring in oil and wine, and set him on his own beast, and brought him to an inn, and took care of him. And on the morrow when he departed, he took out two pence, and gave them to the host, and said unto him, Take care of him ; and whatsoever thou spendest more, when I come again, I will repay thee. Which now of these three, thinkest thou, was neighbour unto him that fell among the thieves? And he said, He that showed mercy on him. Then said Jesus unto him, Go, and do thou likewise."

LOGICALLY this parable may be conveniently associated with that of the unmerciful servant. They constitute a pair; that teaches us to forgive the injurer; and this to help the injured. On the almost pictured page of the evangelic history you may often observe two persons, sometimes in presence of a multitude, and sometimes far apart, engaged in close and earnest conversation. In most cases you discover, when you approach, that one of them is the Lord Jesus, and the other one of the lost whom he came to save. At one time it is a rich Jewish ruler, and at another a poor woman of Samaria; now, it is Nicodemus in a private house, and then Pilate in the judgment hall; here the Saviour, suffering, converses with the thief on the cross, and there the Saviour, reigning, calls to Saul as he is entering Damascus. Many of the precious words of Jesus which now constitute the heritage of the Church, were at first spoken in answer to friends or foes, during the period of his ministry on earth, or after he ascended into heaven.

Thus the Lord's word frequently took its form from the the character and conduct of those with whom he conversed. On their ignorance, or simplicity, or malice, his wisdom and goodness were cast for keeping till the end of time. The temper, and conceptions, and tricks of those Jews, like sand in a foundry, constituted the mould in which the pure gold of our Redeemer's instructions was poured; and like the sand, when they had served that purpose, they were allowed to fall asunder, as being of no further use.

Here is a case in which the question of a self-righteous Jew elicits and gives shape to the subsequent discourse of the Lord; here, accordingly, the meaning of the discourse depends, in a great measure, on the history in which it grows. At some pause in the Lord's discourse, while the multitude still remained on the spot expecting further instruction, a certain lawyer who was watching his opportunity, interposed with the demand, " Master, what shall I do to inherit eternal life?"* The question was not put in simplicity, with a view to obtain information, it was employed knowingly as an experiment and a test.

Very many such questions were addressed to the Lord Jesus during the period of his public ministry by differ-

---

* " How eagerly would the critics seize on this passage, and pronounce the question of a certain lawyer to be identical with the narrative contained in Matt. xix. 16, only differently reported—if St. Luke had not himself subsequently narrated that second incident (xviii. 18) ! This once more shows that many things could naturally, and would necessarily, occur more than once in the life of Jesus."—Stier.

ent persons, and with different motives. We may safely gather from the whole spirit of the narrative that this example, as to the character and motive of the questioner, was neither one of the best nor one of the worst. This scribe was not, on the one hand, like Nicodemus, a meek receptive disciple, prepared to drink the sincere milk of the word that he might grow thereby, nor was he like some, both of the Pharisaic and Sadducean parties, who came with cunning questions to ensnare and destroy. This man seems to have been from his own view point sincere and fair: his tempting aimed not to catch and betray, but simply to put the skill of the new Nazarene prophet to the test. The man was full, not of conscious malice against Jesus, but of ignorant confidence in himself.

The scribe's question is cast in the mould of the most unmitigated self-righteousness: "What shall *I do* that *I may inherit?*" &c. No glimpse had he ever gotten of his own sinfulness, no conception did he ever entertain of the publican's prayer, "God be merciful to me a sinner."

Taking the man on his own terms, and meeting him on his own path, the Lord replies by the question, "What is written? and refers him to the law." The lawyer, a professed theologian, answers well. He gave a correct epitome of all moral duty, showing that love is the fulfilling of the law,—"Thou shalt love the Lord thy God with all thy heart, and with all thy soul, and with all thy strength, and with all thy mind, and thy neighbour as thyself."

The Lord approved the answer, seemed to require as to profession, not another word, and closed for the time the colloquy with the simple announcement, "This do and thou shalt live." A very great question crosses our path here, but we must not discuss it fully lest we should be diverted too far from our immediate object. This answer of the Lord we accept in all simplicity as the great universal cardinal truth in the case. Life was offered at first, and life is offered still as the reward of obedience. It is not safe, it is not needful to apologize for this statement or to explain it away; it is not in any sense contrary to evangelical doctrine. It is really true that the fulfilling of God's law will secure his favour. Nor is this a thing merely to be admitted in its own place when it comes up; it is the truth that lies at the foundation, and on which all other truth leans. The basis of all is,— Obedience deserves life, and disobedience deserves death. Mankind have disobeyed; we have all sinned, and are therefore all under condemnation. Nothing but a perfect obedience can gain God's favour. Hence the covenant, and hence the incarnation and sacrifice of Christ; hence the substitution of the just for the unjust. The Gospel is not an exception to the Law, "This do and thou shalt live;" the Gospel is founded on that Law. This Law Christ came not to destroy but to fulfil.

"This *do* and thou shalt live:" whether by an emphasis on the word, or by an expressive glance at the moment in the speaker's eye, or by the simple majesty of the truth declared, the scribe's conscience was aroused and arrested. The questioner was not altogether comforted by the result of the conversation; he could not allow the matter to drop there. The reason why he continued the dialogue is expressly given; he was "willing to justify himself." Justify himself! But who accused him? Not the Lord: he had only said, "This do and thou shalt live." The man's own conscience was awakened and at work: well he knew at that moment that he had not done what his lips confessed he should do; he had not loved God with all his heart, and his neighbour as himself.

It is interesting to notice the principle on which he proceeds to defend himself: conscious that love to neighbours is in his heart a very narrow thing, he conducts his argument so as to justify its narrowness. If he can show that his neighbours are limited to a small circle of relatives, with the addition perhaps of some chosen individuals beyond the line of blood, he may yet be able to live on good terms with himself as a keeper of the law; accordingly, in order to form a basis for his own defence, he inquires, "Who is my neighbour?"

The parable constitutes the answer. But before we proceed to examine its contents, it is of great importance to observe that it is not a direct answer to the scribe's question. It is the answer which the Lord saw meet to give, but it is not a decision on the case which had been submitted for adjudication. In his question the scribe contemplated other people, and speculated upon who had the right to receive kindness: the answer of Jesus, on the contrary, contemplates the scribe himself, and inquires whether he is prepared to bestow kindness. As to those who should receive our love there is no limit: the real subject of inquiry concerns the man who bestows it. The question is not, Who is my neighbour? but, Am I neighbourly? This is the line in which the parable proceeds. It does not supply the scribe with an answer to the question which he had put; but it supplies him with another question which he desired to evade. He is not permitted to ride off upon a speculative inquiry about the abstract rights of other men; he is pinned down to a personal practical duty. "A certain man went down from Jerusalem," &c. It is a narrow, dreary mountain pass. By nature it is fitted to be a haunt of robbers; if there are any robbers in the country, they will certainly gravitate to this spot. In point of fact it was notoriously unsafe for travellers in that day, and it is equally danger-ous still. A particular portion of the road acquired the name of the *path of blood*, and under the feeble go-vernment of the Turks, as well as in more ancient times, it has well deserved its appellation. The scene of the event therefore is laid in a place which is eminently suit-able to its character: the audience who heard the story first would at once and fully recognise its appropriate-ness.

Robbers assailed the solitary traveller, and after plun-dering him of his money, left him so severely wounded that he could do nothing to help himself, and must soon have died if he had not obtained help. Although it is not expressly stated, it appears from the whole com-plexion of the narrative that this man was a Jew. Indeed this is so obvious and so necessary that the point of the parable would be lost if it were otherwise: I think the nationality of the unfortunate sufferer is not stated, pre-cisely because it could not be mistaken.

" And by chance there came down a certain priest that way," &c. By chance is an unfortunate translation here. It was not by chance that the priest came down by that road at that time, but by a specific arrangement, and in exact fulfilment of a plan; not the plan of the priest, not the plan of the wounded traveller, but the plan of God. By "coincidence" κατα συγκυριαν) the priest came down: that is, by the conjunction of two things, in fact, which were previously constituted a pair in the provi-dence of God. In the result they fell together according to the omniscient designer's plan. This is the true theory of the divine government, and this is the account of the matter which the parable contains.*

By previous appointment and actual exact coincidence that meeting took place between the hale comfortable priest and the wounded half-dead traveller in the bloody path between Jerusalem and Jericho. It is thus that all meetings take place between man and man. "The poor ye have always with you," said Jesus to his disciples. It is not only that once for all the poor and the rich are placed in the same world: but day by day, as life's current flows, by divine unerring purpose those who need are placed in the way of those who have plenty, and the strong are led to the spot where the feeble lie. We are accustomed to admire the wisdom and foresight that spread layers of iron ore and layers of coal near each other in the crust of the earth that the one might give the melting heat which the other needed; but the divine government is a much more minute and pervading thing. The same omniscient provider has appointed each meet-

---

* The analogy between the meetings exhibited in this parable and the meeting of Philip with the Ethiopian (Acts viii.) is interesting and instructive. In both cases the place is a desert, in both a man in great need and a man who has the means of supplying that need meet each other there. Here the want and its supply are material and temporal, there they are moral and spiritual. The man who fell among thieves on the way to Jericho suffered from bodily wounds, and the Samaritan who came to his relief appropriately applied material remedies: the Ethiopian treasurer, in that way towards Gaza which is desert, suffered in his soul, and the name of Christ was the ointment which Philip the evangelist poured into his wound. These two cases are indeed diverse, but as we learn from the Scriptures throughout, they proceed, both as to disease and cure, upon analogous principles, so that the knowledge of the one throws light upon the meaning of the other. The meeting in the desert near Gaza did not happen by chance, it was a tryst duly made and exactly kept, for "the angel of the Lord spake unto Philip, saying, Arise and go toward the south," &c. (Acts viii. 26). The appointment for the meetings in the valley between Jerusalem and Jericho was as certainly made, although it has not been as expressly recorded.

ing between those who are in want and those who have abundance ; and for the same reason, that the one may give what the other needs, and that both may be blessed in the deed.   But he who lays the plan watches its progress, and is displeased when men do not take the opportunity that has been given.   When he has brought the strong to the spot where the weak are lying he is displeased to see them pass by on the other side.   "Lo, I am with you alway even unto the end of the world."   Is that a pleasant promise?   No; if after the Lord has led you to the spot where the needy are perishing, you pass by on the other side; it is a dreadful thing to have him beside us, looking on in such a case as this.

We are led to suppose that the wounded man was not only unable to walk, but that he could not even move his head, so as to observe at a distance the approach of a traveller.   Possibly the sound of footsteps was the first warning he received that a human being was near.   Perhaps he started in terror lest it should be the robbers returning to take what remained of his life away.   But as the priest came and looked upon him, he might well begin to hope.   This is a man who is consecrated to the service of God ; he is even now on his way from his turn of office in the temple.   He who gets so near to God will surely show mercy to man.   No: the priest passed by on the other side.   We are not informed what his excuses were ; but we may be quite sure he had plenty, and that they were very good.   Those who seek a good excuse for neglecting the labour of love always find one.   He was alone ; he could neither cure the unfortunate man there nor carry him away.   To make the attempt might bring the robbers down from their fastnesses upon himself, and thus he should only throw away a good life after a damaged one. Right well would he justify himself that evening as he told his adventure in the pass to his friends or his family in Jericho. Love saw no excuses for leaving the man lying in his blood, for it was not looking for them; but selfishness saw them at a glance, and would have created them in plenty if there had been none at hand.

In like manner also a Levite came to the spot, looked for a moment on the sufferer, and passed on.

At last a Samaritan came up; and when he saw the wounded man "he had compassion on him." The root of the matter lies here: "Out of the abundance of the heart the mouth speaks," and the hand labours; the fountain is opened, and you may expect to see a flowing stream. Love in presence of human suffering takes the form of compassion; and love in all its forms tends to express itself in action: compassion issues in help.

In this case evidently compassion was the secret force that produced all the subsequent beneficence: yet we must not too readily count that all is safe for practical efficiency, when in presence of a brother's suffering this tender emotion begins to flutter about the heart. As the heart itself is deceitful, so also in turn are each of its affections; even those that in name and nature are good may swerve aside after they have sprung, and degenerate into selfishness. Probably both the priest and the Levite experienced some compassion as they looked on the pale and bleeding victim of lawless violence; perhaps they went away pleased with themselves on account of their tenderness, and somewhat angry with the wounded man for being wounded, and so hurting their sensibilities. The best things corrupted become the worst; and sometimes the sight of distress among poorer neighbours stirs into fermentation some of the worst elements of character in the comfortable classes. A little water may spring in the bottom of the well; but if it do not increase so as to fill the cavity, and freely overflow, it will become fetid where it lies, and more noisome than utter dryness. It is quite possible, as to emotion, to be very languishing over the misfortunes of others, and yet do the unfortunate as little good as the misanthrope who laughs at human sorrows.

But while the spurious compassion is thus vile and worthless, the true is beyond expression beautiful and good. It breaks forth in power, and sweeps down whatever obstacles may be thrown in its way. In this parable the Lord expressly points to the fountain of compassion opened before he invites us to follow the stream of beneficence in its course.

The nationality of the compassionate traveller is an important feature of the parable; he was a Samaritan. The Jews and Samaritans were locally nearest neighbours, but morally most unneighbourly. An enmity of peculiar strength and persistency kept the communities asunder from age to age. The alienation, originating in a difference of race, was kept alive by rivalry in religion. The Samaritans endeavoured to cover the defects of their pedigree by a zealous profession of orthodox forms in divine worship. The temple which they presumed to erect on Gerizzim as a rival to that of Jerusalem was naturally more odious to the Jews than others that were more distant in space, and more widely diverse in profession. Distinct traces of the keen reciprocal enmity that raged between the Jews and the Samaritans crop out here and there incidentally in the evangelical history, as in chapter ix. 54.

Most certainly the Lord does not here intend to intimate that all the priests and Levites were cruel, and all
Samaritans tender-hearted : to apply them so would be
to wrest his words. This teacher grasps his instrument
by the extremity, first one extremity and then the other,
that his lesson may reach further than if he had grasped
it by the middle. The honourable office, and even the
generally high character, of priest and Levite will not
cover the sin of selfishly neglecting the sufferings of a
fellow-creature : self-sacrificing love is approved by God
and useful to men as well in a Samaritan as in a Jew.
There is no respect of persons with God. It is quite certain that there were benevolent priests and unkind Samaritans ; and it is also certain that the Lord would not
overlook kindness in the one, nor sanction cruelty in the
other. The lesson was addressed to a Jew ; and therefore the lesson is so constructed as to smite at one blow
the two poles on which a vain Jewish life in that day
turned—"they trusted in themselves that they were righteous, and despised others." That high thing, the scribe's
self-righteous trust in his birth-right, the Lord will by the
parable bring low ; and this low thing, the mean position
of a Samaritan in the estimate of the scribe, he will at the
same moment exalt. He hath done all things well.*

---

* In the case of the ten lepers (Luke xvii. 16), which is not a parable,
but a history, we learn that the one who experienced and expressed gratitude to God for his recovery was a Samaritan. Whether their low and
despised condition had been to some extent blessed in making them more
humble and receptive than their Jewish neighbours, we do not know ; but,
in point of fact, in the historical incident a Samaritan was more ready than
the Jew to give praise to God ; and in the construction of the parable a
Samaritan is represented as also more beneficent to men.

In connection with this case a striking example may be seen of the divine
impartiality of the Scriptures. Some persons, with a view to objects of
their own, take pleasure in representing ministers of religion as more self-
seeking and less generous than those who make no religious profession

The Samaritan had compassion on the wounded man; and the emotion is known to be genuine by the fruits which it immediately bears : he bound up his wounds, pouring in oil and wine. These methods doubtless represent the opinions and practice of the time and place as to the treatment of wounds. They constituted the expression of the Samaritan's painstaking compassion; and for our present purpose no further notice of them is needful.*

The contrast between the Levite and the Samaritan, if this case stood alone, might seem to support their theory. But there is no respect of persons or classes with God; you may learn from the Scriptures—and that, too, from the writings of the same apostle—that the Samaritans were not all kind, and the Levites not all hard-hearted. They were Samaritans (Luke ix. 53) who would not permit Jesus and his disciples, when they were weary, to pass the night in their village; and he was a Levite (Acts iv. 36) who was named Son of Consolation, and sold his property that he might distribute the proceeds among the poor.

* The Samaritan was riding; for he set the wounded man "on his own beast." What of the priest and the Levite ?—were they riding, or performing the journey on foot ? If they were both pedestrians, while the Samaritan had a mule or an ass, it is obvious that the two parties were not on equal terms, and that consequently no fair test of their benevolence could in that transaction be obtained. On that very ground I think it is certain that they were riding as well as he. The parable is not a history, containing the simple facts of any given case, without respect to the lessons which the facts may contain ; it is a picture, constructed according to its Author's mind, and constructed for the purpose of expressing a particular lesson which the Author already had in his mind, and desired to teach. The doctrine which the Teacher intended to declare obviously requires that the two parties whose compassion is compared and contrasted should be on equal terms. The lesson which he meant to convey would slip through and be lost, like water through a leaky vessel, if the priest and Levite were walking when they found the wounded man : we must, therefore, if we would not do violence to the parable, assume that both were mounted. With this conclusion, resulting from the nature of the case, the expressions in their minutest details correspond. The journey of the priest is narrated in the same terms as that of the Samaritan : "A certain priest came down that way," and "A certain Samaritan as he journeyed came where he was : " we never learn that the Samaritan had a beast of burden until he sets the half-dead traveller upon its back. There was no occasion for mentioning the priest's mule, for he made no special or remarkable use of it.

The inn to which the patient was conducted must have been more than a khan built on the way-side, and left empty, a free shelter to each party of travellers who chose to occupy it for a night. It must have been something more nearly allied to our modern system; for there was a resident manager, who kept in store such provisions as travellers needed, and supplied them to customers for money.

The Samaritan remained all night with his patient, and then intrusted the case to the care of the inn-keeper, paying a sum to account, and pledging his credit for the balance, if the expense should ultimately exceed the amount of his deposit. Two denaria (pence) were at the time and in the circumstances of value sufficient to meet the probable outlay.

Now comes the searching question, "Which of these three thinkest thou was neighbour unto him that fell among the thieves?" The scribe, shut up to one answer, gives it rightly, beginning perhaps to be dimly conscious of its bearing upon himself,—" He that showed mercy on him." Here, as has been already noted, the tables are turned upon the questioner. The point on which attention is fixed is not, Who of all mankind have a right to receive kindness? but, Are you willing to show kindness, as far as you have opportunity, to every human being who is in need? The scribe desired to select a few who might rank as his neighbours, hoping that by limiting their number he might show kindness to each, without any substantial sacrifice of his own ease. The Lord shows him that love is like light: wherever it truly burns it shines forth in all directions, and falls on every object that lies in its way. Love that desires to limit its own exercise is not love. Love that is happier if it meet only

354 / Parables of Our Lord

one who needs help than if it met ten, and happiest if it meet none at all, is not love. One of love's essential laws is expressed in those words of the Lord, that the apostles fondly remembered after he had ascended, " It is more blessed to give than to receive."

" Then said Jesus, Go and do thou likewise." Through the self-sufficient Jewish theologian the command is addressed to us. The direct form of the injunction intimates, what might be gathered from the nature of the case, that this parable is more strictly an example than a symbol. It does not convey spiritual lessons under the veil of material imagery : it rather describes a case of practical beneficence, and then plainly demands that we should imitate it. However various the required reduplications may be in their form, they are the same in kind with the sample which is here exhibited.

Besides this more obvious and literal application, almost all the expositors find in the parable an allegorical representation of the world's lost state and Christ's redeeming work. In this scheme the wounded man represents our race ruined by sin ; the robbers, the various classes of our spiritual enemies ; the priest and Levite, the various legal and ineffectual methods by which human wisdom endeavours to cure sin ; and the Samaritan shadows forth the Redeemer in his advent and his office. I mention this scheme in order to intimate that I cannot adopt it. From the nature of the things, there must be some likeness to our Redeemer's mission, wherever a loving heart pities a fallen brother, and a strong hand is stretched out to help him ; but beyond this general analogy I see nothing. I can derive no benefit from even the most cautious and sober prosecution of the details. I find in it a reproving and guiding example of a true and effective compassion ;

but I find nothing more. Nor should we think the lesson unworthy of its place, although it does not directly reveal the redemption of Christ; He who loved us, and whose love to us is the fountain and pattern of all our benevolent love to each other, counted it a suitable exercise of his prophetic office to teach his disciples their relative duties in life. The lesson of this parable is parallel with that other lesson, "Love one another, as I have loved you." *

Some who experience a genuine love are so poor that when they meet a sufferer they cannot supply his wants. In such a case the Lord acknowledges the will, and knows why the deed does not follow. In the example of the widow's mite he has left it on record that he does not despise the gift because of its smallness. Nay, further, he approves and rewards the emotion when it is true, although the means of material help be altogether wanting : "I was sick and in prison, and ye came unto me." †

In the vast mass and complicated relations of modern society, it is extremely difficult to apply right principles in the department of material benevolence. On two opposite sides we are liable to err ; and we ought on either side to watch and pray that we enter not into temptation. (1.) It would be a mischievous mistake to give money, food, and clothes to every importunate beggar who contrives to cross our path and present an appearance of distress. There are men, women, and children

---

* Dräseke has happily expressed the conception that to love is truly to live : " Wir finden hier demnach die Lehre : Willst du leben, liebe."— *Vom Reich*, G. ii. 130.

† " If the robbers had seized the Samaritan before he was able to accomplish his design, his work would have been accomplished in the sight of God ; —and if the priest and Levite had given help on account of approaching spectators, it would have been of no value."—*Stier*.

in our day, who trade upon their sores, and even make sores to trade upon. To give alms indiscriminately, in these circumstances, is both to waste means and propagate improvidence. But (2.) it is not. enough to resist importunities which may proceed from feigned distress. Shut your hand resolutely against the whine ot trained, unreal pauperism; but, at the same time, diligently search out the true sufferers, and liberally supply their wants. If from defective knowledge errors must sometimes be committed, better far that now and then a shilling should be lost, by falling into unworthy hands, than that our hearts should be drained of their compassion and dried hard by the habit of seeing human suffering and leaving it unrelieved. "A man's life consisteth not in the abundance of the things which he possesseth;" it is better that his abundance should be diminished, by an occasional excess of disbursement, than that love, in which his life really lies, should wither in his breast for want of exercise. "The milk of human kindness" this compassion has been called; but let us remember that if no needy child is permitted to draw it, this milk will soon cease to flow.

The Friend at Midnight
(Luke 11:5-10)

"And he said unto them, Which of you shall have a friend, and shall go unto him at midnight, and say unto him, Friend, lend me three loaves; for a friend of mine in his
journey is come to me, and I have nothing to set before him? And he from within
shall answer and say, Trouble me not: the door is now shut, and my children are with
me in bed; I cannot rise and give thee. I say unto you, Though he will not rise and
give him, because he is his friend, yet because of his importunity he will rise and give
him as many as he needeth. And I say unto you, Ask, and it shall be given you;
seek, and you shall find; knock, and it shall be opened unto you. For every one that
asketh receiveth; and he that seeketh findeth; and to him that knocketh it shall be
opened."

IN prayer, as in every other department of his
ministry, the Lord Jesus gave his disciples
both example and precept: he prayed in their
presence, and taught them to pray. The order
of events at the beginning of this chapter is worthy of
notice: it was the Lord's praying that led to the Lord's
Prayer. The disciples heard their Master praying, and
requested him to teach them also to pray: in reply he
imparted to them the brief germinal directory which the
Church has been living on ever since, and which the
Church will live on till her Redeemer come again.

"As he was praying in a certain place;"—the scene
here presented is sublime and mysterious. The Son of
man—the Son of God in our nature, is praying to the
Father, and his followers are standing near. Silently,
reverently they look and listen. They bate their breath
till the prayer is done, and then eagerly press the request.

" Lord, teach us to pray." They observed in their Master while he prayed a strange separation from the world, a conscious nearness to God, a delight in the Father's presence, and a familiarity in communion with the Father, which seemed to them like heaven upon earth. Fondly desiring to partake of these blessed privileges, they besought their Master to show them the way. He complied with their request. He taught them as one teaches children—he put words in their mouths. Behold, the natural history of the Lord's Prayer! Thus sprang that wonderful specimen-prayer, which serves at once as the first lesson for babes beginning, and the fullest exercise of strong men's powers.*

Having taught his followers first by praying in their presence, and then by dictating an example of prayer, he next gives them a specific lesson on importunity and perseverance in praying. This lesson he has been pleased to impart in the form of a parable—" And he said unto them, Which of you shall have a friend," &c.

The picture refers to a simple, primitive condition of society, and reveals corresponding social habits. We must abandon our own modern, artificial view-point, ere we can comprehend and appreciate the facts on which the parable is based. Some cottages, built near each other for common safety, are owned and possessed by the cultivators of the surrounding soil. Daylight has disappeared, and the inhabitants of the hamlet, wearied with their toil, have all retired to rest. Meantime a benighted traveller is threading his way to the spot expecting food and

---

* This seems, however, not to have been the first occasion on which he gave "The Lord's Prayer" to the disciples; it is embodied in the Sermon on the Mount, which belongs to an earlier date. The learners were defective both in understanding and memory; and the Master gave them "line upon line."

shelter in the house of his friend. It is midnight ere he arrives; for, footsore and weary, he has consumed many hours in accomplishing the distance between his resting-place at noon and his destination for the night. The inmates, hearing his knocking and recognising his voice, forthwith open the door and hospitably receive the traveller.

But here a new difficulty occurs: the bread prepared for the household had satisfied their wants for the day, but none remained over. The last remnant had been consumed at the evening meal, and the family had retired to rest with the intention of providing early in the morning for the wants of the following day. They had not a morsel to set before the weary stranger. The head of the house, willing to undergo any amount of trouble rather than seem lacking in hospitality, determined to borrow even at that late hour the necessary supply of bread. To the door of his nearest neighbour, accordingly, he went, and knocked as the traveller had already knocked at his own. Between the two villagers a conversation now takes place, the one lying in bed within, and the other standing on the street without. The request is met at first by a polite but peremptory refusal. The hour is untimely; the children are asleep; unwonted movements in the house will awaken and alarm them: better that one stranger should fast till morning than that a whole family should be disturbed in the night.

But the suppliant at the door has taken the matter much to heart. The customs of society elevate the exercise of hospitality into the highest rank of virtues: he was ashamed to be caught off his guard, and unable to comply with the cardinal social duty of the East. He knew not how to meet his friend and confess that he had no bread in his house ; bread he must have, and will not want; he plies his request accordingly. He will listen to no refusal; he continues to knock and plead. To every answer from within, " I will not give," he sends a reply from without, " I shall have." It was for the sake of shielding his own sleeping family from disturbance at midnight that this neighbour had, in the first instance, refused; but now he discovers that the method which he had adopted to preserve the seemly stillness of night is the surest way of disturbing it. At first, that he might protect his sleeping family from disturbance, he refused; but at last, for the same reason, he complied. Although he would not give from friendship, he gave to importunity.

This parable is remarkable in that the temporal and spiritual, instead of lying parallel throughout their length, touch each other only at one point. They are like two straight rigid rods laid one upon another at right angles; all the weight of the upper rod lies on the under at one spot, and therefore presses there with tenfold intensity. The comparison has been chosen, I think, precisely because of this quality. Because the analogy does not hold good in every feature, it better serves the purpose in hand : the point of comparison delivers its lesson all the more emphatically when it stands alone.

When you have been convinced that God cares for his creatures, and have therefore begun, in the Mediator's name, to pray;—when you have not only said a prayer in fulfilment of a commanded duty, but felt a want, and like a little child requested your Father in heaven to supply it, another lesson concerning prayer remains still to be learned—to persevere. When you have asked once—asked many times, and failed to obtain relief, you are tempted gradually to lose hope and abandon prayer. Here the lesson of the parable comes in : it teaches you to continue asking until you receive. Ask as a hungry child asks his mother for bread. It is not a certain duty prescribed, so that when you have performed it you are at liberty to go away. Nor is it, Ask so many times—whether seven or seventy times seven : it is, Ask until you obtain your desire. When the Lord desired specially to recommend importunity in prayer, he selected a case which teaches importunity and nothing more. He gives us an example in which unceasing pertinacity alone triumphed over all obstacles, and counsels us to go and do likewise when we ask good things from our Father in heaven.

In this parable, as in that of the unjust judge, a human motive that is mean is employed to illustrate a divine motive that is high and holy. In both cases the reason of the choice is the same ; and in both the reason of the choice becomes the explanation of the difficulty. An example of persevering importunity in asking was needed in order to become the vehicle of the spiritual lesson ; but in human affairs such an example cannot be found among the loving and generous : you must descend into some of the lower and harder strata of human character ere you reach a specimen of the pertinacious refusal which generates the pertinacious demand. That feature of the Father's government which the Son here undertakes to explain cannot otherwise be represented by analogies drawn from human experience. If the villager had been more generously benevolent, he would have complied at once with the request of his neighbour ; but in that case no suitable example for the Lord's present purpose could have emerged from his act. In order to find an example of persevering importunity, it was necessary to select a case in which nothing but persevering importunity could prevail

The terms are distinct and emphatic : " Though he will not rise and give him because he is his friend, yet because of his importunity, he will rise and give him as many as he needeth." The term αναιδειαν, translated "importunity," signifies freedom from the bashfulness which cannot ask a second time. The shamefacedness which prevents a modest man from importuning a fellow-creature for a gift, after the first request has been refused, is out of place in the intercourse between an empty but believing suppliant and the God of all grace. If this Jewish country-man in his perplexity had been ashamed to ask a second time, he would have failed to accomplish his object ; but because he was not so ashamed, or at least did not permit the shame to drive him from his purpose, he obtained at length all his desire. Now, his conduct in this respect is specially commended to us for imitation in our prayer : " And I say unto you, Ask and it shall be given you." As that man asked a gift from a brother, we should ask from God. This is the kind of prayer that Christ teaches us to address to God ; and the Son who is in the bosom of the Father will rightly declare the Father's mind.

The lesson is in some of its aspects difficult. We have not experience—we have not faculties sufficient to make us capable of understanding it fully. Our Teacher might have maintained silence regarding it ; or he might have said, as we often in substance say to little children, "What thou knowest not now, thou shalt know hereafter ;" and this not from our unwillingness to teach, but from their incapacity to comprehend. But the Lord does not leave us wholly ignorant, because we are incapable of under-standing all. He makes one point abundantly clear—that persevering importunity in prayer is pleasing to God and profitable to men.

But the lesson is not easy : analogies drawn from sensible objects or human experience cannot express it fully. The two parables which bear upon it—the one now under consideration, and that of the unjust judge—touch only the edges of the theme. The human motive is in the one picture mean, and in the other wicked ; yet these are the best analogies that can be found on earth for expressing this feature of our Father's love.

Knowing the defect of the analogy employed in the parable, the Lord has supported and supplemented it by a fact in his own history. The case of the Syro-phœnician woman (Matt. xv. 21–28), although a historic event, serves also as an allegory. The two parables, one enacted and the other spoken, together make the lesson plain, as far as we are capable of comprehending it. In the mouth of these two witnesses the Lord has established his doctrine regarding importunate pressure in prayer.

When I was a little child I often stood near a forge, and watched a blacksmith at work, admiring the strength and skill of the wonder-working man. He was wont to treat me kindly and bear with me patiently, although I sometimes stood in his way. At one time he would benevolently answer my childish questions ; and at another, instead of answering, would continue to handle his tools with his strong, bare arms, throwing glances of tenderness towards me from time to time out of his deep intelligent eyes, but all in silence. When two pieces of iron, placed in the fire in order to be welded together, became red, I thought and said he should take them out and join them ; but he left them lying still in the fire without speaking a word. They grew redder, hotter ; they threw out angry sparks : now, thought I, he should certainly lay them together and strike ; but the skilful man left them still lying in the fire, and meantime fanned it into a fiercer glow. Not till they were white, and bending with their own weight when lifted, like lilies on their stalks—not till they were at the point of becoming liquid, did he lay the two pieces alongside of each other, and by a few gentle strokes weld them into one. Had he laid them together sooner, however vigorously he had beaten, they would have fallen asunder in his hands.

The Lord knows, as we know not, what preparation we need in order that we may be brought into union with himself. He refuses, delays, disappoints,—all in wise love, that he may bring the seeker's heart up to such a glow of desire as will suffice to unite it permanently with his own.

A father, when his son asks bread, does not give him a stone: when he asks a fish, does not give him a serpent. Thus, our Father in heaven gives good things to them that ask him. "The giving God" (τοῦ διδόντος Θεοῦ James i. 5), is one of his attributes. Why, then, do not all his children get whatever they ask, and when they ask it? One reason, doubtless, is that the child, ignorant and short-sighted, often asks a stone or a serpent because they seem beautiful,—not knowing that the one is destitute of nourishment, and that the other will sting—and then frets when things are given to him wholly different from those which he desired and expected. Hannah asked a son; in that case God saw that the request was wise : the child asked bread, and the Father, after the needful trial of faith, bestowed it freely. Some have asked a son, not knowing that in their case the gift would have been a serpent. All their days they have wondered why the boon was denied, and have learned, perhaps, in the light of the great white throne when their days on earth were done, that He who cared for them shielded their bosoms more tenderly and effectually than themselves could have done, from one of the sharpest stings that pierce the flesh of living men. Abraham believed God, and every step of his life-journey was thereby made plain : some great mountains that stood in the path of the patriarch were obliged to get quickly out of the way as he approached. To him that believeth, all things are possible.

At midnight, in the parable, the cry for help came, and prevailed. It is never out of season to pray, until you be out of life. He that keeps Israel slumbers not nor sleeps. Come we early, he is awake ; come we late, he has not retired to rest. In prayer, the shamefacedness ($\alpha\nu\alpha\iota\delta\epsilon\iota\alpha$) that shrinks from giving trouble should have absolutely no place. We trouble God by our sins, but not by our prayers. Is the sun burdened by the weight of the planets that hang on him as they run their course ? Is he exhausted by the necessity of supplying them with the light in which they shine ? Would you relieve him by covering some of them up, or blotting them out of being ? The infinite God is not wearied by the weight of all the worlds he has made : the God and Father of our Lord Jesus Christ is not exhausted by giving a portion to each of his regenerated children of human kind. Ten lepers were healed by the word of Jesus, and of them one came back to give him praise. That man in his eagerness pushed aside every obstruction, and pressed through the crowd that encircled the great Teacher, demanding and engaging his attention. Did the interruption trouble the Lord ? No. Who troubled him ? Not the one who came, but the nine who remained at a distance. With a sigh the Lord said, "Where are the nine?"

He grieved because they did not come back with praise: therefore he would have rejoiced if they had come. But if they who come to Christ to give thanks please him much, they who come to him asking gifts please him more ; for in his own experience, and according to his own testimony, it is more blessed to give than to receive.

Some additional light is thrown backward on the parable by the discourse that immediately follows. It was with the view of bringing out and pressing home the lesson from his own picture, that the Lord, in continuation of his teaching, said, " And I say unto you, Ask, and it shall be given you," &c. Two things here are most wonderful ;—one is, that needy men should require so many reasonings to induce them to ask good things from God; and the other is, that God should condescend to employ so many reasonings for that end.

One who knew only the pertinacity with which the prodigal held to his hunger, and cold, and nakedness in a foreign land, would be apt to suppose that this son had been harshly treated in his father's house, and that nothing but punishment awaited him on his return. But if such an observer had been able to witness the actual meeting of father and son when the exile returned at last, he would have learned from the fond reception which the yearning father gave to his erring child, that the son had all along grievously misjudged and misrepresented his father.

Suppose, now, the angels, who desire to look into the provisions of the covenant of grace, should have discovered only these two things, the need of men, and the mercy of God, they would expect that all the fallen would flock back to his presence, like doves to their windows when the tempest comes on : but herein they would find themselves mistaken. That complaint which our Redeemer uttered describes in one stroke the essential characteristic of the lost,—" Ye will not come unto me, that ye might have life " (John v. 40).

The Lord, who loves to bestow the blessing, reasons with us from our own experience. Children trust a father, and are not disappointed; why will you not confide in the Father of your spirits, and live ?

In the close of his lesson, he indicates that the best gift of God is the Holy Spirit, and that this gift he is most willing to bestow. More ready than a father is to give bread to a hungry child when it cries, is our Father to give the Holy Spirit to them that ask him.

Let us put him to the proof. Let us come at Christ's bidding, and in Christ's name: let us come boldly to the throne of grace. He who reigneth over all has sent for us, and bidden us come—bidden us ask. He will not dishonour his own promise: treat him as a father, and see whether he will not make you his dear child.

In some respects these two,—this and the unjust judge, —are the most wonderful and most precious of all the parables. The rest present such views of divine grace as may be shadowed forth by the ordinary manifestations of human character and action,—such as a shepherd bringing back his sheep, or a sower casting his seed into the ground: but these two go sheer down through all that lies on the surface of human history—down through all the upper and more ordinary grades of human experience, and penetrate into the lower, darker, meaner things at the bottom, in order to find a longer line wherewith to measure out greater lengths and breadths of God's compassion ; as the shadow in the lake must needs be deepest where the heavens which it represents are highest.

I know nothing more amazing, in all these lessons which Christ gave about the kingdom of grace, than the lesson which these two pictures teach about prayer. It is the same lesson that is embodied in one of the most memorable and mysterious of all the Old Testament facts— Jacob's wrestling with the Angel. Sweet to the Angel of the Covenant was the persistent struggle of the believing man; and sweet to that same Lord to-day is the pressure which an eager suppliant applies to his heart and his hand. In all the Bible you will not find a word that expresses greater loathing than that which tells us how God regards the Laodiceans who asked as if they cared not whether they obtained or not: "Because thou art lukewarm, and art neither cold nor hot, I will spue thee out of my mouth." The Lord loves to be pressed: let us therefore press, assured by his own word that the Hearer of prayer never takes urgency ill.

The Rich Fool
(Luke 12:16-21)

" And he spake a parable unto them, saying, The ground of a certain rich man brought forth plentifully : and he thought within himself, saying, What shall I do, because I have no room where to bestow my fruits? And he said, This will I do : I will pull down my barns, and build greater ; and there will I bestow all my fruits and my goods. And I will say to my soul, Soul, thou hast much goods laid up for many years ; take thine ease, eat, drink, and be merry. But God said unto him, Thou fool, this night thy soul shall be required of thee : then whose shall those things be, which thou hast provided? So is he that layeth up treasure for himself, and is not rich toward God.

WHILE Jesus was, in his wonted way, preaching the kingdom to a great multitude, one of the audience, taking advantage probably of some momentary pause in the discourse, broke in upon the solemn exercises with the inappropriate and incongruous demand, " Master, speak to my brother that he divide the inheritance with me."

In regard to the matter in dispute between himself and his brother, this man probably had both an honest purpose and a righteous cause. For aught that we know to the contrary, he may have been violently or fraudulently deprived of his share in the inheritance of the family. In the answer of the Lord there is not a word that calls in question the justice of his claim. The question of right and wrong as between the brothers does not constitute an element of the case as it is presented to us ; it it intentionally and completely omitted. Dishonesty is a simpler affair, and can be settled in very few words. Elsewhere it is disposed of in a very brief sentence,—" Thou shalt not steal." But here a far more subtle sin is analyzed and exposed. The lesson is not, Take heed and beware of Injustice; but, "Take heed and beware of Covetousness." The warning is directed not against the sin of obtaining wealth by unjust means, but against the sin of setting the heart upon wealth, by what means soever it may have been obtained: this reproof was doubtless a word more in season for the assembly of well-conducted Jews who listened that day to the preaching of Jesus, as it is a word more in season for the members of Christian Churches in this land, than an exhortation to beware of theft.

The appeal so inopportunely made, shows incidentally that the people had begun to look on Jesus as a prophet, and to pay great deference to his word. Had he not been already in some sense recognised as an authority, this man would not have applied to him for relief. He was well aware that Jesus of Nazareth could bring no civil constraint to bear upon his brother ; it was the moral influence of the prophet's word that he counted on as the means of accomplishing his purpose: "Master, *speak* to my brother, that he divide the inheritance with me." He had, perhaps, observed an amazing effect produced by a word from those meek lips; he had, perhaps, himself seen wicked men subdued by it, and heard from others that it had silenced a stormy sea. He may have marked its power in healing the sick and raising the dead. Forthwith he conceived the plan of enlisting this mysterious and mighty word on his own side of a family quarrel. If that word, he thought within himself, were exerted in my behalf, it would induce my brother to give to me the half or the third of the paternal estate, which I claim as my right.

We cannot cast the first stone at this poor simpleton, who had no other use for the Redeemer's word than to gain by means of it a few more acres of the earth for himself: in every age, some men may be found who hang on the skirts of the Church for the sake of some immediate temporal benefit. Nor is it difficult to understand the phenomenon: " No man can serve two masters; " practically each chooses one, and in the main serves him faithfully. If Christ is chosen as Lord and Master, Mammon and all other things are compelled to serve: if Mammon is chosen and seated on the throne, he will not scruple to lay heaven and earth under contribution for the advancement of his designs;—Mammon, when master, will take even the word of Christ and employ it as an instrument wherewith he may rake his rags together.

How simple and helpless is the man who has allowed wealth to become his chief good! Here is an example of ungodly simplicity. Without any apprehension of a reproof from the Lord or his disciples, the poor man betrays all: in the public assembly he unwittingly turns his own heart inside out. Instead of addressing to the preacher the question, What must I do to be saved? showing that the truth had taken effect on his conscience, he preferred a request regarding a disputed property, showing that while the words of Jesus fell on his ears, his heart was going after its covetousness. He attended to the sermon for the purpose of watching when it should be done, that he might then do a stroke of business.

We must not too complacently congratulate ourselves on our superior privileges and more reverent habits. If those who wait upon the ministry of the word in our day were as simple as this man was, some requests savouring as much of the earth as his would be preferred at the

close of the solemnity. If human breasts were trans·
parent, and the thoughts that throng them patent to the
public gaze, many heads would hang down.

From this untimely and intensely earthly interruption
the parable springs: thus the Lord makes the covetousness as well as the wrath of man to praise him, and
restrains the remainder thereof. A fissure has been made
in the mountain by some pent-up internal fire that forced
its way out, and rent the rock in its outgoing; in that
rent a tree may now be seen blooming and bearing fruit,
while all the rest of the mountain-side is bare. "Out of
the eater came forth meat; out of the strong came forth
sweetness." This word of Jesus that liveth and abideth
for ever is a green and fruitful tree to-day; but it was
the outbursting of a scathing, scorching covetousness that
formed the cavity, and supplied the soil in which the tree
might grow.

"The ground of a certain rich man brought forth
plentifully," &c.

The ground was his own: no law, human or divine,
challenged his right. The ground was eminently fruitful;
the unconscious earth gave forth its riches, making no
distinction between one who used it well and one who
abused it. On the fields of the covetous man the rain
fell and the sun shone: God makes his sun to shine on
the evil and on the good. It is not here—it is not now
that he judges the world in righteousness. He giveth to
all men liberally, and upbraideth not.

Mark now what effect the profusion of nature and the
beneficence of God produced on the mind of this pros-
perous man. It set him a thinking: so far, so good. The
expression in the original indicates a dialogue, and a
dialogue is a discourse maintained between two. Dialogue

is, indeed, the original word transferred bodily into the English language: διελογιζετο εν ἑαυτῳ—he dialogued in himself: his soul and he held a conversation on the subject. This was a proper course. When riches increase it is right and necessary to hold a consultation with one's own soul regarding them: in like manner, also, when riches take themselves wings and fly away, a conversation between the same parties should take place regarding their escape.

He said, "What shall I do, I have no room where to bestow my fruits?" The process advances most hopefully: hitherto, no fault can be found with this man's conduct. So great had been his prosperity that he was at a loss for storage. His cup was not only full, but running over, and so running waste; his solicitude now turned upon the question how he might profitably dispose of the surplus. Taking it for granted, as any sensible man in the circumstances would, that something should be done, he puts the question, "What shall I do?" A right question, addressed to the proper person, himself. No other person was so well qualified to answer it,—no other person understood the case, or possessed authority to determine it.

Listen now to the answer: "He said, This will I do: I will pull down my barns, and build greater," &c. This is the turning-point, and on it the poor man turns aside into error. When God's goodness was showered upon him in such abundance, he should have opened his treasures and permitted them to flow: for this end his riches had been bestowed upon him. When rain from heaven has filled a basin on the mountain-top, the reservoir overflows, and so sends down a stream to refresh the valley below: it is for similar purposes that God in his providential government fills the cup of those who stand on the high places of the earth—that they may distribute the blessing among those who occupy a lower place in the scale of prosperity.

But self was this man's pole star : he cared for himself, and for none besides. Self was his god ; for to please himself was practically the chief end of his existence. He proposed to pull down his barns, and build a larger storehouse on the site, in order that he might be able to hoard his increasing treasures. The method that this ancient Jewish self-seeker adopted is rude and unskilful. We understand better the principles of finance, and enjoy more facilities for profitably investing our savings : but the two antagonist principles retain their respective characters under all changes of external circumstances—the principle of selfishness and the principle of benevolence ; the one gathers in, the other spreads out.

The method of reserving all for self, is as unsuccessful as it is unamiable : it cannot succeed. The man who should hoard in his own granary all the corn of Egypt, could not eat more of it than a poor labourer—probably not so much. It is only a very small portion of their wealth that the rich can spend directly on their own personal comfort and pleasure : the remainder becomes, according to the character of the possessor, either a burden which he is compelled to bear, or a store whence he daily draws the luxury of doing good.

The dialogue proceeds : the man has something more to say to his soul : " Soul, thou hast much goods laid up for many years," &c. He counts on riches and time as if both were his own, and at his disposal. The big barn is not yet built ; the golden grain that shall fill it has not yet been sown : and even although no accident should mar the material portion of the plan, how shall he secure the "many years" that constitute its essence on the other side? Does he keep Time under lock and key in his storehouse, that he may at pleasure draw as much as he requires? Many years! These years lie in the future, —that is, in the unseen eternity. They are at God's right hand—they are not within your reach. Why do you permit an uncertain element to go into the foundation of your hope?

There is, indeed, nothing strange here. It is according to law: those who are taught of the Spirit understand it well. The god of this world hath blinded the minds of them that believe not. "Thou hast goods laid up for many years! take thine ease, soul; eat, drink, and be merry!" What simplicity is here! The case is in degree extreme; the letters are written large that even indifferent scholars may be able to read the lesson; but the same spiritual malady, in some of its forms and degrees, is still epidemic in the world: those are least exposed to infection who have their treasures laid up at God's right hand.

It is a useful though a trite remark, that there is great stupidity in the proposal to lay up in a barn the portion of a soul. The soul, when it is hungry, cannot feed on musty grain. Material treasures cannot save a soul from death. The representation in the parable, however, is true to nature and fact: it would be a mistake to attribute to a miser a high appreciation of the dignity of man. Covetousness, in its more advanced stages, eats the pith out of the understanding, and leaves its victim almost fatuous.

This man, in a dialogue with his own soul, had settled matters according to his own mind. The two had agreed together that they would have a royal time on earth, and a long one. The whole business was comfortably arranged. But at this stage another interlocutor, whom they had not invited, breaks in upon the colloquy : " God said unto him, Thou fool, this night thy soul shall be required of thee ; then, whose shall those things be which thou hast provided ?" This is the writing on the wall that puts an end to Belshazzar's feast, and turns his mirth into terror.

The terms run literally, " Unwise, this night they demand from thee thy soul." Those ministering angels and providential laws, represented by the drawers of the net in another parable, to whom the Supreme Governor has committed the task of gathering gradually the generations of men from this sea of time, and casting them for judgment on the borders of eternity—those ministering spirits, and principles pervading nature, arrive in their course this night at your door, and send the message into the midst of the merry festival, The master of this house is wanted immediately ; he must arise and go, in obedience to the summons ; he can neither resist nor delay. He may weep, tremble, rage ; but he must go, and go on the instant. It is not the whole man, but only his soul that is wanted : his body will be left behind. But the body, though left behind, cannot claim, cannot use the goods. When the soul is summoned over into eternity, it cannot carry the hoarded treasures with itself, and the body left behind has no further use for them. A grave to rest in while it returns to dust is all that the body needs or gets ; and the deserted wealth must advertise for an owner—whose shall it be ?

Our Lord Jesus has spoken these piercing words, not for the sake of the pain which they are fitted to inflict. He is the Healer * of diseased humanity, and when he

---

* Der Heiland—the Healer—is the ordinary epithet applied to the Lord Jesus in the religious phraseology of the Germans. The term is suggestive and comforting.

makes an incision he means to cure. This sharp instrument, at whose glance we wince and shrink precisely in proportion to the measure of our malady, he wields for the purpose of piercing the deadly tumour, and so saving the threatened life. "A man's life consisteth not in the abundance of the things which he possesseth" (ver. 15); and the man who places his life therein, loses his life. That is not his life; and if he take that for his life, he is cheated: when a merchant has given all for what seemed a goodly pearl, he has not another fortune in reserve wherewith to begin anew, if that for which he paid all his possessions turns out to be a worthless toy of glass. Our time, our life—this is our fortune, on which we trade for the better world: if these be spent,—be thrown away for what is not life, then life is lost.

Riches are truly enjoyed when they are wisely employed in doing good; but hoarded as the portion of their possessor, they burden him while they remain his, and rend him at the parting.

By way of contrast, the Lord mentions another kind of treasure, which satisfies now, and lasts for ever. Those who are "rich toward God," are rich indeed, and all besides are poor: and this wealth is, in Christ, offered free, —offered to all.

Seeing that an evil spirit possessed this man, the Lord in mercy applied his word to cast the evil spirit out, and make room for his own indwelling. When the spirit of the world refuses to go out at his word, he sometimes interferes as Ruler in providence, and tears out the intruder by his mighty hand: the kingdom of heaven that is "within you" also suffereth violence; and He who is most mighty comes sometimes with merciful strokes to take it by force. "Even so: come, Lord Jesus."

The Barren Fig Tree
(Luke 13:1-9)

" There were present at that season some that told him of the Galileans, whose blood
Pilate had mingled with their sacrifices. And Jesus answering said unto them, Suppose ye that these Galileans were sinners above all the Galileans, because they suffered
such things? I tell you, Nay : but, except ye repent, ye shall all likewise perish. Or
those eighteen, upon whom the tower in Siloam fell, and slew them, think ye that they
were sinners above all men that dwelt in Jerusalem? I tell you, Nay : but, except ye
repent, ye shall all likewise perish. He spake also this parable ; A certain man had a
fig-tree planted in his vineyard ; and he came and sought fruit thereon, and found
none. Then said he unto the dresser of his vineyard, Behold, these three years I come
seeking fruit on this fig-tree, and find none : cut it down ; why cumbereth it the
ground? And he answering said unto him, Lord, let it alone this year also, till I shall
dig about it, and dung it : and if it bear fruit, well : and if not, then after that thou
shalt cut it down."

IT is obvious that the massacre of the Galileans
by Pilate was mentioned on this occasion, not
for its own sake, but for the purpose of sup-
porting a doctrine which the narrators held
and desired to establish. Their meaning is echoed distinctly in the answer of the Lord. These Pharisees seem
to have found grist for their own mill in all events and
all persons; everything was turned to the account of their
own self-righteousness. Peculiar sufferings seemed to
prove peculiar guilt. The logical consequence they did
not express, and perhaps did not distinctly frame even in
thought; but they solaced themselves with it, notwithstanding: they were not visited by such calamities, and
therefore it might be presumed they were not chargeable
with such sins.

The Lord expressly denied the truth of their silent, hidden inference, and fortified his teaching by reference to another analagous case,—the sudden death of some men through the fall of a tower. Leaving untouched the general doctrine that mankind suffer for sin, he clearly and emphatically teaches, that particular calamities do not measure or prove the particular guilt of those who suffer in them. Otherwise, it is obvious that God's government begins and ends in this life ; there is neither the necessity nor the evidence of a judgment to come. He indicated to the Jews that the sudden and unexpected destruction of those sacrificing Galileans, was but an emblem of the sudden and unexpected destruction that would overtake themselves if they were not converted in time, and shielded in mercy from the judgment that sin entailed. To repeat, expand, and enforce this lesson the parable is spoken : "He spake *also* this parable,"—the similitude is given in addition to the more direct instruction which had gone before, and for the same purpose.

"A certain man had a fig-tree planted in his vineyard." This was not a seedling that had sprung accidentally within the fences of the vineyard, and through carelessness been permitted to grow : the language is precise, and indicates that the fig tree had been planted within the vineyard by a deliberate act of the owner. The husband-man planted the fig-tree that he might enjoy its fruit ; and in order more effectually to secure his object, he selected for the tree the most favourable position. It is obvious both from the structure and design of the parable that the position of the fig-tree was the best that it could possibly have obtained.

In countries where the vine is cultivated, not by a few wealthy proprietors with a view to an export trade, but by each family on a small scale with a view to the food of the household, to plant some fruit trees of other kinds within the same enclosure is the rule rather than the exception. The vineyard is not the luxury of the few, but a common necessity of life with the many. It becomes the most cherished possession of the permanent rural population. Its aspect is sunward, its soil is good, its fences are in order. Within this favoured spot the owner is willing to make room for one or more fig-trees, for the sake of the fruit which in such favourable circumstances he expects them to bear.*

When the tree had reached maturity the owner expected that it should bear fruit; but that year, the next, and a third it continued barren. Having waited a reasonable time, he gave orders that it should be destroyed; since it produced nothing, he desired to utilize in another way the portion of ground which it occupied.

The dresser of the vineyard is a person who has the entire charge, subject to the general instructions of the proprietor. He has long occupied this position, and is acquainted with the fig-tree from its infancy; he knows it, as a shepherd in a similarly primitive state of society knows his sheep. He has formed for it a species of attachment; and a sentiment akin to compassion springs up in his heart, when he hears its sentence pronounced. "Woodman, spare that tree," is a species of intercession thoroughly natural and human.

The intercession of the dresser, however, is not senti-

---

* In the valley of the Rhine where the vine is cultivated as the material of a great manufacture, and the staple of a foreign trade, fruit trees of other species are not admitted within the vineyard; but at Botzen in the Tyrol, where the habits of society are more simple and primitive, I have repeatedly seen fig-trees growing within the lofty wall of the carefully cultured vineyard, rewarding the possessor for his care with abundant fruit.

ment merely; it is sentiment completely directed and controlled by just reason. He does not plead for the indefinite prolongation of a useless existence. He asks only another year of trial: he intends and promises to take in the interval the most energetic measures for stimulating the barren tree into fruitfulness. If under these appliances it bear fruit, he knows the owner will gladly permit it to retain its place; if not, he will abandon it to the fate which it deserves and invites.

No peculiar difficulty attends the exposition of this parable: the main features of its meaning are so distinctly marked, that it is hardly possible to miss them. The lesson is easily read; and when read, it is unspeakably solemn and tender.

God is the owner of the vineyard and the fig-tree within its walls. Abraham's seed, natural and mystical, are the fig-tree; and the Mediator between God and man is the Dresser of the vineyard, the intercessor for the barren tree. These points are all so obvious that there can hardly be any difference of opinion regarding them. One point remains, demanding some explanation indeed, but presenting very little difficulty,—the vineyard. The fig-tree was planted within the vineyard, and what is the doctrine indicated by this circumstance in the material frame of the parable? The suggestion that the vineyard means the world, in the midst of which Israel were planted, although supported by some honoured names, does not merit much consideration. In no sense is there any likeness between the vineyard and the world. The essential circumstances involved in the fact that the fig-tree grew within the vineyard are, that in soil, south exposure, care and defence, it was placed in the best possible position for bearing fruit. The one fact that it was planted in the vineyard indicates, and was obviously intended to indicate, that the owner had done the best for his fig-tree. The meaning is precisely the same as that which is more fully expressed in the analogous parable : " Now will I sing to my well-beloved a song of my beloved touching his vineyard," &c. (Isa. v. 1–7). In the prophet's allegory, while in general the vineyard represents the house of Israel, the vine trees more specifically represent the people, and south exposure, soil, care, and defence, represent the peculiar providence and grace of God displayed in their history and institutions. ' The vineyard of the Lord of hosts is the house of Israel, and the men of Judah his pleasant plant" (ver. 7) ; the plants represent the men, and all that the proprietor did in their behalf represents the goodness of God to Israel in redeeming them from bondage and giving them his covenant. On the same principle in our parable the fig-tree represents the people who were favoured, and the advantages of the vineyard represent the privileges which the people enjoyed. The intimation that this barren fig-tree grew within a vineyard, is a short method of informing us that it enjoyed a position on a very fruitful hill, and was there fenced, watched, and watered with the most patient care. Now, obviously, none of these things, in their spiritual signification, were enjoyed by Israel simply in virtue of their existence in this world. The Egyptians, the Babylonians, and the Persians were placed in the world too, and yet they enjoyed no peculiar privileges,—could not be compared to a vineyard on a very fruitful hill. This feature of the parable, so far from merely intimating that Israel were placed in the world, teaches us that they were separated from it ; they were protected by special providences in their history, and cherished by the ordinances of grace. The place of the fig-tree within the vineyard indicates that the people to whom God looked in vain for the fruits of righteousness, were distinguished from the nations by the peculiar religious privileges which they enjoyed : the favourable circumstances of the tree aggravated the guilt of its barrenness.

Three successive years the owner came seeking fruit on this fig-tree, and found none. In regard to the specified period of three years, I do not think we gain much by a particular reference to the well-known natural process by which the fig develops simultaneously the fruit of this season and the germs of the next ; for we do not know in this case whether the germs were never formed, or fell off before they reached maturity. I am not able to perceive that the number three has any necessary reference to the peculiarities of the fig ; I think the same number would have been employed for the purposes of the spiritual lesson, although a fruit tree of another species had been taken as an example. Three years was a reasonable period for the owner to wait, that he might neither on the one hand rashly cut down a tree that might soon have become profitable, nor on the other permit a hopelessly barren tree indefinitely to occupy a position which might otherwise be turned to good account.

While the lesson of the parable bears upon the Church at large, both in ancient and modern times, it is to individuals that it can be most safely and most profitably applied. Most certainly we enjoy at this day the advantages set forth under the figure of the favoured fig-tree. Besides the life and faculties which we possess in common with others, we have spiritual privileges which are peculiar to ourselves. Civil and religious liberty, the Scriptures, the Sabbath, the Church, place us in the position of the fig-tree within the vineyard, while other nations are more or less like a tree rooted in the sand, or exposed on the wayside. The God in whom we live has conferred these advantages upon us, that we might bear fruit unto holiness; and if we remain barren, notwithstanding all his kindness, he will give forth the decree to cut us down. In some he finds bad fruit, and in some no fruit, and even in the best, little fruit. He has not cast out the unfruitful, but has tenderly spared them.

As the fig-tree greedily drank in the riches of earth and air, and wasted all in leaves, so the unconverted in a land of Christian light enjoy God's goodness and employ it in ministering only to their own pleasures. The line of justice, stretched to the utmost,—to the utmost and more, snaps asunder at last: the sentence goes forth, Cut the barren tree down, and cast it out. This is the doom which guilt deserves and justice proclaims: if the sinful were under a government of mere righteousness, it would be inexorably executed upon all.

Here is the turning point: here an intercessor appears, —an Intercessor who cares for man and prevails with God. The first part of his plea is, Spare: he appeals for a respite of definite and limited duration,—one year: less would not afford an opportunity for amendment, and more would in the circumstances confer a bounty on idleness. All who have under the Gospel reached the age of understanding, and are still living without God in the world, enjoy the present respite in virtue of Christ's compassionate intercession. If that Mediator had never taken up the case, or should now abandon it, the sentence already pronounced would descend like the laws of nature and inexorably execute itself. It is Christ's intercession alone, that stands between the unpardoned on earth, and the punishment which is their due.*

But the Intercessor does more than secure for the sinful a space for repentance: He who obtains the respite takes means to render it effectual. The two chief applications employed in husbandry to stimulate growth and fruitfulness are digging and manuring: these accordingly the dresser of the vineyard undertakes to apply in the interval to the barren fig-tree. I think something may be gained here by descending into the particulars. One of these agricultural operations imparts to the tree the elements of fruitfulness, and the other enables the tree to make these elements its own. Digging gives nothing to the tree ; but it makes openings whereby gifts from another quarter may become practically available. The manure contains the food which the plant must receive, and assimilate, and convert into fruit ; but if the hardened earth were not made loose by digging, the needed aliment would never reach its destination.

Similar processes are applied in the spiritual culture : certain diggings take place around and among the roots of barren souls, as well as of barren fig-trees. Bereavements and trials of various kinds strike and rend ; but these cannot by themselves renew and sanctify. They may give pain, but cannot impart fertility : the spirit much distressed may be as unfruitful as the spirits that are at ease in Zion. These rendings, however, are most precious as the means of opening a way whereby the elements of spiritual life conveyed by the word and the Spirit may reach their destination. The Lord who pours

---

* I cannot see any force in the argument by which Stier endeavours to show that the interceding vine-dresser represents primarily the human ministry in the Church.

in the food for the sustenance of a soul, stirs that soul by his providence, so that grace may reach the root and be taken in. As the constituents of fruit, held in solution by air and water, cannot freely reach the plant whose roots lie under a long unbroken and indurated soil, so the grace of God contained in the preached Gospel is kept at bay by a carnal mind and a seared conscience. It is when afflictions rend the heart, as a ploughshare tears up the ground, that the elements of life long offered are at length received. It is thus that providence and grace conspire to achieve the purpose of God in the salvation of men. In this work mercy and judgment meet; and saved sinners, on earth and in heaven, put both together in their song of praise (Ps. ci. 1.)

But a feature appears in the close, well fitted to arouse those who have hitherto presumed upon impunity and neglected Christ. Even this kind Intercessor does not propose that the unfruitful tree should be allowed indefinitely to maintain its place without changing its character: He spontaneously concedes that if this trial prove ineffectual, justice must take its course; "After that thou shalt cut it down." When Jesus lets a sinner go, who shall take him up? But there is love even in this last stern word. Love intercedes for a time of trial, —an opportunity of turning; and love, too, after securing sufficient opportunity, lets go its hold and leaves all hopeless beyond. It is the terrible concession, "thou shalt cut it down," issuing from the Intercessor's lips, that gives power to the invitation, "Now is the accepted time." To warn me now that if I let the day of grace run waste, even Jesus on the morrow of the judgment will not plead for me any more, is surely the most effectual means of urging me to close with his offer to-day.

The Excuses
(Luke 14:16-24)

"Then said he unto him, A certain man made a great supper, and bade many : and sent his servant at supper time to say to them that were bidden, Come ; for all things are now ready. And they all with one consent began to make excuse. The first said unto him, I have bought a piece of ground, and I must needs go and see it : I pray thee have me excused. And another said, I have bought five yoke of oxen. and I go to prove them : I pray thee have me excused. And another said, I have married a wife, and therefore I cannot come. So that servant came, and showed his lord these things. Then the master of the house being angry said to his servant, Go out quickly into the streets and lanes of the city, and bring in hither the poor, and the maimed, and the halt, and the blind. And the servant said, Lord, it is done as thou hast commanded, and yet there is room. And the lord said unto the servant, Go out into the highways and hedges, and compel them to come in, that my house may be filled. For I say unto you, That none of those men which were bidden shall taste of my supper."

A CHAIN of connected lessons, consisting of several links, immediately precedes the parable in the evangelic history ; but we may appreciate all the meaning of the parable without reference to the circumstances in which it sprung. In some cases the connection with the context is such that light from the history preceding is necessary to elucidate the meaning of the lesson that follows ; but it is not so here. Although one thing suggests another in the conversation which the Evangelist records, the lesson ultimately given is independent of the things that suggested it.

Touched by the solemn teaching of the Lord Jesus, one of the company, well-meaning, but dim and confused in his conceptions, made the remark, " Blessed is he that shall eat bread in the kingdom of God." Observing that this man and the Pharisees around him were clinging to the notion that to be invited to enter the kingdom is the same thing as to be in it, he spoke the parable to point out the difference, and to show that the invitation will only aggravate the doom of those who refuse to comply with it. He intends to teach the Jews, and through them to teach us, that those who are near the kingdom may in the end come short of it—that those who stand high in spiritual privileges may be excluded—may exclude themselves from the kingdom of God.

Both in the natural objects employed, and the spiritual lessons which they convey, there is, at some points, a marked resemblance between this parable and that of the royal marriage; but the two, though similar, are manifestly distinct.

" A certain man made a great supper and bade many." In this case it is not a king but a person in a private station who provides the feast ; and the occasion of the rejoicing is not the marriage of the entertainer's son. It is an ordinary example of hospitality exercised by an affluent citizen.

Both here and in the analogous parable of the royal marriage it is assumed, as at least not altogether incongruous with custom, that invitations should be issued some days before, and that the invited guests should a second time be warned by a messenger to repair to the banqueting house when the time drew near. This summons to attend immediately was sent out at supper time. We know that the term δειπνον was in ancient times employed generally to signify the principal meal, without reference to a particular period of the day ; and, from the circumstances of this case, it plainly appears that the feast was a dinner at an early hour, and not a supper in our sense of the word. At the moment when the warning reached him, the man who had bought a field intended to go and see it, and the man who had bought five yoke of oxen intended on that same afternoon to try whether they would go well in harness ; these excuses, although not sincere, must in the nature of the case have appeared plausible, and consequently the feast must have been ready at an early hour of the day.

It is implied that these men had tacitly, or in some other well-understood way, accepted the first invitation. They gave no intimation that they intended to decline— they gave the provider of the feast reason to expect their presence. Probably they were well pleased to be invited ; if they met any of their poorer neighbours in the interval, it is probable they would take occasion to show their own importance. These common people in the town, and these labourers in the country, are not admitted as we are into good society. When the moment arrived they were unwilling ; or rather they were so intently occupied with their own affairs, that the attractions of the feast were not powerful enough to tear them away.

"With one consent" they all made excuses. The servant saw them separately and received their answers. There is no reason to believe that they met together and framed a plan to insult their entertainer. They acted all on the same method, although they did not act in concert. The creatures were of one kind, and though they answered separately they answered similarly. Off one carnal instinct—$\alpha\pi o$ $\mu\iota\alpha\varsigma$ ($\gamma\nu\omega\mu\eta\varsigma$)—the excuses were taken, and accordingly, although spoken by different persons, and moulded by different circumstances, they were all of the same type.

The first had bought a field and must go to examine his bargain ; the second had bought live stock for his farm and must see them tried immediately ; the third had married a wife, and held himself absolved for the time from the ordinary rules of society. They are fair samples of the things that occupy and engross men's hearts and lives.

The servant, having no authority to act, simply reported the facts to his master. The master was angry, and immediately invited all the poor of the neighbourhood to the feast. When many of the most destitute had assembled, the householder, not satisfied as long as there was room at the table, and a poor man within reach to occupy it, sent out another message still more pressing, to sweep into the feast all the homeless wanderers that could be found, the very dregs and outcasts of society Satisfied when his house at length was filled, the owner announced that none of those who had made light of his invitation should now be permitted to partake of the feast.

We are now ready to examine more directly the spiritual meaning of the parable, and as the lesson is in the main coincident with that of the royal marriage in its earlier portion, a brief exposition will suffice.

In the Gospel, God has provided a great feast. Israel, or his Church at any period, are a privileged class, and enjoy, through his sovereign goodness, a perpetual invitation,—a standing right. The charge which the parable brings against this privileged people is, that they were satisfied with the honour of being invited, and refused actually to comply with the invitation. They were content with their name and their outward privileges, and would not in their own hearts and lives obey the Gospel; clinging to the form of godliness, they peremptorily denied its power. Not they who are invited, but they who partake of the feast, are blessed. To get the first invitation will be not a blessing but an aggravation of guilt, if you despise the Giver and refuse his gifts. The last invited shall be first in ultimate position if they accept the invitation, and the first invited will be last and lowest if they refuse to comply : the condition of men, ultimately, turns not on pardon to them offered, but on pardon by them received.

The servant obviously represents the ministry of the Gospel in every form and in all times. The message is addressed in the first instance to them "that were bidden." The Gospel was not first proclaimed to the heathen : begin at Jerusalem was the Master's command, and that command was fulfilled in spirit and letter by his servants. To the lost sheep of the House of Israel the Lord came in person, and to them the apostles addressed their Lord's words at the beginning of their ministry. The history of the event in the Acts of the Apostles corresponds exactly with the prophetic delineation in this parable : it was when the Jews rejected the Gospel, that the messengers turned to the Gentiles.

The invitation addressed to the favoured circle first is, "Come, for all things are now ready;" all preceding dispensations were a preparation for Christ. When the fulness of time had come, those who had been all along brought up within the lines of the privileged people, were invited to behold the Lamb of God that taketh away the sin of the world. This is repeated in the experience of every generation, and every individual, that grows up within the circle of Christian ordinances, as soon as the mind comprehends the message of mercy. As each attains maturity, he is informed that all things are now ready; he is invited and pressed to believe in the Lord Jesus Christ that he may be saved.

To "make excuse," does not here mean to invent an excuse, and falsely state, as a reason, that which is, in point of fact, not the motive of the act. To make excuse, both in the original Greek ($\pi\alpha\rho\alpha\iota\tau\epsilon\iota\sigma\theta\alpha\iota$) and in the English translation, signifies simply to plead to be excused. The grounds on which the plea is urged, may in any case be true or false ; but in this case, it is highly probable that the grounds stated were in themselves facts, and that they were, in part at least, the true grounds of refusal. Whether the first would have gone to the feast, if he had not at that time bought a property, we do not certainly know. A man who is intensely unwilling to go, when one reason fails, will find or make another; but in this case, the probability is, that anxiety to see his purchase was the real, or at least, a real ob-obstacle. The same observation is applicable to the other two examples.

But although we concede that the obstacles are real, we do not thereby help the case of those who neglect the Gospel; we must go one step deeper into the strata of deceit that are piled over each other in a human heart. A secret unwillingness to partake of the feast may induce the invited to time his purchases, so that he may have a good excuse at hand, or at least to abstain from effort to regulate the incidence of other cares, so as to leave a time of leisure for the great concern. Here in the highest matters, as elsewhere in lower, "Where there's a will there's a way." If the desire were pure and true,—the desire to attend the Giver, and receive his unspeakable gift, the field may be inspected and the oxen proved early in the morning, or postponed till the following day. Without supposing a conscious falsehood representing that transactions which had no existence stood in the way, you have the evil in all its bulk and all its virulence, when the deceitful heart tries to persuade neighbours, and to persuade itself, that the emerging necessities of earthly business interfered with the waiting on Christ for the salvation of the soul.

We might be put on our guard against this species of deceit in the highest matters, by observing how readily we glide into it, in things of smaller moment. Deceits of every shade, from the lie direct to the most attenuated equivocation, spring in the complicated intercourse of modern society, like weeds in a moist summer on a fallow field. Assuredly, unless our hand be diligent in digging out these bitter roots, we shall not grow rich in the graces of the Spirit. You are invited to a neighbour's house : you don't like to go, and you determine that you will not go. Forthwith your wits go to work to discover an excuse, and you soon find that which you seek for : you must travel on business that day; or some other excuse equally convenient and plausible occurs. You are invited to the house of another neighbonr; difficulties unforeseen spring up; but being bent on accepting this invitation, you brush them all aside, and contrive to reserve the evening for the company that you love. There is much danger of staining the conscience in affairs like these. The Lord requires truth in the inward parts : watch and pray. But the difficulty of the path should not make any disciple sad : the effort to walk circumspectly, when honestly, prayerfully, lovingly made, is pleasant and healthful exercise to the spirit.

Neither on the natural nor on the spiritual side does the expression, "with one consent," intimate that the parties met and consulted together regarding the terms of their answers. As birds of the same species build their nests of the same material and the same form, without deliberation or concert; so the carnal mind, being in its own nature enmity against God, produces, wherever it operates, substantially the same fruits. In an alienated heart there is an intense unwillingness to be or to abide near to God; and there is, consequently, great fecundity in the conception and production of partition walls to shield the conscience from the glances of his holiness.

The three species* of thorns that grew up and choked the word in this instance, are fair specimens of their class —fair samples from the heap. These and such as these slay their thousands still in the Christian Church. At this point, however, it is of very great importance to observe that all the transactions which are represented in the parable as having come between a sinner and the Saviour, are in themselves lawful; to overlook this would be to miss half the value of the lesson. In point of fact acts and habits of positive vice keep many back from the Gospel; but it is not with these cases that the parable deals —it is not to these persons that the Lord is here addressing his reproof. Everything in its own place and time; the lesson here is not, "A drunkard shall not inherit the king-

---

* I do not set much value on the elaborate and minute discussions which some expositors have raised regarding the distinct and specific significance of the several excuses. It is enough for me that they point to the possessions and the pleasures of life,—the possessions being distinguished into two kinds, the field and oxen, corresponding to the farm and the merchandise of the cognate parable.

dom," but " How shall we escape if we neglect so great salvation ?" When the material of the temptation is lawful and honourable the temptation is less suspected, and the tempted is more easily thrown off his guard. The field and the oxen must be bought and used; the affections of the family must be cherished; but woe to us if we permit these seemly plants to grow so rank that the soul's life shall be overlaid beneath their weight!

The mission of the servants successively to the streets and lanes of the city, and to the highways and hedges, with the urgent invitation to poor labourers and homeless beggars, the maimed, the halt, and the blind, is a vivid picture, given in prophecy, of what the Gospel of Christ does and will do in the world till the end of time. When many, and these the most wretched, are brought in redeemed and sanctified, the Lord is not satisfied; yet there is room, and the servants must go forth again to new, and if possible, more needy objects, with new, and if possible, more urgent appeals. "Whosoever will, let him come." It is thus that the numbers are filled up in the kingdom of God; but let it be well observed that to be in a spiritually wretched state does not confer a favour or imply safety. These men were saved, not because they were spiritually very low, but although they were spiritually very low: they were saved, although the chief of sinners, because Christ invited them, and they came at his call. The more moral, and more privileged, who were first invited, would have been as welcome and as safe if they had come.

Introduction: Lost Sheep,
Lost Coin and Prodigal Son
(Luke 15)

THE three parables of this chapter, like the seven in Matt. xiii., constitute a connected series. As soon as we begin to look into their contents and relations, it becomes obvious that they have been arranged according to a logical scheme, and that the group so framed is not fragmentary but complete. We cannot indeed fully comprehend the reciprocal relations of all until we shall have examined in detail the actual contents of each; and yet, on the other hand, a preliminary survey of the scheme as a whole may facilitate the subsequent examination of its parts. A glance towards the group from a point sufficiently distant to command the whole in one view may aid us afterwards in making a minuter inspection of details; and, reciprocally, the nearer inspection of individual features may throw back light on what shall have been left obscure in the general outline.

The three parables, then, the lost sheep, the lost coin, and the prodigal son, refer all to the same subject and describe the same fact; they contemplate that fact, however, from opposite sides, and produce, accordingly, different pictures. It is important to notice at this stage that the three parables of this group do not constitute a consecutive series of three members. In the logical scheme the stem parts into two branches, and the first of these is afterwards subdivided also into two : the lost sheep and the lost coin contemplate the subject from the same side, and in the main present the same representation.*

The repetition is profitable, for besides the intensity which reiteration imparts, the two parables, although generically the same, are specifically different. Together they represent one side of the fall and the redemption of man, while the other and opposite side is represented by the parable of the prodigal. But while the first two represent the same aspect of the great event, they represent it with specific varieties of feature. This will be more distinctly understood when we shall have examined the parables in detail.

In further indicating the relations which subsist between the two portions of the group, I shall, for the sake of shortness, speak only of the lost sheep and the prodigal, including under the first term also its twin parable of the lost money.

The sin and the salvation of man,—the fall and the rising again, considered as one whole, is here contemplated successively from two different, and in some respects opposite points of view. As the result, we obtain

---

* While the evidence that the main division is twofold, not threefold, lies chiefly in the nature of the several representations, the minute formulae by which the transitions of the narrative are effected, point in the same direction. The parable of the lost sheep is introduced by the phrase, "And he spake this parable," (ειπε δε την παραβολην), and that of the prodigal by the corresponding, "And he said," (ειπε δε). These two are thus balanced over against each other; but the only link between the lost sheep and the lost silver is, Either (η), indicating that the second does not introduce a new subject, but gives another illustration of that which was already expressed in the first.

two very dissimilar pictures; yet the pictures are both
true, and both represent the same object.

In as far as the departure is concerned, the two representations are coincident: it is only in regard to the
return that they are essentially diverse. The sheep and
the prodigal alike depart of their own accord, the one in
ignorance and the other in wilful wickedness. Man
destroys himself; but the hand of God must intervene for
his salvation.*

The conversion of a sinner is, on the contrary, represented by two different pictures. You cannot convey a
correct conception of a solid body by one picture on a
flat surface. The globe itself, for example, cannot be
exhibited on a map except as two distinct hemispheres.
To the right you have a representation of one side, and
to the left a representation of the other; the two pictures
are different, and yet each, as far as it goes, is a true picture
of the same globe. In like manner, the way of a sinner's
return to God is too great and deep for being fully set
forth in one similitude. In particular its aspect towards God
and its aspect towards men are so diverse that both cannot
be represented by one figure. On one side the Redeemer
goes spontaneously forth to seek and bear back again the
lost; on the other side the wanderer repents, arises, and returns. Here, accordingly, you see the shepherd following
the strayed sheep, and bringing it back on his shoulders
to the fold; and there you see the weary prodigal first
coming to himself, and then coming to his Father. The
first picture shows the sovereign self-moving love of God

---

* Bengel, in his usual pointed way, expresses the specific varieties which
characterize the three successive views of men's sin, as stupidity, want of
self-consciousness, and the positive choice of evil by an intelligent but de-
praved being. "Ovis, drachma, filius perditus: peccator stupidus, sui
plane nescius, sciens et voluntarius."

our Saviour; and the second shows the beginning, the progress, and the result of repentance in a sinner's heart.

These two similitudes represent one transaction: first, you are permitted to look upon it from above, and you behold the working of divine compassion; next, you are permitted to look upon it from below, and you behold the struggle of conviction in a sinner's conscience,—the spontaneous return of a repenting man. Here is revealed the sovereign outgoing of divine power; and there in consequence appears a willing people (Ps. cx. 3). It is not that one sinner is brought back by Christ, and another returns of his own accord: both features are present in every example. Of every one who, from this fallen world, shall have entered the eternal rest, it may be said, and will be said in the songs of heaven, both that the Lord his Redeemer, of His own mere mercy, saved him, and that he spontaneously came back to his Father's bosom and his Father's house.*

---

* It is interesting to notice that the same twin doctrines which the Master here exhibited in parables were afterwards taught in the same relation by his servants. Take two examples, one a brief bold allegory, and the other an autobiographic fragment, both from the fervent heart and through the fruitful pen of the apostle Paul. (1.) "Nevertheless the foundation of God standeth sure, having this seal, The Lord knoweth them that are his; and, Let every one that nameth the name of Christ depart from iniquity" (2 Tim. ii. 19). The engraving on the upper side of this seal represents God's part in a sinner's salvation, and corresponds to the shepherd's generous act; the engraving on its under side represents man's part, and corresponds to the repenting and returning of the prodigal. (2.) "Not as though I had already attained, either were already perfect; but I follow after, if that I may apprehend that for which also I am apprehended of Christ Jesus" (Phil. iii. 12). The obscurity which adheres to the sentence as it stands in the English Bible is removed when, instead of "that for which," you substitute the more direct and literal rendering, "for that," meaning "because" or "inasmuch as." The sentence should be read, "I follow after, if that I may (if so be that I may) apprehend, inasmuch as I also have been apprehended by, Christ Jesus," (διωκω δε ει και καταλαβω, εφ ᾧ και κατελημφθην υπο του Χριστοι Ιησου). The apostle intends to state two connected facts; and to intimate

It is proper to notice here also the immediate occasion in our Lord's history whence these instructions sprung, as it belongs not particularly to the first parable, but generally to the whole group. This spark of heavenly light, like many others of similar beauty, has been struck off for us by a rude blow which the Jewish leaders aimed against the character and authority of Jesus. The publicans and sinners of the place,—the home-heathen of the day,—the people whether rich or poor, who had neither the power of religion in their hearts nor the profession of it on their lips,—came out in great numbers to hear this new prophet, Jesus of Nazareth. The word was new: "never man spake like this man" to these poor outcasts before. If at any time they sauntered into the synagogue, and hovered for a few moments on the outskirts of the congregation, the stray words that reached their ears from the desk of the presiding scribe, were harsh supercilious denunciations of themselves and their class. Hitherto their hearts had been like clay, and the Pharisaic teaching, as far as it had reached them, had been like fire: the clay in this furnace grew aye the harder. But now a new sound from the lips of a public teacher saluted their ears. They could not throw these words back in the speaker's face, if they would; and they would not if they could. They permitted themselves to

---

that the one is the cause of the other. He is striving to grasp the Saviour; and what impels or encourages him to make the effort? His own experience that his Saviour has already in sovereign love laid hold of him. Christ has already come to this sinful man, in loving saving power, as the good shepherd came to the lost sheep; therefore the sinful man will arise and go to the Father like the repenting prodigal. The consciousness that like the lost sheep he has been grasped in the Redeemer's arms does not induce him to abstain from effort as unnecessary; on the contrary, by inspiring hope, it nerves his arm and spurs him on. Because he feels that the Shepherd is bearing him, therefore he will arise and go.

be taken, and led. To them Jesus speaks "with authority, and not as the scribes." This word had power; and its power lay in its tenderness: it went sheer through their stony hearts, and made them flow down like water.

Nor did he gain favour among unholy men by making their sins seem lighter than the scribes represented them to be:—he made them heavier. He did not convey to the profane and worldly the conception that their sins were easily forgiven; but he fixed in their hearts the impression that God is a great forgiver. Touched and won by this unwonted tenderness, they came in clouds to sit at Jesus' feet.

The Pharisees counted their presence a blemish in the reputation of the teacher. As for them, they had always so spoken as to keep people of that sort effectually at a distance: the doctrine, they think, that brings them round the preacher cannot be sound. "This man," they said, "receiveth sinners and eateth with them;" and they said no more, for they imagined that Jesus was convicted and condemned by the fact.

The occasion of the parables becomes in a great measure the key to their meaning. These men, the publicans and sinners, are Abraham's seed, and consequently, even according to the showing of the Pharisees themselves, lost sheep,—prodigal sons; and the Redeemer's errand from heaven to earth is to seek and find and bring back such as these to the Father's fold. If they had not strayed, it would not have been necessary that the shepherd should follow them in their wandering, and bear them home: if they had not in a far country spent their substance in riotous living, it would not have been necessary that they should return repenting to their Father.

The Lost Sheep
(Luke 15:1-7)

"Then drew near unto him all the publicans and sinners for to hear him. And the Phari
sees and scribes murmured, saying, This man receiveth sinners, and eateth with them.
And he spake this parable unto them, saying, What man of you, having an hundred sheep, if he lose one of them, doth not leave the ninety and nine in the wilderness, and go after that which is lost, until he find it? And when he hath found it, he
layeth it on his shoulders, rejoicing. And when he cometh home, he calleth together
his friends and neighbours, saying unto them, Rejoice with me ; for I have found my
sheep which was lost. I say unto you, that likewise joy shall be in heaven over one
sinner that repenteth, more than over ninety and nine just persons, which need no
repentance."

ALTHOUGH by another saying of the Lord, it
is rendered certain that hired, and even in a
sinister sense "hireling," shepherds were known
at the time in the country, the presumption
that the flock which this shepherd tended was his own
property is favoured both by the specific phraseology
employed in the narrative, and the special circumstances
of this particular case. The size of this flock, consisting
of only a hundred sheep, points rather to the entire
wealth of a comparatively poor man, than to the stock
of a territorial magnate. The conduct of the shepherd,
moreover, is precisely the reverse of that which is elsewhere ascribed to the "hireling whose own the sheep
are not." The salient feature of the man's character,
as it is represented in the parable, constitutes a specific proof of his ownership,—"he careth for the sheep,"

and that too with a peculiar and self-sacrificing tenderness.*

We assume, therefore, according to the terms of the narrative in their literal acceptation, that this is a man " having an hundred sheep,"—that the sheep are his own. He is feeding them on pasture land far from cultivated fields and human dwellings. Hills impervious to the plough, and patches of vegetation interspersed through rugged stony tracts, have in all countries and ages constituted the appropriate pasture for flocks of sheep. These are indicated here by one word, " the wilderness.' The term is obviously used not in a strict but in a free popular sense; it means simply the region of pasturage, consisting generally of hills and moors, not suitable for being ploughed and sown.

A flock of a hundred sheep, although small, is yet sufficiently considerable to render it impossible for the shepherd to detect the absence of one by merely looking to them in the lump and from a distance; he must have minutely inspected them ere he discovered that one was

---

* In the nature of the case a great and incurable defect adheres to the method of employing a hired servant to keep a flock of sheep, without giving him a material interest in the prosperity of his charge. Such is the nature of the occupation, and such its sphere, that the servant is necessarily far and long removed from the master's inspection, and if suspicion should arise, proof of unfaithfulness could hardly be brought home to the accused. It is the interest of the owner to contrive some method of linking the profit of the shepherd to the prosperity of the flock. It was by attempting to accomplish this object by a defective plan, that Laban afforded to Jacob the opportunity of prosecuting his subtle policy. While conversing lately with some shepherds on the Scottish Cheviots, I learned that masters and servants in that district arrange the matter easily to their mutual profit and satisfaction. The wages of the shepherd are not paid in money; a certain number of the sheep, between forty and fifty according to circumstances, are his own property, and their produce constitutes his hire. Thus his own interest is an ever present motive pressing the man to do his best for the flock, and so to do his best for the master.

amissing.   Knowing them all individually, he knows the one that has strayed ; he loves them all as his children, and grieves when one goes out of sight.

It was no mark of carelessness in the shepherd, as some have erroneously imagined, to leave the ninety and nine in the wilderness while he went to seek the one that was lost.   The main body of the flock was left in its own proper place, where it is often left from morning till night by the most careful shepherd, even when he is not employed on the urgent duty of recovering wanderers.

The shepherd knows the nature of the country in which the sheep is straying ; and also the nature of the sheep that is straying there.   He knows the roughness of the mountain passes, and the silliness of the solitary truant sheep ; he divines accordingly what track it will take. He conjectures beforehand, with a considerable measure of accuracy, the pit in which it will be found lying, or the thicket in which it will be seen struggling.   He follows and finds the fugitive.   Wearied by its journey, and perhaps wounded by its falls, the sheep, when discovered, cannot return to the fold even under the shepherd's guidance ; he takes it on his shoulders and bears the burden home.   He does not upbraid it for its straying ; he does not complain of its weight.   He is glad that he has gotten his own again, after it was "ready to perish." Happy while he bears it homeward, and happy when he has gotten it home, he invites all his neighbours to share in his joy.

Such is the simple and transparent outline of this ancient eastern pastoral scene ; let us now endeavour to see in the symbol those lessons which it at once veils and reveals.

The parable is spoken expressly for the purpose of

determining and manifesting the character and work of the Son in the salvation of sinful men ; it declares the design, the method, and the terms of the incarnate Redeemer in his intercourse with the creatures whom he came to save. But in the fact of accomplishing this its immediate object, it strikes also a chord which runs through the centre—constitutes, as it were, the medulla of the divine government in all places and all times. The parable spoken in order to afford a glance into the heart of Jesus, incidentally at the same time sketches the outline of God's universal rule ; as in drawing the figure of a branch you necessarily exhibit, in its main features and proportions, an image of the tree. This wider subject, certainly and accurately outlined, although incidentally introduced, demands some notice at our hand.

Ever since scientific observation discovered the true system of the material universe, and so, as it were, changed those twinkling sparks of light into central suns, the rulers of tributary worlds, philosophy apart from faith has been, more or less articulately, scattering the question, at once a fruit and a seed of unbelief, How could the Creator of so vast a universe bestow so much of his care on one small spot ? Some have been disposed to say, and perhaps more have been disposed to think, with fear or joy according to their predilection, that modern discovery is gradually putting the Bible out of date. A feeling, if not a judgment, has in some quarters arisen, that in view of the vastness of creation, the Scriptures ascribe to this globe and its concerns a share of its Maker's interest disproportionately great.

This phase of unbelief is refuted both by the necessary attributes of God and by the written revelation of his

will. What relation, capable of being appreciated or calculated, subsists between material bulk and moral character? The question between great and small is totally
distinct from the question between good and evil
Number and extension cannot exercise or illustrate the
moral character either of God or of man. We should ourselves despise the mischievous caprice which should give to
the biggest man in the city the honours that are due to the
best. Right and wrong are matters that move on other
lines and at higher levels than great and small, before
both human tribunals and divine.

There is, perhaps, as much reason for saying that this
earth is too large, as for saying that it is too small, for
being the scene of God's greatest work. The telescope
has opened a long receding vista of wonders, where the
observer is lost in the abyss of distance and magnitude;
the microscope has opened another long receding vista of
wonders, where the observer is lost in the abyss of nearness and minuteness equally beyond his reach. Between
the great and the small, who shall determine and prescribe the centre-point equidistant from both extremes,
which the Infinite ought to have chosen as a theatre for
the display of His greatest glory?

In the divine government generally, as well as in
revealed religion particularly, the aim is not to choose
the widest stage, but on any stage that may be chosen
to execute the Creator's purpose, and achieve the creature's good. A battle is fought, an enemy crushed, and
a kingdom won on some remote and barren moor : no
man suggests, by way of challenging the authenticity of
the record, that a conflict waged between hosts so powerful, and involving interests so momentous, could not have
taken place on an insignificant spot, while the continent

contained many larger and more fertile plains : neither can the loss incurred by the sin of men, and the gain gotten through the redemption of Christ, be measured by the size of the world in which the events emerged. It is enough that here the first Adam fell and the second Adam triumphed ;—that here evil overcame good, and good in turn overcame evil. There was room on this earth for Eden and for Calvary ; this globe supplies the fulcrum whereon all God's government leans. The Redeemer came not to the largest world, but to the lost world : " even so, Father."

" He took not on him the nature of angels." In aggregate numbers they may, for aught we know, be the ninety and nine, while we represent the one that strayed ; but though all these shining stars were peopled worlds, and all their inhabitants angels who kept their first estate, he will leave them in their places in the blue heaven afar, like sheep in the wide moorland, and go forth in search of this one shooting star, to arrest and bring it back. It is his joy to restore it to law and light again. Rejoice with great joy, O inhabitants of the earth! the Saviour Almighty has passed other worlds and other beings, some of whom do not need, and some of whom do not get, salvation,—has passed them and come to us. He has taken hold of the seed of Abraham, that we who partake of Abraham's sinful flesh may partake also of Abraham's saving faith. There is much in this mystery which we do not know, and in our present state could not comprehend; but we know the one thing needful regarding it,— that " Jesus Christ came into the world to save sinners."*

---

* " Should not that great and glorious Shepherd, whose millions of bright sheep fill the universe, leave these millions in order to seek the slightest, poorest, most infirm of those who need his care, and without that

Having noticed cursorily that grand characteristic feature of God's universal government to which the principle of the parable is applicable, we proceed now to examine more particularly the recovery of lost men by the Lord our Redeemer, to which the lesson of the parable is, in point of fact, specifically applied.

1. The shepherd misses one when it has strayed from the flock. The Redeemer's knowledge is infinite; He looks not only over the multitude generally, but into each individual. When I stand on a hillock at the edge of a broad meadow, and look across the sward, it may be said in a general way that I look on all the grass of that field; but the sun in the sky looks on it after another fashion,—shines on every down-spike that protrudes from every blade. It is thus that the Good Shepherd knows the flock. Knowing all, he misses any one that wanders. He missed a world when it fell, although his worlds lie scattered like grains of golden dust on the blue field of heaven,—the open infinite. When the light of moral life went out in one

---

care would utterly perish; does not his boundless love require him to go after it?" Stier, after quoting this sentence in reference to the parable from Kurz, *Bibel und Astronomie*, remarks, "This is a thought quite permissible in itself, but as an exposition of what Eternal Wisdom has spoken, it is not valid." Here, however, the learned critic has incorrectly apprehended the state of the question. A secondary relation is as real in its own place as a primary. It is quite true that the parable, under the picture of the one sheep that strayed and the ninety-nine that remained on the pasture, points directly and immediately to two distinct classes of human kind; but it brings up as legitimately, although more remotely, the distinction, governed by the same principle, which has in God's universal sovereignty been made between the human race on the one hand, and angelic spirits on the other. One expositor may legitimately confine his view to the more immediate and narrower sphere; but another may as legitimately take a wider range, provided he make and mark the necessary distinctions as he proceeds; as one inquirer in physics may limit his speculation to the solid body of this globe, while another, under the same general designation, may, with perfect logical exactness, include also the atmosphere that surrounds it.

of his worlds, he missed its wonted shining in the aggregate of glory that surrounds his throne. With equal perfectness of knowledge he misses one human being who has been formed by his hand, but fails to hang by faith upon his love. The Bible speaks of falling "*into* the hands of the living God," and calls it "a fearful thing" (Heb. x. 31); but an equally fearful thing happened before it,—we fell *out of* the bosom of the living God. He felt, so to speak, the want of our weight when we fell, and said, "Save from going down to the pit." But the omniscience of the Saviour does not stop when it passes through the multitude, and reaches the individual man ; it penetrates the veils that effectually screen us from each other, and so knows the thoughts which congregate like clouds within a human heart, that he misses every one that is not subject to his will. When the mighty volume is coursing along its channel towards the ocean, he marks every drop that leaps aside in spray. It is a solemn thought, and to the reconciled a gladsome one, that, as the shepherd observed when one sheep left the fold, the Shepherd of Israel, who slumbers not nor sleeps, detects every wandering soul, and in that soul every wandering thought. The Physician's thorough knowledge of the ailment lies at the very foundation of the patient's hope.

2. The shepherd cared for the lost sheep ; although he possessed ninety and nine, he was not content to let a unit go. A species of personal affection and the ordinary interest of property, combine to cause grief when the sheep is lost, and to contribute the motive for setting off in search of the wanderer.

In attempting to apply the lesson at this point, we very soon go beyond our depth. Our own weakness

warns us not to attempt too much; but the condescend-
ing kindness of the Lord, in speaking these parables, encourages us to enter into the mystery of redeeming love
on this side as far as our line can reach. In that inscrutable love which induced the Owner of man to become
his saviour when he fell, there must be something corresponding to both of the ingredients which constituted
the shepherd's grief. There was something corresponding—with such correspondence as may exist between the
divine and the human—to the personal affection, and
something to the loss of property. When we think of
the Redeemer's plan and work as wholly apart from self-
interest, and undertaken simply for the benefit of the
fallen race, we form a conception of redemption true as far
as it goes, but the conception is not complete. The object
which we, from our view-point, strive to measure, has
another and opposite side. For his own sake as well as for
ours, the Redeemer undertook and accomplished his work.*
" For the joy that was set before him he endured the cross,
despising the shame." When he wept over Jerusalem, mere
pity for the lost was not the sole fountain of his tears.
Those tears, like some great rivers of the globe, were supplied from two sources lying in opposite directions. As the
possession of the ransomed when they are brought back
affords the Redeemer joy, the want of the lost, while they
are distant, must cause in his heart a corresponding and
equivalent grief. It is true, that if we too strictly apply
to the divine procedure the analogy of human affairs at

---

* You may measure a square surface and find it to contain so many feet
of superficial area : suppose you discover afterwards that it has depth as
well as length and breadth; to take in also this new measurement does not
diminish the old. If we discover that, for his own sake, the Redeemer
accomplished his saving work, it was not on that account less for our
sakes.

this point we shall fatally dilute our conception of the generosity displayed in the Gospel; but on the other hand, if do not apply this analogy at all, we shall inevitably permit some of our sweetest consolation to slip from our grasp. To be merely pitied does not go so kindly or so powerfully about our hearts as to be loved; Christ's regard for fallen men is not merely the compassion of one who is loftily independent. When an infant is lost in a forest, and all the neighbours have, at the mother's call, gone out in search of the wanderer, it would be a miserably inadequate conception of that mother's emotion to think of it as pity for the sufferings of the child: her own suffering for want of her child is greater than the child's for want of his mother; and by the express testimony of Scripture, we learn that the Saviour's remembrance of his people is analogous to the mother's remembrance of her child. If you press the likeness too far, you destroy the essential character of redemption, by representing it as a self-pleasing on the part of the Redeemer; but if you take away the likeness altogether, you leave me sheltered, indeed, under an Almighty arm, but not permitted to lie on a loving breast. My joy in Christ's salvation is tenfold increased, when, after being permitted to think that he is mine, I am also permitted to think that I am his. If it did not please him to get me back, my pleasure would be small in being coldly allowed to return. No: the longing of Christ to get the wanderer into his bosom again, for the satisfaction of his own soul, is the sweetest ingredient in the cup of a returning penitent's joy.*

---

* "In the centre of all lies the profound thought, that in God and Christ love is one with self-interest, and self-interest one with love; no such contrariety existing between them as is found in the case of man."—*Stier, Words of the Lord.*

3. The shepherd left the ninety and nine for the sake of the one that had wandered. I find no difficulty in the interpretation of the parable here. The doctrinal difficulty which some have met at this point, has been imported into the field by a mistake in regard to the material scene. The leaving of the ninety and nine in the wilderness, while the shepherd went out to seek the strayed sheep, implied no dereliction of the shepherd's duty,—no injury to the body of the flock. In this transaction neither kindness nor unkindness was manifested towards those that remained on the pasture;—it had no bearing upon them at all. Nor is it necessary, at this stage, to determine who are represented by the ninety and nine. Be they the unfallen spirits, or the righteous in the abstract, or those who, in ignorance of God's law, count themselves righteous, the parable is constructed for the purpose of teaching us that the mission of Christ has for its special object, not the good, but the evil. As the specific effort of the shepherd, which is recorded in this story, had respect not to the flock that remained on the pasture, but to the one sheep that had gone away, the specific effort of the Son of God, in his incarnation, ministry, death, and resurrection, has respect, not to the worthy, but the unworthy.

Thus the Pharisees were entirely at fault in regard to the first principle of the Gospel. They assumed that, because the publicans and sinners had gone astray, Jesus, if he were the true Messiah, would not have any dealings with them; without either conceding or expressly denying their assumption of superior righteousness—that being precisely the point on which he determined that then and there he would give no judgment—he intimates that the strayed sheep is the peculiar object of his care, and that because it is the strayed sheep, and he is the Good Shepherd;—he intimates, taking the Pharisees at their own word, that the sinners are the objects whom a Saviour should follow, and seek, and find, precisely because they are sinners. It concerns us more to know who are represented by the strayed sheep, than to know who are represented by the sheep that did not stray, for to the former class, and not to the latter, we most certainly belong.

4. How does the shepherd act when he overtakes the wanderer? He does not punish it—he does not even upbraid it for straying; his anxiety and effort are concentrated on one point—to get it home again. Would that guilty suspicious hearts could see through this glass the loving heart of Jesus, as he has himself presented it to their view! He takes no pleasure in the death of them that die. His ministry in general, and this lesson in particular, proclaim that Christ's errand into the world is to win the rebellious back by love. You may suppose the truant sheep to have dreaded punishment when it was overtaken by the injured shepherd; but his look and his act when he came must have immediately dispelled the helpless creature's fears. The Lord has held up this picture before us that in it we may behold his love, and that the sight of his love may at length discharge from our hearts their inborn obdurate suspiciousness.

5. The shepherd lays the sheep upon his shoulders. This feature of the picture affords no ground for the doctrine which has sometimes been founded on it, that the Saviour is burdened with the sinners whom he saves. His suffering lies in another direction, and is not in any form represented here. He weeps when the sinful remain distant and refuse to throw their weight on him; he

never complains of having too much of this work in hand. The parable here points to his power and victory, not to his pain and weariness.

The representation that the shepherd bore the strayed sheep home upon his shoulder, instead of going before and calling on it to follow, is significant in respect both to this parable and its counterpart and complement, the Prodigal Son. In as far as the saving of the lost is portrayed in this similitude, the work is done by the Saviour alone. First and last the sinner does nothing but destroy himself : all the saving work is done for him, none of it by him. This is one side of salvation, and it is the only side that is represented here. It seems hard to conceive how any converted man can be troubled by doubt or difficulty concerning this doctrine. Every one whom Christ has sought and found, and borne to the fold, feels and confesses that, if the Shepherd had not come to the sheep, the sheep would not have come to the Shepherd. If any wanderer still hesitates on the question, Who brought him home ? it is time that he should begin to entertain another question, Whether he has yet been brought home at all ? The acknowledgment of this fundamental truth, that salvation is begun, carried on, and completed by the Saviour alone, does not, of course, come into collision with another fundamental truth, which expatiates on another sphere, and is represented in another parable, that except the sinful do themselves repent, and come to the Father, they shall perish in their sins.

6. Far from being oppressed by the burden of his strayed sheep, the shepherd rejoices when he feels its weight upon his shoulder. His joy begins not when the work is over, but when the work begins. While the lost

one is on his shoulder, and because it is on his shoulder, the shepherd is glad. The doctrinal equivalent of this feature is one of the clearest of revealed truths, and yet it is one of the last that a human heart is willing to receive. The work of saving, far from being done with a grudge in order to keep a covenant, is a present delight to the Saviour. This lesson falls on human minds like a legend written by the finger on dewy glass, which disappears when the sun grows hot ; but when it is graven on the heart as by the Spirit of the living God, it is unspeakably precious. When I habitually realize not only that Christ will keep his word in receiving sinners, but that he has greater delight in bearing my weight than I can ever have in casting it on him, I shall trust fully and trust always. There is great power in this truth, and great weakness in the want of it. Let even an experienced Christian analyze carefully the working of his own heart, not in the act of backsliding towards the world, but in its best efforts to follow the Lord, and he will discover among the lower folds of his experience a persistent suspicion that the great draft which a sinner makes on the Saviour's mercy will, though honoured, be honoured with a grudge because of its greatness. Look on the simple picture of his love which Jesus has in this parable presented—look on the words, " He layeth it on his shoulders rejoicing," --look till you grieve for your own distrust, and the distrust melt in that grief away.

7. The shepherd on reaching home not only himself rejoiced, but invited his neighbours to rejoice with him over his success. To this last intimation of the parable the Lord immediately adds an express exposition of its meaning,—Ver. 7, " I say unto you that likewise joy shall be in heaven over one sinner that repenteth, more than

over ninety and nine just persons which need no repentance." In the parallel explanation appended to the
next parable (ver. 10), an additional feature is expressed,
" There is joy in the presence of the angels of God over
one sinner that repenteth ;" both obviously refer to the
same fact, and should be taken together as one announcement.

The kingdom of God recognises two successive home-
comings in the history of every citizen. The exile discovered and borne back by the discriminating mercy of
the Redeemer, comes home when through the regeneration he enters a state of grace ; and he comes home
under the leading of the same chief, when in the resurrection he enters a state of perfect glory. It is instructive and comforting to observe that, while both home-
comings are joyful, it is of the first that the Lord
expressly speaks when he intimates that over it himself
and the hosts of heaven will rejoice. It is over the repentance of a sinner that a jubilee is held in heaven ; they
do not wait till the ransomed one shall appear in bodily
presence near the great white throne. There is no need :
the entrance into grace ensures the entrance into glory.
The children will all get home. No slip can come between the cup of the Redeemer's glad anticipation when
a sinner is renewed, and the lip of his complete satisfaction when he welcomes the ransomed at length into the
mansions of the Father's house.

In this brief but lucid exposition of his own similitude
which the Lord gave at the moment, and the evangelist
has preserved for us, something is taught first regarding
the companions, and second regarding the measure of his
joy. Both present points of interest which require and
will repay more particular attention.

(1.) In regard to the participation of the angels, in the Redeemer's joy over the salvation of the lost, the intima-tions bear that there is joy " in heaven," and " in the pre-sence of the angels of God." It seems unaccountably to those who look carefully into the terms of the record, to be universally assumed from these expressions that the angels, in the exercise of their inherent faculties, are in some way cognisant of conversion as it proceeds in human souls upon the earth, and that they rejoice accordingly when another heart melts, and another rebel submits to God. Capital has even been made out of this passage by Romanists in support of prayers addressed to unseen created spirits. All this proceeds upon an exegesis, which is, I believe, demon-strably erroneous. In order to settle all questions that can arise here, nothing more is necessary than a simple straight-forward examination of the terms. The rejoicing takes place " in heaven," and " in presence of the angels" (ενωπιον τῶν ἀγγέλων). This is not the form of expres-sion that would naturally be employed to intimate that the angels rejoiced. Expressly it is written, not that they rejoice, but that there is joy in their presence,—before their faces. The question then comes up, Who rejoices there? In as far as the terms of the exposition go, the question is not expressly decided ; but its decision can be easily and certainly gathered from the context. Both in the case of the lost sheep and in that of the lost money the comparison is introduced by the term " likewise " (ὄντω.) In this manner there is joy before the angels ; in what manner? Obviously in the manner of the rejoicing which took place after the strayed sheep was brought home, and the piece of money found. He who sought and found the lost, rejoiced over his gain ; but, not con-tented therewith, he told his neighbours about his happiness and its cause ; he manifested his joy in their presence, and invited them to rejoice in sympathy with himself. It is after this manner that joy in heaven over a repenting sinner begins and spreads. We are not obliged,—we are not permitted to guess who the rejoicers are, or how they came by the news that gladdens them. The shepherd himself, and himself alone, knows that the strayed sheep is safe in the fold again, for he has borne it back on his shoulder : his neighbours did not know the fact until he told them, and invited them to participate in his joy. It is expressly in this manner, and none other, that there shall be joy in heaven over one sinner that repenteth. The angels do not become aware of the fact by a species of subordinate omniscience. He who saved the sinner knows that the sinner is saved ; rejoicing in the fact, he makes it known to his attendants, and invites them to share in his joy.

The gladness that thrills in the angels is a secondary thing, caught by sympathy from that which glows in the heart and beams in the countenance of Jesus. The Son of God the Saviour having won a sinner by the power of his love, and brought the wanderer back forgiven and renewed, rejoices on his throne over this fruit of his soul's travail. Ere the ransomed sinner has risen from his knees or wiped his tears away ;—ere he has had time to sing a hymn or sit down at the communion table on earth, the Lord in heaven, feeling life flowing from himself into that living soul, rejoices already in the fact, and calls upon his friends, whether the spirits of just men or angels unfallen, or both in concert, to participate in his joy. The Apocalyptic witness saw no sun in the new heaven; "the Lamb is the light thereof:" from that sun the light streams down on the sea of upturned faces that surround the

throne, and the sympathetic gladness that sparkles in the
members is a reflection from the gladness that first glows
in the Head, as a separate sun glances on the crest of
every wavelet, when the breeze is gentle and the sky is
bright.

(2.) The intimation that there is greater joy in heaven
over the return of a single wanderer than over ninety and
nine who never strayed, presents indeed a difficulty ; but
here, as in many other similar cases, the difficulty lies
more in the way of the scientific expositor, whose task is
to express the meaning in the form of logical definitions
than in the way of the simple reader of the Bible, who
desires to sit at the feet of Jesus, and learn the one thing
needful from his lips.   In this, as in many other portions
of Scripture, a hungry labourer may live upon the bread,
while it may baffle a philosopher to analyze its constituents, and expound its nutritive qualities.   A devout
reader may get the meaning of the parable in power upon
his heart, while the logical interpreter expends much pro-
fitless labour in the dissection of a dead letter.

Who are the just persons who need no repentance ?
The suggestion* that they are the members of the Old
Testament Church, who really possessed the righteousness of the Law, although they had not attained the righteousness of the Gospel, creates a greater difficulty than
that which it proposes to remove.   There is not any such
essential difference between the righteousness of Abraham, who looked unto Jesus coming, and the righteousness of Paul, who looked unto Jesus come.

The true solution I apprehend to be that in the mind
of the Lord this declaration had a double reference.   It
expressed an absolute and universal truth, known to him-

* Made or adopted by Dr. Trench.

self and to his enlightened disciples ; and also, at the
same time, took the Pharisees on their own terms, condemning them out of their own mouth.   The parable was
spoken expressly to the Pharisees, and spoken specifically
in answer to their objection, " This man receiveth sinners."
They meant to intimate that it became the Messiah to
shun the evil and associate only with the good.   From
their own view-point he exposes their mistake ;   even
granting their assumption that themselves were the righteous, their sentence was erroneous.   According to the
principles of human nature, and the ordinary practice of
men, they might have perceived that the chief care of the
shepherd must be bestowed on the sheep that has gone
astray, and his greatest joy be experienced when it has
been discovered and restored.   The Saviour's delight over
a publican's return to piety should be more vivid than
his joy over a Pharisee, who, by the supposition, has been
pious all his days.

Had the Lord then and there intimated to the Pharisees that they were deceiving themselves in regard to
justifying righteousness,—that they needed repentance
as much as the publicans, his word would have been true,
but that truth, he perceived, was not suitable in the circumstances.   It pleased him at this time not to fling a
sharp reproof in their faces, but rather to drop a living
seed gently into their ears, that it might find its way in
secret to some broken place in their hearts.   A certain
portion of the truth he communicated to them ;   more
they would not have received.   The whole truth on this
subject, if it had been bluntly declared, would have driven
them away in disgust.

Elsewhere the Master expresses his mind very clearly,
Except your righteousness exceed the righteousness of the

Scribes and Pharisees, ye shall in no case enter into the kingdom of heaven;" but it pleased him on this occasion to teach another lesson, namely, that even although they were as righteous as they deemed themselves to be, the recovery of a lost one would afford the Redeemer a greater joy than the retention of the virtuous. Beyond expression precious is the doctrine unequivocally taught here that so far from receiving prodigals with a grudge, the Saviour experiences a peculiar delight when a sinner listens to his voice and accepts pardon at his hand. This doctrine we learn is divine; we know it is also human: almost every family can, supply an example of the familiar principle that the mother loves most fondly the child who has cost her most in suffering and care.

The Lost Coin
(Luke 15:8-10)

" Either what woman having ten pieces of silver, if she lose one piece, doth not light a
candle, and sweep the house, and seek diligently till she find it ? And when she hath
found it, she calleth her friends and her neighbours together, saying, Rejoice with
me ; for I have found the piece which I had lost. Likewise, I say unto you, there is
joy in the presence of the angels of God over one sinner that repenteth."

THE three parables of this group, as has been
already intimated, do not constitute a simple
consecutive series of first, second, and third :
the group consists of two parts, and the
first part contains two parables. The saving of the lost
is represented in the first division as it is seen from God's
side, and in the second as it is seen from man's. In
the first, the Saviour appears seeking, finding, and
bearing back the lost ; in the second, the lost appears
reflecting, repenting, resolving, and returning to the
Father.

The two parables which constitute the first division
are generically coincident, but specifically distinct. Both
represent the side on which the sinner is passive in the
matter of his own salvation, and the parable of the prodigal alone represents the aspect in which he is spontaneously active ; but while the first two agree in their
main feature, they differ in subordinate details. The
second goes partly over the same ground that has already

been traversed by the first, and partly takes a new and independent track of its own.*

From the similarity of structure and the studied identity of expression in the two cases, I gather surely that

---

* Recognising in the lost coin mainly a repetition of the same lesson which the lost sheep contained, but justly anticipating from the mere fact of a repetition, that the second will present some features which were not contained in the first, Dr. Trench finds the expected difference in this,— that "if the shepherd in the last parable was Christ, the woman in this may, perhaps, be the Church." After suggesting as an alternative that the woman may represent the Holy Spirit, he remarks that these two are in effect substantially identical, and finally rests in the conclusion that it is "the Church because and in so far as it is dwelt in by the Spirit, which appears as the woman seeking her lost." This able expositor speaks with evident hesitation when he represents the Church as the seeker here ; and accordingly we find him with a happy inconsistency affirming in a subsequent paragraph that "as the woman, having lost her drachm, will light a candle and sweep the house, and seek diligently till she find it, even so the Lord, through the ministrations of his Church, gives diligence to recover the lost sinner," &c. I am willing to accept the phraseology of this sentence, but it is obviously at variance with the view which he had previously presented, and to which he recurs in the close, that in this parable it is the Church which seeks the lost, while in the preceding parable it is the Saviour. Further, if he maintain that the woman seeking the lost coin represents the Lord seeking sinners through the ministrations of the Church, he must also maintain that the shepherd seeking the lost sheep represents the Lord seeking sinners through the ministrations of the Church. If the Lord himself is in both cases equally the seeker, there is no reason in the text of Scripture, and Dr. Trench suggests none from any other quarter, why he should be represented as seeking through the ministrations of the Church in one case and not in the other. The letter of the word and the nature of the case peremptorily demand that the qualification regarding the instrumentality of the Church should be attached to both or to neither. In either case it remains that, in respect to the person who seeks the lost, these two parables teach precisely the same lesson.

The house in which the coin is lost means, according to Dr. Trench, the visible Church : the result is that the Church (invisible) searches in the Church (visible) for sinners that have been lost there, and restores them when found to the Church, but whether the visible or invisible I cannot discover. The Church then calls upon the angels to rejoice with her over the recovery of the lost. This exposition seems confused and inconsistent ; and it is a dim mysterious conception of "the Church" that constitutes the disturbing element.

the persons who seek and find the lost in those two parables both represent the same Seeker of lost men, the
Lord Jesus Christ. On any other supposition, I cannot
find a spot on which the foundation of a satisfactory
exegesis can be laid. The introduction of the second
parable by the particle either (η) in the eighth verse, prepares us to expect, not another subject, but another illustration of the same subject ; whereas, when the Prodigal
Son is introduced in the eleventh verse, the connecting
link distinctly indicates a change of theme.*

Assuming from the fact of its repetition that some
feature or features of the lesson must be contained in
the second picture which the first was not fitted to display; and finding in the possessors, with their misfor-
tune, their success and their joy, no difference, but on
the contrary, a studied balanced parallelism, I look for
the distinction in the nature of the property which, in the
two cases respectively, was lost and found. The sheep
is an animated being, with desires, and appetites, and
habits, and locomotive powers; when it is lost, it is lost
in virtue of its own will and activity. The silver coin, on
the other hand, is a piece of inanimate matter; and when
it is lost, it is lost through its own gravity and inertia.

---

* Nor do I see any force in the minute criticism by which Dr Trench
endeavours to make out that while the sheep were the shepherd's property,
the money did not belong to the woman. He says, " I have found my
sheep which was lost;" while she says, " I have found the piece which I
had lost;" but these are nothing more than varieties of expression. The
absolute identity of the terms in which the two cases are introduced, proves
that these seemly and slight variations of phraseology at the close, do not
indicate a substantial difference. " What man of you having an hundred
sheep, if he lose one of them ? " and " What woman, having ten pieces
of silver, if she lose one piece ? "—these questions, so carefully and completely parallel, conclusively show that, after making allowance for the
necessary difference in the nature of the subjects, the two cases, in relation
to possession, loss, and finding, are precisely the same.

When support fails, it falls to the ground. Here lies an inherent and essential difference between the two cases. It is through this opening mainly that light comes to me regarding the specific difference between the lessons which these two cognate parables respectively convey. The inquiry at present concerns this difference only, for the doctrine which is taught in common by both is abundantly obvious. While in both examples alike the property is lost and found again, the manner of the loss and the finding corresponds in each case to the nature of the subject. In the case of the living creature, the loss is sustained through its spontaneous wandering; in the case of the inanimate silver, the loss is sustained through its inherent inertia. The one strays in the exercise of its own will, and the other sinks in obedience to the laws of matter; the method of search varies accordingly.

Both parables alike represent the sinner lost and the Saviour finding him; but in the one case the loss appears due to the postive activity of an evil will, and in the other to the passive law of gravitation. Not that, in the spiritual sphere, one sinner departs from God by an exercise of his corrupt will, and another is drawn away by the operation of an irresistible law; it is one transaction represented successively on two sides. The representations are different, but both are true. In the fallen, sin is both active and passive. The sinful select their own course and go astray in the exercise of a self-determining power; they also gravitate to evil in virtue of an inborn corruption, which acts like a law in their members. In connection with these two sides or features of sin, the two doctrines opposite and yet not contrary, the sovereignty of God and the responsibility of man, meet and embrace each other in the work of redemption. To the disease of sin in both its phases,—as an active choice and an innate tendency,—the divine physician has prepared an antidote; He brings the wanderer home, and lifts the fallen up.

Compare once more the lost sheep and the lost coin : in both the sinful are lost, and in both the Saviour saves; but there we see a spontaneous error, and here the effect of inherited corruption. These, when kept together like the right and left sides of a living man, constitute, in this matter, the whole truth : to tear them asunder is to kill both.

The number of the coins is appropriately fixed at ten, while the number of sheep was a hundred. Ten sheep would not have required or repaid the care of a shepherd; and a hundred pieces of silver would not, in ordinary circumstances, have been at one time in the hands of a working woman. The difference of numbers is fully accounted for by the natural circumstances, and no benefit is obtained by squeezing from it a distinct spiritual signification. The numbers, I think, belong to the adjuncts of the material pictures, and they constitute only elements of disturbance when they are brought into the interpretation.

The lessons which some draw from the preciousness of the metal on the one hand, and the image of the king which it bears on the other, although attractive and useful in themselves, are not relevant here. It is better to forego for the time even precious morsels of instruction, than to obtain them by doing violence to those exquisite analogies which the parables present.

The Prodigal Son
(Luke 15:11-32)

" And he said, A certain man had two sons: and the younger of them said to his father, Father, give me the portion of goods that falleth to me. And he divided unto them his living. And not many days after the younger son gathered all together, and took his journey into a far country, and there wasted his substance with riotous living. And when he had spent all, there arose a mighty famine in that land; and he began to be in want. And he went and joined himself to a citizen of that country; and he sent him into his fields to feed swine. And he would fain have filled his belly with the husks that the swine did eat: and no man gave unto him. And when he came to himself, he said, How many hired servants of my father's have bread enough and to spare, and I perish with hunger! I will arise and go to my father, and will say unto him, Father, I have sinned against heaven and before thee, and am no more worthy to be called thy son : make me as one of thy hired servants. And he arose, and came to his father. But when he was yet a great way off, his father saw him, and had compassion, and ran, and fell on his neck, and kissed him. And the son said unto him, Father, I have sinned against heaven, and in thy sight, and am no more worthy to be called thy son. But the father said to his servants, Bring forth the best robe, and put it on him ; and put a ring on his hand, and shoes on his feet ; and bring hither the fatted calf, and kill it : and let us eat, and be merry : for this my son was dead, and is alive again ; he was lost, and is found. And they began to be merry. Now his elder son was in the field : and as he came and drew nigh to the house, he heard musick and dancing. And he called one of the servants, and asked what these things meant. And he said unto him, Thy brother is come : and thy father hath killed the fatted calf, because he hath received him safe and sound. And he was angry, and would not go in : therefore came his father out and intreated him. And he answering said to his father, Lo, these many years do I serve thee, neither transgressed I at any time thy commandment : and yet thou never gavest me a kid, that I might make merry with my friends : but as soon as this thy son was come, which hath devoured thy living with harlots, thou hast killed for him the fatted calf. And he said unto him, Son, thou art ever with me, and all that I have is thine. It was meet that we should make merry, and be glad : for this thy brother was dead, and is alive again ; and was lost, and is found."

RECALL the relation that subsists between this parable on the one hand, and the two that immediately precede it on the other. These two divisions of the group contain two different and in some respects opposite representations. Both exhibit the salvation of lost men ; but in the first, that deliverance appears as the effect of the Redeemer's sovereign love and care ; in the second, it appears to spring in the depths of the sinner's own soul. There the wanderer is sought and found and borne back ; here he spontaneously repents and returns. There the Saviour's part is revealed ; and here the sinner's.

These examples represent not two distinct experiences, but two sides of the same fact. It is not that some of fallen human kind are saved after the manner of the strayed sheep, and others after the manner of the prodigal son ; not that the Saviour bears one wanderer home by his power, and another of his own accord arises and returns to the Father. Both these processes are accomplished in every conversion. The man comes, yet Christ brings him ; Christ brings him, yet he comes. In the two pictures which we have last examined, the sovereign love and power of the Redeemer occupied the front, while the subjective experience of a repenting man was thrown scarcely visible into the back-ground ; in the picture which is now under inspection the view is reversed—the subjective experience of the sinning man is brought full size into the centre of the field, while the compassion of a forgiving God, although distinctly visible, lies in smaller bulk behind.

Among the parables that of the prodigal is remarkable for the grandeur of the whole, and the exquisite beauty of the parts. The sower is the only one that can be compared with it in comprehensive completeness of outline and articulate distinctness of detail. These two greatest parables, however, are thoroughly diverse in kind. The two chief elements which generally go into the composition of a parable are the processes of nature and the actions of living men—parables, in short, as to their constituents, are composed of history and natural history. In the tares, for example, both these elements are combined in nearly equal proportions. In the malicious sowing of the darnel, the zealous proposal of the servants, and the cautious decision of the master, you have threads of human motive and action running through the whole ; but in the growth of the darnel, its likeness to the wheat in spring, and the decisive difference between them in the harvest, you have the processes of nature profusely intertwined. A parable is ordinarily woven of human action and the unconscious development of nature, as warp and woof. In the two greatest parables those twin ingredients are in a great measure separated : the sower is almost wholly composed of processes in nature, the prodigal almost wholly of human motive and act.

This parable reveals one of the brightest glimpses of God's character and way that men in the body can obtain. There are greater and less among the parts of God's word as well as among the parts of his creation. Taking the discourses of the Lord Jesus, as the little child took the stars, for " gimlet-holes in heaven to let the glory shine through," we find in the prodigal the largest of them all. It differs from other stars in the same firmament by its bulk and its brightness. Never man spake like this man ; and nowhere else has even this man spoken more fully or more winsomely of man's need and God's mercy. Both the departure and the return—both the fall and the rising again, are depicted here. The lesson sweeps the whole horizon of time from the unfallen state at first to the glory that shall at last be revealed. The way is laid open with marvellous precision from the lowest state of sin and misery to a heavenly Father's heart and home. Here a gate is opened by the Mediator's hand, and no man can shut it, until the angel shall proclaim that time shall be no more. Here resounds a voice clear, human, memorable—a voice that all the hum of the world cannot drown, proclaiming to the lowest, furthest outcasts, and to the latest generations, " Whosoever will, let him come." *

It is not necessary in this case to submit a sketch of the material frame-work : there it lies, and the simplest may see it for himself. The least learned may go round without a guide, and not miss any essential feature of the scene. In this case the bare reading of the story from the Bible leaves the image sharply outlined, and permanently impressed upon the reader's mind. Assuming that the body of the lesson may be easily seen, let us proceed at once to seek for its soul in the spiritual meaning, which the picture covers and yet reveals.

"A certain man had two sons : " one of the greatest difficulties meets us in the first line. It is evident that

---

* A curious illustration of the bondage to which an indurated Erastianism has reduced many of the Protestant Churches of the Continent, is incidentally afforded in a remark made by Stier regarding the peculiar fulness and preciousness of this parable :—" That this parable, which Lange beautifully terms a gospel within a gospel, this universal text for preaching about the lost and recovered sons of our heavenly Father (and the hopelessly lost first-born to the rich possessions of the house), should be wanting in the pericopæ of the Sunday Kalendar, is an omission which is utterly unjustifiable on any ground whatever, which is not compensated by the insertion of the previous similitudes, and which of itself is ample reason for that reformation of the Kalendar which Palmer desires."—*Words of the Lord Jesus, in loc.* The successors of Luther must, it seems, tread the mill from year to year on the same limited curriculum of texts which their Kalendar contains ; and those of them who are weary of the restraint long in vain for an opportunity to preach on such a subject as the prodigal, for it is not set down in the bond. That Church surely is greatly defective both in godliness and manliness, that cannot or will not throw open all the Word of God alike, at all times, to its ministers and congregations in their Sabbath solemnities.

God, as specially manifested in the Gospel, is represented by the father ; but who are represented by the two sons, —the elder, who remained at home, and the younger, who went away ?   On this point three distinct interpretations have been suggested: the two brothers of the parable may represent angels and'men, Jews and Gentiles, or Pharisees and publicans.   I do not think it is a profitable method to send these three into the field to fight until two are destroyed, and one is left in undisputed possession.   I am convinced that we shall more fully and more correctly ascertain the mind of the Lord by employing them all than by selecting one.

In representing the human figure, an artist may proceed upon either of two distinct principles, according to the object which, for the time, he may have in view.   He may, on the one hand, delineate the likeness of an individual, producing a copy of his particular features, with all their beauties and all their blemishes alike : or he may, on the other hand, conceive and execute an ideal picture of man, the portrait of no person in particular, with features selected from many specimens of the race, and combined in one complete figure.   The parable of the prodigal is a picture of the latter kind.   It is not out and out the picture of any man ; but it is, to a certain extent, the picture of every man.   This prophecy of Scripture is not of private construction ; and therefore it is not of private interpretation.   As the ideal portrait is in one feature the likeness of this man, and in another the likeness of that man, while it is not throughout the likeness of any ; so the elder and younger sons of this parable find at one point their closest counterpart in angels and men, at another in Jews and Gentiles, at a third in Pharisees and publicans, and indefinitely in as many pairs of correspond·

ing characters as have been, or may yet be, found in the world.

In the first act of the drama,—the departure of the younger son, the case of angels and men, presents by far the most exact counterpart to the case of the two brothers. Man is the youngest child of God's intelligent family. Elder and younger remained together in the house awhile. You may observe sometimes in human families that the children who have reached the years of understanding at the birth of the youngest rejoice over the infant with a fondness second only to that of the mother. Thus the elder brother angels of our Father's house,—the morning stars of creation, sang together over the advent of man. But the younger son did not remain in the house : having become alienated in heart from the Father, he was uneasy in his presence, and sought relief by going out of sight.

In the description of the younger son's conduct, we find a picture both of the first fall and of the actual apostasy of each separate sinner. "The younger said to his father, Father give me the portion," &c. Only his words are preserved in the record ; but we know that thoughts unseen in his soul were the seeds whence these words sprang. He desired to please himself, and therefore grew unhappy under the restraints of home. Bent on enjoying the pleasures of sin, he determined to avoid the presence of his father : alienated in heart, he becomes vicious in life.

The same two elements go to constitute the character and condition of the sinful before he is reconciled to God. There is a lower and a higher link in the chain that binds the slave. There is a body of this death, and a soul : there is a spiritual wickedness in high places, and a bodily wickedness in low places. The one is guilt, the other sin the heart is at enmity, and the life is disobedient.

The younger son did not humbly sue for a gift from his father's bounty: he claimed a share of the property as of right. The terms are significant ; "Give me the portion of goods that *falleth* (τὸ ἐπιβάλλον μέρος) to me." The phrase faithfully depicts the atheism of an unbelieving human heart; the fool hath said in his heart, "No God." He has become brutish: as swine gather the acorns from the ground, heedless of the oak from which they fell; alienated men snatch God's gifts for the gratification of their appetites, and forget the giving God. This seeing eye, and this hearing ear, and these cunning hands, the irreverent son counts his own, and determines to employ them in ministering to his own pleasure.

The father might justly have refused to comply with his son's demand : although a certain part of the property might by law "fall" to the younger son at the death of the father, there was no law or custom that gave the youth a right to any of it during his father's life. In this case, however, the father saw meet to let the young man have his own way ; he threw the reins loose upon the neck of the prodigal. Although the father of his flesh could not see the end from the beginning, the Father of his spirit, in permitting his departure, already planned the glad return.

"Not many days after :" weary of paternal restraint, he made off as soon as possible. He gathered all ; for he needed all as a price in his hand to pay for his pleasure. He went into a far country, and there wasted his substance with riotous living. Even a large substance may in this manner soon be consumed ; money and health waste away quickly when they are employed as fuel to feed the flame of lust. An interesting parallel to this portion of the parable occurs in Luke xii. 45. A servant to whom much had been intrusted thought his master was at a great distance, and would remain a long time away ; then and therefore he began "to beat the men-servants and maidens, and to eat and drink, and to be drunken." It is when a man is, or imagines himself to be, far from God that he dares to indulge freely his vicious propensities : and conversely, those who are secretly bent upon a life of sin, put God far from their thoughts, in order that they may not be interrupted in their pleasures.

The crisis came. The "season" of pleasure did not last long ; and the man who had "sowed to the flesh" was compelled to fill his bosom with an early harvest of misery. The hunger, nakedness, and shame that accumulated on the head of this wayward youth aptly represent the bitter fruits which sin, even in this life, bears as an earnest of the full wages in the second death, which it promises to pay its servants.

His sufferings did not in the first instance turn him from his sin : human sorrow is not all or always godly sorrow. Although the prodigal was in want, he did not return to his father. Convictions and terrors in the conscience seldom bring the wanderer at once to the door of mercy : he generally tries in succession several other methods in order to obtain relief. As the prodigal attempted to keep body and soul together by the most desperate and loathsome expedients, rather than throw himself on his father's compassion ; so an alienated human soul, conscious of having wantonly offended a good God, and therefore hating deeply the Holy One, will bear and do the will of the wicked one to the utmost extremity of misery rather than come home a beggar, and be indebted for all to a father's love. The picture, although drawn by the Master's own hand, is necessarily drawn in the colours of external nature, and therefore it comes far short of the original, which is a spiritual wickedness. The cherished son of an affluent and honourable house in Israel has become the swineherd of a stranger in a famine-stricken land: the transition is as great as could be displayed on the limited stage of the present world; but when he who was made in God's image and treated as God's child is bound by the chain of his own passions, and indentured as a slave in the devil's service, the fall is greater, as heaven is higher than the earth, and the world of spirit deeper than the world of flesh. "No man gave unto him:" when a son deserts the Father of lights, from whom every good gift comes down, his soul cannot be satisfied from other sources: the world's breasts are dry, or yield only poison to the eager drawing of the famished child.

There is a blank in the history here. The later stages of the prodigal's misery are not exhibited in the light: fully exposed, they might have been shocking rather than impressive. Every height has its opposite and corresponding depth: as eye has not seen nor ear heard in all its fulness the blessedness that God hath prepared for them that love him; so neither can our faculties measure the miseries of sin, in their foretastes here and their fulness hereafter. How the prodigal fared under that veil, as his misery day by day increased to its climax, we know not; but at length he suddenly emerges another man. "He came to himself:" the wild foul stream that had sunk into the earth and flowed for a space under ground, bursts to the surface again, agitated still indeed, but now comparatively pure. We learn for the first time that the man has been mad, by learning that his reason is restored. It is a characteristic of the insane that they never know or confess their insanity until it has passed away: it is when he has come to himself that he first discovers he has been beside himself. The two beings to whom a man living in sin is most a stranger are himself and God; when the right mind returns, he becomes acquainted with both again. The first act of the prodigal, when light dawned on his darkness, was to converse with himself, and the second to return to his father.

A man can scarcely find a more profitable companion than himself. These two should be well acquainted, and deal frankly with each other; in the case of the prodigal how disastrous was the estrangement, how blessed the reconciliation between them! The young man, during the period of his exile, was as much a stranger to himself as to his father. His return to himself became the crisis of his fate; from the interview sprang the burning thought, "I will arise and go to my father," and the resolute deed, "he arose and went."

When he had determined to return, he returned at once, and returned as he was. Emaciated by prolonged want,—naked, filthy, hungry, he came as he was. He did not remain at a distance until by efforts of his own he should make himself in some measure worthy to resume his original place in the family; he came in want of all things, that out of his father's fulness all his wants might be supplied. The signification of this feature on the spiritual side is obvious; it exhibits a cardinal point in the way of a sinner's return to God.

But while the repenting youth did not pretend to bring anything good to his father's house, neither did he presume to bring thither anything evil: his poverty and hunger were brought with him, but the companions and instruments of his lusts were left behind. This is a distinctive discriminating feature of true repentance. In the act of fleeing to his father the prodigal leaves his associates, and his habits, and his tastes behind : and conversely, as long as he clings to these he will not—he cannot return to his father.

In the narrative it is made evident that a return to his father was the son's last resort ; he did not adopt it—he did not even entertain it, until all others had failed. The grief which he must have known his unnatural exile caused in the bosom of the family at home did not move him : even want, when it came upon him like an armed man, failed to overcome his stubborn spirit. He will be the servant of a stranger rather than his father's son ; he would live on swine's food, if it had power to sustain a human life, rather than sit at his father's table. It was not till death stared him in the face that he consented to return. He encountered all extremities of privation rather than come home ; no thanks to him, then, for coming at last. Yet he was received with an ardent welcome, and without upbraiding. The son's sullen, obdurate, desperate resistance becomes a measure and a monument of the father's forbearing, forgiving love. It is thus that sinful men return to God in Christ to-day ; and thus that God in Christ to-day receives sinful men. Prodigals returning deserve nothing, and yet obtain all. Of even the last rag of merit that the imagination can conjure up—the merit of being willing to receive favour—they are utterly destitute. Though we do not come back to our father until all other resources have failed—although we come, as it were, only when we cannot help coming, he receives us with open arms ; he takes the sin away, and does not cast it up.

" When he was yet a great way off his father saw him."
He must have been looking out.   Often, doubtless every
day, his eye turned and strained wistfully in the direction
of his son's retiring footsteps.   While that son was starv-
ing in a foreign land, his father was weeping at the window, longing for his return ; when at last the prodigal
appeared, the watchful father caught sight of his form in
the distance, and ran to meet him.   Behold again in this
glass another feature of redeeming love !   Jesus, looking
down on Jerusalem, wept for sorrow, because its giddy
multitude would not turn and live ; if they had with one
accord come forth to accept the pardon which he offered,
he would have wept again for joy.   In his tears, as well
as in his teaching he showed us the Father.

The reconciliation is immediate and complete.   The
parable reveals an extraordinary outburst of paternal
tenderness.   The son, melted, and in some measure confused by the undeserved, unexpected warmth of his reception, bethought of the speech which, at the turning
point of his repentance, he had resolved to address to his
father, and began to recite it as he had conned the words
in exile :—" Father, I have sinned against heaven, and in
thy sight, and am no more worthy to be called thy son;"
but there stopped short, omitting the portion about being
content with the position of a hired servant.   Bengel
suggests that the father may have cut the prodigal's
speech short by giving aloud an order to the servants for
the kind and honourable reception of his child ; but
another thought, also suggested by the same acute and
experimental expositor, brings out, I think, more truly the
deep significance of the omission :—The son lying on the
father's bosom, with the father's tears falling warm on his
upturned face, is some degrees further advanced in the

spirit of adoption than when he first planned repentance beside the swine in his master's field.   There and then the legal spirit of fear because of guilt still lingered in his heart ; he ventured to hope for exemption from deserved punishment, but not for restoration to the place of a beloved son.   Now the spirit of bondage has been conclusively cast out by the experience of his father's love ; the fragments of stone that had hitherto remained even in a broken heart are utterly melted at last, as if by fire from heaven.   He could not now complete the speech which he had prepared ; its later words faltered and fell inarticulate.   He could not now ask for the place of a servant, for he was already in the place of a son.*

---

* The paraphrase of this Scripture, in a selection employed in most of the Presbyterian Churches of Scotland, stumbles at this point, and misses the meaning of the text.   Overlooking the mighty step of progress which the prodigal had made between the time when his accummulating convictions turned the balance first in favour of repentance, and the time when the last fragment of distrust melted away in the flood of a full reconciliation, the hymn represents the son as still pleading specifically to be sent away into the place of a servant, after the embrace, and the kiss, and the tears of his father had bestowed and triply sealed his sonship.

> " He ran and fell upon his neck,
>   Embraced and kissed his son :
>   The grieving prodigal bewailed
>   The follies he had done.
>
> " No more, my father, can I hope
>   To find paternal grace ;
>   My utmost wish is to obtain
>   A servant's humble place."

No ; after the meeting the youth did indeed say that he was not worthy to be called a son, but he did not say he had abandoned the hope or the desire of being reinstated.   Yet, notwithstanding this and other errors that have crept into the collection, and the superior character of many that are excluded from it, no vigorous effort has been made to obtain a revision in order to exclude the faulty and introduce better in their stead.   Conservative inertia—an instinct to keep unchanged what has descended to us from our fathers—is a great and curious power in human nature, operating both on Church and State.   Although not creditable to the wisdom and courage of men. it is doubtless overruled for good by the providence of God.

The father's command regarding the son's reception represents the complete reconciliation of the Gospel—the total oblivion of the prodigal's past sins, and his admission into the favour and the family of God, as a dear child. Even the details at this point have been framed after the pattern of spiritual privileges as they are elsewhere represented in the Scriptures ; and they admit, consequently, of being minutely examined and applied. The best Robe points to the Redeemer's righteousness which the believer puts on, and wherein he is justified ; the Ring is the signet of a king, the seal of the Spirit in the regeneration ; the Shoes suggest that the sinner, forgiven and renewed, shall walk with God in newness of life ; the Feast indicates the joy of a forgiving God over a forgiven man, and the joy of a forgiven man in a forgiving God.

These two lessons Christ has tenderly and plainly taught in this parable,—first, that God receives and forgives a sinner who comes back repenting; and second, that he delights in the act of so forgiving repentant sinners : on these points no ambiguity is left, and no room for controversy. These features of our Father's character, if they were fully perceived and frankly accepted, would soon change the face of the world. Guilt makes the guilty suspicious and distrustful. For the chief ailment of humanity the parable supplies a specific antidote : let the aspect of God's character, which is here displayed, take possession of a sinful heart, and it is forthwith won.

A young person is in want of employment; and a great man lives in the neighbourhood who could give him both work and wages. To this man the youth is advised in his distress to apply; but this is the man whom the youth has injured and offended,—the man whose just resentment he dreads. But it is known and reported that this possessor of great wealth is kind, generous, forgiving; that he does not retain resentment for injuries received; that he delights to bestow favour on those who have offended him. Convinced by these representations, the youth determines to venture, and accordingly sets out on his journey toward the great man's house. As he approaches it, however, his limbs grow feeble, his heart beats high, and he lacks courage to go near and knock. He halts, and is about to turn back in despair. What would suffice to encourage the trembler at that moment, and bear him through? If then and there he could in any way be thoroughly convinced that the man whom he formerly injured, and therefore now dreads, is not only in general tender-hearted and open-handed, but is at that moment specifically thinking of this individual transgressor, grieving over his impenitence, watching from his window for his coming, yearning to receive his confession, and enjoy the blessedness in his own heart of forgiving and satisfying the penitent; this will be effectual; the youth will go forward to the door now with a firm step.

It is such a conviction regarding the mind of God towards erring men that is needed, in order to bring them in clouds to his mercy-seat, like doves to their windows; and it is in order to work this conviction in our hearts that Jesus, who has authority to declare the Father, has given us the parable of the Prodigal Son. May the Spirit take this word, and make it in us quick and powerful.

Here we are not left to deal with curious or doubtful speculation. Nothing in heaven or earth can be truer, surer, plainer than this. The view that Jesus gives is the true view of the Father, as he turns his face to-day toward the children of men.

Here is a youth who has discovered suddenly that a

disease has fatally stricken him, deep in the springs of life. After struggling some days against conviction, and clinging to false hopes, he has at length acknowledged that sentence of death has been passed. When the first tumult subsides, a species of calm succeeds,—the calm of earnest occupation with one over-riding and absorbing theme. The world, with its hopes and fears, is conclusively cut off : his business with time is closed. He has bidden farewell to the crowd that he has left behind, and has entered the solemn vestibule which at the other end opens on eternity. With all the energy of his being, he applies himself now to the question, Am I lost or saved?

He looks alternately backward on his own life, and upward to God's throne; both prospects trouble him. Backward he sees only sin; forward, only judgment. Himself seems the stubble, and the Judge a consuming fire. As these two approach, and their meeting seems near, he fears with an exceeding great fear, and cries with an exceeding bitter cry. He greatly wonders, meanwhile, that he never saw things in this light before. Now, in man's extremity, is God's opportunity to show him the Father. While the eyes of the body are closed in weariness, the mental vision remains active; and a picture appears, as if it were hung in light upon the wall. To the soul's eye Christ appears, and appears in the act of revealing the Father. The Father whom Christ reveals runs forth to meet his prodigal son, falls on his neck, weeps, and kisses him. There is no upbraiding, no bargaining for terms. The returning son is forgiven, accepted, clothed, honoured, loved. He has all, and abounds. This is doubtless a true picture, the dying youth reflects, for it is Christ that displays it; but, alas, it brings no hope to me. I have stifled convictions, and lived for my own pleasure; and though I often heard of mercy, I never sought it, until I found that death was on my track. How can I expect that God should receive me, when I make him a do-no-better, for I never thought of seeking him until all my chosen idols had forsaken me, and I was left destitute?

Brother, look; what good thing was in the lost son, that served to recommend him to his father? He would not remain at home; he could not enjoy his abundance as long as the father, whose face he loathed, abode under the same roof. He went away, that he might enjoy the pleasures of sin. He did not return while he had enough; he did not return when he began to be in want; he endured the extreme of misery and shame rather than return; he came back to his father only when all other resources failed;—and yet his father received him with great gladness. Sinner, look on this love,—look on it till you live in its light. It is not him that never departed, or came back while he yet had plenty, or came back soon, or came back with an improved heart,—it is, " *Him that cometh* I will in no wise cast out."

Those who from this parable conclude that God receives sinners into favour without a propitiation, and those who endeavour to escape from that conclusion by affirming that the father in the parable represents Christ, err equally, although on opposite sides.*

---

* Stier's observations on this point are excellent:—" The well-meaning efforts which are made to explain the absence of reference to the mediating *propitiation* of the Son of God in this instant exhibition of the *Father's mercy*, are altogether needless ; they rest fundamentally on false dogmatic views of this propitiation, as if there were not existing in the Father's being the same love which is expressed in the Son,—as if the Father needed abstractly to be propitiated in order to entertain this love ! We are not to seek *Christ himself* as mediator in the person of this father; nor (though Melancthon has strangely ventured to affirm it), afterwards in the fatted calf, as

The notion that a mediator is not needed, because a mediator is not here specifically represented, proceeds upon the assumption, obviously and inexcusably erroneous, that all truth must be taught in every parable. While occasionally visiting the printing works of the publishers as these sheets are passing through the press, I have observed the process of printing coloured landscapes by lithograph. One stone by one impression deposits the outline of the land ; another stone, by another impression, fills in the sea ; and a third stone, on a different machine, subsequently adds the sky to the picture. No observer is so foolish as to complain, while he sees the process in its earlier stages, that there is no sea or no sky in the landscape. It is thus with the parables in general, and with this group in particular. By the two first, certain portions and aspects of the scene are represented ; and by the last one, when it is impressed on the same field, the remaining features are completed.

Hitherto we have been occupied exclusively with the younger of the two sons ; but the notice given in the first

sacrificially slain. *His* place here is rather to be sought in his thus authoritatively testifying of the Father's mercy. As Nitzsch excellently says :—
'If he seems to conceal himself here, he is all the more manifest there, where the Shepherd seeks the lost sheep. For *the* Son—who is neither an elder nor a *younger*, the *eternal* Son of the Father, one with him, his eye and his heart towards the lost—is come into this world, although invisible and unnamed in the parable, to reveal the Father where he had been ever invisible, and where no man knew him : and he is to the children of the law and the curse, not only a living herald of the propitiable—we shall rather say of the already propitiated—Father, but the (that is *our*) propitiation itself, and the way whereby every one of us may come back to God.' The mediation of Christ is no more denied by this silence than the seduction of Satan was denied in the sinner's apostasy at the beginning of the parable. We may also say with Von Gerlach that the 'coming out of the father to meet his son, here figuratively exhibits the sending of the Son.'"—*Stier in loc.*

sentence of the parable prepares us for meeting with the elder in some significant capacity ere it close; and here, accordingly, he comes up to sustain his part.

At the moment of the prodigal's return, his elder brother was in the field, whether for his father's profit or his own pleasure we are not informed. When he came home in the evening, and before he had entered the house, he heard the sound of the festival within. Surprised and displeased that a feast on so large a scale should have been instituted without his privity and participation, he assumed and maintained an attitude of haughty reserve. Instead of going in at once and seeing all with his own eyes as a son, he went to a servant, and in the spirit of an alien, inquired the reason of the mirth. Having learned the leading facts, instead of imitating his father's generosity, he abandoned himself to selfish jealousy, and went away in a pet. The father, on every side true to his character, came out and pleaded with him to enter and share the common joy. Hereupon the true character of the *soi-disant* model son is revealed; he peevishly casts it in his father's face, as a reproach, that he had never provided such a feast for his immaculate and superlatively dutiful child.

The elder son, in his statement of the case, introduces an elaborately constructed double contrast between his brother's experience and his own, which is peculiarly interesting in relation to the mercy of God and the methods of the Gospel. To the jaundiced eye of this sour-tempered pharisaic youth, it seemed that his father gave much to him that deserved least, and little to him that deserved most: to the profligate son, the fatted calf; to the eminently dutiful child, not even a kid. Here the hard, self-satisfied formalist, like Pilate and Caiaphas, preaches the Christ whom he did not know. The envious contrast portrayed by the elder son is a dark shadow which takes its shape from the Light of life. It is a law of the Gospel that nothing is given to the man in reward for the righteousness which he brings forward as his boast; but all is given to the man who has flung away his own righteousness with loathing as filthy rags, and come, " wretched, and miserable, and poor, and blind, and naked," to cast himself on the mercy of God. The greatest gift is bestowed on the most worthless; for " God commendeth his love toward us, in that while we were yet sinners, Christ died for us" (Rom. v. 8).

At this point the line of our parable touches that of the lost sheep, and thenceforth runs coincident with it to the close : it points to the same features of human cha- racter, and teaches the same principles of divine truth. In the first place, it repeats the answer already given in the two preceding parables to the question embodied in the complaint of the Pharisees,—" This man receiveth sinners and eateth with them." The father announces with great clearness and fulness, the grounds on which he rejoiced more that day over the prodigal restored than over the elder son, who had never left home. It is a rule in human experience, universally understood and appreciated, that though a son never lost is as precious as one who has been lost and found, parents experience a more vivid joy in the act of receiving the exile back than in the continuous possession of a son who has been always in their sight.*

---

* This law may be illustrated by an analagous fact in the material depart- ment of creation. Lay a ball, such as a boy's marble, on an extended sheet of thin paper, and the paper, though fixed at the edges and unsupported in the midst, will bear easily the weight : take now another ball of the same

In the meantime, it is very sweet to learn from the lips of Jesus that this law, which may be clearly traced on earth, penetrates to heaven, and there prepares for repenting sinners, not a bare escape from wrath, but an abundant entrance into the joy of their Lord.

But while the parable thus demonstrates that even though the claim of the Pharisees were granted their objection falls to the ground, it most certainly does not grant that claim. So far from conceding that they needed no repentance, the Lord makes it evident that they kept company with the publicans in sin, and only differed in this, that they did not repent and forsake it. The elder brother, towards the close of the parable, presents a life-likeness of the Pharisees ; in him they might have seen their own shadow on the wall.

The self-righteousness, the pride, the peevishness, the jealousy of the elder brother in the close of the parable represent, in its most distinctive features, the character of the Jewish people and their leaders, in the beginning of the Gospel. One of their leading reasons for refusing to own Jesus as the Messiah was his manifested willingness to extend the blessings of redemption to the needy of every condition and every name. When the Lord reminded them that Elijah was sent past many suffering widows in Israel to relieve a stranger at Sarepta, and that Elisha left many lepers uncured among his own countrymen when he healed the Syrian soldier, they were so exaspe-

___

shape and weight, and let it drop upon the sheet of paper from a height, it will go sheer through. The two balls are of the same weight and figure ; but the motion gave to one a momentum tenfold greater than that of the other at rest. It is in a similar way that the return of a lost son goes through a loving father's heart, and makes all its affections thrill ; while the continued possession of another son, equally valuable and equally valued, produces no such commotion either in the heart of the father or his home.

448 / Parables of Our Lord

rated by the suggestion that God's favour had already

rated by the suggestion that God's favour had already
flowed out to the Gentiles, and might flow in the same
direction again, that they "rose up and thrust him out of
the city, and led him unto the brow of the hill whereon
their city was built, that they might cast him down head-
long" (Luke iv. 29). The same spirit burst forth when they
were touched on the same tender point in the ministry of
the apostles. Paul was permitted from the stairs of the
fortress attached to the temple at Jerusalem to address
an excited multitude on the faith as it is in Jesus. Loving
the Hebrew tongue in which he spoke better than the
Greek, which they had expected him to employ, they
listened with interest and in silence to the story of his
conversion through the appearing of the risen Jesus;
but when in the progress of the narrative he found it
necessary to inform them that the Lord his Saviour gave
him a commission to preach the Gospel beyond the
boundaries of Israel, saying, "Depart, for I will send thee
far hence unto the Gentiles, they gave him audience
unto this word, and then lifted up their voices and said,
Away with such a fellow from the earth, for it is not fit
that he should live" (Acts xxii. 21, 22). In this invete-
rate prejudice of the Pharisaic Jews against the admission
of persons or communities other than themselves into the
privileges of Messiah's kingdom, we see the reason
why the Lord gave his parable the turn which it takes
in the extraordinary conduct of the elder brother. Counting that the kingdom belonged exclusively to themselves,
the Jewish hierarchs violently resented every suggestion
that pointed to the reception of strangers. It was to
them that this series of parables was addressed; and to
them, in immediate relation to their stupid and impudent
cry, "He receiveth sinners!"

But we have not exhausted this portion of the lesson when we have pointed out that those whom the elder brother represents fret proudly and peevishly against the admission of their neighbours into the kingdom : by that very fact they unconsciously but surely demonstrate that themselves have not entered yet. The spirit that in regard to self is satisfied, before God unhumbled, and towards men unloving, has no part with Christ: this is the proud whom God knoweth afar off, not the meek whom he delights to honour.

Ah, woe to the man who serves God as that son served his father, with a mercenary mind and an unbroken heart, —who thinks his obedience praiseworthy, and would be surprised if it should go without reward. The elder son was lost as well as the younger ; but as far as the parable reveals his history, he was not like him found again : he, like his brother, went astray ; but unlike him, refused to come back. The father was grieved as much by the sullen, dry, hard, cold, dead formality of his elder son, as by the prodigal wastefulness of the younger, without getting the sorrow balanced by a subsequent joy. Whited sepulchre! what will thy residence in the house, and thy constant and punctilious profession avail thee while thou art planting daggers in thy father's heart, and nursing vile hypocrisy in thy own ? It is the empty open vessel that gets itself filled when it is plunged into a well of living water ; the vessel that is full and shut, although it is overflowed by rivers of privileges, does not receive and retain a drop. Before God and under the Gospel, the turning-point of each man's destiny is not the number or the aggravation of his sins, but the discovery of his own guilt, and the consequent cry out of the depths for mercy. That which really in the last resort hinders a man's sal-

vation and secures his doom is not his sin, but his refusal
to know and own that he is a sinner. All the excesses
of the prodigal will not shut him out of heaven, for he
came repenting to the father; but all the virtues of
the elder brother will not let him into heaven, for he
cherished pride in his heart, and taunted his father for
overlooking his worth. The ground on which the Laodiceans were condemned was not the sinfulness of their
state, but their stolid satisfaction with the state they
were in. "Because thou sayest, I am rich and increased
with goods, and have need of nothing; and knowest not
that thou art wretched and miserable, and poor, and
blind, and naked" (Rev. iii. 17). What although they
were not rich;—if they had known their poverty, all the
treasures of the Godhead were at their disposal: what
although they were wretched;—all the blessings that are
at God's right hand were theirs for the asking. What
although this son was prodigal;—there is a place for him
in God's favour,—a place for him in the mansions of the
Father's house for ever when he comes back repenting,
confiding; but what although he never strayed—never
missed a diet of worship or a deed of alms, the elder
brother by holding to his own righteousness, rejects the
righteousness which is of God by faith, and shuts himself
out of the kingdom. Him who thought he was poor and
miserable, and wretched, and blind, and naked, the father
runs to meet with kisses of love and tears of joy: but
him who thought himself rich and increased with goods,
and in need of nothing, the father puts away, with the
most piercing expressions of loathing which the whole
Scriptures contain, "I will spue thee out of my mouth."

The Prudent Steward
(Luke 16:1-9)

" And he said also unto his disciples, There was a certain rich man, which had a steward ;
and the same was accused unto him that he had wasted his goods. And he called
him, and said unto him, How is it that I hear this of thee? give an account of thy
stewardship ; for thou mayest be no longer steward. Then the steward said within
himself, What shall I do? for my lord taketh away from me the stewardship : I cannot dig ; to beg I am ashamed. I am resolved what to do, that, when I am put out
of the stewardship, they may receive me into their houses. So he called every one
of his lord's debtors unto him, and said unto the first, How much owest thou unto my
lord? And he said, An hundred measures of oil. And he said unto him, Take thy
bill, and sit down quickly, and write fifty. Then said he to another, And how much
owest thou? And he said, An hundred measures of wheat. And he said unto him,
Take thy bill, and write fourscore. And the lord commended the unjust steward,
because he had done wisely : for the children of this world are in their generation
wiser than the children of light. And I say unto you, Make to yourselves friends of
the mammon of unrighteousness ; that, when ye fail, they may receive you into everlasting habitations."

O N the face of this parable a difficulty presents
itself, all the more formidable in that it lies
not in the critical, but in the moral department. In almost all the other examples, the
acts attributed to human agents are either morally blame-
less in themselves, or are manifestly exhibited in order
to be condemned : but here, an element of injustice is
inseparably mixed up with the prudence which is commended in the conduct of the steward. The difficulty
lies in this, that the specimen of worldly prudence presented in order to suggest and stimulate spiritual prudence in securing the interests of the soul, is dyed through
and through with the loathsome vice of dishonesty. It

is not easy, at least for us, to gather the lesson which this man's prudence contained, out of the dishonesty in which in was steeped.

When we read the parable we may detect a feeling of surprise creeping over our minds, that the Lord, who had the whole world and its history before him whence to select his examples, should have chosen a specimen of worldly wisdom, damaged by an admixture of downright falsehood, in order to stimulate thereby the spiritual zeal of his own disciples. The three following observations will, in my judgment, explain and completely remove the difficulty :—(1.) The Holy One, precisely because he is perfectly holy, can come closer to the unholy than we who are infected with sin and susceptible of injury from contact with impurity. Jesus talked with the Samaritan at the well, and permitted the sinner to wash his feet with tears in Simon's house. His own disciples and the Pharisees wondered by turns why he came so close to the unclean ; but if they had been free from sin as he was, they could have handled it freely when in their ordinary ministry it crossed their path. Inflammable matter must be kept far from fire ; whereas matter that is incombustible may, when a necessary cause occurs, safely pass through the midst of the flame. (2.) A shorter parable in another place presents and explains the same difficulty : " Be ye wise as serpents, and harmless as doves." Serpents are proposed to the disciples as examples to be imitated ; but it is the wisdom only and not the hurtfulness of the serpent that their Master enjoins them to imitate. Foresight and dishonesty are not more closely or inseparably united in the character of the cunning steward than wisdom and hurtfulness in the nature of the serpent. In both alike the Master meant that one quality which is commendable should be selected for imitation, and the other quality which is vile should be cast away with loathing. (3.) The key-note of the parable is expressed in verse 8 : " The children of this world are wiser in their generation than the children of light." The line of interpretation must be drawn through this point, and all the scattered features of the picture brought up or brought down to meet it. Thus the tinge of dishonesty that runs through the prudence of the steward, so far from rendering his case unsuitable for the purpose of the Lord, imparted to it additional appropriateness and point. The methods, as well as the ends of the worldly, were different from those of the spiritual. This example shows that, from the ungodly man's own viewpoint, and according to his own maxims, he prosecutes his object with energy and skill. Let the Christian, with his clearer, purer light, prosecute his high aim by holy means with an energy and zeal similar to those which the ungodly exhibit in the pursuit of their gains or pleasures. It was the design of the Lord not simply to give his disciples generally an example of wisdom, but to give them specifically an example of the wisdom of the world —the wisdom that neither fears God nor regards man. An example of prudence taken from a good man's history, and exercised under submission to the law of God, would not have suited the Master's purpose so well as the one that has been chosen.

It is important to notice at the outset, that in this instance the Lord addresses his instructions specifically to his own disciples. The three parables which are recorded in the preceding chapter were spoken to the Pharisees ; immediately after these, and in continuation of the history, the evangelist intimates that " he said also unto his disciples, There was a certain rich man," &c. Besides those lessons which he gave to the multitude, teaching how the distant may come near, he gave this lesson to those who had already come near, in order to incite them to diligence in the course which they had chosen : this Teacher rightly divides the word of truth, giving to each his portion in due season. In this lesson the diligence of worldly men is employed to rebuke the slothfulness of Christians. Those who make perishing things their portion are thoughtful, inventive, energetic, decisive in prosecuting their object ; how thoughtless and slow are the heirs of the kingdom in the work of their high calling !

"A certain rich man had a steward." We learn here, incidentally, how evenly balanced are the various conditions of life in a community, and how little of substantial advantage wealth can confer on its possessor. As your property increases, your personal control over it diminishes ; the more you possess, the more you must entrust to others. Those who do their own work are not troubled with disobedient servants ; those who look after their own affairs, are not troubled with unfaithful overseers.*

This overseer cheated his master, and concealed the fraud for a time under the folds of complicated accounts ; but, as in all similar cases, this career of wickedness came suddenly to an end. Some person discovered the facts and informed the proprietor. When suspicion was raised inquiry could not be resisted ; and, when an inquiry was

---

* A case came up lately in an English court of justice, in which a certain duke prosecuted his butler for malversation in his charge. It appeared in evidence that the defalcation on the account for wine alone amounted to L. 1500. This fact incidentally reveals two things :—How great is the wealth of these British princes ; and how little that wealth is under their own control.

instituted, the crime could not be hid. The steward seems to have given up his case as soon as he was accused; he uttered not a word in his own defence. There was no proof on one side, and no denial on the other. The case was clear, and the process summary; sentence of dismissal was pronounced on the spot. But the proprietor was still in a great measure at the mercy of this unfaithful servant; the accounts were all in his hand, and the owner could not instantly resume the power which he had delegated. The agent accordingly was ordered to prepare and submit a balance-sheet, on which his successor might proceed to administer the estate.

There was not much time for deliberation: the decree of dismissal had already passed, and as soon as the state of accounts could be made up, this once comfortable and important personage must be cast penniless upon the world. Now or never, he must do something for him·self. With habits, both mental and physical, cast in another mould, he cannot win his bread as a labourer; and his pride revolted against the prospect of becoming a beggar on the spot where he had long been owned as master by the multitude. His resolution is quickly formed, and as quickly carried into effect. He will employ his present opportunity, so as to provide a refuge for himself in his future need: he will so deal with the money while it is still in his hand, as that he shall not be left destitute when he is driven from his place.

In prosecution of his purpose, the steward summoned his master's debtors one by one into his presence. He held their acknowledgments for goods received, or their signatures for the amount of rent which they had agreed to pay for their lands. Having in his hands the documents which bound the debtors, he might have read off from these the amount due by each ; but it suited his purpose better to ask the obligants what sums they owed, and to proceed wholly upon their voluntary acknowledgments. The first owed a hundred measures of oil, the second a hundred measures of wheat. What these quantities may have been in relation to our standards is a question which possesses only a critical and antiquarian interest : it has no bearing on the interpretation of the parable, and therefore we pass it without further notice. The absolute amount of the debt has no influence on the meaning of the parable ; the point which is really important is the proportion between the amount owned by the debtors and the amount exacted by the steward. Olive oil and wheat were two of the staple products of the country, and the obligations in regard to them may have been incurred either in transactions of a mercantile character, or in those which intervene between landlord and tenant.*

The method of the overseer is short and simple : apart from considerations of morality, conscience, and divine retribution, it seemed a short road to the accomplishment of his purpose. He surrendered to the debtors their obligations, and received in return obligations for smaller amounts, in one case for fifty, and in another for eighty, instead of a hundred. These two cases are submitted as specimens : others were treated in a similar way. Of course the steward could not obtain from these debtors any obligation in his own favour for the portion remitted, which could be enforced in a court of justice ; for the proof of the claim on the one side would have revealed

---

* Probably the rents were paid in kind, and these were the arrears which the tenants acknowledged.

his guilt on the other : but it was assumed between the parties that the benefit conferred should in due time be substantially acknowledged and repaid. The steward counted that in the day of his distress those men on whom he had conferred favours would receive him into their houses.*

It was expected, moreover, that the proprietor, or the steward whom he might afterwards employ, could not exact more than the smaller sums, for which they possessed the acknowledgments of the parties. We could indeed conceive a case in which the injured owner could lead a proof of fraud in the transaction, and enforce from the obligants the original amounts ; but it is not probable that, in an age when records were defective, and the two parties immediately connected with the fraudulent transaction deeply interested in concealing it, such a suit could be successfully carried through.†

The lord, that is the injured proprietor, commended the unjust steward, because, or in that, he had done wisely. The difficulty here lies on the surface,—lies, as it were, in the sound ; upon a close examination it vanishes. First of all, the lord who praised the steward is, as the translators have indicated by printing the word without a capital, not the Lord Jesus, the speaker of the parable,

---

* Of the same nature were the long leases of ecclesiastical property in England at low rents, granted by the living incumbents, in consideration of a sum of money in name of fine paid to themselves.

† A case emerged lately in the courts of this country, in which a proprietor, who had lost very large sums by the unfaithfulness of his agent, prosecuted the parties for restitution, on the ground of the agent's bad faith in the transactions. The case was protracted, and I lost sight of it before the solution was reached ; but it is enough for my present purpose that a plea was actually raised to obtain from one debtor the price of a hundred measures of oil instead of fifty, which he acknowledged, on the alleged ground that the absconded steward had corruptly and for his own interest sacrificed the rights of his employer.

but the master, whom the cunning agent had robbed. Further, this praise obviously did not indicate moral approval. The master praised the servant when all was over, not for the faithfulness with which he had been served, but for the cleverness with which he had been cheated. The commendation which the master bestowed upon the servant was that of sharply looking after himself. It is the commendation which one whose house has been robbed during the night might bestow in the morning upon the robber, after noticing how adroitly he had opened the locks, and carried off the booty.

This nefarious transaction was, from the perpetrator's view-point, cleverly planned and promptly executed. It was no sooner said than done; delay might have ruined the steward's prospects. He must have everything done before he is summoned actually to transfer his books to his successor's hands. He provided in his own way for his own future need; the plan was well-contrived, and successfully carried into effect. This praise, but expressly and only this, the injured master bestowed upon the man.

" And I say unto you, Make to yourselves friends of the mammon of unrighteousness; that when ye fail, they may receive you into everlasting habitations." Such is the lesson which the Lord draws from the picture. Difficulties, indeed, adhere to the phraseology in its details; but the interpretation, in its main line, is determined and made evident by landmarks which can neither be overlooked nor removed. The mammon of unrighteousness means the world with all its business and its possessions; mammon is denominated unrighteous, generally on account of the manner in which it is employed by worldly men, and specially on account of the case in hand, where a gross injustice was perpetrated without scruple, and as an ordinary matter of business. Alas, how prevalent is this form of unrighteousness still! Although justice in a large measure pervades and so sustains the vast commerce of the country, many mean tricks insinuate themselves between its mighty strata, corroding its fabric, and undermining its strength.

In counselling the disciples to acquire for themselves friends from the mammon of unrighteousness ($\pi o\iota\eta\sigma\alpha\tau\epsilon$ $\dot{\epsilon}\alpha\nu\tau o\iota\varsigma$ $\phi\iota\lambda o\upsilon\varsigma$ $\epsilon\kappa$ $\tau o\upsilon$ $\mu\alpha\mu\omega\nu\alpha$ $\tau\eta\varsigma$ $\alpha\delta\iota\kappa\iota\alpha\varsigma$), the Lord obviously adopts the terms of his spiritual lesson from the structure of the parable which conveys it. By remitting part of their debts the steward made the debtors his friends; he won them to his side, and made sure of their sympathy when his day of need should come. His prudence and skill were commendable, but the fraud which was mingled with them is neither approved by the Lord, nor prescribed as a pattern for the disciples.* Nor is it difficult to lift the pure lesson from the impure ground on which it lies. The steward could not reach his unrighteous object except by a crooked path; but the ends which a Christian strives to attain neither require nor admit the employment of falsehood. Use the world in such a way that it shall help and not hinder the interests of your soul and of the world to come.

The position of the phrase, $\epsilon\iota\varsigma$ $\tau\grave{\eta}\nu$ $\gamma\epsilon\nu\epsilon\grave{\alpha}\nu$ $\tau\grave{\eta}\nu$ $\dot{\epsilon}\alpha\upsilon\tau\omega\nu$, in or for their own generation, near the end of the sentence, determines that it is applied equally to both

---

* The Emperor Julian adduced this parable in order to prove that the doctrines of Christ were adverse to good morals. This is precisely the place where the apostate, seeking reasons to justify his apostasy, will most readily find what he seeks.

parties. It is implied that both classes, the children of the world and the children of light, look after their own affairs ; and it is intimated that the one class attends to its business more earnestly and more skilfully than the other. This man cleaves to the world as his portion, and that man has chosen the Saviour as his : but, in point of fact, he who has chosen the inferior object prosecutes it with the greater zeal. The superior energy of the worldling in the acquisition of gains is employed to rebuke the Christian for his slackness in winning the true riches. This is the main lesson of the parable.

The specific form which the lesson assumes is,—Provide now for future need, and make the opportunities of time subservient to the interests of eternity.

The characteristic features of the steward's skill were, that when his dismissal was near, he occupied the short time that remained, and the resources still at his disposal, in skilfully providing for the future. We are stewards in possession still, but under warning; do we employ the time and the opportunities that remain in making our calling and election sure ?

Many precious possessions have been placed in our hands by the owner of all ; health of body and soundness of mind ; home and friends ; good name or great riches, or both conjoined ;—these and many others have been by their owner placed under our charge, that we should lay them out for him. Soon the stewardship will be taken from us. "When ye fail,"—that is, when we can no longer retain our hold of time and life ; when flesh and heart are failing ; when a mist comes over the eye, so that it can no longer see the circle of weeping friends that stand round the bed of death,—have we an everlasting habitation ready to receive the departing spirit ?

More particularly the practical question is, Have we disposed of earthly possessions and opportunities, so that they helped and did not hinder the acquisition of an incorruptible inheritance ?

There is a place and a use for temporal things in making sure of the life eternal. How constant has been the tendency of fallen humanity to run wildly into opposite extremes of error ; because the Popish system gives worldly possessions too high a place in the concerns of the soul, we may readily fall into the error of giving them no place at all. We lean hard over against the superstition that expects by alms, and money paid for masses, to smooth the spirit's path to peace beyond the grave ; but when we have refused to make money directly the price of our admission into heaven, we have not exhausted our duty in regard to its bearing on our eternal weal. The property, and money, and occupations of time may instrumentally affect for good or evil our efforts to lay up the true riches. According as they are employed, they may become a stumbling-stone over which their possessor shall fall, or a shield to cover his head from some fiery darts of the wicked one.*

Could it be truly said of any who are lost that the

---

* For example, their competence and the comforts which it brings shield women of the higher and middle classes in this country, in a great measure, from certain snares of the devil in which multitudes of their poorer sisters miserably fall. If those who enjoy this protection throw away their advantage by turning that which is a protection on one side into a temptation on the other, and so bring themselves to an equality over all with the less favoured classes, the fault is their own. It is proved by obvious facts that worldly possessions may be placed between you and temptation, as cotton bales and sand bags may be employed to ward off cannon shot from stone walls. They are capable of being turned to some account in advancing our eternal interests ; for our inheritance in heaven, the world is useful, if it is rightly used.

mammon of unrighteousness brought them to the place of woe? or, conversely could it be truly said of any who now stand round the throne in white, that the mammon of unrighteousness became the friend who introduced them to that everlasting habitation? I reply, this mammon is not and cannot be a cause either of being saved or being lost; but it, as well as all other things in time, may become instruments in the saving or destroying of a soul, according as it is wisely used or foolishly abused. For example, in the next parable, it was sin and not wealth that ruined the rich man; many richer men than he have walked with God on earth, and entered rest when they departed. Wealth was not his destroyer, yet he so used his wealth as to permit the wicked one to bind his soul with it as with chains over to the second death. On the other hand, it was neither the poverty nor the sores of Lazarus, nor both together, that saved him; many as destitute of money and as full of sores as he are never saved. Christ was this man's Saviour,—Christ alone; yet, his poverty became in God's hands, and through his servant's faith, the instrument of shielding him from temptation and purging his dross away. In the same subordinate and instrumental sense in which the rich man's wealth was his ruin, the poverty of the poor man saved him. But these results are not uniform—are not necessary; they may be—they often are reversed. The wealth of a rich man may help him heavenward, and the poverty of a poor man may press him down toward the pit. The cardinal point of the parable is, employ the mammon of unrighteousness—this world's affairs all, with forethought, skill, decision, and energy, to further your own salvation; turn all to account for the gain of godliness.

A ship leaves our shores bound westward to an

Atlantic port : the wind, being from the north, beats on her right side all the way. She makes a quick voyage and reaches her destination in safety. Another ship at another time leaves these shores for the same destination: the wind, blowing from the south, beats on her left side. She wanders from her course and is shipwrecked. Whence these opposite results ? Was the first ship saved because she met a north wind, and the second lost because she fell in with a wind from the south ? Nay, verily : but because the one so received the wind, from whatever point of the compass it might blow, as to be impelled by it onward in her course : and the other, instead of wisely employing every wind to help her forward, allowed herself to drift before the wind that happened to blow.

Mammon, the world—ah, is it not adverse to the interests of our souls ? What then ? Believer, adversary though it be, you may make it your friend. A skilful seaman, when once fairly out to sea, can make a wind from the west carry him westward! he can make the wind that blows right in his face bear him onward to the very point from which it blows. When he arrives at home, he is able to say the wind from the west impelled me westward, and led me into my desired haven.

Thus if we were skilful, and watchful, and earnest, we might make the unrighteous mammon our friend ; we might so turn our side to each of its tortuous impulses, that willing or unwilling, conscious or unconscious, it should from day to day drive us nearer home.

The parable is in this peculiar, that in the moral lesson which the Master enforces at the close, he retains and employs the phraseology of the story. " Make to yourselves friends of the mammon of unrighteousness," &c

The meaning is by the context made plain, and the reader may translate the metaphor as he proceeds. The steward, while he remained in his place, so handled the property in his power as to secure for himself a home when he should be removed from his place : in like manner let men so use material possessions while they live on earth, that these very possessions shall be found to have helped them toward their eternal rest. When a man's ways please God, he maketh even his enemies to be at peace with him. These things that are enemies, and that overcome many, you may make your friends ; you may turn to them such a side, that every time they strike they shall press you nearer rest, and at their last stroke impel you through the narrow entrance into the joy of your Lord.

The Rich Man and Lazarus
(Luke 16:19-31)

"There was a certain rich man, which was clothed in purple and fine linen, and fared sumptuously every day : and there was a certain beggar named Lazarus, which was laid at his gate, full of sores, and desiring to be fed with the crumbs which fell from the rich man's table : moreover the dogs came and licked his sores. And it came to pass, that the beggar died, and was carried by the angels into Abraham's bosom : the rich man also died and was buried ; and in hell he lift up his eyes, being in torments, and seeth Abraham afar off, and Lazarus in his bosom. And he cried and said, Father Abraham, have mercy on me, and send Lazarus, that he may dip the tip of his finger in water, and cool my tongue ; for I am tormented in this flame. But Abraham said, Son, remember that thou in thy lifetime receivedst thy good things, and likewise Lazarus evil things : but now he is comforted, and thou art tormented. And beside all this, between us and you there is a great gulf fixed : so that they which would pass from hence to you cannot ; neither can they pass to us, that would come from thence. Then he said, I pray thee therefore, father, that thou wouldest send him to my father's house : for I have five brethren ; that he may testify unto them, lest they also come into this place of torment. Abraham saith unto him, They have Moses and the prophets ; let them hear them. And he said, Nay, father Abraham ; but if one went unto them from the dead, they will repent. And he said unto him, If they hear not Moses and the prophets, neither will they be persuaded, though one rose from the dead."

THE intervening portion of history, contained in verses 14–18, should not be permitted to conceal from us the intimate relation that subsists between this and the preceding parable. The application of the first for the reproof of covetousness, touched a besetting sin of the Pharisees, and stung them to the quick. Unable to bear in silence a rebuke which their own consciences recognised as just, they interrupted the preacher with rude derision. They attempted to shield their own open sores from painful probing by raising a laugh at the expense of the reprover. I suspect they reckoned without their host in this matter. This man spake with authority, and not as the scribes; the common people heard him gladly. His speech was too divinely grave, and too palpably true, to be turned aside by the clumsy wit of the men whom it condemned. Intermitting for a moment the thread of his parabolic preaching, he turned aside and addressed a few withering words directly to these uneasy interrupters.*

When this episode was over, the Lord resumed his theme where it had been broken off. I think it probable, both from the terms of the narrative, and the nature of the case, that if these Pharisees had not been present, or if they had held their peace when the preaching galled them, the matter of verse 19th would have touched that of verse 13th—the parable of the rich man and Lazarus would have been connected in place as well as in purport with that of the prudent steward.

When he had followed up the first parable with a pungent application regarding the abuse of riches, "the Pharisees, also, who were covetous, heard all these things, and they derided him." To them, in reply to their jesting, he spoke the words verses 14–18, and then resumed, in verse 19th, " There was a certain rich man," &c.†

---

* From the introduction of a new subject abruptly in the 18th verse the much agitated question regarding a man's right to put away his wife— I think it probable that the interruption had been repeated and continued ; that it took the form of a dialogue, the Pharisees throwing in what they considered a damaging question, and Jesus giving an answer by turns—a scene which is frequently repeated in modern missions among the heathen.

† Dr Trench's disquisition regarding the latent union between covetousness and prodigality, involving a proof that the discourse about the rich man was applicable to the Pharisees who were not of prodigal habits, although very good in itself, is scarcely relevant ; inasmuch as it is not the parable of the rich man, but the reproofs intervening between it and the unjust steward that are expressly addressed to the Pharisees.

At the beginning of the chapter, addressing his own disciples particularly, although some of the Pharisees were present, he had taught them from the case of the prudent steward to use the possessions of this world with a view to their bearing on the next; and now, to complete the lesson, he will teach them, by a terrible example, the consequences of neglecting that rule.

But before we proceed to examine the parable in detail, it is important to determine generally regarding its nature whether it is an allegory in which spiritual things are represented by sensible objects, or simply an instructive example, historic or poetic, charged like other examples with moral warning and reproof. The parable of the sower is an allegory: the sower represents not a sower, but a preacher; the seed represents not seed, but the Gospel: whereas in the inner substance, as well as the outward form of the lesson, the good Samaritan is simply a good Samaritan, and the wounded traveller is simply a wounded traveller. The parable of the rich man and Lazarus is not allegory; it belongs to the class of the Samaritan, and not to that of the sower. It is not like a type, which a man cannot read until it is turned; but like a manuscript, which delivers its sense directly and at first hand.*

---

* It is true a figurative meaning has been applied to it, as to all the rest, both in ancient and modern times. In this case the lesson, when metaphorically rendered, possesses a remarkable measure of beauty, truth, and appropriateness. The rich man is the Jewish nation, by God's gift rich in position and privilege, but selfishly keeping all to itself, despising and neglecting others. Lazarus represents the Gentiles, spiritually poor, naked, hungry, homeless, within reach of the privileged people, yet by them left destitute. Both die: the old dispensation runs out, and Jews and Gentiles are together launched into "the last times." By apostolic messengers, the poor outcasts are now led unto the blessed privileges of the Gospel; these stones become children of Abraham; while the Jews, who enjoyed so good a portion in the former dispensation, are cast out. In this case, as in that

The description of the rich man is short, but full. He "was clothed in purple and fine linen, and fared sumptuously every day." He maintained a royal state and a prodigal expenditure. This excess of luxury was not confined to great occasions; it was the habit of every day.

Here, as in other cognate parables, great wisdom is displayed in bringing the whole force of the rebuke to bear on one point. It is not intimated that this man made free with other people's money, or that he had gained his fortune in a dishonest way. All other charges are removed, that the weight lying all on one point may more effectually imprint the intended lesson. To have represented him as dishonest or drunken, would have blunted the weapon's edge. Here is an affluent citizen, on whose fair fame the breath of scandal can affix no blot. He had a large portion in this world, and did not seek—did not desire any other. He spent his wealth in pleasing himself, and did not lay it out in serving God or helping man. It is not of essential importance whether such a man miserably hoard his money, or voluptuously spend it in feasts and fine clothing. Some men take more pleasure in wealth accumulated, and others more in wealth as the means of obtaining luxuries. These are two branches from one root; the difference is superficial and accidental: the essence of the evil is the same in both—a life of self-pleasing—"without God in the world."

By a transition, purposely made very abrupt, we learn

---

of the Samaritan, it is easy so to turn the polished instrument in the light, that it shall throw off bright glimpses of great evangelic facts and doctrines. Perhaps the Lord, in constructing it, kept this capability in view; but we must take the parable as in the first instance and mainly a direct moral lesson, accounting its allegorical capabilities secondary, and to us uncertain.

next that a beggar named Lazarus* was laid at this rich man's gate, full of sores. Whether the position was chosen by the man himself, or by his friends for him, the motive is obvious—it was expected that where so much was expended, perhaps also wasted, some crumbs might come the beggar's way.

"The dogs came and licked his sores;" perhaps the dogs always plentiful in eastern cities, that had no master; perhaps the dogs that belonged to the rich man, and had turned aside to lick the beggar's sores when their master rode past on the other side, and hid from the sight of misery within the drapery of his stately mansion. The act attributed to the dogs accords, as is well known, with their instincts and habits. It is soothing to the sufferer in the sensations of the moment, and healthful in its effects. When the beggar's fortunate brother took no notice of his distress, the dumb brutes did what they could to show their sympathy. The stroke, though it wears all the simplicity of nature, is in the parable due to consummate art ; the kindness of the brute brings out in deep relief the inhumanity of man.

---

* The name of the poor man is given, while the rich man is left nameless. Generally, Christ's kingdom is not of this world, and, in particular, it does not imitate this world's kingdoms in throwing the common people into anonymous heaps, and recording the names of only the great. I saw in an extension of the parish churchyard the graves of the two hundred men who perished in the pit accident at Hartley a few years ago. They were grouped in families of two, three, four, or five, and these family groups were arranged in extended rows ; but all were nameless. Near them slept the dust of the hereditary owners of the soil under monumental marble, loaded with statuary and inscriptions. Subjects of Christ's kingdom, "it shall not be so among you." Nor is the law which obtains in the heavenly the direct reverse of that which obtains in the earthly kingdom ; it is not the poor, but the "poor in spirit," to whom the kingdom of heaven belongs. The names that are recorded in the Lamb's book of life are neither those who have nor those who lack this world's wealth, but those who are poor in spirit and rich in grace.

"And it came to pass that the beggar died." Towards this point the narrative hastens. Here on the border is the hinge on which the lesson turns. The whole parable is constructed and spoken in order to show how this life bears on eternity ; and to make eternity, thus unveiled, bear reciprocally on the present life. The death of Lazarus happened in the ordinary course of things : his sufferings came to an end. Not a word of his dust, whether it was buried, or how. Of design, and with deep meaning, the body is left unnoticed, and the history of his soul is continued beyond the boundary of life, as the real and uninterrupted history of the man : in the same breath and in the same sentence that intimates his death, we are informed that he was carried by angels into Abraham's bosom. The dying and the entrance into the rest that remaineth are expressed in one sentence, the two clauses connected by a copulative conjunction : the Lord means manifestly to teach us, as he afterwards taught the repenting malefactor on the cross, that there is no interval to his people between departing from the body and being with Christ.

Nor did Jesus then reveal the immortality of the soul : the doctrine was already accepted, and he assumed it in his discourse as a truth known and acknowledged. Even the resurrection of the body was a commonplace among the immediate disciples of Jesus during the period of his ministry : " Thy brother shall rise again," said the Lord to Martha. " I know that he shall rise again," she replied, " in the resurrection at the last day :" this was a belief that she previously possessed."

Abraham's bosom, we may assume, was already an expression employed by the Jews to designate the place of the blessed beyond the grave. It accords much better with the Lord's purpose and method to suppose that this phrase and the term paradise, which he afterwards employed to express the same idea, were adopted by him from the current custom, than that they were then first introduced.

" The rich man also died and was buried." Here, for once, the rich and the poor meet together : the beggar died, and the rich man died too. The same event happened to both, and in both cases the same terms are employed to record the events ; but very remarkable is the difference introduced immediately after the article of death. What came after death in the case of Lazarus ? He was carried by angels into Abraham's bosom. What came after death in the case of this rich man ? He was buried. Perhaps as much could not have been said of Lazarus. The rich man was carried from a sumptuous table to a sumptuous tomb ; and the poor man perhaps had not where to lay his head, when its aching had ceased at length. It may be that his body did not find a grave. His spirit found happy rest and holy company ; and we can afford therefore to lose sight of the dissolving dust. First and last the one had excellent earthly accommodation, and the other had none ; but conversely, he who had neither a house when living nor a tomb when dead, walked with God while the tabernacle stood, and went to God when it fell ; whereas he who made the earth his portion got nothing for his portion but earth.

It would be a mischievous perversion of the parable to suppose that because the one was rich he was cast out, and because the other was poor he was admitted into heaven : the true lesson is in one aspect the reverse proposition : an ungodly man is in the highest sense poor in spite of his wealth ; and a godly man is in the highest sense rich, in spite of his poverty.

We enter now, or rather have already entered, the region where the parable must needs glide, not indeed from the literal into the metaphorical, but from a foreground where every object is distinctly seen to a background where the real objects cannot be seen at all, and where, accordingly, only signals are thrown up to tell what is their bulk and their bearing. When the line of the instruction goes through the separating veil and expatiates in the unseen eternity, it must become dim and indistinct to our vision. The moment that the parable in its progress goes beyond the sphere of the present life, our effort to follow it is like the struggle of a living creature out of its element. Even when the Lord of that unseen world is our instructor, our conceptions regarding it are necessarily indirect, second hand, and obscure. In this region the capacity of the scholar is infantile, and, consequently, the ability of the teacher cannot find scope. While, therefore, those parts of the parable which lay within our sphere were direct and literal, the latter portion, lying beyond our sphere, is necessarily indirect and expressed by signs : consequently, though sufficiently precise in its larger leading features, it is, in its minor details, indistinct, inarticulate.

"The beggar died ;" this is sufficiently direct and literal : "and was carried by angels into Abraham's bosom,"—there we are already beyond our depth. The horizon is dim now, by reason of distance and intervening clouds. Equally obscure is the other line of information when it has crossed the boundary of time. The rich man died and was buried : this we clearly comprehend : but "in hell he lifted up his eyes, being in torment."—

these are events of the eternal world, shadowed forth in the language and according to the conceptions of the present. We perceive the direction in which they lie, and can understand the moral lesson which they contain, but the things themselves are shrouded from our intellectual vision in impenetrable darkness. Not perhaps intentionally in the structure of the parable, but necessarily, on account of the place where its scene is latterly laid, a veil thicker than that of allegory is wrapped around it.

In accordance with the use of the word in classic Greek, and of the corresponding term in the Hebrew Scriptures, we might assume that "hell" (Hades) only indicates generally the world of spirits, as distinguished from this life in the body ; while the expression "being in torment," serves to determine the specific region or condition in that world to which the rich man was consigned : the term, however, wherever it occurs in the New Testament, seems to be applied, in point of fact, to the place of punishment, except in passages that are directly quoted from the Old Testament. Both were now in the world of spirits; but the beggar in that world was in Abraham's bosom, and the rich man in torment. Both spirits near the same time passed from this world by the same narrow passage ; beyond the boundary their paths diverged in opposite directions. Each went to his own place as certainly and as necessarily as vapour rises up, and water flows down. The ransomed man entered the Father's house and joined the company of the holy ; the ungodly gravitated, according to his kind, into the place of woe.

Having lifted up his eyes, "he seeth Abraham afar off and Lazarus in his bosom, and he cried and said, Father Abraham, have mercy on me." Deeper and deeper into the mystery we are led at every step. While the outline of the landscape is defined sufficiently for the purpose of affording a landmark to direct our course, all the lesser objects are entirely concealed by the distance. We must beware lest, in straining to get a glimpse of the invisible, we should mistake the flitting shadows that the unnatural effort sets afloat in the humours of our own eyes for the veritable objects of the spiritual world.

Here I would fain arrest attention on one guiding and dominating consideration, which may become a thread to lead us safely through the labyrinth, saving us the trouble of working out difficult speculations, and averting from us the danger of injuring ourselves by falls in the dark. The Lord delivered and the evangelist recorded this parable for the purpose of teaching, warning, directing, not spirits disembodied in the other world, but men in the body here. "All things are for your sakes;" the great Teacher determined all his words and acts by a regard to the benefit of his people. Even when Lazarus died at Bethany, he said to his followers, "I am glad for your sakes that I was not there, to the intent that ye might believe;" his absence led to the resurrection of Lazarus, and that event, he foresaw, would confirm their faith. So here, his aim is not to show how much he knows of the separate state, or to astonish the world by the display of its secrets; it is to give men while they are in the body those views of the separate state which will tell most effectually in leading the wicked to repentance, and in establishing believers in the faith.

Taking the Teacher's aim as the determinating principle in the interpretation of his discourse, I gather that the dialogue between the rich man and Abraham does not describe absolutely what is possible and actually takes place in the world of spirits, as if it were addressed to an inhabitant of that world, but gives such pictures of it, or signs regarding it, as are intelligible to an inhabitant of this world, and as will best bring the realities of the future to bear with beneficial effect upon the present character of men. By a system of coloured lights we contrive to warn the conductors of engines on our railways of danger to be avoided on the one hand, and to intimate the line of safety on the other. The things regarding which the engineers get instruction are not within their view. A red or a white light are not like the things in the distance that are to be dreaded or desired ; but a red or a white light displayed serves the purpose when the things themselves cannot be made known. There everything is determined with a view to immediate practical benefit. I think this helps me to grasp the difficult portions of the parable. The purpose of the Lord was not to display his own knowledge or gratify our curiosity. He ever acted as the Saviour of the lost ; he never swerved from that aim. It was his meat to do the Father's will, and to finish his work. In this particular case, accordingly, the object which he kept in view was not to convey to men in the body the absolute knowledge of a state, for knowing which their faculties are unfit, but to convey to them in time such shadows or signals of danger and safety as the actual state of matters in the unseen world truly suggested, and in such forms as that living men, from their view-point, and with their mixed constitution, could comprehend and appreciate.

When this principle is permitted to dominate, the exposition of the dialogue becomes comparatively both short and easy.

I do not know whether the saved are within view of

the lost in a future state, or whether any communication can pass between them; I only know that this parabolic picture, constructed as from a view-point within the present world, is the exhibition best fitted to make the diverse conditions of the good and the evil beyond the grave effectual to warn and instruct living men in the body. If any one should curiously inquire about flame, what is its nature, and how it can hurt a spirit, I can give no information on the subject, and I can gather none from the parable. One thing I know, that this representation is a red light hung out before me, as I am rushing forward on the line of life—hung out to warn me of danger, and hung out by the hand of him who came to save the lost. I understand perfectly what the beacon means to me : it is my part to take the warning which it gives ; and, as to the exact state of events and capabilities in the world to come, I shall learn all when I enter it. It may be quite true that there is not a flame like that which we are accustomed to see, and not a body, previous to the resurrection, that may be burned in it. But he who gave the word is my Friend ; and he is true ; I shall trust him. He knows what I understand by a flame ; he knows how I am affected by the thought of the pain which it inflicts. Knowing all these, he has employed that word in order to apply the terrors of the Lord for my warning ; he has done all things well. The minute features of the dialogue all serve to give point to the main conception. The request for a drop of water contributes to bring out the intensity of the suffering ; the answer of Abraham shows that, beyond the boundary of this life, there is no hope of relief. Jesus Christ came into the world to save sinners—it was to this world he came ; but no Saviour goes to that other world to win back the lost who have permitted the day of grace to run out. Christ is the way unto the Father; but there is no way of passing from death unto life, if the passage has not been made in this present world.

Interpreting the rich man's intercession for his brothers on the same principle, I do not know and cannot learn here, whether those who have passed through death into the next world unsaved, remember the character of the relatives whom they left behind on earth, or whether, remembering their condition, they will or can make intercession in their behalf. All that I gather certainly on the subject from this parable is, that although a brother may permit his brother to abide in sin without instruction or reproof, while all are living here and walking by sight; yet, if the fate that awaits the impenitent were adequately believed and realized, he who believed and realized it, could not refrain from effort to arouse the slumberers, and lead them to repentance. Again, as in previous parts, I am taught here not what I shall wish when I shall be in the world of spirits, but what I should do now while I am in the body and under grace. I should get the message sent to every heedless brother who is wasting his day of grace, while a messenger of flesh and blood may be found, and there is a way by which I may reach the objects of my solicitude.

By aid of the same machinery—the dialogue between the rich man and Abraham—another lesson is brought from the world of spirits to the land of living men—the lesson that those who refuse to believe and obey under the means of grace which God has appointed in the Church, would not be more pliable if prodigies were shown to them by way of overcoming their unbelief. The conception, although conveyed by the lips of the rich man after he had gone to his own place, that a miracle of power would, if it were exhibited, bring alienated hearts submissively back to God, springs native here in time. It is the deceit with which many sing themselves to sleep—they would believe if one rose from the dead. There are two answers to it :—one is, it would not be effectual although it were granted ; and the other is, even though it were fitted to accomplish the object, it will not be given.

The conclusion of the whole matter is, delays are dangerous ; " Now is the accepted time, now is the day of salvation.

Some lessons still remain, that invite our attention, and will repay it.

1. For mankind, after this life is done, another world remains, consisting of two opposite spheres or conditions, one of holiness and happiness, the other of sin and misery. The Jewish people and their rulers persistently demanded of Jesus that he would show them a sign from heaven ; and this demand he as steadily refused to gratify. Unlike all false prophets, the Lord Jesus maintained silence in regard to the particular characteristics of the unseen world ; but one thing in compassionate love he made known with abundant clearness, that there is an absolute and permanent separation between good and evil in the world to come, and that there are distinct places of rewards and punishments.

Some people labour hard to shake from their own minds the belief in a place and state of retribution. To these I would affectionately suggest that to disbelieve it will not destroy it. Even in Scotland—the narrow end of an island nowhere very broad—I have met with persons well advanced in life, of good common education and good common sense, who had never seen the sea. Suppose that these persons should have cause greatly to dread the sea, and should therefore ardently desire that there were no such thing in existence. Suppose further, that, in the common way of the world, the wish should become father to the thought, and that they at last should firmly believe that there is not a sea. Would their sentiment change the state of the fact? Sinners, to whom the name and nature of a place of punishment are disagreeable, have no more power to annihilate the object of their aversion than the shepherds of the Cheviots to wipe out the sea by a wish. The sea is near those men though they have never seen it; and, if they were cast into it, they would perish, notwithstanding their opinion. Ah! the thing which by God's appointment is, cannot by our arguments be blotted out of being.

2. There is a way from this present life to the place of future misery, and also a way to the place of future blessedness. The way from this world to the place of woe was made by man's sin; the way from this world to the place of rest was made by the incarnation, death, and resurrection of Christ. By the one way you can glide easily down; by the other you may climb toilsomely, but surely up. The one goes with the corrupt affections; the other against them. But let it be remembered that the way of life, though hard, is not unhappy; the struggle, when once fairly begun, is a grand, gladsome thing. Forth from this world there are only two paths; by one or other of these two all men take their departure; on one or other of these two paths we all are treading now. We owe it to Christ that a way into safety has been opened for our sinful world: " I am the way, ... no man cometh unto the Father but by me."

3. There is no way over from one of these future states to the other. The great gulf between them is fixed. This is the main fact of the parable, and hereon its greatest lesson grows. The great gulf is fixed, and after death none can change his place. This fact we now know without further revelation, and if we believe it not on the testimony of Jesus, neither would we believe it although one should rise from the dead to declare it. This parable, in some of its minute features, is to our vision necessarily obscure, because the scene is laid in the life to come, but its main outline is as clearly visible as any temporal object could be. It teaches with great perspicuity that when immortal spirits, at the dissolution of the body, are thrown into the eternal world, it is no longer possible that their place or their condition should be changed: those who will not learn from this word of Christ that the condition of the departed is for ever fixed at death will not learn it in time to profit by the lesson.

4. Our Lord has thus emphatically taught us that there is no possibility of passing from one state to another beyond the boundary of this life in order that he may thereby constrain us to make the needful transition now. The impassable gulf between the saved and the outcast in eternity is a dreadful sight; it was the compassionate Jesus who drew aside the curtain and exposed it to view, and it was his great love that moved him to make this revelation. There is a line that crosses our path a little way forward from the spot where we stand to-day—a line that divides our time from our eternity—invisible to our eyes, but known unto God. We never know as we advance what step of the journey will carry us over this line. Christ has told us that if we pass it unsaved we cannot obtain a change of condition beyond it; and

he has revealed to us this truth in order that we might be induced now to make our calling and election sure. These terrors of the Lord are displayed in order to persuade men. There is no impassable gulf now between a sinner and the Saviour; the way is open, and the perennial invitation resounds from the Gospel, " Come unto me;" but to those who pass from this life without having obeyed that call, there remaineth no more sacrifice for sin, no more a refuge from judgment.

This word of Christ is not of any private interpretation; it may have pointed to Herod or to the Pharisees in the first instance, but it was of the nature of a seed, and its applications multiply a hundred times a hundred fold down through the history of the world. We may find the rich man in this land to-day as certainly as in the circle that listened that day to the preaching of Jesus. We find the counterpart of this picture, not only in individuals, but in associated churches; and if Christians, both in their private and corporate capacities, are rich both in temporal means and spiritual privileges, they need not go far to seek for the Lazarus who is laid at their gate. Lazarus lies in the streets and lanes of our opulent cities; and, oh, he is full of sores! For his sake, for Christ's sake, for our own sake, we must go out and show him kindness. Dives lost his opportunity,—lost it for ever: we must " haste to the rescue" lest we lose ours too. If we love the Lord, our love will stir and burst out and overflow in life. The life that will exercise itself in Christ-like charity must begin now; and if a new life in the Lord begin, it will reveal itself in love's labour. If we are bought with a price and quickened by the Spirit, the beggar at our gate will soon discover the change. He will not be left longer to the mere promptings of natural instinct among his neighbours for the soothing of his sorrows; the warm skilful hand of intelligent and affectionate brotherhood will raise him up and minister to his wants. Lazarus, instead of having only a dog to lick his sores, will be compassed about with human affections, and all his wants supplied. As a diseased, miserable, neglected lazar world felt the coming of Christ, the poor and destitute of the world's inhabitants will know when a loving, hopeful Christian comes within reach. Who touched me? might the huge world have said, if it had possessed intelligence, when God became man and dwelt among us. Who touched me? will the outcasts on the earth begin to cry as they awaken to consciousness, when a revived Church has visited them in their prison, and brought to them the bread of life.

Unprofitable Servants
(Luke 17:1-10)

"Then said he unto the disciples, It is impossible but that offences will come : but woe unto him, through whom they come ! It were better for him that a millstone were hanged about his neck, and he cast into the sea, than that he should offend one of these little ones. Take heed to yourselves : If thy brother trespass against thee, rebuke him ; and if he repent, forgive him. And if he trespass against thee seven times in a day, and seven times in a day turn again to thee, saying, I repent ; thou shalt forgive him. And the apostles said unto the Lord, Increase our faith. And the Lord said, If ye had faith as a grain of mustard seed, ye might say unto this sycamine tree, Be thou plucked up by the root, and be thou planted in the sea ; and it should obey you. But which of you, having a servant plowing or feeding cattle, will say unto him by and by, when he is come from the field, Go and sit down to meat? And will not rather say unto him, Make ready wherewith I may sup, and gird thyself, and serve me, till I have eaten and drunken ; and afterward thou shalt eat and drink ? Doth he thank that servant because he did the things that were commanded him ? I trow not. So likewise ye, when ye shall have done all those things which are commanded you, say, We are unprofitable servants : we have done that which was our duty to do."

WE are accustomed to observe a connection, more or less intimate, between the parable and the history that precedes it. Generally, some recent event, or some question by friend or foe, suggests the similitude. In almost every case we are able to trace the natural history, as it were, of the parable,—to determine what feature of the events or discourses preceding called up the image and gave it shape. Here the relation between the parable and the antecedent instruction is closer still : in this case there is not merely a connection, but an absolute union. The direct and the metaphorical are here successively employed to enforce one continuous lesson. The lesson is one : the first portion of it is delivered in simple didactic language, and the second in parabolic figure. Some instruments are made of two different kinds of metal, not mixed in the crucible, but each occupying its own separate place : one part consists of steel, and another of brass, soldered together, so as to constitute one rod. The nature of the work is such that steel suits best for one extremity of the tool, and brass for the other. It is in a similar way that two different forms of speech are employed here to impart one lesson : the discourse begins with literal expressions, and ends with a similitude.

The passage 1–10 as a whole, teaches the double truth, That God requires of men a complete obedience, and that even though a complete obedience were rendered, the master would not be laid under any obligation—the servants would have no claim to praise or reward. While the rule towards the close is made universal, in the beginning the demand is particular and specific—to bear meekly and forgive generously the injuries which neighbours may inflict in the multifarious intercourse of life. Besides the point which constitutes the main scope of the discourse, several matters of the very highest importance are incidentally involved, and must be noticed, each in its proper place.

First of all, in order to prepare his disciples for meeting the trials that lay before them, he warned them that offences will come, and pronounced a solemn woe on those who should cast them in their neighbour's way. Looking to his own—alike those who were then in his sight, and those who should believe on him down to the end of the world—he calls them, tenderly, little ones, and intimates that it would go ill with all who should dare to hurt them.

This, however, appears to be laid down as a basis for the lesson which he intended at that time to teach, rather than the lesson itself. Speaking expressly for the benefit of his own followers, he was more concerned to teach them how to bear injuries than to command them to beware of inflicting injuries on others. The chief part of a Christian's duty consists in bearing well ; and when that part of his duty is successfully performed, it is more effectual in serving God and convincing men than any kind or degree of active effort. The disciple is like his Lord in this, that he conquers by suffering.

Accordingly, the Teacher soon glides from the precept which forbids his people to inflict injuries, into the precept which teaches how they should bear injuries inflicted by others. " Take heed to yourselves :" this is his main design : towards this he was hastening ; as a basis for this word, the previous injunction had been given. But, mark well, it is not after the manner of men that Jesus warns his disciples to take heed to themselves. He does not mean that they should be solicitous to protect themselves from receiving injury: he leaves that to the natural instincts of self-preservation, and warns them against danger on another side, where nature supplies no defence. He does not mean, Take heed lest you suffer by the stroke which an enemy may deal against you ; he means, Take heed lest you sin in spirit and conduct when you suffer unjustly. You suffer one injury when a neighbour treats you unfairly : and another when you proudly, impatiently retaliate. The loss that you thus inflict on yourself is far heavier than the loss which has been inflicted by a neighbour : the little finger of the one damage is thicker than the loins of the other.

After the outpouring of the Spirit at the Pentecost, we

find these scholars far advanced in this lesson, which their Master taught them while he remained at their head. The believers of those days had, especially in the persons of Peter and John, been cruelly persecuted by the Jewish authorities, and when they met after their suffering to pray, their petition ran: "And now, Lord, behold their threatenings: and grant unto thy servants, that with all boldness they may speak thy word" (Acts iv. 29). An injury had been inflicted: they innocently suffered; and observe what in these circumstances they feared: not more suffering, but lest by the suffering they should be tempted to be silent or wavering when called to be witnesses of Christ. Not the pain they endured, but the right state of their own spirits under the endurance, exercised their minds, and stimulated their prayers.

We must not suppose, however, that the Lord has commanded his disciples to bear injuries as a clod bears blows Mere softness in yielding to the wicked is not a Christian grace; it is, on the contrary, a mischievous indolence: it suffers sin upon a brother: it deprives him of the benefit of reproof, and so encourages him to continue in his sin. " If thy brother trespass against thee, rebuke him; and if he repent, forgive him." This Teacher does not obliterate the lines which separate righteousness from unrighteousness. He enjoins tenderness: but much as he loves to see that feature in his disciples, he places it second to faithfulness. The order of precedence as regards these two has been determined by royal ordinance—" first pure, then peaceable." " Have salt in youselves, and have peace one with another," said the Lord at another time (Mark ix.), plainly giving faithfulness the first place, and requiring that gentleness should press hard up behind. Rebuke the brother who does a wrong to you; if under

your reproof and the working of the truth on his conscience, he be led to repentance and confession, forgive
him in your heart, and express your forgiveness, that he
may be encouraged and relieved. The precept "forgive"
must, from the nature of the case, refer to the articulate
expression of forgiveness ; for in his heart and before God,
a Christian forgives his enemy, although that enemy continue obdurate.

Next comes the precept, given in similar terms already
in another place (Matt. xviii. 15–22), regarding the repetition of injuries. The duty of forgiving a repenting
injurer is not modified by the frequency of his sin; the
form of the expression "seven times in a day," is manifestly
intended to intimate that there is on that side absolutely
no limit. It is not the part of a Christian to count the
number of the injuries he has received, and to refuse forgiveness after a certain point; it is his part to be of a forgiving spirit, and to give forth forgiveness to all like the
sunlight. The example of the Lord is the pattern for
his servants; "Love one another as I have loved you."

The conception of unlimited forgiving, which in Matthew's narrative is expressed by "seventy times seven,"
is here with equal emphasis expressed by "seven times
in a day." When we understand the terms as a formula
for an indefinite number, we exclude the minute question,
How could we believe a man sincere, who should seven
times in a day do us an injury, and as often come and
express sorrow for his fault ? The words should not be
literally taken; and besides if any one should trifle with
his neighbour by frequent and manifestly false professions
of repentance, his meaning would and should be read, not
by his words, but by his conduct; the rule would and should
be understood in its spirit, and not in its letter merely.

Ver. 5. "And the apostles said unto the Lord, Increase our faith." An interesting and instructive view emerges here, of the relation between faith and practice. When they heard the measure of the demand which their Master made upon them in the matter of bearing and forgiving injuries, the apostles felt instantly that the weight was heavier than they could bear. They had not in their hearts such an amount of patience and love, as would enable them to fulfil this commandment of the Lord. Having already learned that faith is the secret fountain whence the stream of obedience flows, they asked with equal simplicity and correctness that their faith might be increased. In this short prayer they assumed, first, that they already believed, asking for an addition to the faith which they already possessed; and second, that it is more faith that will produce more obedience; and third, that the faith which worketh by love is not of themselves, but is the gift of God through his Son. In all this, having been secretly taught of the Spirit, these apostles are deeply intelligent, and completely correct. The appetites are generally sure guides to living creatures for the sustenance of their life; and here the appetite of the new creature, points surely to the source of supply: " Blessed are they that hunger and thirst after righteousness, for they shall be filled."

Both in the request of the scholars (ver. 5), and in the answer of the Master (ver. 6), it is distinctly assumed as a fundamental truth in religion, that faith lies at the root of obedience. When a requisition is made upon them for an amount of meek endurance and forgiving love which their own stores cannot supply, they cry not directly for more power of enduring and forgiving, but for more faith which will strengthen them on this side, and on all other sides at the same time. It is as if you had a cistern meant to supply twelve streams, running in various directions, from whose lip twelve conduits were accordingly led: and when water from one of these was suddenly wanted, you opened it but found that little or none could be obtained. You cry out for a new supply to the cistern; that supply given will fill this channel which is for the the moment in requisition, and all the other channels at the same time. Endurance and forgiving—more than we are able to bear and bestow—are at this moment required of us; but if we had more faith, we should exhibit more of these graces, and more of all graces.

The Lord in his answer acknowledges that their inference is correct. By another form of expression, similar in character to the " seven times in a day," he intimates that faith possesses an unlimited power of production in the department of doing. To intensify the result he employs a double hyperbole, as engineers employ two pairs of wheels to generate extreme rapidity of motion; the smallest spark of faith will overcome the greatest obstacles that may lie across a Christian's path. Again, the same idea which appeared before in Matt. xvii. 20, is expressed here by a different figure: in both cases the Lord intends to intimate that what without faith is impossible, may with faith be done. In Matthew the impossible is represented by the removal of a mountain; in Luke by the planting of a sycamore in the sea. By these forms our Teacher conveys his meaning with amazing distinctness. The letters of his lessons thus sharply, deeply cut, remain indeed dead letters to those who have not experienced the grace of God; as letters of a book, the largest and loveliest lie meaningless before the eyes of a savage or a little child; but in either case, as soon as tne scholar becomes capable of understanding, the meaning shines forth like light. It would be a great transition from our present position of impotence, if we should become able to remove a mountain, or plant a sycamore in the sea; such and so great is the transition when a man passes from death in sin to life in Christ; such and so great the difference between what he could bear, and hope, and do while he was at emnity with God, and what he can bear, and hope, and do when he is reconciled to God through the death of his Son.

The particular requirement which on this occasion put the faith of the disciples under a strain greater than it was able to meet, was the endurance and the forgiving of injuries; but this Scripture must not be limited to a private interpretation; this is a specimen shown in illustration of a general rule. There are diversities of operation, under the providence of God our Father; now the faith of Christians is tested in one way, and then in another. At one time they are called actively to do a great work; and at another time passively to bear a great burden. The work required of one disciple is a mission to the dark places of the earth; and the work required of another is to bear patiently many years of pain and weariness, in his own home, it may be on his own bed. By both alike the kingdom of Christ may be advanced: from both equally when they are bruised,—the one by great effort, and the other by a heavy weight,—the odour of a holy temper may be diffused all around.

We are not masters; we are servants. The Lord appoints to each his place, and his work.

The lesson now passes into the parable. When he had pointed out how great is God's claim, and how large faith's performance might become in the life of a disciple, Jesus warns them, on the other side, that the greatest possible, the greatest conceivable attainment in the direction of a believing obedience, implies absolutely no independent merit in man; obedience, although it reached the utmost point of perfection, would still leave God indebted to man for nothing, and man indebted to God for all.

" But which of you having a servant ploughing or feeding cattle." The state of society which supplies the ground-work of this parable is in many respects different from that which prevails in modern Europe. It is especially important here to notice the difference in these two features:—

1. It is a simple pastoral life that constitutes the basis of this picture. The principle of division of labour exists there in its lowest stages of development. It is assumed as a common and proper thing to employ a shepherd or a ploughman in serving his master at table—a practice entirely unknown among us. 2. The servitude in the instance supposed was not a voluntary limited engagement, but a species of slavery: the master's control was much more absolute and complete than it is among us. The servant's toil might be, and probably in many cases actually was, on the whole, not heavier than that to which our hired servants are subjected; but the measure of the labour, both as to its endurance and its severity, depended there on the master's will rather than on the servant's freedom. The master, under the species of relation which then largely prevailed, could demand of his servant on occasion an amount and continuity of service which now is not demanded on the one side, and would not be rendered on the other.

It should be noticed, however, that the service which is

in the parable required and rendered, is both in character and quantity extreme. An ordinary example of a servant's work would not have suited the purpose of the Lord ; he needed a line stretched to its utmost limits. His purpose is to teach that the utmost conceivable amount of obedience on man's part is not independently meritorious before God ; and, in searching among temporal things for a suitable analogy, he selected a case in which the line stretched from one extremity to the other.

When the servant has finished his day's work on the pasture or in the field, at his return, and before he obtain either rest or food, he is compelled to wait upon his master at table. Even this extreme measure of work is required by the master and rendered by the servant as within the limits of their respective rights : the servant even in that case has done no more than was due.

" So likewise ye, when ye shall have done all these things which are commanded you, say, We are unprofitable servants."

God has given all, owns all, has a right to all. We are his by right of creation, and his by redemption, when we are in Christ. Christians are not their own ; they are bought with a price. Themselves, and their faculties, and their capabilities belong to God, their Creator and Redeemer. When they have rendered all their powers, and all the product of these powers, absolutely up to God's will, they have done no more than rendered to him his own. " Will a man rob God ? yet ye have robbed me " (Mal. iii. 8). It is an aggravated sin to rob God of what is his ; but it is no merit or ground of praise simply to refrain from robbing him ; and this is all that the creature's obedience would amount to, although it were complete.

Our Master ordinarily makes our work easy; he is gentle, and easy to be entreated. "As a father pitieth his children, so the Lord pitieth them that fear him:" but at his pleasure, and doubtless in deep ways for their good, he sometimes lays extraordinary burdens on his own. He may permit offences to come, trying your temper; he may permit sickness to overtake you, trying your patience; he may permit temptations to assail you, trying your faith even at its foundations; he may require of you great and varied activity, trying your willingness to run at his call. These burdens seem heavy, as the master's demand of service in the house seemed heavy to the servant when he returned weary and hungry from field labour; but although we should bear them all with complete uncomplaining alacrity, we should acquire thereby no right to reward.

There is absolutely no such thing as a surplus of merit in man. The imagination of it has ever been rife in man-made religions, as weeds spring thick and spontaneous from the ground; but never and nowhere is there any substantial foundation for this human conceit. It springs in the deepest ignorance, and it withers when the light of knowledge begins to shine. It rests on an entire misapprehension of the relations between God and man. If a man on ship-board, thinking that the ship was about to sink, on account of being too heavily loaded, should grasp the shrouds, and hang on them with all his weight, by way of lightening the ship, the bystanders would count him fatuous; and yet such is the folly of him who, getting all from God, imagines that he has conferred on God a favour by a surplus of goodness. I have seen grown people, in possession of all their faculties, able to read, if not further educated, when, in crossing a river by a ferry, they apprehended danger, applying both their hands to the side of the boat in which they stood, and, pushing with all their might, in order to push it towards a place of safety. This implies the grossest ignorance, or at least the total forgetfulness for the time of the most obvious and ordinary of the natural laws; and yet I have found that these persons had quite enough of wit to manage all their ordinary affairs, and to get along respectably in society. I think there is some analogy between this case and the case of those who, intelligent on other points, yet blindly imagine that they merit praise for not squandering God's gifts that have been placed under their care.

"When ye have done all, say, We are unprofitable servants"—servants whom the master did not need, and who contribute nothing to him. The question whether the Lord conceded that in point of fact any man ever does perfectly perform all his duty is out of place here; The Lord's meaning is, even although a man should do all, he would still be destitute of merit before God; much more are those destitute of merit who come far short of perfection, and to this class belong all, even the best of the children of men.

Means and opportunities of bearing evil and doing good are in providence conceded to every one of us; and the law announced in another parable holds good here; If we improve aright the talents which we possess, more will forthwith be entrusted to us.

There is room for advancement; and, when grace is begun, it is sweet to grow in grace. If we had power to add cubit by cubit to our stature, we should have far to grow ere our head should strike the heavens; and in bearing meekly, and acting righteously, and living purely, we have room enough to expand: it will be long ere we have done all, and so our progress be stopped by striking the boundary. Forgetting the things that are behind, and reaching forth to those that are before, we may press on and ever on ; yet there is room.

Nor let any one think that bearing and doing God's will must be less blessed when we learn that God did not need this at our hand, and that we do not thereby lay him under obligation to us. When one is truly taught of the Spirit, it will increase and not diminish the pleasure which he enjoys in obedience, to learn that all he is, and has, and does, comes from God. A dependent is happier than an independent position for human beings, if he on whom they hang is great and good. The life of a child is happiest during the period when he has no possession of his own, and desires none,—when he gets all as he needs from his father ; on this side, as well as on others, we must receive the kingdom as a little child.

Here is a little stream trickling down the mountain side. As it proceeds, other streams join it in succession from the right and left until it becomes a river. Ever flowing, and ever increasing as it flows, it thinks it will make a great contribution to the ocean when it shall reach the shore at length. No, river, you are an unprofitable servant ; the ocean does not need you ; could do as well and be as full without you ; is not in any measure made up by you. True, rejoins the river, the ocean is so great that all my volume poured into it makes no sensible difference ; but still I contribute so much, and this, as far as it goes, increases the amount of the ocean's supply. No : this indeed is the seeming to the ignorant observer on the spot ; but whoever obtains deeper knowledge and a wider range, will discover and confess that the river is an unprofitable servant to the sea—that it contributes absolutely nothing to the sea's store. From the ocean came every drop of water that rolls down in that river's bed, alike those that fell into it in rain from the sky, and those that flowed into it from tributary rivers, and those that sprang from hidden veins in the earth. Even although it should restore all, it gives only what it received. It could not flow, it could not be, without the free gift of all from the sea. To the sea it owes its existence and power. The sea owes it nothing ; would be as broad and deep although this river had never been. But all this natural process goes on, sweetly and beneficently, notwithstanding : the river gets and gives ; the ocean gives and gets. Thus the circle goes round, beneficent to creation, glorious to God.

Thus, in the spiritual sphere,—in the world that God has created by the Spirit of his Son, circulations beautiful and beneficent continually play. From him, and by him, and to him are all things. To the saved man through whom God's mercy flows, the activity is unspeakably precious : to him the profit, but to God the praise.

The Persistent Widow
(Luke 18:1-8)

" And he spake a parable unto them to this end, that men ought always to pray, and not to faint : saying, There was in a city a judge, which feared not God, neither regarded man : and there was a widow in that city ; and she came unto him, saying, Avenge me of mine adversary. And he would not for a while : but afterwards he said within himself, Though I fear not God, nor regard man ; yet because this widow troubleth me, I will avenge her, lest by her continual coming she weary me. And the Lord said, Hear what the unjust judge saith. And shall not God avenge his own elect, which cry day and night unto him, though he bear long with them? I tell you that he will avenge them speedily. Nevertheless when the Son of man cometh; shall he find faith on the earth ?"

AMONG the parables this one is signalized by the distinctness with which its object is announced at the commencement, and the principle of its interpretation at the close. No room is left here for diversity of opinion regarding the lesson which the Lord intended to teach, or the manner in which the parable should be expounded. The design is expressed in verse first ; the rule of interpretation in verses sixth and seventh. Why did the Master tell this story to his disciples ? To teach them " that men ought to pray always, and not to faint." How may this lesson be derived from it ? As the widow by her unremitting cry obtained her desire from the judge, God's own redeemed children will obtain from their Father in heaven all that they need, if they ask it eagerly, persistently, unwearyingly.

When we rightly comprehend the design of the

parable, the difficulty connected with the bad character of the judge at once disappears. It was necessary to
go to a corrupt tribunal in order to find a suitable case ;
a pure judgment seat supplies no such example. In
certain circumstances you might gather from a dunghill
a medicinal herb which cleaner ground would never bear.
The grain which becomes our bread grows best when its
roots are spread in unseen corruption ; and so perfect is
the chemistry of nature, that the yellow ears of harvest
retain absolutely no taint of the putrescence whence they
sprung. Thus easily and perfectly the Lord brings lessons
of holiness from examples of sin. He pauses not to
apologize or explain : majestically the instruction advances, like the processes of nature, until the unrighteousness of man defines and illustrates the mercy of God.

It is not by accident,—it is by choice that this seed of
the word is sown on filthy ground : it is sown there, because
it will grow best there. The experience of a righteous
human tribunal does not supply the material of this lesson.
Where the presiding judge is just, a poor injured widow
will obtain redress at once, and her perseverance will never
be put to the test. The characteristic feature of the case
which the Lord needed, was a persistent, unyielding perseverance in the cry for redress ; for such a case he must
go to a court where law does not regulate the judge, but
where the judge for his own ease or interest makes his
own law. The feature of Christ's teaching which most
arrested intelligent listeners in his own day, was its inherent, self-evidencing majesty. Instead of seeking props,
it stood forth alone, obviously divine. He taught with
authority, and not as the scribes. Here is an example of
that simple supremeness that is at once a witness to itself.
He compares explicitly and broadly the method of God's

dealing, as the hearer of prayer, with the practice of a judge who is manifestly vile and venal. Nor is a word of explanation or apology interposed. He who thus simply brings sweet food from noisome carrion, has all power in heaven and in earth; His ways are not as our ways, nor his thoughts as our thoughts.

As he needed for his purpose an example of judicial corruption, examples lay ready to his hand in human history; especially in the practice of oriental empires, ancient and modern, it is easy to find cases in which the supreme authority, civil and criminal, is vested in a deputy who habitually sacrifices justice to his own ease or interest.

The thorough badness of this judge, although stated distinctly, is stated briefly; it is not made prominent in the parable, and should not be made prominent in the interpretation of the parable. That badness on both sides, towards God and man, is I apprehend not introduced here for its own sake, but for the sake of a particular effect that resulted from it;—the frequent, persevering appeals of the widow for redress. This is the thing that is needed and used in the Lord's lesson; and although the injustice of the judge stands distinctly out on the face of the parable, it is like the forest tree in the vineyards of Italy, used only to hold up the vine. Earnest, repeated, unyielding appeal by a needy, feeble suppliant before the throne of power;—this is the fruit which is precious for the Teacher's purpose, and the hollow heart of the epicurean judge is employed only as the trunk to bear it. When it has held up that fruit to be ripened, itself may be thrown away.

At certain points in frequented routes through romantic scenery it is customary to fire a gun in order to afford the tourists an opportunity of hearing the echoes answering each other in the neighbouring mountains. The explosion is in place nearest, in time first, and as to sound loudest, but this the most articulate and arrestive fact is employed exclusively for the purpose of producing the subsequent and more distant echo. The explosion is instantly dismissed from the mind and attention concentrated on the reverberation which it called forth. The conduct of the judge in this parable stands precisely in the place of that explosion. When it has produced the widow's importunity it is of no further use; it must be thrown aside.

Let us hear now the interpretation,—" And the Lord said, Hear what the unjust judge saith," &c. God's own chosen and redeemed people correspond to the suppliant widow in the parable. They are like her in her suffering and her weakness; they should be like her too in her unintermittent, persevering cry.

Like other similar lessons, this one bears equally on the Church as a body, and on an individual Christian. The Church collective, in times of persecution, and a soul surrounded by temptations, stand equally in the place of the poor widow; they are in need and in danger. They have no resources in themselves; help must come from one that is mighty. It is their interest to plead with him who has all power in heaven and in earth,—to plead as men plead for life.

The lesson here is very specific; it bears on one point, and in order that all its force may be concentrated on one point, others are for the time omitted. This parable is not spoken with the view of teaching that Christians ought to pray; that duty is assumed here, not enjoined. Neither does it prescribe what the suppliant should ask, or on whose merits he should lean. Taking for granted all these things which the Scriptures elsewhere explicitly teach, the Master in this lesson confines his attention to one thing,—perseverance in prayer when the answer does not come at first, perseverance and pertinacity aye and until the object is attained.

It is expressly intimated in the narrative that there is sometimes a long, and from our view-point inexplicable delay. This is the meaning of the expression "though he bear long with them." This phrase is not taken here in its ordinary signification,—an endurance of injuries; it means that he holds back long, and resists their pressure for relief.

Here are the two sides over against each other: they cry day and night, and he, hearing their continuous cry, refrains from bestowing the relief for which they passionately plead. As God keeps back the answer, they redouble the cry; as they redouble the cry, God still withholds the answer. Expressly we are informed he will give answer; he will avenge his own elect. The eternal Father treasures up all the supplications of his children, and he will yet give them deliverance. When his time comes the deliverance will be complete; but in the meantime the interesting inquiry presents itself, Why does he delay at all? In the light of Scripture we are able to give a satisfactory answer to this inquiry.

The reason why the widow's claims were left long unsettled in the court was the self-pleasing indolence of the judge. The love of his own ease was the motive that induced him both to refuse redress at first and to grant it afterwards. He refused to avenge her until he perceived that to do her justice would afford him less trouble than to withhold it. In the treatment which the petitions of the elect receive at the throne of God there is nothing in common with the conduct of the unjust judge, except the delay. The fact that the petitions lie for some time unanswered is common to both tribunals, but on all other points they are wholly diverse, and even the single feature of coincidence springs in the two cases from opposite grounds.

When God withholds the deliverance for which his children plead he acts with wisdom and love combined. It would be, so to speak, easier for a father who is at once rich and benevolent to comply immediately and fully with all the child's demands; it requires and exercises a deeper, stronger love to leave the child crying and knocking for a time in vain that the bounty given at the proper time may in the end be a greater boon. I once knew two men who lived near each other in similar worldly circumstances, but adopted opposite methods in the treatment of their children. The boys of this family obtained money from their father when they asked it, and spent it according to their own pleasure, without his knowledge or control: the boys of that family often asked, but seldom received a similar supply. The father who frequently thwarted his children's desires loved his children more deeply, and as the result showed, more wisely than the father who could not summon courage sufficient to say No. The wise parent bore with his own when they pleaded for some dangerous indulgence, and the bearing wounded his tender heart; but by reason of his greater love, he bore the pain of hearing their cry without granting their request. The other parent was too indolent and self-pleasing to endure such a strain, and he lived to taste bitter fruit from the evil seed which his own hand had sown

For the same reason, and in the same manner, our Father in heaven bears with his own when they cry night and day to him for something on which their hearts are set. Because he loves us he endures to hear our cry and see our tears. We do not certainly know what thorn it was that penetrated Paul's flesh, but we know that it pained him much, that he eagerly desired to be quit of it, and that he besought the Lord thrice to take it away. From the fact that the child pleaded three times for the same boon, we learn that the Father bore with him awhile,—bore, so to speak, the pain of refusing, because he knew that the refusal was needful for Paul. The thorn was left in the flesh until its discipline was done, and then it was plucked out by a strong and gentle hand. "My grace is sufficient for thee:" there are no thorns in Paul's flesh now.

The case of the Syro-Phœnician woman (Matt. xv. 21–28) runs parallel with this as well as with the "Friend at midnight." Mark how the Lord bore with the woman. He delighted in her faith; it was his happiness to give, and yet he refused; in denying her he denied himself. But by withholding a while, he kindled her love into a brighter, stronger flame. By refusing what she asked, he reduplicated her asking; this is sweet to him and profitable to her. By the long delay on his part and the consequent eager repetition of the request on her part, a richer boon was prepared and bestowed. Her appetite was greatly quickened, and her satisfying was more full. Who shall be filled most abundantly from the treasures of divine mercy at last? Those who hungered and thirsted most for these treasures in the house of their pilgrimage.

Think of the plainness of this lesson, and the authority which it possesses. Its meaning cannot be mistaken; we know what is spoken here, and we know who speaks

Hath he spoken, and shall he not make it good? The only begotten Son who is in the bosom of the Father, he hath declared him. Show us the Father, said Philip, and it sufficeth us; here Christ, in answer to his disciples' prayer, is showing the Father.

To reveal the Father's heart he spoke this parable. The helpless, needy woman came and came again, and cried, and would take no refusal, until the judge was compelled by her importunity to grant her request: and this is the picture chosen by the Lord Jesus when he desires to show how God regards suppliant disciples as they plead at his footstool. It is an amazing revelation, and the best of it is its truth. He who gave it has authority to speak. The Son will not misrepresent the Father; the Father's honour is safe in this Teacher's hands. We learn here, then, that the Hearer of prayer puts himself in the power of a suppliant. He permitted Jacob to wrestle, and the firmer he felt the grasp the more he loved the wrestler. The words, " I will not let thee go except thou bless me," dropping in broken fragments from his lips at intervals as he paused and panted, were sweeter than angels' songs in the ears of the Lord of Hosts. He is the same still, as he is in the New Testament revealed by Jesus. The spirit in man that will take no denial is his special delight; the spirit that asks once and ceases he cannot away with. As the Lord loveth a cheerful giver, he loveth too an eager persevering asker. The door seems narrow, but its narrowness was not meant to keep us out; they please him best who press most heavily on its yielding sides. "The kingdom of heaven suffereth violence, and the violent take it by force." The King of Glory feels well pleased the warriors' onset,— gladly welcomes the conqueror in.

It is indeed blessed to give: but the giver's blessedness is greatly marred by the listlessness of the needy creatures on whom he has bestowed his bounty. If they who need and get the goodness are insensible, and cold, and ungrateful, the joy of the benefactor is proportionally diminished. It is thus with "the giving God." When the receiver values the bounty, the delight of the bestower is increased. Thus the Lord Jesus was specially pleased as he healed the daughter of the Syro-Phœnician mother because she gave evidence by her importunity how much she valued the boon; and, on the other hand, his plaintive question, "Where are the nine?" when the lepers took their cure so lightly, shows that he did not much enjoy the act of healing because the diseased made light both of their ailment and their cure.

Come near, press hard, open your mouth wide, pray without ceasing; for this is the kind of asking that the great Giver loves. Unforgiven sin on the conscience keeps the sinful distant, and Satan calls the silence modesty. It is not; they most honour God who show by their importunity in asking that they value his gifts.

While it is true that prayer should be a continuous fulness in the heart, ever pressing outward and upward, flowing wherever it can find an opening, it is not specifically that characteristic to which this parable points. This is not the lesson, "In everything by prayer and supplication, with thanksgiving, let your requests be made known unto God:" the lesson here points not to the breadth of a whole spiritual life, but to the length of one line that runs through it. Whatever it be that a disciple desires, and is bent upon obtaining, he should ask not once, or twice, or twenty times, but ask until he obtain it; or until he die with the request upon his lips: and in that case he will get his desire, and more. Trust in God: trust in his love. He who has not spared his own Son, how shall he not with him freely give us all things ? Do not deem that delay is proof of his indifference. Delaying to bestow is not proof of indifference in God; but ceasing to ask is proof of indifference in man. Christ assures us he will give : that should induce us to continue asking.

Give me these links—1. Sense of need ; 2. Desire to get ; 3. Belief that God has it in store ; 4. Belief that though he withholds awhile, he loves to be asked ; and 5. Belief that asking will obtain ;—give me these links, and the chain will reach from earth to heaven, bringing heaven all down to me, or bearing me up into heaven.

While it is right to generalize the lesson, as we have already done, it is our duty also to notice the special form of the widow's prayer and the Lord's promise : in both cases it is vengeance against an adversary. The pleading is that the enemy who wronged the widow should be punished by the hand of power : the promise is that God will avenge his chosen ones, who cry to him.

The case is clearly one in which the weak are overpowered by an adversary too strong for them : unable to defend themselves, or strike down their foe, they betake themselves to God in prayer. The ailment is specific ; such also is the request. Do justice upon this enemy—rid me of his oppression and his presence.

Ah, when a soul feels sin's power a bondage, and sin's presence a loathsome defilement ;—when a soul so oppressed flees to the Saviour for deliverance, the Lord will entertain the case, and grant redress. He will avenge. "The God of peace will bruise Satan under your feet shortly."

No cry that rises from earth to heaven sounds so

sweetly in the ear of God as the cry for vengeance upon the enemy of souls. When there is peace between man and his destroyer, the closet is silent, and no groan of distress from the deep beats against the gate of heaven. This is not what Jesus loves. He came not to send this peace on earth, or in heaven ; he came to send a sword. His errand was to produce a deadly quarrel between the captive soul and the wicked one, its captivator. When the cry rises, broken and stifled, but eager, as uttered by one engaged in deadly strife—when the cry, "Avenge me," rises from earth, God in heaven hears it well pleased. He delights when his people, hating the adversary of their souls, ask him for vengeance ; and he will grant it. Long to the struggling combatant the battle seems to last, but speedily, according to God's just reckoning, the avenging stroke will fall. If there is delay it is but for a moment, and because this added moment of conflict will make the everlasting victory more sweet.

It is worthy of notice, incidentally, that where an indolent judge, in order to avoid trouble, gives a just sentence to-day, he may, from the same motive, give an unjust sentence to-morrow. He who taught this lesson, knowing all that should befall himself, and hastening forward to his final suffering, knew well that deepest sorrow may spring from the selfishness of an unjust judge which happened for that time to bring deliverance to the widow. Pilate was precisely such a magistrate. Neither fear of God nor regard for man was the ultimate reason that determined his decision : the love of his own ease and safety was the hinge on which his judgment turned. He was disposed to do justly rather than unjustly in the case, when the Jewish rulers dragged Jesus to his bar. He would have pronounced a righteous judgment if that course had seemed to promise greater or equal advantage to himself. But the priests and people were, like this widow, very importunate and persevering. "Crucify him, crucify him," they cried. "Why, what evil hath he done?" "Crucify him, crucify him," rose again in a sound like the voice of many waters from the heaving throng. "Shall I release Jesus?" interposed the irresolute Pilate; "Away with this man, and give us Barabbas," was the instant reply. "Shall I crucify your king?" said Pilate, making yet another effort to escape the toils that were closing round him; but this fence laid him open to the heaviest blow of all: "If thou let this man go, thou art not Cæsar's friend." He gave way at last: by their continual coming they wearied him, and he abandoned the innocent to their will.

Thus the unjust as well as the just judgment seat has two sides. Jesus gave the safe side to the poor widow, and accepted the other for himself. He became poor that we might be rich: he was condemned that we might be set free.

The Pharisee and the Publican
(Luke 18:9-14)

" And he spake this parable unto certain which trusted in themselves that they were right
eous, and despised others : Two men went up into the temple to pray ; the one a
Pharisee, and the other a publican. The Pharisee stood and prayed thus with himself, God, I thank thee, that I am not as other men are, extortioners, unjust, adulterers, or even as this publican. I fast twice in the week, I give tithes of all that I
possess. And the publican, standing afar off, would not lift up so much as his eyes unto
heaven, but smote upon his breast, saying, God be merciful to me a sinner. I tell you,
this man went down to his house justified rather than the other : for every one that
exalteth himself shall be abased ; and he that humbleth himself shall be exalted."

IN this parable two great classes are represented, not by symbols, but by specimens. Self-righteous men are here represented by a self-righteous man, and repenting sinners by a repenting sinner. The instruction is communicated, not obliquely by a figure, but directly by a fact. The quality of the harvest is shown by samples taken from the heap.

If allegory were deemed an essential ingredient of a parable, this lesson of the Lord would necessarily be excluded from the list ; but I am not disposed to adopt such a narrow and artificial definition. Taking a general view of its substance, rather than making a minute inspection of its form, I accept the Pharisee and the publican as a parable according to the common consent of the Church.

It is almost entirely free from critical and exegetical difficulties : he may run who reads its lesson.

In announcing the class of persons for whose reproof

it was spoken, the evangelist at the outset supplies us with a key that opens all its meaning :—" Certain which trusted in themselves that they were righteous and despised others," were clustering round the Teacher, and mingling with his disciples. He spoke this parable for the purpose of crushing their pride : he will not suffer sin upon them. For their instruction and reproof, these examples are selected and described.

It is not necessary to suppose that the parable pointed exclusively to those who were Pharisees, or exclusively to those who were not : it concerned all who were self-righteous, to whatever sect they externally belonged. We know that within the circle of Christ's devoted followers much of this spirit still lingered. Peter enumerated the sacrifices which he and his comrades had made for their Master, and bluntly demanded what reward they might expect for their fidelity. It is expressly to his own disciples that the Lord, on another occasion, addresses the warning, " Beware of the leaven of the Pharisees, which is hypocrisy." For our benefit, then, even though we be true Christians—for our benefit, and not only for some particular sect, is this instruction given.

" Two men went up into the temple to pray." The temple was the acknowledged place of prayer ; to it the devout Jews went at the hour of prayer, if they were near; toward it they looked if they were distant. The appointment was a help to prayer in the preparatory dispensation: it would be a hindrance if it were maintained still. Not in that one place, but in all places, the true worshippers pray to the Father.

" The one a Pharisee, and the other a publican." The two characters are represented in deep relief : there is no confusion, and no ambiguity. Each is exhibited in his own colour, and the two are sharply distinguished from each other.

Nor are these two men in all their features diverse : there are points of likeness as well as of difference. It is as profitable to observe wherein they are like as wherein they are unlike. The distinction does not lie in that the one was good while the other was bad : both were evil, and perhaps it would be safe to say, both alike evil. In the end, the one was a sinner forgiven, and the other a sinner unforgiven ; but at the beginning both and both equally were sinners. Their sins as to outward form were diverse ; but in essential character the sinfulness was in both the same. The Pharisee said and did not ; the publican neither said nor did. The Pharisee pretended to a righteousness which he did not possess ; the publican neither professed righteousness nor possessed it. While one maintained the form of godliness, but denied its power, the other denied both the form and the power of godliness. At first there is nothing to determine our choice between the two men as to their state before God : the one was a hypocrite, and the other a worldling. Both alike need pardon, and to both alike pardon is offered in the Gospel. "The blood of Christ cleanseth us from all sin ;" but no effort of our own will cleanse us from any. With the forgiveness that comes through Christ, the Pharisee would have been accepted ; but wanting it, the publican would have been cast out. The hinge on which the essential distinction between these two men turned was not the different quantities of sin which they had severally committed, but the opposite grounds on which they severally placed their trust.*

* There is a strong resemblance between this pair and the two sons who were severally asked by their father to work in his vineyard. — page 223.

Both go at the same time to the same place to pray, and both adopt in the main the same attitude in this exercise ; they stood while they prayed. This was the ordinary attitude ; but kneeling and prostration were also practised. Each of these postures has its own peculiar appropriateness ; either is a seemly and a Scriptural method of bringing the position of the body into significant harmony with the desire of the soul. Among those attitudes which are true and right, we are at liberty to adopt that which is in our circumstances most convenient and seemly. Alas ! there has always been a tendency in man to lay a yoke upon himself and his fellow. Why should we judge one another where our Master has left us free ? We may safely lay it down as an absolute rule, without stipulating for even a single exception, that the best position for praying in is the position in which we can best pray.*

"The Pharisee stood and prayed thus with himself, God, I thank thee," &c. Those expositors are probably right who think that "with himself" is connected with "stood," rather than "prayed." It is in perfect accord with the narrative to intimate that he stood by himself— he was not the man to mingle with the common herd of worshippers ; but it does not seem congruous to intimate that he prayed with himself. His prayer is addressed to

---

* This question has begun of late to attract a considerable measure of attention in the Presbyterian Churches of this country. It needs a wise treatment, and, alas ! we lack wisdom. For convenience and order, all the members of a worshipping assembly ought evidently to adopt the same method ; but this is not a matter for arbitrary ecclesiastical enactment. The Pharisee and the publican both stood while they prayed ; but their prayers seem to have been short. To enact that the congregation must stand during prayer, and then to keep them praying for twenty minutes or half-an-hour, which is sometimes done, seems to be in effect turning prayer into penance.

God ; he has no doubt much to do with himself while he utters it, but so has his neighbour the publican. As much as the proud man deals with himself to contemplate his own goodness during prayer, so much does the humble man deal with himself to contemplate his own badness. It is not then intimated that he prayed by himself, but that he stood by himself while he was praying. He counted that he belonged to the aristocracy in the kingdom of God, and must get a position apart from the multitude.*

In yet one other point the two suppliants are like each other ; both alike look into their own hearts and lives ; and both permit the judgment thus formed to determine the form and matter of their prayer. Both addressed themselves to the work of self-examination, and the prayers that follow are the fruits of their research.

At this point the two men part company, and move in opposite directions—the one found in himself only good, the other found in himself only evil. In both, and in both alike, there was only evil ; but the publican discovered and confessed the truth regarding himself, while the Pharisee either blindly failed to see his own sin, or falsely refused to confess it.

The error of the Pharisee does not lie in the form or

---

* Σταθεις προς ἑαυτον, standing by himself, as if it were καθ' ἑαυτον. Thus the relation is preserved with the position of the publican, μακροθεν ἑστως. Either stood alone, but for opposite reasons : the Pharisee stood forward alone, because he thought other worshippers were not fit to be in his company ; the publican stood back alone, because he considered himseli unworthy to mingle with other worshippers. It may be worth while to mention, for the sake of the English reader, the order of the words in the original is, "The Pharisee standing with himself, thus prayed." You must be guided entirely by the sense in determining whether to read it, Standing with himself, thus prayed ; or standing, with himself thus prayed.

matter of his prayer. It is substantially a song of thanksgiving. This is never out of place ; praise is comely.
There is not a living man on the earth who has not
ground for giving praise to God every day, and all day.
Nor does his prayer necessarily transgress the strict limits
of truth when he says, " God, I thank thee that I am not
as other men." If he had been employed in numbering
the mercies of God—if he had meditated on his privileges,
till he was lost in wonder, that so many benefits had been
conferred on one so worthless, he might with truth have
burst into the exclamation, " I am not as other men."
As a true penitent, when employed in considering his
own sin, truly describes himself as the chief of sinners; so
a thankful man, lost in the multitude of God's mercies,
thinks in all simplicity that none in all the world have been
so highly favoured as himself. From his own view-point
a true worshipper truly counts both his sins and his
mercies greater than those of other men. When he confesses his sins he counts and calls them deeper than those
of others ; when he recounts the benefits he has received
from God, he says that they are greater than others have
enjoyed. Glad praise and weeping confession correspond
to each other in a true heart, as correspond the height of
the sky and the depth of its shadow in still waters.
When the clouds above you become high, the shadow of
them beneath you becomes correspondingly deep. The
same man who said, " I am chief of sinners," said also,
" Thanks be to God for his unspeakable gift."

It is not, then, for what he has said that the Pharisee is
condemned, even when he announces that he is not as
other men. If conscious of unworthiness, and amazed at
God's long-suffering, he had exclaimed, I am not like
other men—I have been spared and instructed, and in-

vited and taught and led with a paternal tenderness that others do not enjoy, his thanksgiving would have been sweet incense as it rose to the throne of the Most High. He presumes to give thanks not for what he has received, but for what he is and does. Here lies his condemnation. It is not in the thanks but in the reason for the thanks that the old serpent lurks; he is delighted not with what God has graciously bestowed on him, but with what he has meritoriously given to God.

The sense in the original is more comprehensive than that which the English conveys; other men here mean all others. On one side he places himself, and on the other side the rest of human kind: the result of the comparison in his judgment is that he is better than all.

Three of the more articulate and manifest forms of wickedness he enumerates, in order by the contrast to set forth his own purity. "Extortioners" are officials having a right to something, who unjustly force from an oppressed people more than is due; the "unjust" are those who deal unfairly in the ordinary intercourse of life; and adulterers are, in fact, and were then accounted the deepest and most daring transgressors of the laws both human and divine. Probably the Pharisee was in point of fact free in his conduct from all these vices; there is nothing in the parable that forbids us in these matters to take him at his word.

Instead of extending the list of vices of which he felt himself free, he cuts the matter short by a general comparison between himself and the publican. The contempt in which the tax-farmers were held by the stricter Jews shines out in every page of the Gospel, and is well understood by the readers of the Scriptures. By way of purging himself from sin in the lump, he says shortly, "I am not as this publican." In order to condemn the Pharisee on this point, it is not necessary to suppose that he made a wrong estimate of his neighbour. Granted that this publican had up to this hour been stained with all these three vices, and that the Pharisee, knowing his character, formed a correct judgment regarding it ; still his condemnation remains the same; it is not the part of one sinner to judge and condemn another.

" I fast twice in the week, I give tithes of all that I possess,"—all that I acquire; it is not capital but income. It is a picture of mere self-righteousness. His judgment was wrong from the root ; he knew neither his own heart nor God's law. Pharisee as he was, he might have learned from the prophet Isaiah the true state of the case, " We are all as an unclean thing ; and all our righteousnesses are as filthy rags."*

" The publican standing afar off," &c. The difference does not lie in that this was a good man while the other was bad. This is a sinner too ; but he has come to know it, and therein lies the distinction between him and the Pharisee. His judgment of himself accords with his actual state and character ; he knows and owns the truth regarding his own sinfulness. There is no merit in this discovery, and in itself it cannot save. If two men should both take poison, and one of them should become aware of the fact ere the poison had time to operate ; the one who knows the truth is more miserable than the one who is ignorant, but not more safe. If there be a physician within reach who can cure, the knowledge of his

---

* He obtained this self-confidence by comparing himself not with the law of God, but with others who seemed worse than himself. When a man compares himself with robbers and adulterers, for whom the sword and the prison are prepared, he may easily seem to himself like an angel.—*Arndt.*

danger will send one man to the source of help, while the ignorance of the other will keep him lingering where he is, till it is too late to flee. But even in that case it was not the man's knowledge of his danger that saved him. Another saved him ; his knowledge of his own need only led him to a deliverer.

It is so here. There is no merit and no salvation in the publican's conviction and confession; although he confesses his sin, he is still a sinner. His own tears are not the fountain in which his guilt can be washed away. If there were no Saviour, his penitence would do him no good; if Christ had not come to save the lost, the lost, though alarmed, would not have been saved.

If we take care to notice that there was neither merit nor safety in the man's confession, we may profitably listen to the confession, and learn what it was.

" He stood afar aff." Here we begin to observe external marks of an inward penitence ; he judged and condemned himself. He had the same right with other worshippers to come near; but a consciousness of his uncleanness before God compelled him to take the lowest place even among men. Such was the tenderness of his spirit, that he thought everybody better than himself. Humility is the exact opposite of pride; as the one man counted himself better than all, the other counted himself worse than all. When he obtained a sight of his own vileness before God, his feeling was that even his brother would be polluted by his presence. As love of God, when we have tasted his grace, carries love to men after it, like a shadow; so shame before God, because of sin in his sight, diffuses humility and modesty through the spirit and conduct in the ordinary intercourse of life.

He was unwilling to lift up his eyes to heaven. He

looked down to the earth; but his heart was rising up to heaven the while. His eyes could not bear at that moment to look, as it were, on the light of the great white throne; but his soul ascended, and pressed with violence on the gate of the kingdom. Against that strait gate his spirit is now striving; the King of glory from within feels the pressure well pleased, and opens to let the agonizer in.

"Smote upon his breast;" it is like other signs of grace, precious if it is true, worthless when it is false. A worshipper will not be heard for his much beating, any more than for his much speaking: but when it is the true external symptom of a broken heart within, the knocking on his own breast is reckoned a knocking at the gate of heaven. To him that knocketh at this lower gate, the highest will be opened.

His prayer was short and suitable; "God be merciful to me, the sinner" ($\tau\hat{\omega}$ $\dot{\alpha}\mu\alpha\rho\tau\omega\lambda\hat{\omega}$). The contrast continues to the last; as the Pharisee had compared himself with all mankind, and concluded that he alone was good; so the Publican in the depth of his shame seems to count himself the only sinner.

The steps are few and simple by which a sinner finds or misses the way into eternal life. Not perceiving his own sin, a Pharisee comes to God, as one who deserves favour; he seeks to enter heaven where the wall of righteousness frowns in his face, and is cast away. The publican, conscious of his unworthiness, counting himself altogether evil, flees from his own sin to God's provided mercy; he tries where the door is open, and passes in a moment through. I tell you, "This man went down to his house justified," &c.; he, but not the other.* The

---

* He brought with him, what the Pharisee left at home, the book of his own guilt, and exhibited all that stood against him there.—*Arndt.*

Pharisee forgave himself; who is this that forgiveth sin? and who is this whose sins he forgives? He asked no forgiveness from God, and got none. He departed from the temple as full and satisfied, or rather as empty and poor, as he entered it. For aught that we learn to the contrary, he went on, tithing his mint, anise, and cummin,— went on blindfold till he stumbled on the judgment-seat.

The penitent Publican went down to his house a justified man; he sat in the circle of his family, retired to rest at night, rose in the morning to his labour, at peace with God. On the morrow he looked on the sun-light without being in terror of the mighty One whose word had made it shine; he walked abroad on the fields, in conscious, loving companionship with Him who spread them out and covered them with green; he looked from the mountain-side on the great sea when "it wrought and was tempestuous," the confiding child of Him who holds its waters in the hollow of his hand; and when again he laid his head upon the pillow for rest to his wearied body, he laid his soul on the love of his Saviour, as an infant leans on a mother's breast. When the hand that led him through the wilderness leads him at length down the dark sides of the swelling Jordan, he looks up with languid eye, but bright, burning spirit, and whispers to his guide, "I will not fear, for Thou art with me;" when the judgment is set and the books are opened, he stands before the Judge in white clothing, accepted in the Beloved; the voice of the Eternal, tenderly human, yet clothed with divine authority, utters the welcome,—"Come, thou blessed of my Father, inherit the kingdom."

The Servants and the Pounds
(Luke 19:11-27)

' And as they heard these things, he added and spake a parable, because he was nigh to
Jerusalem, and because they thought that the kingdom of God should immediately
appear. He said therefore, A certain nobleman went into a far country to receive for
himself a kingdom, and to return. And he called his ten servants, and delivered them
ten pounds, and said unto them, Occupy till I come. But his citizens hated him, and
sent a message after him, saying, We will not have this man to reign over us. And it
came to pass, that when he was returned, having received the kingdom, then he commanded these servants to be called unto him, to whom he had given the money, that
he might know how much every man had gained by trading. Then came the first,
saying, Lord, thy pound hath gained ten pounds. And he said unto him, Well, thou
good servant : because thou hast been faithful in a very little, have thou authority over
ten cities. And the second came, saying, Lord, thy pound hath gained five pounds.
And he said likewise to him, Be thou also over five cities. And another came, saying,
Lord, behold, here is thy pound, which I have kept laid up in a napkin : for I feared
thee, because thou art an austere man : thou takest up that thou layedst not down, and
reapest that thou didst not sow. And he saith unto him, Out of thine own mouth will
I judge thee, thou wicked servant. Thou knewest that I was an austere man, taking
up that I laid not down, and reaping that I did not sow : wherefore then gavest not
thou my money into the bank, that at my coming I might have required mine own
with usury ? And he said unto them that stood by, Take from him the pound, and
give it to him that hath ten pounds. (And they said unto him, Lord, he hath ten
pounds.) For I say unto you, That unto every one which hath shall be given : and
from him that hath not, even that he hath shall be taken away from him. But those
mine enemies, which would not that I should reign over them, bring hither, and slay
them before me."

I T is necessary at the outset to indicate the
relation which subsists between this parable
and that of the talents, (Matt. xxv). Although
in many of their features they are the same,
in others there is a decisive difference. Both show that
the Lord bestows privileges on his servants, and demands
faithfulness in return ; and both show that the diligent

are rewarded and the unprofitable condemned. But the one supposes a case, in which all the servants receive equal privileges, and shows that even those of them who are faithful, may be unequal as to the amount of their success; the other supposes a case in which unequal privileges are bestowed upon the servants, and shows that when unequal gifts are employed with equal diligence, the approval is equal in the day of account. Both alike exhibit the grand cardinal distinction between the faithful and the faithless; but in pointing out also the diversities that obtain among true disciples, they view the subject from opposite sides, each presenting that aspect of it which the other omits. The parable of the talents teaches that Christians differ from each other in the amount of gifts which they receive ; and the parable of the pounds teaches that they differ from each other in the diligence which they display.*

The incident connected with Zaccheus, although it occurred on the spot and at the moment, did not, I think, supply the occasion of this parable, and does not contain the key of its meaning. The Lord's interview with that interesting and earnest tax-farmer in the neighbourhood of Jericho rather constituted an episodical interruption to the continuity of his thought and the narrative of his journey. He had passed through Jericho on his way to Jerusalem for the last time. An expectation, intense in character though vague in outline, was spreading through the neighbourhood, that great events would emerge on

---

* The man who cannot perceive, or will not own that these are two distinct cases, charged with different, though cognate lessons, is not fit to be an expositor of any writing, either sacred or profane. Enough for the critics who persist in the theory, that these two parables are different, and consequently incorrect, reports of one discourse spoken only once by the Lord ; the conceit is not worthy of more minute refutation.

his arrival at the capital. It was the crowd already on this account assembled that gave prominence to the case of Zaccheus. It is not from that episode that the parable springs; rather, when the interruption which it caused was over, the current of thought, displaced for a moment, returns to its former channel, and flows as it had flowed before. The crowd had assembled before the conversation with Zaccheus took place, and the cause of the excitement was the expectation that "the kingdom of God should immediately appear." It was on account of this expectation that the parable was spoken. The purpose of the Lord was to correct the popular impression in as far as it was erroneous, and to turn it to account in as far as it contained a basis of truth. They expected that Jesus was about to proclaim himself king, and occupy David's throne at Jerusalem: he teaches them by the parable that his kingdom is not of this world—that he, the king, will depart from their sight for a while, and that it behoves his subjects to occupy their talents and opportunities till he return.

"A certain nobleman went into a far country to receive for himself a kingdom, and to return." His errand when he went abroad was not to seek a kingdom in another quarter of the world, but to obtain from a foreign power nomination to the sovereignty of his native land. In the first place, it is not probable that, after having become king of another country, he would return to reside where he was only a subject; but a much more decisive indication is given by the message which his fellow-citizens sent after him, "We will not have this man to reign over us." They do not interfere with his prospects in a foreign country; it is his sovereignty over themselves that they dread and deprecate

This outspoken repudiation of his government by his fellow-citizens makes it both certain and manifest that, though he sought investiture abroad, the kingdom which he expected to receive was in his own native land, and over his former fellow-citizens.

In those days both the Jews and other nations subject to the supremacy of Rome were familiar with the transaction which forms the basis of this parable. After the nobleman's departure, his countrymen, aware of his design, endeavoured to thwart it. With this view they sent a message, or rather an embassy ($\pi\rho\epsilon\sigma\beta\epsilon\iota\alpha\nu$) after him ; they commissioned some of their own number to appear along with him before the power paramount, and oppose his claim. It is a mistake to suppose that the protest of these citizens was addressed to the nobleman who sought to become their king; the deputies are instructed to address themselves not to him, but to the foreign power from whom he intends to seek investiture. They will appear at court along with him when his petition is presented, and plead that it may be rejected. Such debates were in point of fact held before the republican and imperial tribunals of Rome.*

Before setting out on his journey " he called his ten servants," &c. These men were his servants or slaves. In different countries, and at different times, the bond of servitude has been indefinitely varied both in stringency and duration. In all probability these servants were the bondsmen of the nobleman, although law and practice might not accord to the owner a power so absolute as that with

---

* Herod and his son Archelaus had both in succession repaired personally to Rome to obtain their authority. Precisely similar scenes are enacted between the British government and the protected potentates of India ; the agents for rival princes contend for regal rights in London, where the government of India is in the last resort controlled.

which we are too familiar in modern slavery. But the more nearly that the master's rights approached the point of absolute ownership of property, the more suitable becomes the picture to represent the relation that subsists between the redeeming Lord and his ransomed people.*

This nobleman, desiring that no part of his property or capital should lie unproductive during his absence, made the best arrangement, of which the circumstances admitted, before he left the country. His method was the same as that which appears in the cognate parable, the entrusted talents, with the exception that in this case the master made all his servants equal. A mina, in value equal to about £2, 3s. 6d., was entrusted to each man, with the intimation that, according to his diligence and

---

* It is altogether a mistake to conclude from the allusions made here and elsewhere in the Scriptures to the actually existing servitude of the times and places, that any modern system of slavery may claim the sanction of divine approval. It was the custom of Jesus to seize existing facts on the right and on the left as they lay around, and employ them as vehicles for conveying his meaning. Sometimes he so employed a good thing, and sometimes a bad thing, but by the mere fact of using a human act or habit as a metaphor, he pronounced no judgment regarding its moral character. It was enough for him that the thing was well known, and that it served as a letter with which he might indicate his mind. Printers make their types of any material that may be most suitable for the purpose, and most readily obtained; and with these types they multiply the Scriptures. They use a cheap mixture of lead and tin ; and this base alloy serves their purpose better than more precious metals. Their only question in determining the choice of material is, Will it print our meaning clearly ? Thus the Lord Jesus dealt with the habits which he found in society, and the events that were passing at the time. He selected and employed them with a regard not to their own intrinsic moral worth but to their fitness for expressing the idea which he meant to convey. No matter whether it be lead or gold ; what he wanted was material suitable for types. A steward has no Scriptural warrant for cheating his master, because the trick of an astute agent is employed to print one of the parables ; neither have men-stealers, men-sellers, and men-buyers any authority from the Bible to treat their fellow-men like cattle, because the relation of master and slave was employed by the Lord to express a conception in the course of his teaching.

faithfulness in the management of this capital, would be his reward when the owner should return.*

Such is the arrangement which this nobleman made with those who are described as "his own servants," on the eve of his departure; but with his neighbours, who were free and independent, he had either neglected to seek, or failed to obtain, an understanding. Aware of his object, they sent after him a deputation of their own number, instructed to appear along with him at the imperial court, and oppose his request. They were not willing to become his subjects, and therefore endeavoured to prevent him from obtaining a regal title and despotic power.

Their opposition, however, had no other effect than to betray their enmity, and so expose them to the King's displeasure. His first act after he returned with supreme authority was to call his servants into his presence, and reward them according to their merits; and his second, to issue an order for the punishment of those who had opposed his elevation. The remaining portion of the scene is so similar to the corresponding parts of the cognate parable already expounded, that it is unnecessary to trace the narrative further; rather let us hasten now to ascertain and enforce the spiritual lesson from the whole.

While the Master was setting his face towards Jerusalem for the last time, a dim presentiment of coming change occupied his disciples. In their minds, the expectation of his kingdom had taken a wrong direction, and tended to put them off their guard. To correct their error, and bind them to patient watchfulness, he spoke this parable. Because they imagined he was about to assume kingly power, and give them places of temporal

---

* For fuller notice of the methods adopted, see the exposition of the corresponding parable on page 299.

dignity on his right hand and on his left, he taught them by this similitude, that he must go away, and that they must remain behind, working and watching.

The nobleman represents the Lord himself. While he prosecuted his ministry on earth, he had not fully attained possession of the kingdom. The departure of the nobleman represents the exodus which the Lord soon afterwards accomplished at Jerusalem, comprising his death, resurrection, and ascension. In the parable, the power paramount who could withhold or bestow a kingdom is not named : it is intimated only that this transaction took place out of sight in a far country. When the Son of God ascended after his mediatorial work on earth was complete, all power was given to him in heaven and on earth. Beyond his disciples' sight he received the kingdom from the Father. Now he has right to rule supreme over that world, on which before he had not where to lay his head. He will come to this world again as its King, with power and great glory.

Two classes of persons are mentioned as having remained in the country while the prince was absent :— these are his servants and his adversaries. In the material scene, there might be many who neither served nor opposed him ; but these are not mentioned in the parable, because there are none to correspond with them on the spiritual side. There only two classes exist,—those who serve Christ as the Lord that bought them, and those who, being at enmity with God, refuse to obey the Gospel of his Son.

The parable has not much to do with them that are without. At the beginning, it shortly indicates their rebellion, and at the close as shortly predicts their doom ; but the circumstances, the character, the life, and the reward of the Lord's disciples are more expressly and more fully declared.

The master who owns them places some of his treasures at their disposal, and with the general injunction, "Occupy," goes out of their sight. The servants are those who, at least in profession, are the disciples of Christ, and the pounds are the faculties which they possess, and the opportunities which they enjoy. The place and age in which our lot has been cast, our early education, our bodily members and mental powers, our station in society and the circle of our homes, our money and our health, and, in addition, the graces of the Spirit, in whatever measure they may have been conferred,—all that we are and have belongs to God. He is the owner, and we are tenants at will.

While a general law has been laid down to determine, in the main, the direction of our course, the details are left to our own discretion. One man may invest his master's capital in land, and another in merchandise, and both may be equally faithful, equally successful : so in various lines of effort, different disciples may, in diverse manners, but with equal faithfulness, serve the Lord. There is freedom in the choice of departments, provided always there be loyalty to the King.

In the relation between Christ and Christians, opposites meet without hostile collision. His ownership is absolute, and yet there is freedom in full. His lordship does not limit their liberty; their liberty does not infringe his rights. What a glorious liberty this earth-ball enjoys ! How it careers along through space, threading its way through thronging worlds, and giving each a safe wide berth in the ocean of the infinite ! Yet the sun holds the earth all the while in absolute and entire control. Like that glory in the visible heavens is the glory of the

Everlasting Covenant. The largest liberty conceded to the sons of God consists with sovereignty complete and constant exercised over them by the Redeemer, who bought them with his blood. He is their owner, and yet they are free. The union of opposites is possible with God: " He is wonderful in counsel, and excellent in working."

The sons serve; and yet they are sons. Ransomed men are instruments of a higher order, than other agencies through which the reign of Providence is administered. Although the Lord requires of his regenerated people as complete submission to his law, as he demands and obtains from the elements of nature and the brutes that perish, he does not require from them an equally uniform and mechanical routine. The streams that course over continents, and the tides that swell upon their shores, must render the same service every day; but these sons of God are not held to labour by a bridle so short and rigid. They are endowed with reason and will; they are set at liberty, and permitted to expatiate over a wider field. Their master goes out of sight, and trusts to a renewed, loving heart for the diligent outlay and faithful return of all the talents. The Gospel requires and generates not a legal, but an evangelical obedience.

When the king returns, or the servants are summoned one by one through death to meet their master, they are tried as to faithfulness and diligence in laying out their talents. Although ten were mentioned at the beginning, it is not necessary to report on more than three at the close. These are sufficient to show that some were diligent, and some slothful; and that among the diligent there were different measures of effort, success, and reward.

What hast thou that thou didst not receive? Occupy; occupy all, and occupy it all the time till the Giver come to claim his own. All that God gives us is given for use. There is much evil, moral and material, in the world. He who made it and saw it fall by sin, has its restoration and renewal much at heart. When he has gotten some of the fallen restored to favour and renewed in spirit, he endows them with various riches from his own treasury, that the capital wisely invested may yield a large return at his coming. Let each according to his means and opportunity lay himself and his talents out to leave the world better than he found it;—to diminish the amount of sin and suffering, to feed hungry mouths, and cover naked backs, to enlighten dark minds and save perishing souls. It is a high calling to be fellow-workers with God, to be instruments of righteousness in his hands.

One, by trading with his pound gained ten, before the king returned, and another five. Both are equally approved, but unequally rewarded; each receives as his recompense all that he had won. Two principles which operate in the spiritual kingdom are symbolized here; one, that various degrees of efficiency and success obtain among the faithful disciples of Christ; another that reward in his kingdom springs from work and is proportioned to it.

The parable of the talents recorded by Matthew represented one fact in the history of the kingdom, that different persons receive differing gifts from the sovereign God: this parable, recorded by Luke, represents another fact in the history of the kingdom, that among those who possess equal gifts varieties occur in the skill and success with which the gifts are employed. The practical lesson from the former parable is, If with all your efforts you fall far behind your neighbour in the result of your labour, you need not on that account be cast down, for equal diligence will meet equal approval, whether it be applied to a large capital or a small; the lesson of the latter parable is, If others are obtaining greater results than you, strive to imitate and equal them, lest your opportunity not have having been fully occupied, you should obtain at last only a small reward. The first puts in a spring to keep the truly faithful from sinking into despondency because their talents are few; and the second puts in a spring to keep the indolent from lagging behind. The two together, one on this side and one on that, shut all up to diligence in the work of the Lord.

A glimpse is given here of the method in which rewards are bestowed upon faithful servants; each receives what he has won. The work of the saved in their Master's service measures in some way their recompense at their Master's side. In all cases the wages given, seeing they depend on the merits of the Mediator, must be immeasureably greater than the work done; but it would appear that the differences which shall obtain in heaven will bear some proportion to the productiveness of the service here: the whole continent will be elevated as by the immediate power of God: but certain points will stand out above others in the celestial landscape on account of great talents greatly used. How much a city is greater in value than a pound we cannot calculate exactly, but the difference represents the gain that all the true servants will make at the coming of the king. All the faithful are made great; but the greatest worker is the greatest winner when the accounts are closed. Hold on, disciples; every grace that grows into strength, through bearing and doing your Redeemer's will here, is a seed that will multiply your enjoyment manifold when you come to the inheritance. Nor is this a mercenary motive. A true Christian can never separate his interests from Christ: he serves his Lord in love to-day, and will discover at last that in serving his Lord, he has been enriching himself.

The case of the servant who allowed his pound to lie unused is not different from the corresponding case in the parable of the talents except in one thing; in this parable the pound which the indolent servant had permitted to lie idle is simply taken out of his hands, while, in the other parable, the unprofitable servant is cast into outer darkness.

The lesson, in as far as it is the same in both, is, that not only those who do positive wickedness, but those also who fail to do good, are counted guilty in God's sight. Inasmuch as in this parable no other punishment is inflicted on the indolent servant than the deprivation of his capital, it may possibly be intended to intimate that culpable unfaithfulness in a true believer may sometimes descend so far as to be undistinguishable by human eyes from the entire neglect of the unbelieving. There is, however, in all cases, a dividing line, although we may not be able to trace it—"the Lord knoweth them that are his." Nor does this conception really weaken the motive to diligence; for if any one should slacken in his efforts to serve the Lord on the ground that a great degree of negligence, although it may diminish his reward, does not imperil his safety, this very thing would conclusively prove that he has no part in Christ. It is the nature of the new creature to be forgetting the things behind, and reaching forth to those that are before; when the leaning of a man's heart goes in the opposite direction—that is, when he deliberately endeavours to make matters as pleasant as possible for himself, by escaping from all service to Christ, except as much as is necessary to carry him safe to heaven, he certainly has not yet been born again, and in this state shall not see the kingdom. He who sails along the sea of Christian profession, loving the neighbouring land of worldly indulgence, and therefore hugging the shore as closely as he thinks consistent with safety, will certainly make shipwreck. Ah! the ship that thus seeks the shore is drawn by the unseen power of a magnet-mountain—drawn directly to her doom; he who is truly bound for the better land gives these treacherous headlands a wide berth.

The last lesson is the judgment pronounced and the punishment inflicted on the adversaries. They who will not submit to Christ the crucified will be crushed by Christ the king. Every eye shall see him; they also who pierced him. Meekly now he stands at the door and knocks; then he comes as the lightning comes.

One hope remains,—one door stands wide open yet. His enemies must be slain, either now or then. The enemies of the Lord's reign in the present world are the evil desires that occupy a man's heart, and close it against its rightful sovereign; drag them forth and slay them before him, that he may enter and possess his own. Surrender his enemies into his hands to-day, and you will henceforth be among his friends; if sins be sheltered in the day of grace, the sinners will find no shelter in the day of judgment.